ESLANDA

Eslanda

THE LARGE AND UNCONVENTIONAL LIFE
OF MRS. PAUL ROBESON

BARBARA RANSBY

Haymarket Books
Chicago, Illinois

First published in 2013 by Yale University Press
with assistance from the foundation established in memory of
Amasa Stone Mather of the Class of 1907, Yale College.

Published in 2022 by
Haymarket Books
P.O. Box 180165
Chicago, IL 60618
773-583-7884
www.haymarketbooks.org
info@haymarketbooks.org

ISBN: 978-1-64259-582-6

Distributed to the trade in the US through Consortium Book Sales
and Distribution (www.cbsd.com) and internationally through Ingram
Publisher Services International (www.ingramcontent.com).

This book was published with the generous support of Lannan Foundation
and Wallace Action Fund.

Special discounts are available for bulk purchases by organizations and
institutions. Please call 773-583-7884 or email info@haymarketbooks.org
for more information.

Cover photograph of Eslanda Robeson taken in 1952 by Hyman Rothman,
published by permission from NY Daily News Archive via Getty Images.

Cover design by Rachel Cohen.

Library of Congress Cataloging-in-Publication data is available.

Entered into digital printing March, 2022.

For Peter, Jason, and Asha

CONTENTS

Photo galleries follow pages 80 and 204

PREFACE

Since the publication of *Eslanda: The Large and Unconventional Life of Mrs. Paul Robeson* in 2013, I have spoken to thousands of people in audiences all over the world about this tough, tenacious, and fascinating woman. Eslanda Cardozo Goode Robeson died in 1968, as Africa was emerging from the yoke of colonialism and the rest of the world felt on the verge of revolution. She was proud of her decades of crusading for racial justice and African independence. She knew in 1968 that the work to which she had devoted her life was far from done. Alongside her husband, colleague, and comrade, the acclaimed artist Paul Robeson, Eslanda allied herself with the struggle against imperialism, capitalism, and white supremacy from the 1930s on. She was also uncompromising in her resistance to the McCarthy-era repression that almost destroyed her family and her husband's career. In her own way, she was also a feminist, paving a career path as a journalist, activist, and anthropologist, and establishing a political voice that was all her own. She allied with and advocated for women's rights wherever she went.

Eslanda was a world traveler. She moved across the planet not as a tourist but as an act of solidarity: to the front lines of the antifascist forces in the Spanish Civil War; to Uganda as a respectful researcher; and to meetings in Ghana, China, Russia, Guyana, London, and New Zealand. To her mind, she was born a Negro American woman and became a Black global citizen. She forged strong relationships throughout the African continent and beyond, establishing herself as a pathbreaking Black woman internationalist. She wrote, spoke, worked, and lived in the venerable and rich Black radical tradition, a tradition that continues to this day.

In the mid- to late twentieth century, groups like the Black Panther Party and the Student Non-Violent Coordinating Committee and the Black feminist internationalists like June Jordan, Angela Davis, and Eslanda's friend and contemporary Claudia Jones were exemplars of this tradition, expressing principled solidarity with "people's struggles" for freedom all over the world.

I have had the honor to work closely with the Movement for Black Lives (M4BL) coalition for the past several years. It is one of the largest coalitions of contemporary Black freedom movement formations in the U.S. today. Very much in Eslanda's tradition, Black internationalism has been central to M4BL since its inception. Several delegations have gone to Palestine, and statements were crafted in solidarity with the peoples of Tigray, Sudan, Haiti, and Cuba. A Haiti material aid campaign was launched, and solidarity projects with African Diasporic communities in Brazil and southern Africa have been hallmarks of M4BL's internationalist praxis. Eslanda would have been proud.

As for me, I take Eslanda with me wherever I go. I spent many years digging into the corners and crevices of her life and came to respect her greatly for what she accomplished, as much as I was humbled by her mistakes and contradictions. Since 2013 the world has changed greatly. We saw the election of a proto-fascist maniac to the White House and witnessed explosions of protest in the United States and around the world. After the murder of an unarmed Black man in Minneapolis in 2020, more than twenty million protesters flooded the streets across the United States. We also endured a global pandemic that reminded us with acuity of our interconnectedness and interdependency, and the precarity of our very existence.

When I move around the world and when I map my own sense of obligations and commitments to global justice, I continue to be inspired by Eslanda's bold curiosity, her staunch loyalty to the dispossessed of the world, her uncompromising spirit, her refusal to be silent about what she knew, saw, believed, and felt, and the way her fierce confidence coexisted with her humility. Those of us in the U.S.-based Black freedom movement and a part of Black internationalist and Black left feminist traditions are challenged to embrace and, to the degree possible, match her example. The bar is set and the stakes are high. Her life is but one more example that what we do matters, standing on the right side of history matters, and a life of consistent praxis helps to change the world. She is in good company: Ella Baker, Toni Cade Bambara, Claudia Jones, Fannie Lou Hamer, Marielle Franco, Lorraine Hansberry, Olive Morris, Shirley Graham Du Bois, Funmilayo Ransome-Kuti, and others.

The relationship between a biographer and her subject is a unique one. My experience with Eslanda, Ella Baker, and the women whose activism I wrote about in my most recent book, *Making All Black Lives Matter*, are special to me. I had the privilege of delving into their lives, and they, in turn, changed mine. I once gave a talk about Ella Baker called "A Conversation between Sisters, Living and Dead." I feel biography and movement narration is a kind of intergenerational conversation that touches, shapes, and changes the participants. I think Eslanda's influence on me has been to push me to resist parochialism or nationalism in my view of the world and in my view of Black struggle. I will always appreciate that about her.

In thinking about the preface to this special Haymarket edition of this book, nearly ten years after *Eslanda* was launched into the world, I think of how my relationship with the subject has evolved, and what her legacy means to all of us today. Since Eslanda was a devoted diarist and diligent letter writer, I thought of how might I craft a letter to her from the vantage point of 2022, more than a half-century after her death. I would tell her this.

> Essie, my dear . . . The bad news is the world is still a mess! Black people are still fighting for our freedom, and up against some nasty and violent opposition. You would have cheered on the many young people who took to the streets in Ferguson, Missouri, and in Minneapolis, Chicago, and Baltimore to protest racist police murders. New coalitions and networks of resistance are being created as a result of the intense times in which we are living. There are women like you, all over the world: women who refuse to be silenced or sidelined. And while the independence struggles of the mid-twentieth century did not win the robust, full-bodied freedom that you and so many had hoped for, the African Diaspora—on the continent of Africa and beyond—is still a cauldron of resistance. This phase of struggle is resistance to neocolonialism and neoliberalism, to corruption by new elites and collaborations with old ones. There are eloquent young voices speaking out against the pillage and polluting of the land and water. There are labor struggles and student

protests and women's campaigns. The radical tradition of Black women's resistance continues! Your contributions remind us that each phase of struggle and each generation confronts its own challenges, but the struggle perseveres. Thank you for your provocative and inspiring example.

ACKNOWLEDGMENTS

There are always many people to thank for a research project that stretches over many years and across several continents. First and foremost, I would like to thank the Robeson family—Paul Jr., Marilyn, and Susan—for opening up the Robeson family archives to me, and for sharing their memories and insights about Essie. Paul and Marilyn have spent decades maintaining and overseeing the Paul and Eslanda Robeson archive, an extensive collection housed at the Moorland-Spingarn Research Center at Howard University. Their groundwork was of enormous help to me, as were my conversations with both of them. Paul's two-volume biography of his father's life, along with Martin Duberman's extensively researched life history of Paul Robeson, served as great resources for me in mapping Eslanda Robeson's life. Susan Robeson became involved the last year of the project, and truly embraced it. She was especially helpful in figuring out how to visually represent her grandmother as a way of complementing her own earlier photographic tribute to her grandfather, her book *The Whole World in His Hands: A Pictorial Biography of Paul Robeson*. I delighted in getting each of her emails that celebrated another photographic "find" in the Robeson family photo collection.

There are many librarians, archivists, research assistants, and colleagues to thank, some of whom I know well, and others I worked with only fleetingly. Collectively they advised, guided, and aided me in my search for sources at various stages of the project. Others read and gave feedback on the manuscript. Research assistants included Toussaint

Losier, Tiffany Fanning, Ainsley Lesure, Gillian Wu, Anna Klebine, Leena Odeh, Sussan Navabi, and Ellen Kang (who went beyond the call of duty), and Ferzana Chavda. Adam Kuranishi, Deana Lewis, and Joseph Lipari deserve special thanks for their many labors, off and on, over several years. Adam worked tirelessly day after day for many months as he juggled his own involvement in the immigrant rights movement. Deana became my photo detective, locating and documenting images of Essie in obscure places, then obtaining permissions from near and far: no simple task. She was also my technology expert and sounding board. Joey picked up where Deana left off and endured my obsession and angst as we brought the book to closure. He dotted the i's and crossed the t's with all the photos and images. Another special word of gratitude goes to Rose Horwitz, who provided a last-minute and very helpful translation of the introduction to the Russian edition of *African Journey*.

Archivists at the Moorland-Spingarn Library at Howard University, Joellen El Bashir and Ida Jones, provided enormous assistance and patient support for this project over several years. Librarians and archivists at the Nehru Memorial Museum and Library in Delhi; the University of the Witswatersrand Special Collections in Johannesburg, South Africa; and the Emma Goldman Papers in Amsterdam were also generous with their time and expertise. Archivists at the Tamiment Collection and Robert F. Wagner Labor Archives at New York University—especially Erika Gottfried—and at the Schomburg Center for Research in Black Culture were also extremely helpful, knowledgeable, and patient. A special word of thanks to Dan Schneider, Ryan Burner, and Dr. Anita Ghai, as well as my colleague Gayatri Reddy, who helped me obtain access to materials from the Nehru Archives in Delhi, which turned out to be a complicated and time-consuming endeavor. I owe words of appreciation to my German colleagues at the Musikarchiv of the Akademie der Künste in Berlin: Werner Gruenzweig, for his long-distance collegiality; Christiane Niklew, who painstakingly catalogued the Berlin Robeson collection; and Anouk Jeschke for making me feel welcome during my stay in Berlin. Janet Jagan's daughter, Nadira Jagan-Brancier, kindly sent from her family's archive letters exchanged between her mother and Essie Robeson. Jack O'Dell and Esther Cooper Jackson, inspiring icons in their own right after so many decades of struggle, were also generous with their memories of Essie.

Friends and colleagues shared tips, facts, and primary documents. I extend my sincere thanks and appreciation to Erik McDuffie, who sent documents from Johannesburg; Carol Anderson, who turned me on to the M15 declassified documents; and Holly Peters-Golden, who found a class roster for the London School of Economics with Essie and Jomo Kenyatta listed. Nikhil Singh put me in touch with Jack O'Dell, and Jordan Goodman in the United Kingdom, who is working on a parallel project, shared tips with me. A number of scholars aided me in trying to decipher unlabeled photos: my thanks go to Arnold Rampersad, Houston Baker, Lovalerie King, Steven Fullwod, Joanne Gabin, and Randall Burkett. Many time zones away, Professor Dmitri Bodarenko and retired professor Artyom Letnev of the Institute for African Studies of the Russian Academy of Sciences in Moscow were generous with their time and knowledge. Closer to home, my colleagues in the Gender and Women's Studies Program and the African American Studies Department at the University of Illinois at Chicago, and my former dean, Dwight McBride, provided material and moral support for this effort. Having two hundred photos of Essie spread out on our department conference table for more than a week while I decided which images to select for the book was only one of many inconveniences that my colleagues endured with good-natured tolerance.

I am enormously grateful to the readers who sifted through all or part of the manuscript in its earlier iteration, including Penny Von Eschen, Dayo Gore, Peter Sporn, Vijay Prashad, Premilla Nadasen, Jan Susler, Linda Hillman, Beth Richie, Lisa Yun Lee, Pam Sporn, Jason Ransby-Sporn, Prexy Nesbitt, Eric Johnson, Paul Robeson Jr., Robin D.G. Kelley, Gerald Horne, Jarvis Tyner, Anthony Monteiro, and Horace Campbell. My dear friend Martha Biondi lovingly encouraged me while contributing her wonderfully critical eye. Jonah Horwitz took time away from his legal duties to give the manuscript an extremely rigorous read, which was enormously helpful. And Asha Ransby-Sporn offered razor-sharp copyediting for various sections.

Then there are my friends who provided love and encouragement during the research and writing process, and reminded me of the importance both of telling untold stories from the past, and of making the world a better place for ourselves and our children. Those special friends include Alice, Beth, Cathy, Ella, Bill, Bernardine, Adam and Tessie, James and Martha, Prexy, Premilla, Billy, Tyler, Indira, Linda and John, Lisa, Harishi, Tracye, Chandra, Beverly, Kim and Michelle, Lynette, Jan, Iasha and Elena, Joel and Teresa, Adam K., Kim and Mary, Camilia—and the list goes on.

Essie took on and championed social justice issues and issues of oppression and injustice. She did so in every corner of the globe and around a multiplicity of issues. I am proud to write that my community of activist friends, colleagues, and compañeras has done the same, and one day, someone will tell their stories too with passion and admiration. The immigrant rights struggle and the brave young people who have stood up to declare themselves "undocumented and unafraid" (Reyna, Tania, Rigo, Nadia, to name a few), will be a part of that story. Aisha, Wisdom, Leena, Mika, Latoya, Maria, and so many other founding Ella's Daughters are the kind of smart and committed young women activists whom Essie hoped and dreamed would eventually change the world. I remain confident that they will.

I am indebted to the inspiring courage of my sister-colleagues who traveled with me on a feminists of color human-rights delegation to Palestine in the summer of 2011 to bear witness to the injustices there. The Essie project traveled with us in my suitcase. During the more than five years that I worked on this book, my eclectic little political tribe has traveled the world standing up to repression and injustice, speaking out and building ties from Palestine/Israel to Egypt, from South Africa to Honduras to India, and all parts in between. Essie would have been quite at home among them.

I thank my editor, Chris Rogers, and my agent, Sandy Dijkstra, for having faith that readers would want to know Essie Robeson's story, and that I had the skill and ability to tell it in an honest and compelling way—as well as for their patience with numerous delays and missed deadlines. I thank Jill Marsal for placing the book with Yale. Additional appreciation goes to Christina Tucker at Yale for her help and support along the way. Editors Julie Carlson and Margaret Otzel lent their skills to the project and provided warm encouragement in the final stretch.

And then there is family. For me, like Essie, family has always meant extended family. There were those who adopted me and those whom I adopted over time. First and foremost of these is my life partner of over thirty years, Peter Sporn, whose compassion for suffering—that of his patients, and of strangers he has never met in places around the world—continues to inspire and humble me. He sets a high moral and political standard that I aspire to every day. I am honored to be making this journey with him by my side. Our children—an adult and a young adult—have been supporters and loving cheerleaders for this book project since it began. Love is always a choice. I am ever grateful that such awesome people have chosen to love me, and to believe in the work that I do as they each continue to do important work of their own: Jason as an energy analyst and advocate for conservation and renewable resources;

and Asha as a teen journalist, blogger, writer, photographer, and spoken-word poet. She entered her first year of college just as *Eslanda* went to press. Asha and Jason have grown into two amazing young people over the years since Essie came into our lives: people of integrity and verve, of many curiosities and many talents.

My extended family includes Pam Sporn, Pablo Foster, Lelanie and Paul Foster Jr. (Papito), and Lisa. They too deserve many thanks for being a special part of my life and for sitting through endless discussions about Essie Robeson. The memories of the family that raised me (all of whom have passed), Charlie and Ethel Ransby, and Rosia and Henry Pittman, are ever with me. They were factory workers, sharecroppers, and maids. They never heard of most of the places Essie traveled to. They would not have known quite what to make of her life, so very different from their own, but I know they would have adored her all the same. My in-laws and friends for many years, Jo and Paul Sporn, now gone, would have also enjoyed Essie's life story. Paul was proud to have been a part of the large security team that defended Paul Robeson at Peekskill in 1949.

Finally, I am indebted to Eslanda Cardozo Goode Robeson. What a life. What guts. What resilience. What perspective. What a passion to live and speak and know and understand the world in all its amazing complexity. I did not agree with, or even fully understand, all of the personal or political choices she made, and that is not important, really. But in the final analysis, I stood in awe of the life she made for herself. And what a capacity to love, to remain loyal, and to speak out with emphatic eloquence and steel-willed resolve against so many of the injustices of her day: McCarthyism, colonialism, sexism, racism, fascism, imperialism, wars (cold and hot), and class exploitation. Until her last days, she was tireless, unrelenting, vigilant, as well as thinking and "living large," in the most meaningful sense of the term.

INTRODUCTION

At a time when most Black women suffered painfully circumscribed lives, Eslanda (Essie) Cardozo Goode Robeson enjoyed enormous mobility, even if this mobility was conditional, rife with contradictions, and sometimes costly. For most of her adult life, Essie was a traveler, both literally and metaphorically. She transcended class and cultural boundaries and crossed international borders; she conversed in multiple languages and traveled to nearly every corner of the globe. Essie Robeson's story is about one woman's journey across the vast and volatile landscape of twentieth-century world politics and culture, how that landscape looked to her, and how it changed beneath her feet. It is also a chronicle of love and loss, of grand ideals and unyielding principles, of loyalty and betrayal, of resilience and survival. It is the story of a woman grappling with how to make her mark in a rapidly changing world, and of how she herself changed in the process. But it is not a singular story. It is a story of a marriage and a partnership that was fraught with complications, but which ultimately endured. And it is a story that reflects the embeddedness of Essie Robeson's life in the major global struggles of her time.

Essie Robeson's life was set against the backdrop of the Harlem Renaissance, World War II, the Cold War, African decolonization, and the early rumblings of the U.S. Black Freedom movement. She witnessed, engaged in, and was shaped by these historic events. While she may have been best known for her marriage to world-famous artist and activist Paul Robeson, Essie was an independent and accomplished trailblazer in her own right; an anthropologist, an outspoken anti-colonial and anti-racist activist, a strong advocate for women's leadership, and a prolific writer and sought-after public speaker.

College educated when most Black women were working as domestics, Essie in the 1920s became the first Black woman chemist to work in a pathology laboratory at Columbia Presbyterian Hospital in New York City, and the first Black woman to head such a unit. In the 1930s, she studied with renowned anthropologist Bronislaw Malinowski at the London School of Economics and later pursued a Ph.D. in anthropology. She published three books, one of which was co-authored with the Nobel Prize–winning China scholar Pearl Buck. For nearly twenty years, she worked as a freelance journalist, a U.N. correspondent, and a writer, analyzing international affairs and domestic politics. She wrote hundreds of essays and articles and delivered hundreds of lectures throughout the United States and around the world in which she spoke out against racism and injustice. By the 1940s, she had become an outspoken and uncompromising voice for a range of progressive and left-wing causes, most notably independence for African nations still suffering under colonial rule. She publicly allied herself with militant anti-colonial campaigns, and with the world communist movement, at a time when such stances were both controversial and dangerous.

"There's nothing like a trip to get your mind wandering," Essie Robeson once wrote in a meandering essay about travel and self-discovery.[1] And wander she did. She set foot in nearly forty countries on five continents between 1930 and 1960. For Essie, the journey was as important as the destination. She relished "the thrill when the plane revved up, gathered speed, and then was airborne." The unease and uncertainty were inseparable from the excitement. "You are most certainly on a magic carpet," she once enthused to a fellow passenger who was flying for the first time.[2] Essie explored such far-flung places as Beijing, Moscow, Capetown, Mexico City, Sydney, and Brazzaville, and lived overseas for extended periods of time. She trudged through the Ituri Rainforest, visited the front lines of the Spanish Civil War, and took a ten-day boat trek down the crocodile-infested Congo River.

How was Essie able to move with such fluidity and fearlessness across cultural and political divides, as well as international time zones? What "set her flowin'" (as literary critic Farah Jasmine Griffin might ask)? In her early travels, Essie was searching. Sometimes she roamed for personal reasons, other times she had political and professional goals in mind. She traveled in search of grand adventures and new challenges, and sometimes to seek refuge from the debilitating racism in the United

States that stunted her personal and professional aspirations. Essie moved through the world with courage, curiosity, ambition, a keen eye, and an open mind. She was never a disinterested spectator or a voyeur; she was an itinerant traveler but never a tourist. Later in life her travels were driven by her intellectual and political interests and commitments. As a writer and anthropologist, Essie sought to connect with and understand the cultures of people whom she encountered across the globe, and she felt particular empathy for those living under the yoke of colonialism and oppression, from the Maori people of New Zealand to the multi-ethnic Black working class of South Africa.

Over time, Essie became an ally and advocate for the oppressed and disenfranchised. She left the United States for London in 1928 with limited ideas of what the Black experience meant beyond the U.S. borders, and with her political views still in formation. She returned nearly twelve years later with not only a richer understanding of the African Diaspora and the world, but also a deep appreciation for the limits of capitalism and the dangers of fascism and colonialism.

Essie was born on December 15, 1895, a year before the historic *Plessy v. Ferguson* Supreme Court decision that inscribed Jim Crow segregation as federal law.[3] Her middle-class family, based in Washington, D.C., was defined by both privilege and struggle. Essie's maternal grandfather was a famed Reconstruction-era politician, and Essie was a distant relative of U.S. Supreme Court Justice Benjamin Cardozo.[4] Her father was a federal government employee with a law degree from Howard University.

Essie's family fortunes changed irrevocably when, on January 23, 1901, her father died suddenly at the age of thirty-nine.[5] Essie was only five years old, and the tragedy meant that her mother had to raise three young children on her own. Supporting the family by working as a beautician and entrepreneur, Essie's mother, also named Eslanda, moved to New York City soon after her husband's death, and it is there that Essie and her brothers spent most of their childhood. She and her mother later moved to Chicago, where Essie finished high school and enrolled in the University of Illinois on scholarship. During her third year, she transferred to Columbia University's Teachers College in New York City, a move that would change her life in immeasurable ways.[6]

Essie met Paul Robeson in New York in 1919, in 1920 she fell in love with him, and in 1921 they married. Paul went on to become an internationally acclaimed actor, singer, artist, and beloved icon of both the Black American freedom movement and the worldwide anti-colonial and communist movements. With Essie as his business manager and the architect of his early career, Paul became perhaps the best-known Black artist of his generation. Widely celebrated, he performed regularly on the stages of New York, London, and Paris, and Essie often traveled with him.

A fiercely independent woman with savvy, determination, and smarts, Essie was a ubiquitous figure in international arts circles during the 1920s, 1930s, and 1940s. She developed personal and professional relationships with a wide variety of writers, performers, producers, and patrons. Her correspondence and appointment books included a who's who of the theater and literary world of the early 1900s: Countee Cullen, Langston Hughes, Carl Van Vechten, Zora Neale Hurston, Noel Coward, Eugene O'Neill, Virginia Woolf, and more. By the early 1940s, she had found her political voice and, along with Paul, became an unwavering advocate for racial justice in the United States and for freedom and self-determination globally. Essie and Paul enjoyed an eclectic group of friends and associates whose political affiliations ranged from the National Association for the Advancement of Colored People (NAACP) to communist parties around the world.

Three sets of experiences in the 1930s profoundly influenced Essie's life and worldview. One was her 1934 trip to the Soviet Union, where she and Paul got a glimpse of a predominately white society where official state policy stood in opposition to racism and colonialism. Her second life-altering experience occurred in 1936, when she spent three months living and traveling in South Africa and Uganda, supplemented a decade later by travels in the Congo. Her time in Africa represented an intensive political education for Essie, who saw up close the ugly realities of colonialism and the complex and hopeful face of African resistance. Essie made three trips to sub-Saharan Africa: to South Africa and Uganda in 1936, to Congo in 1946, and to Ghana in 1958. And the final set of pivotal experiences occurred during Essie's twelve years in London and Europe, where she enjoyed a rich and stimulating cultural and intellectual environment. The "Blacks" (Jomo Kenyatta, Kojo Touvalou Houénou, and dozens of African students), "Browns" (Jawaharlal Nehru, Vijaya Lakshmi Pandit, and Cheddi Jagan), and a few "reds" (most notably Emma Goldman) formed Essie's intellectual community and profoundly influenced her evolving sense of politics and the world.

In the 1940s, along with W. E. B. Du Bois, Max Yergan, and Paul Robeson, Essie became an important contributor to the Council on

African Affairs (CAA), a prominent anti-colonial organization. In 1945, she was an unofficial CAA delegate to the founding convention of the United Nations in San Francisco. Her identity, which was grounded in the Black American and global Black experiences, led her to side with the downtrodden and oppressed of the world, whatever their color, as well as with communist ideals and leftist movements because in her eyes they represented hope for the future. In the 1950s, Essie worked as a writer for *New World Review*, covering the United Nations, and eventually became the publication's editorial consultant on Negro and colonial issues.[7] She also contributed to numerous African American newspapers, including the *Afro-American*, the *Amsterdam News*, and the *Pittsburgh Courier*. And she contributed articles to the *Daily Worker*, the U.S. Communist Party's newspaper, as well as Claude Barnet's Associated Negro Press, a more mainstream Black news service. Essie was a sought-after public speaker in the 1940s and 1950s, giving lectures to sororities, church groups, labor unions, civic associations, and political organizations. In 1948 she joined the newly formed Progressive Party; toured the country with its political candidate, Henry Wallace; and ran for office twice on the party's antiwar ticket.

Throughout the Cold War years, the Robesons refused to renounce either their radical friends or their own radical ideas, even when it would have been convenient and expedient to do so.[8] They also refused to be silent about the persistent scourge of American racism. As a result, they were targeted as subversives by their own government, spied on by the FBI, blacklisted by the U.S. State Department, and, in 1950, had their passports confiscated, which dealt Paul's career a severe blow, slashed their income dramatically, and turned their lives upside down.

In 1953, Essie Robeson appeared as an uncooperative witness in front of Senator Joseph McCarthy's infamous anti-communist committee, which had been set up to root out alleged communist sympathizers from the government, arts, and public life. Far from being intimidated, Essie used her highly publicized testimony to challenge the credibility of the committee itself and to indict its conveners on the grounds of racism and repression.[9] When their passports were returned in 1958, Essie and Paul relocated overseas, spending time in England and the Soviet Union, but retaining a residence in Harlem. They returned to the States in 1963.

With his bass-baritone voice, towering frame, powerful intellect, and irrepressible charm, Paul Robeson cast a large and imposing shadow. He was, in many ways, the most influential person in Essie's life. He was her first love, the father of her only child, an artistic genius whom she greatly admired, and a hero in the struggles for peace and freedom that she ardently supported. Her identity as Mrs. Paul Robeson was extremely important to her. That title gave her access to otherwise unreachable people and places and honored her role in their partnership. Whatever it meant to "be" Paul Robeson, Essie felt she had had a hand in creating that status. Incredibly, even as she defended, supported, promoted, and advanced Paul's interests and career for over four decades, she never lost herself. She did not see herself as an appendage of Paul, but rather recognized that her privileged position in his circle enabled her to amplify her own creative voice and later, promote her vision for a different kind of world. Over time, she forged her own career, made her own friends, and reached an unconventional marital accord—all while remaining steadfastly devoted to Paul.

For most of their forty-four-year partnership, Paul had romantic relationships and long-term affairs with other women, some of whom were married themselves and some of whom Essie knew and befriended. As is clear from her diaries, Essie was aware of Paul's infidelities and alternately tolerated, protested, and ignored them. At one critical point in 1932, their eleven-year marriage teetered on the brink of divorce. They eventually overcame that obstacle and settled into an open marriage of sorts, with Paul pursuing other intimate relationships and Essie, on occasion, doing the same. The marriage survived because there were ties between them more enduring than sexual attraction and more fundamental than a marital contract: friendship, respect, commitment, and intellectual camaraderie. Later there would be political camaraderie as well.

As complicated as her private life may have been at times, Essie managed to maintain an outward focus. She traveled frequently, crossing the Atlantic at least thirty times over the course of her life and documenting her experiences in her diaries, spiral notebooks, fine leather journals, and even on makeshift scraps of neatly labeled paper. She may initially have traveled out of curiosity or to bask in her beloved husband's fame, but later she traveled to enact her principles and bear witness to injustice. Along the way, she saw history unfold: fascism emerged, colonialism eroded, socialism arose, and empires unraveled.

Essie visited countries in transition, those engaged in civil war, socialist, or communist experiments or postcolonial nation-building. She went to the newly independent Ghana, war-torn Spain, post-revolutionary China, and the Soviet Union. Her support of the Soviet

Union was the most controversial of her political associations, given its Cold War rivalry with the United States after World War II. But the Robesons had a special attachment to the country and its people that lasted to the end of their lives. Many Black American supporters of the Soviet Union in the 1930s and 1940s felt that a strong Kremlin was a necessary bulwark against Western imperialism and white supremacist practices, especially as the prospect of decolonization loomed large.[10] Despite the problems and contradictions in the Soviet system, Essie felt that it was important to offer her support, not only because of her anti-racist and anti-colonial views, but also because of her growing sympathy with the plight of poor and working-class people of all races. Many later broke with the Soviet Union over Stalin's dictatorial policies and purges. But for complicated reasons, some of them still unclear, the Robesons never did.

Many historians, including Paul Gilroy, Dayo Gore, Brenda Gayle Plummer, Gerald Horne, Robin D. G. Kelley, Nikhil Singh, Carol Anderson, and Penny Von Eschen, have written about how certain African Americans helped to internationalize Black American politics and identity through their travels, writings, migrations, social networks, and political affiliations. Essie Robeson was one such figure. In September 1943, she wrote of her international views and identity: "In my travels about the world I have come to realize that we are not only lumped together as Negroes, 13 million of us, we are lumped together, in the world view, as Colored Peoples. . . . Whether we want to be or not, you and I are not only brothers and sisters in our little American Negro family, we are also fellow members in the very big family of Colored Peoples."[11] She increasingly viewed herself as a part of a "world family" as well as an African Diasporic and Third World family.

In fact, while much of the discussion of the Robesons' global politics in the postwar years focuses on the politics of East versus West, a more careful look at Essie's writings, speeches, and activism forces us to shift our attention from the Soviet Union to the growing sense of community and solidarity that was being forged in the global South. Essie's strong ties to and interest in India and the Caribbean were superseded only by her deep and abiding passion for, and commitment to, the cause of African freedom and liberation. Through her three significant visits to western, southern, and central Africa, Essie developed some enduring relationships on the continent, furthered her understanding of its complex political landscape, and deepened her Pan-Africanist views.[12]

No matter how far from home Essie's journeys took her, she always found her way back to New York City and to Harlem. She felt a sense of comfort and place there that eluded her in Europe, Russia, and even Africa. Upon her return to the United States, Essie was often overcome with a sense of reassurance and affirmation. In her words, "When the ship enters New York harbor, I am excited." When "the ship begins slowly to come to berth against one of the largest piers in the world, and gradually in the smiling, shouting and waiting people, the face of John and Frank, my brothers, of Minnie Sumner, Corrine Cook, Buddy Bolling come into focus, my gates are open and I am overwhelmed with a grand feeling that I am home again."[13]

The following chapters chronicle Essie Robeson's life, although not always in a perfectly neat timeline, in part because the overlapping themes, patterns, and ideas that stretch across multiple decades sometimes need to be discussed together, and in part because not every year in Essie's life was equally eventful or equally well documented. Overall, however, Essie Robeson lived what biographers call a well-preserved life. She made sure of it. She marked her journey, maintained and saved voluminous correspondence and news clippings, published her thoughts and ideas as widely as she could, and saved many of her public speeches and private diaries. To his enormous credit, Essie's son, Paul Jr., a researcher and biographer in his own right, and his wife, Marilyn Robeson, have devoted untold hours and resources to preserving the historical record of the lives of Essie and Paul Robeson. Therefore I had a wealth of material to draw on: the Paul and Eslanda Robeson Collection at the Moorland-Spingarn Manuscript Collection, Howard University (which includes many of the powerful and revealing photographic images that I have used to help tell Essie's story), and the smaller and overlapping Robeson collection, mainly on microfilm, at the Schomburg Center for Research in Black Culture in New York City. But the primary sources do not stop there. Essie lived a dynamic and engaged life and she was constantly on the move, with friendships that stretched from Delhi to London to Accra to Harlem. Her way of keeping in touch was to write, and thus there is a treasure trove of letters scattered around the globe that document and map Essie's political and social networks and relationships. There are also international archives that have offered me a window into Essie's world: the Robeson Collection at the Akademie der Künste in Berlin, the Emma Goldman Papers in Amsterdam, the Nehru Archives in Delhi, and the A. B. Xuma Papers in Johannesburg. Finally, through their painstakingly detailed documentation of Paul's life, his two principal biographers—Martin Duberman in his more than seven-hundred-page tome published in 1988, and Paul Robeson Jr. in his subsequent two-volume portrait of his father—have offered a partial but substantial roadmap to Essie's life. Both biographers rely heavily on the material that Essie had preserved and the diaries and papers that she left behind.

Still, for me, the story becomes most interesting when we travel off the beaten path. Essie's journey is perhaps most exciting, and most telling, when she is on her own—in Paris in the summer of 1932 meeting an array of extraordinary and colorful characters; in South Africa and Uganda in 1936 where her real passion for Africa and politics were ignited; and in the Congo in 1946, interviewing an eclectic group of Africans and then making her way down the Congo River in the fierce heat and rain.

In the following pages I will privilege Essie's own words in retelling her story, largely because she was such a talented and underappreciated writer and she can, in many instances, write for herself better than I can paraphrase her ideas. I will also rely on Essie's writings, published and unpublished, because too few of them ever reached a wide audience. Her correspondence alone deserves an edited volume, and her many novels and plays that publishers rejected for a variety of reasons (some fair, some unfair) tell yet another story.

But even though I have foregrounded Essie's own articulated views, and situated her in a wider world, I understand that I still have another job to do. And that is to add myself to the mix (however humbly). This happens whether we biographers admit to it or not, so I admit it: this story is also in part about me. It is biased in favor of my curiosities and questions, my passions and predilections, and it is subject to my judgment calls and assessments of what matters and what does not. In a sense, for every page written there is another page that could have been written, with details and caveats added, or with simply a view of the same moment captured through a different lens. But I have made choices. And one of these was not to create a mammoth text that attempts to transcribe Essie Robeson's life, but rather to offer a narrated and annotated chronicle punctuated with observations and analyses. In the end, I hope the story I have crafted is a fair and honest portrait of an amazing, talented, tough, and complex woman.

I should also underscore the obvious, that this is not another biography of Paul Robeson. Many people I have talked to over the years about this project start off talking about Essie, but in five minutes end up asking, telling, or theorizing about Paul. Enough of that. There are already two very fine biographies of Essie's "fabulously talented" and "terrifically brave" husband, and many more articles, book chapters, smaller biographical portraits, and even children's books about him. So even though I, like many others, was captivated by Paul long before I ever got to know Essie, this is her story, and Paul is a supporting actor in it.

What follows, then, are fourteen chapters arranged in general chronological order. Chapter 1 skims the surface of Essie's youth and family history, offering what little is known about this period. Chapters 2 through 5 give the highlights of Essie's early life with Paul, including her role as hard-working and determined manager of his theatrical and musical career, their marital woes, and their growing ambitions. As Essie herself articulates in a letter to Carl Van Vechten years later, her early life goals were social, artistic, and professional, and centered around Paul. Later her ambitions became political and looked out to the larger world. Chapters 6 through 10 chronicle her growing engagement with that wider world and how she evolved and changed as a result. Chapters 11 and 12 examine the repression and political persecution Essie and Paul experienced in the 1950s, the toll it took on their health and well-being, and how, above all, Essie responded with dogged resilience, unwavering strength, and a renewed commitment to her political views and to her family. Paul and Essie's passports were confiscated in 1950, and for eight long years Paul's career and income suffered severely because the couple could not travel overseas. Essie helped to coordinate a campaign against the travel ban and continued to speak out vociferously against U.S. government policies.

When the passport battle was finally won, the Robesons left the United States for a five-year stay abroad. Chapters 13 and 14 chronicle this time of new possibilities and new limitations, when the possibilities were political, and the limitations physical and personal. Essie wrote to a friend in the early 1960s that she had more ideas than ever before and less and less energy to implement them. During the couple's time in London from 1958 to 1963, Essie reconnected with old friends and reached out to new ones, particularly in the African Diasporic and expatriate communities. She supported numerous organizations and wrote prolifically about Africa, African Americans, and the world.

When the Robesons returned to the United States in 1963, the world was in flux. Essie's relationship to the resurgent U.S. Black Freedom movement and the postcolonial world during this time is also highlighted in the final chapters of the book. Despite Paul's poor health, Essie continued to write extensively about the burgeoning civil rights and Black Power movements and international affairs. She even trekked to the United Nations to sit in on certain sessions, see old colleagues, and bear witness to the historic events that were being debated and discussed. Essie delighted in the upsurge of activity on the part of Black activists, artists, and intellectuals in the mid-1960s. She saw the world shifting and changing before her eyes, yet again and there must have been some satisfaction in the knowledge that she had played a role.

Essie Robeson lived a life that was complicated and vibrant, rich and full, privileged but often difficult. Along the way she made some hard choices about the path she was going to follow, and about the kind of woman she was going to be. Tough and determined, Essie fought long and hard for the ideas she believed in and on behalf of the people she loved and admired. She won some battles and lost others, but she was a fighter to the end.

one

GROWING UP ALONG THE COLOR LINE, 1895-1918

Ever since I can remember, I have always been determined
never to let anyone push me around.
Eslanda Robeson

Eslanda Cardozo Goode (or Essie, as her friends and family called her) came from a long line of Black educators who placed a high premium on literacy and learning—and who had to fight for their place in the world every step of the way. Essie, named after her mother, would become the most academically accomplished of the three Goode siblings, but she would also mature into a fearless and tenacious fighter when circumstances called for it. And circumstances often did. "My grandfather Cardozo went to prison for his beliefs, so I have it in my blood," she once told a friend.[1] She inherited her fighting spirit and her love of learning from both her maternal grandfather and her mother, the two Cardozos who had the most lasting influence on her life and thinking.[2]

Essie recalled her first run-in with racism, which happened when she was a little girl, not yet five years old, living in an integrated neighborhood in the nation's capital. She recounted the incident this way: "One of the earliest things I remember is playing with a little boy who lived across the street from us . . . it was about the year 1900. The boy was white but I had not yet realized that there was any color difference between us. . . . One day while we were playing I wanted my turn at something—a game or a toy, I don't remember exactly what it was. I had waited for my turn, but he wouldn't let me have it. I insisted and he got angry and called me a 'nigger.' I asked what it meant. He said it meant something bad—and something black. That infuriated me, for I knew I wasn't bad and I wasn't black. I pushed him and then I chased him home. His mother asked me why we were fighting and I told her what he had called me and that I was going to kill him if he called me any more bad names."[3]

Despite a few more fights and scuffles, Essie had mostly fond memories of her childhood growing up in Washington, D.C., and New York City in the late 1890s and early 1900s. She was the youngest of three children, and the only girl, born on December 15, 1895. Eslanda and John Goode had four children but only three survived. A baby girl, Dorothy, born in 1897, lived only a few short months.[4] Her eldest brother was John Cardozo Goode, born on April 20, 1892, and named after his father. The middle child, Francis Cardozo Goode, the largest and most athletic of the three, was born May 14, 1894.[5] The Goode family settled into a comfortable life in Washington but the stability and good fortune was short-lived. John Goode died suddenly when Essie was only five years old.[6] Even though he had been a successful man and a hard worker, according to relatives he had also been a heavy drinker, which may have contributed to his early death.[7]

After she lost her husband, Essie's mother moved the family to New York for better job opportunities. In Essie's words, her mother "rose to the occasion when she was left a penniless widow with three children, gathered us into her arms and ventured forth to New York (where everyone went and still goes to make a fortune)."[8] They lived for a time in what Essie later described as "a cold-water railroad flat." But her mother worked hard and soon reestablished her footing in the Black middle class. Essie recalled an essentially happy childhood. She described herself as a "fat, healthy tomboyish little girl" accomplished in academics and in sports.[9] But life for Essie and her family was not always carefree or simple. Like most educated Black people in this period, her family's accomplishments were precariously maintained. They were relatively advantaged, but still constrained by the strictures of racism that applied to poor and prosperous alike. Even in cosmopolitan New York City in 1900 there were racist restrictions on where Negroes could eat, live, work, and socialize. The Cardozo-Goode family felt the sting of discrimination like everyone else.

On her mother's side, Essie came from a long line of prominent, highly educated Black people who had managed to attain success during the nineteenth and twentieth centuries, despite rampant racism. They were proud of being Negroes, but also proud of their Spanish ancestry. The Cardozos traced their heritage to a clan of wealthy Sephardic Jews who had been expelled from the Iberian Peninsula centuries earlier. The family was not wealthy, but was on the whole better off than many of their Negro counterparts. Essie's maternal grandfather, Francis Lewis Cardozo, was a notable South Carolina politician during Reconstruction who later became a respected educator in Washington, D.C. His legacy loomed large in the family lore. Even though Essie barely knew her maternal grandfather, she knew his illustrious life story well and recounted it often as an adult.[10]

Francis Lewis Cardozo, a man so light-skinned that he could have passed for white if he had chosen to do so, was the son of a free Black mother of mixed ancestry, Lydia Williams, and a rich, white Charleston businessman, Isaac Nunez Cardozo.[11] Not much is known about Lydia's background or whether she was ever enslaved, but as an adult she lived the life of a free "colored" woman. When Isaac died, Lydia and the couple's seven children fell on hard times. There is no firm evidence that Isaac was actually married to Lydia, since interracial marriage was illegal in the state of South Carolina at that time. Rumor had it that they had traveled to Ohio to marry and returned to Charleston to live quietly as husband and wife. Essie's accounts of her great-grandparents are of the "happy couple" living in a "beautiful home" before Isaac's death. Isaac passed away when Francis was still a boy, and the children were not recognized as legal heirs to the Cardozo family estate.[12] Regardless of the legalities, Essie's mother nurtured a strong connection to the Cardozo lineage. Essie observed proudly that she had "Spanish blood," and from the antebellum period onward, family names were preserved: "There has always been a Francis and an Eslanda in every generation of the Cardozos."[13] Essie and her two brothers also bore Cardozo as their legal middle name.

Despite his father's death and his family's financial struggles, young Francis did well for himself. He worked as a shipbuilder's apprentice and carpenter in South Carolina, eventually making his way to Scotland, where he attended the University of Edinburgh and earned academic accolades. He subsequently moved to England and studied briefly at Oxford. Upon his return to the United States, Francis settled in New Haven, Connecticut. There, he met and married Catharine Romena Howell, a "pure white looking woman with patrician features" who was of Scotch, Danish, and West Indian descent. The couple had five children: the four boys, George, Francis, William, and Henry; and a girl, Eslanda.[14] Along the way, Francis had become a Presbyterian minister, so the new couple spent a short time in New Haven before they accepted an offer from the American Missionary Association to open a religious school in Charleston, South Carolina, in the immediate aftermath of the Civil War. Under Cardozo's leadership, the Saxon School evolved into a highly respected institution, and was eventually renamed the Avery Institute of South Carolina.[15]

Based on his career as an educator and given the racial reforms of Reconstruction, Francis was able to launch a short but distinguished political career. He was elected state treasurer of South Carolina, becoming the first African American to hold statewide office. After two terms as treasurer, during which he pushed for educational and land reforms to benefit freed Blacks, he became Secretary of State, a position he held until 1877. Historians have described Francis Cardozo as both "a symbol of integrity" and a rigorous proponent of the rights of Black freed people.[16] By the time he became Secretary of State, however, former Confederate leaders had begun to regain political power in the South, staging targeted and effective misinformation campaigns to unseat progressive Blacks like Francis who had managed to secure positions of influence during Reconstruction. Francis fought back hard against the resurgent white elites, but was unable to hold on. As the Cardozos' own family history would have it, Francis Cardozo's persecution centered on his refusal to be complicit in the notorious Tilden-Hayes presidential compromise of 1877. That compromise followed the presidential election of 1876, which was a near tie. To resolve the deadlock, Republican Rutherford B. Hayes essentially agreed to an unsavory compromise: to pull federal troops from the South, effectively ending Reconstruction and the political inclusion and enfranchisement of Blacks. The Democrats, the forces that had supported slavery and opposed Black citizenship rights, asked Francis to throw his support behind Tilden in exchange for a crude cash reward. As the story was recounted to future generations of Cardozos, he would not even consider such an unprincipled proposition. Consequently, he was soon arrested on trumped-up embezzlement charges, tried, convicted, and jailed for one year. After his release from prison, he resettled in Washington, D.C., where racism was less harsh and the color line a bit less rigid.[17] Indeed, the racial tensions were so high in South Carolina at the end of Reconstruction in 1876 that his immediate family had to flee the state the night after he was arrested for fear of Ku Klux Klan reprisals. They spent a year in Washington, D.C., awaiting Cardozo's release.

When Francis first arrived in Washington, D.C., despite having been an elected official and having impressive academic credentials, the only job he was offered was as a janitor in a government building. He declined the offer, secured a position as a clerk, and after a short time was able to return to the field of education, which he loved. Francis Cardozo went on to found two prominent high schools in Washington and to establish himself as a preeminent and pioneering Negro educator.[18] Cardozo High School in northwest Washington, D.C., still bears his name.

Francis shared a special relationship with his only daughter, Eslanda (Essie's mother). He was a father, a teacher, mentor, role model, and gentle patriarch. When she was a young woman, Eslanda often took long walks with her father after dinner, during which they would exchange ideas about history, culture, and politics. Francis Cardozo respected his daughter's views and opinions and encouraged her to express them openly. The two of them "talked long and earnestly about the Negro problem," and Francis made sure his daughter had a good sense of Negro history.[19] Eslanda Cardozo was deeply influenced both by her father and by the illustrious guests whom he frequently hosted in their home, including on at least one occasion the revered abolitionist and statesman Frederick Douglass, and his wife, Helen Pitts Douglass.[20]

Writing about her grandfather many years after his death, Essie Robeson's recollections were vivid, more vivid than her own childhood memories could explain. Her mother, it seems, told and retold stories of her own father with such vigor that they became ingrained in each of her children. Decades after her grandfather's death, Essie recalled, "All during my childhood I heard and read about Francis Lewis Cardozo and his great contribution to the making of Reconstruction history. . . .We are all very proud of his great dignity and integrity."[21] Essie's mother followed in her father's footsteps to pursue a career, albeit short-lived, as an educator, before marriage and motherhood. So important was Francis Cardozo's legacy to his descendants that Essie and her mother actually had an argument decades after his death about who had a right to tell his story in book form.[22] By contrast, very few family stories are recounted about Eslanda's mother, Essie's grandmother, Catharine Romena Howell, who lived well into her eighties. We know that she was born in Connecticut in about 1843, met Francis Cardozo while singing in the church choir, then married and moved to South Carolina with him.[23]

Color was important to the Cardozos. In a lengthy section that Essie wrote for her 1930 book *Paul Robeson, Negro*—and later omitted—she explored the nuances of color consciousness among Negroes of her class and generation. Every family she knew had a light-skinned relative who, as she put it, had "crossed over." Her own great uncle Jacob Cardozo had merged into white Louisiana society, marrying and raising a family, most of whom, as Essie put it, "never knew of his Negro blood." Years later one of Jacob's sons came to Washington, D.C., and, somewhat inadvertently, met his Negro cousins, one of whom was Essie's mother.[24] Such discoveries were not uncommon, Essie insisted. She recounted in detail the findings of an investigative report (no citation given) that documented how some Negro individuals had disappeared from the census records only to have whites with the same names and birth dates surface ten years later. These "disappearances" were part of the widespread practice of light-skinned Blacks passing for white in order to obtain better jobs, opportunities, and social status. The families of these individuals, Essie insisted, were usually complicit in the deception, or defection, as it were. In her words, "If today a Negro meets his fairer brother in the company of a white person in a downtown street, the darker one gives no sign of recognition unless the fair one does so first. This has been an unwritten law among Negroes for years: one must never speak to a fair brother or sister on the street unless spoken to first; the fair one might be 'passing,' and if he is greeted familiarly by a Negro his secret may be revealed."[25]

Whether Essie's account of this so-called unwritten rule is fully accurate, or whether the reality is a bit more nuanced, is up for debate. What is known is that the color line was taken seriously in America and among American Negroes, and that individual decisions about whether or how to cross that line were always complex and fraught with anxiety. At the same time, a sense of fairness and equity pervaded the Cardozo family's values. One historian of nineteenth-century South Carolina schools noted that although he lived in a color-conscious world where light-skinned Negroes experienced real privileges, Francis Cardozo was an anti-racist educator who "ridiculed the notion that (so-called) mulattos learned more quickly than darker students" and "harbored no racial prejudice" toward dark-skinned Blacks. He believed that all students had similar abilities and the same rights to an education.[26] Needless to say not all of his contemporaries agreed.

Eslanda Elbert Cardozo married John Jacob Astor Goode on June 16, 1890, ended her brief teaching career, and began to raise a family.[27] It was the eve of the twentieth century; a century that W. E. B. Du Bois wrote would be divided and defined by the color line. It was a line that Essie's family alternately walked, crossed, ignored, and challenged.

Essie's mother was so light-skinned herself that a 1900 census taker mistook her for a white woman, most likely further confused by the fact that all of the family's immediate neighbors were white.[28] Eslanda Cardozo had rebelled against elitist attitudes about skin color within some quarters of her own family by marrying a dark-skinned man. John Goode was handsome and well educated, and Eslanda had great expectations for his future success, perhaps to prove her color-conscious relatives wrong as much as anything else. Ironically, Eslanda was still not completely free of her own subtle color bias, and would one day frown upon her own daughter's choice of a dark-skinned husband.[29]

John Goode could not claim as aristocratic a lineage as his wife, and his children knew far less about his family history. The one thing Essie did know is that her paternal grandparents claimed partial American Indian ancestry, although she did not know which tribe or ethnicity they belonged to.[30] She also knew that her father was an accomplished man. Born in Cook County, Illinois, in 1861, just as the Civil War commenced, John J. A. Goode was raised in Chicago.[31] He graduated from Evanston Township High School (in a northern Chicago suburb), and later earned degrees from both Northwestern University in Evanston, Illinois, and Howard University Law School in Washington, D.C. Records from the National Archives indicate that John Jacob Astor Goode—his "robber baron" name hints that his parents had grand ambitions for his future—enjoyed a solid career as a government employee. He was appointed to a position as a federal government clerk in 1885 at a decent salary of $1,000 a year. After a promotion and raise, that figure went up to $1,200 a few years later.[32] Census records, newspaper social pages, and other primary and secondary sources paint a picture of Washington, D.C.'s African American community in the late 1800s as highly stratified and intensely class and color conscious.[33] The Goodes navigated that social landscape with great care.

We can only imagine what family life must have been like for Eslanda Goode and her children during her decade-long marriage, given her husband's alcohol addiction. It could not have been easy. Perhaps the fact that John and his extended family were rarely discussed when Essie was growing up is evidence that some memories were too painful to hold on to, even for the tough and preserving Mrs. Goode. It wasn't until more than two decades after her father's passing that Essie finally had a "long talk with mother about father's death. Got some interesting facts about him that I never knew before."[34]

After John's premature death in 1901, Eslanda Goode's life changed dramatically. She was forced reluctantly back into the workforce as a young widow. Teaching no longer seemed like an option. It was a profession for young single women, or older women who were never married. And besides, it did not pay terribly well. After casting about for a suitable and adequately lucrative career, she decided to work in the growing beauty industry. Eslanda began as a beautician and beauty consultant, but soon advanced to running her own salon and managing a beauty consultancy that catered to a very elite clientele of mainly white women, including "Mrs. Joseph Pulitzer and Mrs. George Gould." Most of her clients assumed that Essie's mother was white too, and she told them no different. Hard work, grit, and an entrepreneurial spirit carried her through challenging times.[35]

Essie's recollections of how her mother began her entry into the business world are telling. She proudly described "the almost masculine intelligence with which Eslanda attacked her [career] problem," referring to her mother's methodical study of the beauty services market in her native Washington. After soberly assessing her options, Eslanda decided to move her children from Washington, D.C., to New York City where she determined that there were better business opportunities. "The genteel trades such as dressmaking and millinery did not appeal to her," but once she decided on her career path, "she built up a fine private trade and charged and received high prices for her work."[36] Her mother was a strong-willed, formidable person who railed against defeat and was reluctant to ask for help. She managed to wrestle her way out of a very bleak situation to make a decent life for herself and her children. Eslanda Cardozo's pragmatic and highly disciplined manner had an enormous effect on young Essie. She would come to embrace these traits as the cornerstones of survival (and success) for a Black woman in an often hostile and unpredictable world.

The elder Eslanda was a tough, resilient person who eschewed frills and frivolous behavior. For example, "In 1900, when women were wearing voluminous skirts, enormous hats, tight corsets and an absurd femininity that went with those inconvenient and ridiculous garments," Essie's mother rejected all that. It is true that with few options open to her, she found her career niche in the female-dominated beauty industry.[37] But in Essie's mind, her mother was defined less by the type of work she did, and more by her discipline and hard work, which were important ingredients for her success. Even though Essie's mother was a good provider for her three children, she did not pamper them. And much of the responsibility for cooking and cleaning fell on Essie, as the only girl among the three siblings. By the time she entered college, Essie "knew all about housekeeping, having kept house for our little family for several years while my mother went out to work."[38]

Essie and her brothers did not enjoy many luxuries growing up, but they never wanted for the basics. According to Essie, these "basics" included: "ice skates, roller skates, bicycles, baseballs . . . sleds, tennis racquets and a bathing house at the seashore in summer."[39] Her mother made sure that the children had sports equipment and books, which she regarded as tools for a healthy life and windows into the larger world, but when it came to stylish clothes, there was none of that. Later in life, Essie would write that this "deprivation" was helpful because it toughened her up and forced her to prioritize substance over the superficial. She remembered one afternoon when she and her brothers were being teased and taunted by other children for wearing out-of-date clothing. Essie decided she had had enough. With words, wit, and two fists ready for action, the chubby little girl walked right into the center of the jeering crowd of children and told them off. "My mother says she is dressing up our minds," not our bodies, she proclaimed, quieting the crowd. The message was that the Goode siblings were A students because they worried about matters more important than clothes and accessories.[40] The bullies backed off.

Essie described herself as a tough little girl and a modest and serious-minded teenager. "I remember when I was a girl growing up in Harlem, I had to make up my mind what I wanted to be. Did I want to dress well, or did I want to develop my personality rather than my appearance? . . . Most of the girls were concerned about how their faces, hair, and clothes looked as they passed the boys, but I was more concerned about my behavior." Essie did not want to appear, in her words, to be "available" to local boys. She wanted their respect more than their amorous attention, or so she wrote many years later.[41] Essie grew into a no-nonsense teenager who was unafraid to challenge things that were, to her mind, simply unacceptable—like racism. She had vowed at an early age never to let anyone "push me around," but the segregation laws and customs of the 1910s were pushing her and her fellow Negroes around at every turn. One day, tired and thirsty after an afternoon of shopping, Essie marched up to the whites-only counter in Liggett's Drug Store "and in a firm voice ordered an ice cream soda." She likely raised a few eyebrows, but she got her vanilla ice cream soda and enjoyed her first taste of effective political action.[42]

Essie witnessed other political actions on the streets of New York—

collective ones—and they were not always peaceful. When she was eleven years old she saw an explosive protest against police brutality outside of her apartment. Looking out her window, she noticed a group of police gathering and angry Harlem residents yelling at them. "At first I thought it was a parade," she recollected years later, "but there was tenseness in the air that didn't go with parades. Then the police came in the street in pairs. Bottles and bricks and hot water were thrown at them from windows and rooftops. I asked people what this was all about and they told me, 'we're sick of these Irish cops beating up Negroes and we are going to teach them a lesson.' We thought all the police in New York were Irish. I learned afterwards that trigger-happy or mean white policemen often abused the people of Harlem."[43] Such protests were not uncommon in the 1910s as a growing Black urban population demanded more space and greater respect.

Essie's family lived on 135th Street and she and her brothers attended Public School 119. After that she attended Wadleigh High School and played basketball on the girl's team at St. Christopher's Parish House, while John attended Townsend Harris Hall High School, the feeder school for the College of the City of New York, where he later enrolled.[44] The children went to racially integrated schools, some of which were mostly white.[45] Essie also held treasured memories of exploring all of New York City as a young girl. She and her friends went skating at City College near her apartment, then farther south in Central Park as well as in the northerly Bronx at Van Cortlandt Park. She and her brothers also went swimming at the beach in the summer.[46]

In addition to her emphasis on hard work, Essie's mother also instilled a sense of collective obligation and reciprocity in her children. They were responsible not just for themselves, she insisted, but for each other as well. They played together, stood up for each other, and helped one another with homework. If one of the Goode siblings came home with a poor report card, they all suffered the consequences. The family's routine Friday night "party," which included games, candy, and cards, was summarily canceled if any one of the children brought home grades that were not up to par. The lesson was that they had to rely on one another and support one another. They rose or fell together. This message of family loyalty stuck with Essie as well.[47]

In 1912 Essie and her mother relocated to Chicago in pursuit of greater financial opportunity. Essie's mother agreed to take over and manage a beauty salon on the South Side of Chicago on a one-year trial basis. As a result, Essie and her mother moved to Illinois, where

Essie finished high school and enrolled in college the following year. Her brothers were several years older than she, and by this time they had both already completed high school, so they stayed behind in New York. John, the elder of the two, had been enrolled at City College the year before, but was forced to withdraw after his first semester because he could not afford the tuition.[48] We can only assume from this that Essie's mother was struggling to support herself and her children and that the move to Chicago may have been her only option.

Once Essie and her mother had arrived in the city and settled into a house at 2959 Wabash Avenue on Chicago's South Side, Essie's mother enrolled her teenage daughter in the newly opened Lucy L. Flower Technical High School for girls, named after the turn-of-the-century social reformer.[49] It was one of three high schools in the city that accepted Negro children, and in each case the Black students were a minority. Essie was one of thirty-eight Negroes in her school, which enrolled hundreds of students.[50] While attending Lucy Flower High School, Essie met a gifted and devoted music teacher, Teresa Armitage, who would become a mentor and lifelong friend.[51] Essie had a beautiful contralto singing voice as a child and even briefly considered a career in music. Armitage was an accomplished musician and educator who was the author of several texts on musical instruction and was much sought after as a vocal coach.[52] She took a special interest in Essie and went so far as to make preliminary arrangements for her to study voice one summer in Italy. But it would never come to pass. The pragmatic Mrs. Goode deemed this career path entirely too impractical for her daughter and the idea was cast aside. Still Essie was so fond of Armitage that she kept in touch for decades. Years later, Essie would hire Armitage to coach Paul Robeson as he sought to expand his vocal range for concert performances.[53]

For some unexplained reason, Essie transferred from Flower High School in Chicago to Urbana High School in Urbana, Illinois, during her senior year.[54] But at both schools, Essie excelled in academics and sports. She won a highly competitive four-year scholarship to attend the University of Illinois, a well-respected public college in the cornfields of Urbana, Illinois, several hours' drive south of Chicago. Fierce and determined, she was one of fourteen students (among them only three women) who took a rigorous examination for the much sought-after public scholarship.[55] She learned about the test entirely by chance from a boy she met one night at a graduation party. Although the test was being given the very next morning, Essie rushed home to study for the exam, aided by her mother. She was one of three to win the coveted scholarship, guiltily edging out the boy who had given her the tip.[56] When she arrived on campus, she was among only a handful of Negro students. A chilling indicator of the racial climate at the time was that the Ku Klux Klan had an open and active chapter on campus.[57]

Racism notwithstanding, Essie migrated to the farmlands of the Midwest eager to immerse herself in the college experience. She initially gravitated to the humanities, studying what proved to be a rather boring "domestic science" curriculum that consisted of classes designed to train young women to be good wives, mothers, and caretakers. Essie had a different trajectory in mind and ultimately found that the hard science courses were the most intriguing and challenging. She chose chemistry as her major and was often one of the few women, and in most cases the only Negro, in her classes at the University of Illinois.[58]

While Essie was away at college, her mother decided to move back to New York City to pursue other business opportunities. She developed various beauty products and even managed to patent a beauty cream that she had invented.[59] Mrs. Goode also became involved in the civic life of Harlem, where she lived. Both of her sons served in the military during World War I, so in 1918 she volunteered as a supervisor at a military canteen at 6 West 131st Street. The Mayor's Committee of Women oversaw canteens throughout the city, and the Harlem canteen served one thousand Black soldiers a week. Mrs. Goode eventually resigned from her voluntary post because she felt that the Harlem canteen was underutilized. She was a notable enough person that her resignation from one volunteer position warranted mention in the national edition of the *Chicago Defender*, a prominent Black newspaper.[60] More relevant to the political views that her daughter would embrace later in life, in the 1910s Mrs. Goode was a supporter of Black socialist internationalist Hubert Harrison. After she moved back to New York, she was a volunteer for Harrison's *The Voice* newspaper and possibly a member of the Harlem-based Liberty League, which produced the paper. She also organized young girls in the neighborhood to sell the paper and to solicit subscriptions. The content of the paper reflected Harrison's ideas and politics. He was a Caribbean-born radical intellectual and independent thinker, and a powerful orator, who opposed "capitalism, White supremacy, and the Christian church," and "supported socialism, 'race consciousness,' racial equality, women's equality, freethought, and birth control."[61] It is interesting and significant that Mrs. Goode was associated with Harrison; this connection might explain young Essie's nascent exposure to radical ideas.

Essie's mother's involvement with Harrison was not an aberration but an extension of other political organizing and advocacy that she was involved in during and after World War I. She was one of the leaders of the "new group of suffrage workers" of New York. She spoke at numerous venues and forums around Harlem, including at a Liberty League meeting on Lenox Avenue on September 30, 1917, where she delivered a talk on "The New Negro Woman," and at the Harlem People's Forum at Lafayette Hall on November 4, 1917, when she raised her voice as a representative of "the new group of suffrage workers." Mrs. Goode was not simply interested in women's rights generically; rather she wanted to make sure that "colored women" were included in any demand for rights. In fact when woman suffrage was on the state ballot in New York in 1917, Goode advocated that Negro voters not support it as a strategic challenge to white women leaders who were not factoring Black women into their agenda as Goode felt they should. She insisted that the white woman suffragists had to take a public stand "on the status of colored women" before they could enjoy her support.[62]

Never a woman to bite her tongue or shy away from a challenge, and an active and outspoken opponent of injustice, as her father was, Mrs. Goode was a role model for the young Essie, who likewise prided herself on being assertive, ambitious, and engaged. Her mother encouraged Essie to be bold but never reckless. This advice applied to life in general, but to Essie's career plans in particular. Once Essie had changed her major to chemistry, "she had long talks with her mother, and between them, they decided she would be happiest working in a laboratory."[63] The best opportunities for scientific laboratory work were in New York, they determined. So, Essie transferred to Columbia University's Teachers College, a few short blocks from Harlem, for her final year of college. She loved the intellectual stimulation and cultural dynamism of New York City, and she enjoyed her classes at Teachers College. Essie dropped out of school in the spring of 1917 due to an unspecified illness but she returned in 1918 and officially completed her degree in the spring of 1920.[64] She took pre-med courses that summer.

Just as Essie was about to finish her bachelor's degree, she struck out on her own. She found an apartment, a roommate, and a job that she would continue after graduation. She wanted to be her own woman and make her mark on the world. Essie conscientiously worked to expand her social and intellectual horizons beyond her small group of medical coworkers and former Columbia classmates. She had joined the Delta Sigma Theta Sorority for Negro women when she was a student at the University of Illinois, and she began volunteering to serve on various committees of the organization in New York. She attended the group's annual conventions, and her sorority sisters were, for a time, like a second family to her. The constellation of people whom Essie met during the early 1920s in Harlem became her social anchors and sources of moral and emotional sustenance as the years went by. Harlem would remain her home base for the rest of her life: the place to which she returned time and again to rejuvenate and regain her bearings.

When summing up her early life, Essie often painted her family portrait in convenient broad strokes: they were proud and accomplished people with a legacy of service, struggle, and success. Her actual family history was more complicated. The daughter of a single mother, a widow, and an alcoholic father, Essie lived in three different cities growing up and the family was at times insecure financially. She witnessed her first Black protest against police harassment at a young age and engaged in self-styled protests of her own by the time she was a teenager. With her sharp tongue and quick wit, she was not one to shy away from a fight or to let anyone intimidate her. Essie's mother set a strong example. She was a formidable woman, a woman who refused to be defeated by circumstances or self-pity. She made her own path and followed it unflinchingly. She was a tough and self-reliant person but one who gravitated to collective action and radical ideas. A supporter of women's rights and an ally of Black Socialists, nationalists, and internationalists through her association with *The Voice*, Eslanda Goode was a powerful figure in her daughter's life. As young Essie pursued her career and made a life for herself, she was ever reminded that she was, inescapably, her mother's daughter.

two

A HARLEM LOVE STORY,
1919–1927

We'll try to climb that ladder to fame and fortune.
Eslanda Robeson

In 1919, Essie lived in a tiny studio apartment at 250 Seventh Avenue near 133rd Street, a prime location in the center of Harlem, New York. On humid summer nights, people would hang out of their windows, trying to catch a breeze, or gather on the stoops and street corners to mingle and commiserate about the heat. That strip of Seventh Avenue would earn a lofty place in African American history. It had been the site of massive anti-lynching rallies and fiery speeches by leaders such as A. Philip Randolph and Marcus Garvey. By the end of World War I, Harlem was a center of Black social and cultural activity. Within a half mile of the lively intersection where Essie lived, Langston Hughes would pen his elegant poetry; James Weldon Johnson would write the Black national anthem, "Lift Every Voice and Sing"; Zora Neale Hurston and Jessie Fauset would pioneer a Black women's literary tradition; and jazz legends Duke Ellington, Billie Holiday, and Thelonious Monk would perform some of the century's most unforgettable music.

It was in fact the beginning of a new, more hopeful era for many Black Americans. Educated and ambitious young Negroes were flocking to urban cities in the North in search of new opportunities. Black soldiers were returning from the battlefields of Europe with heightened expectations. Harlem was a vibrant and diverse Diasporic enclave of Jamaicans, Antiguans, Bahamians, and Black Americans. It was the dawning of the Harlem Renaissance and the emergence of the "New Negro."

Essie loved the energy and sense of possibility that was Harlem in the 1920s. And she became a close acquaintance of many of its legendary figures.

Her first apartment, Essie remembered with tempered fondness, was "the most inconvenient little flat."[1] It consisted of a kitchen, a bathroom, a closet, and one large room that doubled as a bedroom and living room. She and her roommate, Minnie Sumner, shared a pullout bed that served as a sofa by day. Entertaining unannounced guests was a challenge and a production because "there was always a scramble" to get dressed, put the bed away, and make the room presentable. But entertain they did. The two young women garnered a reputation for themselves the first week they moved in by throwing a large and lively party in their apartment, which was still empty because their furniture had not yet arrived. Essie, in one of her rare wild and spontaneous moments, agreed to play chemist and liquor distiller by concocting some homemade "bathtub" gin in honor of the occasion. People danced and drank until the wee hours of the morning. One of them was the future sociologist E. Franklin Frazier, who would become a pioneer in research on Negro families. He lived one building over. Other neighbors were artists, writers, musicians, and students.[2]

Essie remembered this period of 1919 as "that hectic summer after the war when everyone was so gay."[3] In fact, everyone was not so 'gay.' It was also the summer of the Palmer Raids against suspected communists and race riots targeting Black returning soldiers. But none of this was at the forefront of Essie's mind in 1919. For her it was a carefree time of new relationships and exciting opportunities. At this point, Essie was preparing to begin her senior year as a chemistry major at Columbia's Teachers College, after which she planned to apply to medical school. She was a serious student but not too serious to have fun. Out of this swirling, colorful Harlem scene strode Paul Bustill Robeson. Essie first met the devilishly handsome Robeson on a warm evening during that summer of 1919, as he sauntered down bustling Seventh Avenue near 135th Street.[4] Essie was with two girlfriends, and Paul was strolling along with a woman whom Essie knew just well enough to stop and greet—perhaps as an excuse to meet the handsome stranger to whose arm the woman was securely attached. Essie noticed Paul that day, and he likely noticed her as well.[5] Essie was a distinctively beautiful woman who presented herself with great confidence and poise. She stood only five feet four inches tall, and had a full, shapely figure. She wore her thick, jet-black hair straight, short, and smoothed back or tucked under a stylish hat. She wore very little make-up. Her eyes were deep set, and her flawless olive skin made her look Mediterranean, and in some sense racially ambiguous. Within Harlem's eclectic and international Black community, however, her skin tone was just another shade in the continuum of colors that ran from beige to deep brown to black.

Even before he made a name for himself on the stage, Paul was a popular and highly visible figure—"Harlem's darling" as Essie would recall. He was six feet three inches tall, had a creamy dark-chocolate complexion, a seductive bass-baritone voice, and a warm smile. His friend and collaborator Lloyd Brown would later write, "There was always a largeness about Paul Robeson."[6] A young woman who worked with Paul in the early 1920s described him as flat-out "the most beautiful man" she had ever encountered.[7] More than his physical presence, though, his personality was captivating. He was smart, engaging, and utterly charming. Conversant in sports (he had been an all-American college athlete at Rutgers), music (he had the voice of a deep-throated angel), and academics (he was the only Black student attending the prestigious Columbia University Law School), Paul was a man of many impressive talents. A friend of his reflected years later that it was almost impossible not to be enamored of Paul, and women just loved him.[8]

As much as Essie prided herself on being sensible and sober in matters of romance, after a series of casual encounters, she too was smitten. At the time she met Paul, Essie was dating a young doctor at Harlem Hospital, Grant Lucas. They had been seeing each other for nearly a year. But once Essie met Paul and learned of all his stellar accomplishments, she simply couldn't get him out of her mind. After awhile she even began orchestrating ways to casually bump into him. One such occasion was the Gingham Dance, an annual Harlem springtime affair. Thinking that Paul might be there, Essie wore a frilly white dress with "an enormous white organdie sash." Both her mother, who was never one to mince words, and her fashion-savvy friend, Minnie, discouraged her from wearing the dress, insisting she was too short and full-figured to pull it off gracefully. Stubborn even in matters of fashion, Essie ignored their advice and donned the dress anyway. In a triumph of sweet vindication, Essie was given the award for the best-dressed woman at the dance. Even more thrilling, "the popular young person of note, Paul Robeson," personally presented the prize of ten dollars in gold coins.[9]

Essie's relationship with Paul further intensified when they were both enrolled in summer school classes at Columbia University in the summer of 1920. Essie was taking additional science courses anticipating application to medical school. They met for dinners at the YWCA cafeteria, across the street from the apartment where Paul lived with his friend Jimmy Lightfoot. They attended parties together, as well as "all Negro" tennis matches. Over the summer, their romance began to bloom. To others, they seemed an unlikely pair, since at first glance these two handsome and talented young people couldn't have seemed more different. Paul was robust and jovial; Essie was short and serious. Paul was easy-going and informal; Essie was a meticulous planner. But there was a strong attraction between them. They were both intellectuals and interested in the world of ideas. She was the scientist and he was the legal scholar. Despite, or perhaps because of, their differences, they soon became a "couple."

On a typical Saturday afternoon, Paul and Essie would sit and talk on the living room floor of Essie and Minnie's apartment. Essie would tell Paul about the science classes she was taking and the experiments she observed in the lab. He would talk about his legal studies, explaining the logic and intricate details of the cases he was reading. Each one seemed to appreciate the intellectual appetite of the other. There was a strong physical attraction as well. Essie's soon-to-be former boyfriend, Grant Lucas, whom Essie would remain friends with for decades, saw less and less of her that summer as she devoted more of her time and attention to Paul, with whom she became a lover.[10]

As their romance bloomed, Essie and Paul played cards with friends, had quiet dinners together, walked arm-in-arm down the avenues of New York, and occasionally took in shows, concerts, and plays. They also enjoyed skating in the winter, and attending sports events in the spring and summer. They even went to the beach, where Essie attempted unsuccessfully to teach Paul to swim. As their relationship deepened, they weren't afraid to disagree. "They argued eternally," Essie recalled, but it was "friendly and stimulating, & impersonal."[11] They also confided in one another about their dreams and aspirations. Paul was aiming for a legal career, and Essie wanted to become a pioneering Black female doctor. In a few short years all of those dreams would be abandoned for new ones, and their two separate paths would meld together.

Essie arrived at the conclusion that they should marry probably well before Paul did, but she did not want to present the idea to him before she was sure that the feeling was mutual. She did not want a conventional marriage and was not looking solely for security. She wanted a husband who would be her friend, companion, partner, and lover.

As Essie told an interviewer many years later, "American women look to men to do things for them, to support them. I could and did support myself"—and for her, this meant both before and after marriage.[12] While these comments, made in 1949, may not have wholly reflected what she thought and felt as a young woman in 1921, this is how she came to understand and represent her own attitudes about marriage and independence.

One piece of evidence supporting the idea that early on in their relationship Essie was wary of trapping Paul into a traditional marriage is that she hid an unplanned pregnancy (and illegal abortion) from him in the spring of 1921. She wanted a life and a family with Paul, but only under the right circumstances and on the right terms. Their relationship was still unsettled when she first became pregnant, and she did not want Paul to feel obligated to marry her. So she surreptitiously enlisted her friend May Chinn, a young Harlem medical student and later physician, to help her obtain a dangerous illegal abortion. She did not tell Paul until after the procedure was over. He was not pleased with the decision and they separated briefly, but it did not permanently derail their relationship.[13]

Several months later, in August 1921, Paul proposed marriage to Essie and the couple eloped. Essie remembered vividly the day Paul proposed. He appeared unexpectedly on the doorstep of her building, professed his love, and asked her to marry him that very day. His visit was a surprise because their romance had been off and on the whole summer, which had caused Essie great anxiety. At one point, Paul had resumed seeing his old girlfriend, Gerry Neale (later Gerry Bledsoe), and Essie was frustrated and "deeply hurt" that his affections had been diverted. Their courtship had not always been smooth sailing, but they had always managed to find their way back to one another.[14] Essie was delighted that Paul had come back to her, and was thrilled with the marriage proposal.[15]

Paul's reasons for coming to Essie with such urgency that August day were complicated. Gerry Neale, the former girlfriend Paul still had feelings for, had just told him to pursue Essie instead of her because she thought Essie would be a better match for him, and after thinking it over, Paul apparently had agreed.[16] But Gerry Neale's advice was not the only reason Paul was drawn, or pushed, to Essie. By all indications, he deeply loved her. She was a formidable woman: smart, determined, and confident, all qualities that Paul found appealing and exciting. An added bonus was her haunting beauty. By the end of summer

1921, "Essie seemed to be in his blood," and he succumbed to the desire to have her in his life on a permanent basis.[17]

August 21, 1921, was a rainy summer day. Essie was recovering from a cold and a bad case of the blues, likely the result of Paul's erratic affections. She was disheveled and disoriented when her handsome suitor arrived, and she had to run around the apartment to find decent clothes to put on. When Paul asked Essie to marry him, she answered yes with such uncharacteristic abandon that the discussion quickly became not whether or when to marry but how and where. The couple went to a nearby restaurant to figure out the details. They decided to go to the clerk's office in Greenwich, Connecticut, instead of the more crowded office in New York City. Moreover, New York marriage officials had a practice of publishing the names of newlyweds in the daily paper, so they worried that the whole world would know they had married before they had a chance to tell their families and friends directly. That prospect was complicated by the fact that neither of their families would be terribly excited about the news. Paul's brother, Ben, "didn't think she [Essie] was the right woman for him." To Ben, she seemed "too abrasive" and "too ambitious." Essie's mother, for her part, was skeptical about Paul Robeson.[18] Mrs. Goode would come to respect and love him a great deal as the years went by, but her initial impression was not altogether positive.

Essie and Paul's "wedding day," as it were, was as hectic and unconventional as their lives together would be. They made two stops on their way to the train station. First, they went to the apartment of Essie's longtime friend Hattie Bolling. Hattie was a bit older than Essie and already married to Buddy, a "wonderful," generous, and affable man in Essie's view. Hattie, one of the first people whom Essie had befriended when she moved back to Harlem, had been Essie's rock: the one she turned to when she was sick or broke or both. Hattie would make chicken soup, take Essie to the doctor, and loan her money until the next payday. Hattie was like family, and Essie trusted her completely. Essie and Paul nearly dragged Hattie out of her apartment to serve as their witness in a kind of crazed gush of spontaneity. Hattie first thought they were either "mad" or playing a joke on her. When she realized they were serious, she agreed—then hesitated. She wanted to make sure that Essie was confident about this big decision and she wanted to add something special to the occasion. "She took Essie into her bedroom, and looked her in the eye and asked her if she really was going to be married. Essie replied that she thot [sic] she was but wasn't quite sure. Then Hattie said with the utmost seriousness, 'something old, something new, something borrowed, something blue,'" referring to an old tradition of what a bride needs on her wedding day to ensure good luck. She scrounged up a handkerchief, a pair of stockings, and a blue garter for Essie that would give her all the luck she should need. On the way to the train station, the trio stopped at a Woolworth's drugstore and bought a cheap tin wedding band that they could use to make the wedding official.[19]

While Hattie lamented the fact that Essie would not have a white gown and flowers, running away somehow felt right to Paul and Essie. They were running away from Paul's summer of indecision, away from all their other obligations, and away from the disapproval of their families. Essie was trying, perhaps, to outrun all the questions she might have asked herself in a more logical and sober state of mind. She let her excitement and relief overwhelm any misgivings. Starting soon after she met Paul, she had contemplated what it would mean to marry this exquisite dark giant of a man. For nearly a year, she had thought it would never happen. But as they sat and laughed on the train to Greenwich, everything fell into place. She basked in the tender charms of her soon-to-be husband, a man desired by almost every eligible woman in Harlem.

After the short train ride to Greenwich, they made their way to the local courthouse, paid a five-dollar fee, and only then learned that there was a five-day waiting period for New York residents to marry in Connecticut. Still determined to be married that very day, the determined duo traveled back to New York State, "got off the [train] car in the town of Port Chester, just over the Connecticut border, and went through the doorway under a sign that read 'town clerk.'" Fifteen minutes, a couple of "I do's," and another small fee later, they were pronounced husband and wife. Their "honeymoon" was anticlimactic. They returned to Harlem by train and parted ways with Hattie. The couple then bumped into a friend who invited them along to a tennis match, and after the match they went with a larger crowd of friends to a casual dinner at the YWCA cafeteria, never revealing that they had just officially married.[20] In fact, they would keep their marriage a secret for nearly four months, eventually telling Essie's mother, then Paul's brother and sister, and finally going public with the news in Philadelphia in December 1921, at the annual joint conventions of their sorority and fraternity, the Delta Sigma Thetas and Alpha Phi Alphas. But despite the lack of pomp and ceremony, Essie knew that her life had changed forever that day.

She was Mrs. Paul Robeson, a title she would always cherish, despite the challenges that would later come with it.

By 1949, after twenty-eight years of marriage, Essie would be blunt and pragmatic about matters of romance and fidelity. By then she knew both Paul and herself much better than she did in 1921. She knew how far she could bend and where she had to draw the line. In 1949 she wrote, "I believe that in marriage the partners have to decide what they want, find out how much of what they want they have a fair chance of getting, and then settle for that. Most people want it all roses. There just aren't that many roses."[21] But in the summer of 1921 the roses were in full bloom for Essie and Paul.

After their secret nuptials, Essie continued to work full-time in the hospital for several years to support the two of them. Paul was still in law school at Columbia, earning extra money playing football on the weekends. He even worked briefly as a postal clerk to supplement their household income. But continuing her job was not a big sacrifice for Essie. She liked her work and enjoyed her co-workers, even her eccentric boss, a much-beloved physician nicknamed "Wild Bill Clark." Essie eventually stopped taking the science classes she would have needed to prepare for medical school—that would have to wait, she reasoned—but she still found her laboratory work intellectually stimulating. Her pathology laboratory was near one of the operating rooms in the hospital that had an observer's gallery for students. Essie would sometimes wander over and watch the surgeons at work when things were not busy in the lab. Although she was still toying with the idea of medical school, that dream would grow fainter and fainter.

What Essie increasingly found fascinating was the art and culture of the Harlem Renaissance, the personalities that surrounded it, and the progress she thought it represented for Negroes. Even though she did not know it yet, she was about to be swept out of the world of science and into some of the most dynamic literary and arts circles in New York City and London. An ambitious and adventurous young woman, she had already calculated that she would go further in the world as Mrs. Paul Robeson than a smart, hard-working, attractive Negro girl could go on her own. She was practical and forward-looking if she was anything, and besides, she was totally in love with Paul and with all that was going on in Harlem. Wherever Paul Robeson was headed in 1922, whether to a comfortable life as a respected lawyer or someplace else altogether, Essie Cordozo Goode Robeson wanted to go too, not as an appendage but as a partner.

Essie and Paul's first apartment together was simple and modest, but

Essie loved it. It was a large studio on the top floor of an old Harlem brownstone on West 138th Street. Their bathroom and telephone were on the floor below, and their quarters had a sitting area, bedroom, and small kitchen. Essie kept their domestic life in order so that her new husband could excel in his studies. She managed the apartment, took care of the bills, kept food on the table, and laundered the clothes. She even developed a shopping strategy to buy suits and shirts that would complement rather than hide his natural good looks. One thing that had bothered Essie from the outset of their relationship was that Paul's clothes didn't fit properly and his shoes were rarely shined. He frequently had a rather unkempt look about him. She took care of that immediately. Within a few short months Paul Robeson had a new wife, a new residence, a new look, and would soon embrace a whole new career.[22]

Paul always loved to sing and enjoyed the theater. In some ways he was a stage director's dream: visually compelling, confident and poised in his movement, and thoroughly charismatic. He had already tried his hand at an amateur production of *Simon the Cyrenian* staged at the Harlem YWCA in 1920, and realized he was good at acting and rather enjoyed it. While still in law school, Paul accepted his first professional acting job: a part in an ill-conceived musical called *Taboo* (later renamed *Voodoo*). The musical was directed by Augustin Duncan, brother of the famed dancer Isadora Duncan, and set on a Louisiana plantation after the Civil War. Paul was cast as the nomadic minstrel named Jim and required to wear a leopard loincloth and what could only be described as a wooly "fright wig." These humble theatrical beginnings were a far cry from the complex and dignified roles he would later play. Yet Essie, ever the pragmatist, urged him to take the part, arguing that it was a necessary first step in what might be a new and very successful career.

When Essie saw Paul on stage at the Sam Harris Theatre in the opening of *Taboo*, something clicked in her mind. She realized the scope of Paul's raw talent and potential. She saw the way he moved so effortlessly on the stage, the way audiences responded to him, the way listeners were riveted by his voice. Even though the play had a short run, Essie was becoming convinced that Paul had a better chance for success on stage than in the courtroom. She began encouraging him to put his legal career on the back burner and invest more time and energy into singing and acting. As his career evolved, she would become his most astute critic and his most devoted fan. She sat in on every rehearsal, observing Paul and taking notes on his movement, intonation, weaknesses, and strengths.[23]

What was to become Paul's new career was a team effort from the very start. "We'll investigate its possibilities thoroly [*sic*], and if they look promising, we'll try to climb that ladder to fame and fortune," Essie wrote in her diary. The use of the pronoun "we" is as telling as it was deliberate. Essie was an active and dedicated partner in developing Paul's talent and promoting his nascent career; and she had no doubt that the benefits of Paul's stardom would be shared fully as well. Over the next few years, Essie remembered setting her "heart and mind more and more surely on [a] dramatic career for him."[24]

The cultural scene in Harlem in the 1920s only added to Essie's growing sense of what was possible for Paul as an artist. The Harlem Renaissance was in full swing, and the couple's vibrant social circle was populated by poets like Countee Cullen and Langston Hughes; artists like Augusta Savage; writers like Zora Neale Hurston; and musicians and composers like Roland Hayes. There were literary readings, concerts, and increasingly, stage plays and musicals featuring Black actors. Paul and Essie not only read and viewed work by these artists and writers; they also were guests at small dinners, receptions, and cocktail parties with this lively, talented bunch. Black creativity and intellectual and cultural projects of various kinds had found fertile ground in postwar Harlem.

Essie's own professional ambitions were set aside temporarily in favor of pursuing the career she began to envision for Paul. Convinced that he could be "one of the greatest actors in the world," she nudged, coaxed, and cajoled him to pursue what she had determined was his destined vocation. She clipped newspaper articles about Negroes who were enjoying successful careers in the theater. She bought tickets to Broadway plays to further entice him. When offers to perform came along, she encouraged him to accept.[25]

Essie also began to attend other stage performances around town, scouting the competition and looking for possible roles for Paul. In the process, she became a bit of an amateur theater critic. She kept a notebook in which she meticulously documented all the minute details of performances she attended. She noted costumes that didn't fit, lighting that was less than optimal, and staging that failed to fully capture the drama on stage. This artistic reconnaissance work was part of her effort to help Paul perfect his craft, expand his options, and beat out the competition.[26] It would all pay off handsomely.

Taboo drew criticism from some Black writers for its stereotypical portrayals of Black people, but Paul's performance received praise from all quarters. His skill and confidence as an actor was so evident that when the show was booked for a European tour in the summer of 1922 (with the name then changed from *Taboo* to *Voodoo*), Paul was asked to remain with the cast despite his relative inexperience. He was not entirely happy with the plot and message of *Voodoo*—neither was Essie—but they both saw this as a big break and were loathe to pass it up. In the 1920s, a handful of Negro actors found steady work in London and Paris and a refuge from Jim Crow racism. The couple agreed that Paul would travel to England after the end of his school year and remain there for the duration of the summer tour. After that, they would decide on their next move.

In June 1922, Essie saw Paul off at New York Harbor. Two weeks earlier, she had gone to the doctor with stomach pain, which turned out to be a complication from an old appendectomy. She was told she needed to have a serious operation to correct the problem. Essie kept all of this a secret from Paul and planned to have the procedure two days after his ship set sail for England. Standing on the pier that day, sick and in growing discomfort, Essie remained composed. She waved, blew kisses, and wished her "baby" well. They had been married only a year. Paul's late-night and weekend performances and his hours in the law library meant that their time together had been already limited and strained, and here they faced a long separation. A tough-minded, determined woman, Essie knew the importance of Paul's first European tour and was not about to let him miss the opportunity or be distracted due to her ill health. This attitude did not reflect the martyr in Essie; it was the manager in her.

After Paul was on his way, Essie went back to their apartment and stayed up most of the night carefully writing twenty-one letters that her neighbor would mail to Paul during her hospitalization and convalescence, one letter every few days. Each letter had some slight variations and gave a sense of advancing time. She hoped that Paul would not suspect that anything was awry. After she finished the last letter she sat down and cried, hoping all would go well, hoping she had made the right decision, but fearful that she was taking a risk and was doing so all on her own. Still, Essie had made a plan and she was sticking to it.[27] Some things proved beyond her control, however. The surgery did not go smoothly, and her plan unraveled.

Two weeks after Paul's departure, she was still in the hospital. Essie's mother tended to her devotedly, visiting her every day and sitting at her bedside for hours at a time. Hattie and Minnie visited as well, bringing her flowers and culinary contraband (namely some of Hattie's home-cooked meals).[28] Paul was so focused on making his European debut a success that he was slow to realize that something was amiss back home. He wrote to Essie dutifully and effusively, but her return letters lacked her usual attention to detail. He asked specific questions and described the people and places he saw, but Essie's replies were bland and vague. Throughout their separation, Paul expressed his love and gratitude for his "Dolly" and his "precious little wife," signing his letters "Dubby," for darling hubby. "How I long for my little girl. Always and always," he wrote.[29] He also missed Essie's talent as a critic and confidante: "So anxious for you to see me and criticize. Know you can help me. I feel awkward in new positions. I want you and only you to help me."[30]

Feeling lonely and adrift, especially since the play was not going well, Paul pressed Essie to join him in England. Finally, she wrote to him from her hospital bed, confessing everything and letting him know the extent of her illness. Still concerned about what any disruption might mean at this critical stage of Paul's career, Essie encouraged him to stay in England and finish what he had started. He was staying at a guest-house in Plymouth, England, when Essie's letter reached him telling him about her condition, and he broke down in tears. He did try to follow Essie's advice to make the best of his time in England. But when his acting gig ended abruptly, Paul booked passage back to New York immediately. He sat by Essie's hospital bedside for days, until she was finally well enough to be taken home.[31]

Essie had stoically endured the first few weeks of her illness alone, not wanting to burden her husband. In her mind, she did what she did as much for herself as for Paul. She had big plans for both of them and was not going to allow anything to stand in the way. Essie was not simply a selfless and adoring wife; she was a fully active and engaged spouse and business partner. She played a pivotal and indispensable role in Paul's early success. Without her, his career trajectory may well have been quite different. As her 1922 illness shows, her contributions took a toll. But her discipline, perseverance, and willingness to sacrifice—traits she had learned from her mother—were hard-wired into her very being. Any other course was simply unthinkable.

After Paul finished Columbia Law School in the spring of 1923, he managed to secure a job at a New York law firm through one of his school contacts. Negro lawyers were a rarity in predominately white downtown firms, and Paul's first few months at the firm were bumpy at best. Even the secretaries and stenographers in the office snubbed him, declining to take dictation from him and ignoring his questions about mundane matters like phone messages and office supplies. One even called him a "nigger" outright.[32] With the legal world proving a less dignified and rewarding place than Paul had hoped, and the lure of the stage looming large, he grew increasingly persuaded by Essie's gentle nudging to return to the theater.

In 1923 and 1924, Paul was cast in several prestigious stage productions. He did *Roseanne* with the well-known Negro actress Rose McClendon and the even more well-known Charles Gilpin; a short run of *Emperor Jones* put on by Eugene O'Neill's highly respected Provincetown Players, with Paul in the lead role of Brutus Jones; and another O'Neill play, *All God's Chillun Got Wings*, in which Paul's character, Jim Harris, has an interracial relationship with a white woman, a provocative act in the 1920s. Paul even received death threats when *Chillun* was announced.[33] Even though both of these productions featured better writing than *Taboo*, Black political leaders still criticized both *Chillun* and *Emperor Jones* for promoting negative racial stereotypes. But at that stage of their lives both Essie and Paul were more concerned with career issues than with politics, and they were willing to have Paul take less desirable parts early on with the hope that better opportunities would come later. Moreover, Paul felt that Black life should be portrayed in its entirety, the bad along with the good. In the case of *Chillun* he told one Black reporter in 1924 that O'Neill was liberal in matters of race and that the play actually mocked "petty prejudice" of any kind.[34] In terms of Paul's career, a Eugene O'Neill play with other noted actors was, Essie and Paul agreed, a step in the right direction. The reviews of Paul's acting were once again wonderful, and Essie was pleased.

While Paul was learning his craft, Essie was learning how to get his work noticed. Armed with thick skin and unshakable determination, she began to network and navigate her way into post–World War I high society. Essie was a small woman, but she made sure people noticed her when she entered a room. Her good looks, sharp tongue, and persistence served her well. Essie was engaging, opinionated, and impossible to ignore or intimidate. She looked folks directly in the eye and lingered on handshakes with people she wanted to know better to make sure they registered the encounter. She was described as "aggressive," "brisk," and pushy, as well as witty, insightful, and irresistibly charming.[35] She could be each of these things when she needed to be. She used these qualities in equal measure to make sure that she and her "fabulously talented" Paul met all the right people, went to all the right parties, and seized all the ripest opportunities.

On January 3, 1925, during a Harlem soirée at the trendy Edge-comb Avenue apartment of NAACP leader Walter White, Essie met two people who would become very important to Paul and her: the writer and arts patron Carl Van Vechten and his Russian wife, actress Fania Marinoff.[36] They became fast friends, with Essie soon referring affectionately to Van Vechten by his nickname "Carlo." In the years to come, she would use her friendship with Van Vechten to gain access to a wider circle of white and Black writers, artists, and patrons on both sides of the Atlantic. Through him she met Otto Khan, an eccentric Pennsylvania industrialist who would become an important Robeson patron, albeit a hardnosed and demanding one.[37] Another contact she made through the pair was Carolyn Dudley Reagan, the producer of Josephine Baker's *Negro Revue*. (Essie would later lock horns with Reagan over a broken promise for Paul to appear in one of her shows.)

Van Vechten, a wealthy white man of unconventional interests, became so infatuated with African American culture and artists in the 1920s and 1930s that the sardonic writer Zora Neale Hurston, also an acquaintance of Essie's, deemed him one of Harlem's white "Negro-ologists." In his own words, he was "enamored with all things Negro."[38] White-haired and pale-skinned, Van Vechten stood out in the streets and taverns of New York's Black enclave, and he enjoyed the attention he drew. At times, Van Vechten exoticized as much as he adored his Black friends and acquaintances. His controversial 1926 novel *Nigger Heaven* garnered stiff criticism from some Black intellectuals and political people. W. E. B. Du Bois was disgusted by the novel's title and its content. For her part, Essie liked the novel, presumably viewing its seemingly racist title as provocative and twisted sarcasm, rather than malevolence.[39]

Controversy notwithstanding, Van Vechten was a force to be reckoned with in the labyrinthine arts world of the 1920s. He introduced many Black writers to downtown publishers, including his friend Alfred Knopf, the publisher and philanthropist, and played the unofficial role of publicist and agent for others.

Van Vechten's wife had her own colorful past. Fania Marinoff was born to a Jewish family in Russia and when she was quite young moved first to Boston, then out West. She ran away as a teenager to perform in a traveling theater, only be stranded in Omaha before making her way to New York City, where she launched a career as an actress and married Van Vechten, settling into a nontraditional but loving partnership that included a number of extramarital affairs for Carl. Known for her "extraordinary sense of drama" and "flair," Fania would also become a close and devoted friend to Essie for a good many years.[40]

When they met, Carl Van Vechten was almost as captivated by Essie as he was in awe of the many talents of her handsome husband. One evening, at a party at Marinoff and Van Vechten's home, he and Essie got better acquainted. With the young and talented George Gershwin playing "Rhapsody in Blue" on the piano in the background and Essie wearing a black silk dress with matching hat that Minnie Sumner had made for her, they chatted about life, art, race, culture, and the wildly talented people that animated their world.[41] Although quirky and eccentric, Carlo became a lifelong friend and confidante of Essie's. Even when living on different continents, and even as the gulf between their respective political views widened, they kept up an active correspondence for nearly thirty years. In the 1920s and 1930s their relationship was deeply personal, as reflected in the tone and content of their letters. "Dearest Carlo, we are marvelously happy . . . we feel we could take the world apart and put it back together," Essie wrote from England in 1928. "Dear Carlo and Fania, I am at my wits' end," she confessed only two years later. "I don't know what to do about Paul." Her letters to Van Vechten chronicled the ups and downs of her life and marriage.[42]

Another couple the Robesons grew quite close to, and spent quite a bit of time with in the 1920s, was Walter and Gladys White. Walter was a blonde-haired, blue-eyed Negro who, after witnessing a race riot as a child, became a lifelong crusader for racial justice. A writer and assistant secretary of the NAACP in 1924, he would soon ascend to the helm of the organization in 1931 and become its most influential leader for over two decades. During the early years of their marriage, Essie and Paul shared many meals with the Whites and attended many parties at their Harlem apartment, where talented and distinguished guests were commonplace. Walter and Gladys applauded Paul and Essie's successes and vice versa. When White's first novel, *Fire in the Flint*, a tale of racism and lynching in the South, came out in 1924, Paul read it immediately and was moved to tears. The Whites hosted a farewell dinner for Paul and Essie when they departed for England in 1925 and Walter was at the dock, with other friends, to see them off when their ship set sail.[43]

One summer evening in August 1924, Essie and Paul were invited to a dinner party at the Whites' home, one of many such invitations. The writer Jessie Fauset was there, as was the famed tenor Roland Hayes. It was a lively gathering, and the highlight for Essie was an hour-long conversation with Prince Kojo Touvalou Houénou, a descendent of Dahomean royalty, publisher, and admirer of Marcus Garvey. While the others talked about art, literature, and theater, she and Kojo talked about Africa and the African Diaspora. She was especially interested in the work he was doing with the French Guyanese writer René Maran on the new journal *Les Continents*. Based in Paris, as was Kojo himself, the journal aimed to create a global community of Black writers and artists in opposition to racism and colonial domination.[44] A few weeks later, Essie met up with Kojo again at a party given by actor Bob Greer. After that she took him to see Paul's performance in *All God's Chillun Got Wings* at the Greenwich Village Theatre. They spent several more afternoons and evenings together before he departed for France. By the time he left, a solid friendship had been forged.[45]

Harlem in the 1920s was buzzing with cultural activity and many publications were launched that showcased Black talent, recognized the import of Black culture and history, and affirmed the skill of Negro writers and artists in a way that contradicted some of the basic ideological underpinnings of white supremacy. There were also rumblings of a new political energy that drew from the radical ideas and experiences of Caribbean-born Blacks who were settling in Harlem and making their presence felt. But just as there was debate among the political actors, there was also debate among the coterie of educated Harlem Renaissance artists, writers, and intellectuals about what form Black art should take, who was its primary audience, and whether its cultural products fairly represented the experience and aspirations of the Black majority. Discussions about "primitivism" and authenticity, as well as class and privilege, were at the center of the verbal fray, along with the eclecticism of the African Diaspora. Essie and Paul were both aware of the arguments that were going on but did not formally or forcefully weigh in, at least not yet.[46]

By 1924, Essie had begun to serve in a more official capacity as Paul's manager, publicist, agent, and sometimes acting coach. It was a new profession for her, and she was good at it. One of the more interesting deals that she brokered for Paul in 1924 was his screen debut in Oscar Micheaux's landmark silent film *Body and Soul*, in which Paul had two starring roles as estranged twin brothers, with opposite values and temperaments, who loved the same woman. Essie negotiated for Paul to receive $100 a week and a percentage of the revenues after the film earned its first $40,000.[47] The film was never a box office success, so the royalties never materialized. Moreover, Paul may have been disappointed with the final version of *Body and Soul*, which Micheaux edited heavily. In fact, film scholar Charles Musser goes so far as to suggest that "Robeson's involvement in this motion picture proved so distasteful . . . that he and his wife avoided mentioning it in writings and interviews. It became a taboo subject. Indeed for many years people believed that the 1933 version of *The Emperor Jones* was Robeson's cinematic debut." Musser explains that Paul and Essie had three reasons for their negative reaction to the film: it was a financial failure and critics were less than kind; Micheaux did not treat Paul as an equal but rather as the clay he would mold to his own artistic statement; and finally, Micheaux was trying to make a convoluted political statement about the need for greater Black political consciousness and principled leadership, a message that in 1925 neither Paul nor Essie were, in Musser's words, "ready to hear."[48] Indeed, Essie and Paul rarely mentioned *Body and Soul* or Oscar Micheaux after 1925.

Micheaux, raised in Kansas, the son of former slaves, was the first African American feature filmmaker, and he would go on to make dozens of films before his death in 1951.[49] Essie was fascinated by the filmmaking process. She stayed on set as Paul did his scenes, watching and taking notes.[50] She was intrigued by the techniques that Micheaux employed to manufacture "virtual reality," from using fans to create the illusion of a windstorm, to the use of make-up and lighting to create mood. The film industry was still fairly young and unpredictable at this time, so Essie continued to hunt for new venues and outlets for Paul's talent.

Essie not only handled the business side of Paul's career—bookings, logistics and money—she also embraced the creative end of things as well, determined to do all she could to help sharpen Paul's skills and to hone his talent. When he had difficulty committing the script of *Emperor Jones* to memory, Essie stayed up late and woke up early rehearsing Paul's lines with him. They both became obsessed with making sure that Paul mastered the part to perfection—so much so that one morning while he was taking a bath, script in hand, he called out for Essie to come into the bathroom, sit on the side of the tub, and run through a section of the play with him. Without hesitation she left her breakfast and did just that. "They set to work right there," Essie recounts, in the third person: "he immersed in his bath and she perched nearby; they took the speech sentence by sentence and phrase by phrase, word by word, digging down to the meaning of every single comma, until they both understood it thoroughly."[51] Paul appreciated all that Essie did for him, and the excitement of his ascendant career and all the new opportunities that were coming his way only added to his love and desire for her. It is clear from Paul's own words that his feelings for Essie were deep, passionate, and heartfelt. In one note he wrote "I need you more than you could ever know. Need you because I love you and cannot be completely happy with you away."[52] The romance was intellectual as well as physical: "What joy to talk to you and rehearse with you and watch the workings of your mind," Paul wrote.[53] He not only praised Essie in private; he also publicly acknowledged her instrumental role in his early career. At a party in Paul's honor to celebrate his performances in *Chillun* and *Emperor Jones*, he made an eloquent and memorable toast to his "dynamic, clever, intelligent little wife," to whom he gave "major credit" for his success.[54] They were an unbeatable team, and their passions for one another and what they hoped to accomplish together were mutual and intertwined.

Essie and Paul had personal ambitions, to be sure, but they were also launching their careers during a time of great political energy and activity. Very few of Essie's early writings indicate adherence to a specific political ideology, but she was in close and frequent contact with some people who were very political: activists in the NAACP, Pan-Africanists and Garveyites like Kojo Touvalou Houénou, as well as women's rights activists. Among the women's rights activists, Stella Bloch Hanau stands out. Born in 1890, the daughter of European Jewish immigrants, Stella became an active supporter of the Provincetown Players and helped Essie organize Paul's first musical concert at the Greenwich Theatre in 1924. Significantly, Stella was a leftist and a feminist, a graduate of Barnard women's college, an advocate of birth control and reproductive rights, and an active suffragist before 1920. While there is no transcript of her conversations and exchanges with Essie, we do know that there were many. From 1924 through 1926 in numerous diary entries Essie chronicled a close and intense relationship with Stella. They saw one another regularly, attended plays and concerts together, lunched and dined together, and met for tea and conversation. It is inconceivable that the two women did not discuss, at least to some extent, the ideas about women's rights and women's sexual freedom that so animated Stella's thinking in those days. So in addition to her communication with anti-colonialists like Kojo, and anti-racist leaders like Walter White, Essie was exposed to women like Stella Hanau. All of these experiences were layered on top of a family tradition of resistance to racial repression and restrictive gender roles. Her maternal grandfather had fought the good fight during Reconstruction in South Carolina, and her mother had forged her own path, pioneered an independent career after her husband's death, and supported the radical political actors in Harlem in the World War I era. Essie was influenced by a myriad of ideas, movements, and personalities in the 1920s, and many longings and curiosities had been aroused.[55] Above all else, she loved not only Paul and the great talent she saw in him, but also Harlem and all that it represented in the third decade of the twentieth century.

three

ONTO THE WORLD STAGE, 1920s

I almost melt away with happiness when I think
of the beautiful days we have before us.
Paul Robeson, to Eslanda

Paul's professional acting career began in 1922, and as he added new media to his portfolio he became ever more successful. When Paul's old acquaintance Lawrence Brown returned to New York in 1925 and the two men began singing together informally in Essie's living room, she started to think of ways to showcase the beautiful music they made together. Paul had displayed his amazing singing voice for friends and at parties while he was still in law school, accompanied on piano by his and Essie's friend May Chinn, a virtuoso pianist and medical student. He had even had a brief singing career as a member of the Four Harmony Kings in the stage show *Shuffle Along*. But his musical collaboration with Brown was on a whole different level. Brown was a highly accomplished pianist and had been an accompanist for the celebrated singer Roland Hayes. He and Paul quickly developed a personal and a musical rapport, making, as Essie put it, "a perfect combination."[1] Larry thought Paul was a "unique genius," and they drew upon one another's talents.[2] They also began to sing a special kind of music together: a revised and revitalized form of Negro spirituals to which Paul's deep, soul-stirring voice was perfectly suited. They had other music in their repertoire as well.

The duo sang at private parties while Essie made contacts with prospective supporters in the audience, including artists, writers, pro-

ducers, and patrons. At a party at the Van Vechtens' home, Essie introduced Larry Brown to Carlo and told him that he had to hear the new
musical team. Two days later, at a Sunday gathering at the same venue,
Larry and Paul gave an informal concert that blew their audience away.
The reaction was just as Essie had hoped. As she later wrote, Carlo was
"amazed": he "raved about Paul's voice," and literally "jump[ed] up and
down" for more.[3] With a debut public concert for the two men already
in the works, Essie used their newfound admirers to make it a raging
success.

The Robesons and Brown attended a party hosted by Alfred Knopf,
the publisher and arts patron, and his wife, Blanche. There, they met
and dined with actress Rita Romilly; Equity Actor's Union head John
Emerson; author Theodore Dreiser; and journalist Heywood Broun.
(Broun would later write a favorable review of Paul and Larry's first
concert performance.) Essie also booked the duo a radio performance
on station WGBS as a preview to the concert.[4] Their growing circle of
acquaintances included a long list of wealthy and well-connected New
Yorkers, Black and white.

Sunday, April 19, 1925, was the date of Paul and Larry's first public
concert at the Greenwich Village Theatre. Essie wrote in her diary:
"Today is one of the most significant times in our lives." She had worked
tirelessly to promote the event and her efforts paid off. It was sold out,
with standing room only. "At 8:15 P.M., when the theatre doors opened,
the lobby, sidewalk and vicinity was packed," Essie reported. After the
final song in a program featuring Negro spirituals and secular bal-
lads, "There was thunderous applause, lasting three minutes." Paul had
transformed and revived a genre of Negro spirituals that had a powerful, visceral and cerebral effect on his listeners. His audience was exuberant. Essie was "very, very happy," seeing Paul's huge potential as an
artist.[5]

During the weeks that followed, there were two more public concerts and many private ones. Essie negotiated a $250 fee for private
parties, and Paul and Larry sang in Fifth Avenue drawing rooms, at
dinner parties on the Upper East Side of Manhattan, for teas at the
Hotel Astor, and at the home of Mrs. Murray Crane, the newspaper
heiress and art collector who hosted a regular salon in her elegant apartment. Essie found Crane to be particularly generous and affable. "She
made me think of those old fashioned, wholesome philanthropists, just
big souled, appreciative, attractive and a simple personality, and the
personification of good taste," Essie wrote.[6] Around that same time, a

young sculptor named Antonio Salemme began work on a sculpture of Paul, the sale of which, Essie ensured, would yield profits for sculptor and subject alike. It was an exciting time for Essie, who ate clams and drank champagne for the first time in the company of millionaires. The fun and adventure of their new lives notwithstanding, the Robesons' own "lack of money" was still a problem. Essie arranged for personal loans to tide them over and hoped that, even if their present financial situation was bleak, all of their hard work would all pay off in the future.[7]

Paul and Larry's 1925 concert series solidified a friendship and a creative partnership that would last for many decades. Over time Essie would develop her own relationship with Larry, whom she treated as a part of the Robesons' extended family—and as her trusted confidante when she and Paul were not on the best terms.[8] Many years later Essie would look back on their friendship with affection and gratitude, thanking Larry for "having been my loyal fan for lo [sic] these many years. . . . you always encouraged me when I was down, and nobody paid me any mind."[9] In another letter around the same time, Essie promised Larry, "Someday I myself will write a proper tribute to you. I know what you have done, and I think I will find the way to say it well."[10]

When Paul and Larry Brown teamed up in the mid-1920s, Essie served as their booking agent and manager. She negotiated an arrangement where the two men would split their earnings fifty-fifty, and she would take 10 percent from each as a fee for her services. She took care of the logistics related to their public appearances, negotiated contracts, made travel arrangements, and coordinated publicity. She also served as bookkeeper and accountant. Eventually, Essie hired James Pond to provide additional booking services that she could no longer handle by herself.[11] For Paul, she also remained an invaluable coach and career strategist. He came to rely enormously on her artistic and business acumen.[12]

Essie brought the same toughness to her new job that she had to the school playground and to her chemistry classes in college. In fact, one day when Paul and Larry were preparing to depart for a concert tour, Essie literally wrestled a would-be purse-snatcher to the ground on the streets of New York to stop him from stealing Paul and Larry's travel money. She had just gone downtown to a bank on Fifth Avenue to withdraw several thousand dollars to cover their expenses. Feeling in no danger, Essie casually went about her other business, shopping and running errands with the wad of cash tucked in her purse. She went to Altman's department store on Thirty-Fifth Street to purchase some lingerie and stockings, and exited the store when all of a sudden she was shoved from behind and "elbowed violently against the plate glass window" by a mugger who had apparently stalked her all the way from the bank. Essie refused to be his victim. "How dare you!" she screamed. "I won't give it to you!" Reacting before she had a chance to think, she lashed out and pummeled the man who was attempting to rob her. More than anything, Essie was galled that someone would see her as easy prey. A crowd gathered, the police were called, and the man was eventually taken away in handcuffs. "I collected myself and continued shopping," she wrote later. "I have never started a fight, but I have always defended myself vigorously."[13]

In the summer of 1925, after a whirlwind of concerts and other public appearances, as well as recording sessions with Victor Records, Paul was offered another chance to go to England: Essie had negotiated for Paul to appear in the London production of *Emperor Jones*.[14] With this great opportunity in their sights, Essie finally quit her job at the hospital and arranged to accompany Paul to England. In the weeks leading up to their departure, Essie excitedly shopped with her new friend Bert McGhee, and asked her former roommate, Minnie Sumner, to sew and alter an entirely new wardrobe for her. Essie was happy that Bert and her husband, Harold [Gig] McGhee, were going to be in London at the same time. Not only had Essie and Bert become friends, but also Gig had worked as a stage manager for Eugene O'Neill's Provincetown Players and had agreed to work on the London production of *Emperor* as well. There was a farewell dinner for Essie and Paul, which included Walter and Gladys White and other New York City notables, and another smaller party hosted by the Van Vechtens. The Robesons borrowed $5,000 from the German-Jewish banker Otto Kahn to carry them until the *Emperor* checks began to arrive.[15]

On August 5, 1925, Essie and Paul began the six-day voyage to England, the first of Essie's many trips across the Atlantic. When they arrived, they settled into a comfortable furnished flat at 12 Glebe Place in Chelsea that Bert McGhee had helped Essie to find.[16] It had high ceilings, elegant carpets, a fireplace, and a small garden. To Essie, it was "just too lovely."[17] She and Paul remained there for three months. Because racial barriers were not as strictly enforced in England in the 1920s as in America, the Robesons experienced a level of comfort and respect unknown to them back home. Essie recalled the humiliation and inconvenience of searching for a decent place to dine after one of Paul's performances in New York City.[18] London was so much better.

In addition to the more hospitable social scene, Paul's work in *Emperor* went very well. The play, which centers on a Black American convict who becomes the dictator of a small Caribbean island, received mixed reviews, but Paul's performances garnered high praise and standing ovations. Essie wrote to friends back home about the thrill of seeing Paul's name in lights in London: "Ambassador Theatre, Paul Robeson, Emperor Jones, the prettiest thing in London. He's an honest to God Star now," she effused.[19] Essie beamed as Paul enjoyed the success she felt he so rightly deserved and that they had both worked so hard to attain.

They had arrived on England's shores, however, at an unsettling moment in the history of the British Empire. In the late nineteenth and early twentieth centuries, numerous grand "exhibitions" were held to showcase the prowess and progress of Western nations. These exhibitions were notoriously racist and pro-imperialist, but in 1924 and 1925 England put on an exhibition to exceed all others: the British Empire Exhibition held at Wembley Stadium in northwest London that was attended, over the course of two years, by some 27 million people.[20] One of the goals was to promote awareness of the colonies, but in essence it was a homage to colonialism. There were photos and displays depicting the lives of "the natives." The whole spectacle was so insulting to African students living in London that they held demonstrations in protest.[21] Even though Essie was a voracious reader and prided herself on keeping abreast of the news, there is no indication of her reaction, in either her diaries or letters, to the Empire Exhibition, one of the biggest news events to greet them upon their arrival in London in 1925. Perhaps she was taking it all in and trying to make sense of it all.

During their time in England and Europe, Paul and Essie's world expanded greatly. Paul's celebrity and success as a stage actor and singer opened many doors for them. They lunched with Sylvia Beach, owner of the Shakespeare and Company bookstore, and attended parties with Ernest Hemingway, James Joyce, and Rebecca West.[22] They also spent time with an impressive bunch of Bohemian artists, writers, and intellectuals that included Gertrude Stein, the American writer, poet, art collector, and host of a famous Paris salon.[23] Over the previous three years, the Robesons' fortunes had changed dramatically from sharing a small studio apartment and living month to month to being wined and dined by American cultural elites and European nobility. Essie loved the glamour of it all, meticulously documenting in her diary all the luncheons, dinners, and parties with famous people. Yet she had an intellectual hunger that she was still trying to satisfy.

One relationship that Essie formed in London in the summer of 1925 partially sated that hunger. It was her friendship with the feminist and anarchist Emma Goldman, whom she and Paul had met her at a dinner party at Estelle Langer Healy's home in Hempstead soon after they arrived.[24] More than twenty-five years Essie's senior, Emma already had lived quite a colorful life by the time they met. A serious thinker and a bold political actor, Goldman had been jailed several times for her left-wing activism, once for allegedly plotting to assassinate President McKinley and once for distributing banned literature about birth control to women on the streets of New York City. She was eventually deported to Russia, where she at first supported the Bolshevik Revolution and then sharply criticized the new regime as repressive and undemocratic. Goldman was forced to leave the Soviet Union too. She was so thoroughly angry and disgusted by what she viewed as the corruption and betrayal of the ideals of the revolution that she wrote the book *My Disillusionment in Russia*, which was published by Doubleday in 1923.[25] In it she blasted Lenin and other Soviet leaders for their persecution of Anarchists, deemed "petit bourgeois," and their autocratic tactics. Many of her comrades had been jailed, killed, or exiled in the aftermath of the Bolshevik Revolution, she wrote.[26] By 1925, Emma was living alone in London, spending a good part of the year in France. Essie thought Emma had a "fine mind," and found her both stimulating and provocative.

Emma had Essie and Paul to her small London flat for dinner on several occasions, and the three became incredibly fond of one another. She was in the audience for many of Paul's performances and backstage for the celebrations afterward.[27] One night the Robesons took her out for dinner to one of their favorite restaurants, Villa Villa, and then to see *Gold Rush*, starring Charlie Chaplin.[28] "It will be more dreary and lonely in this town when you two are gone than it is now," Emma confessed.[29] After the Robesons returned to New York, Essie and Emma kept in touch for years.[30] Emma's letters were filled with both political commentary and personal news. She signed them "devotedly" and "affectionately." Although the relationship between Emma and Essie was largely personal—Essie's political views had not fully taken shape in 1925—Essie did recognize and admire Emma Goldman as a radical thinker. She loved hearing Emma talk about her ideas, and found it "thrilling," actually, even though she "disagreed violently" with some of the positions Emma espoused (she did not specify which ones). Emma did share with Essie and Paul copies of essays she had written on various topics ranging from feminism to socialism to the arts. She talked to them about "the disheartening experiences" she had had in Russia.[31] Overall, there was much tenderness and mutual admiration between the two women in particular. Other political differences would develop later. But when the Robesons left England in 1925, Essie and Emma felt they had forged a treasured friendship, one that Emma recognized by giving Essie an antique brooch as a token of her affection.[32] The two friends would keep one another up to date on their lives throughout the decade.

It was during Essie and Paul's time in London in 1925 that Essie made her first trip to Paris, and what a trip it was. She and Bert McGhee bought their train tickets, booked a modest hotel, and excitedly snuck off to Paris for five glorious days. Essie was eager to see all that she could, and their schedule was full every day from morning until after midnight. They "taxied all over," took a boat down the Seine, went to the Louvre, "dressed up and went to the Moulin Rouge" and the risqué Folies Bergère, and consumed lots of French wine and Benedictine, a sweet cognac-based liqueur that Essie thoroughly enjoyed.[33] The friends were so enthusiastic about experiencing Paris that Essie actually "fainted" (or passed out) after one particularly indulgent evening.[34]

When the London production of *Emperor* closed unexpectedly after only five weeks due to financial missteps (and despite Paul's rave reviews), Essie and Paul decided to stay in Europe for awhile longer to see some of the sights, and to relax and rejuvenate. They left London and after another brief stay in Paris traveled by train to the quaint seaside village of Villefranche-sur-Mer on the French Riviera for a wonderful six-week vacation that Essie would never forget. The vistas were beautiful and the climate idyllic, even if a bit chilly in the winter months. "Villefranche is a lovely quiet village at the foot of the southern Alps . . . [and] one of the most beautiful harbours in the world," Essie wrote.[35]

They rented a room with a balcony in a small hotel in the center of town. They got up at 5 A.M. to watch the glorious sunrise and sat naked by the window to feel the sun on their bodies. In the evening, the temperature plummeted and they bundled up and awaited the next morning's sunshine.[36] Out their window they could see the penetrating blue waters of the Mediterranean Sea and the hills of Cap Ferrat off in the distance. In the afternoon, the local fishermen would spread their nets on the embankment next to the water to let them dry. Some mornings Essie would cause a stir on the street below by sitting on her balcony and letting her full, thick hair dry freely in the sunshine. "What's the matter with your hair?" a neighbor called up to her one day. "It's so fat." Essie was amused and quipped back, "We Negroes use hot irons to 'straighten' out the kinks and wool in our hair . . . you white people use hot irons and permanent waving to put the curl and kinks into yours, to make it like ours."[37]

There were a number of expatriates and world travelers who migrated to this part of France in the 1920s—writers, artists, and intellectuals, Black and white. It was during that winter in Europe that the Robesons encountered Max Eastman and Claude McKay.[38] Eastman was a radical socialist publisher and writer who had edited *The Masses* magazine until it was shut down by the U.S. government during World War I for its dissident and radical views—after which he founded *The Liberator*, a socialist magazine focused on politics, philosophy, and art that featured equally dissident views. He was accompanied by his new wife, Elena (Eliena) Krylenko, a Russian artist whom he had met during his stay in the Soviet Union.[39] After having lived in Harlem for several years, the Jamaican-born Claude McKay was in a kind of self-imposed exile in Nice, France (a short train ride from Villefranche-sur-Mer), writing sharp and biting criticisms of U.S. politics and culture. McKay's militant protest poem "If We Must Die," published in *The Liberator* in 1919, had established him as the angry and eloquent icon of a new generation of Black artists and writers. In 1922 he had traveled to the Soviet Union and during almost a year there had met some of the leading revolutionary intellectuals, including Nikolai Bukharin, and delivered a speech before the Fourth Congress of the Third International (Congress of Deputies) in Moscow.[40] The experience had a powerful effect on McKay and it was still very much in the forefront of his thinking two years later. Essie and Paul spent many evenings and afternoons with McKay and with Max and Elena Eastman listening to them "talk about Russia and Socialism," among other things.[41]

Paul hit it off with McKay right away. Essie liked him too, at first, and described him as "charming . . . with beauty all through him." The first evening that the Robesons spent with Eastman and McKay, the group of four had a lovely quiet dinner in a tiny restaurant in Nice, walked the narrow streets to a late night café for coffee, then danced at the Casino.[42] After one of their late-night dinner conversations McKay sent a message to Essie by way of a letter to Paul. It implied that Essie had offered to contact the noted bibliophile Arturo Schomburg on McKay's behalf about a manuscript he had sent to him. McKay asked Paul to tell Essie she need not do him the favor since he had finally heard from Schomburg indirectly himself. The reference to Essie, at that point, was cordial and collegial. Before long, however, friction developed between McKay and Essie. Essie was straightforward and opinionated, and McKay took exception to some of her views. They differed sharply over the condition of Black artists in the United States, the role of white patrons, and the state of Black arts generally. McKay was cynical and pessimistic, while Essie was hopeful, perhaps naively so, about the fate and future of Negro artists like Paul. The precise content of their disagreement was not recorded, but the tone of the exchange was. She and McKay exchanged several heated letters with those penned by him subtly accusing her of being parochial and "racial" in her thinking rather than "universal."[43]

A week later McKay wrote to Paul "to apologize" to both Paul and Essie for his apparently rude behavior during one of their evenings together, presumably related to his ongoing exchanges with Essie. He assured Paul that any perceived insult was unintentional, and expressed his hope that neither Paul nor "Eslanda" were "angry over the incident." The "incident" may well have referred to what both Essie and Max Eastman described as loud, obnoxious, and argumentative behavior by McKay after an evening of drinking. Paul either forgave McKay or did not take offense. Essie, however, reconsidered her earlier impression of McKay and decided she flat-out did not like him. At one point Essie concluded that McKay was "crude and common," confiding to her diary at one point in even more blunt and caustic language that he was "an illbred horrid nigger"—and she wanted nothing more to do with him.[44] Whatever McKay really thought of Essie, and his private descriptions of her might have been just as biting as hers were of him, he obviously respected her enough as a peer to engage her about serious intellectual questions, and to offer an apology when he felt he had overstepped. Significantly, the apology was filtered through Paul and may have been offered more for his benefit than for Essie's. Still the one word McKay used in print to describe Essie was "formidable."[45] That she was.

Such was the effect Essie sometimes had on people: she was at once infuriating and impossible to ignore. She was vocal and vehement and not overly concerned with diplomacy. She once declared that the stage performance of the often scantily clad performer Josephine Baker was "cheap, dirty and stupid;" and she referred to one New York acquaintance, Lenore Ulric, who performed in the Broadway production of *Lula Belle* in blackface, as "an utter ass," albeit a nice one.[46] Many years later, civil rights organizer Bayard Rustin said that Essie "bulldozed her way through" obstacles and was a classic "I don't take shit from anybody" type of Black woman.[47] Rustin, of course, only knew one side of her and saw her through his own lens. Smart and talented men with a great sense of their own importance, men like Rustin and McKay, often experienced Essie as a bulldozer. Another way to view her manner, however, is that she simply refused to be bulldozed herself.

Intellectual debates and personal friction aside, Essie relished her time in France. She felt both calm enough and stimulated enough during their brief time there to focus on her own nascent literary aspirations. Somewhere along the way she had decided she wanted to try her hand at creative writing. She managed to complete an entire play during her time in France, and she hoped to shop it around to producers when she returned home. The Robesons set sail for the States on December 16, 1925, the day after Essie's thirtieth birthday, which was marked by a small celebration with friends in Paris. They arrived in New York Harbor three days before Christmas.

The end of 1925 and start of 1926 was a period of turmoil and adjustment in Essie and Paul's intimate relationship. They were figuring out how to handle Paul's new fame and their demanding schedules, as well as facing the normal difficulties and challenges of married life. They spent Christmas 1925 apart, with Paul visiting his sister, Marian, in Philadelphia and Essie having dinner with friends in New York. The day after Christmas, Essie confessed in her diary that she was contemplating having an affair, implying that she felt Paul was not paying enough attention to her. She abandoned that idea once his affections became more forthcoming. Still, they sometimes slept in separate beds and socialized independently of one another.[48]

After the beautiful and pristine villages of Europe, it was difficult to return to the States and to immediately begin a grueling three-month concert tour through the wintry Northeast and Midwest, including to Detroit, Milwaukee, Pittsburgh, Philadelphia, and Chicago.[49] It was a tough and hectic tour with both of them grinding through every day. Paul sang his heart out for crowds big and small, and Essie hustled as publicist, travel manager, and personal assistant. On this tour and many tours to come, Essie worked the phones, handled reporters, networked with potential benefactors, and looked after Paul physically and emotionally. When he got a cold, she tucked him into bed and found a doctor to prescribe medication. When he felt that new material was testing his vocal range, she found a voice coach to tutor him and nurture his development as a singer. And of course they continued to suffer the indignities of American racism in blatant and subtle forms. While walking down the streets of Chicago during the 1926 tour, a car of rowdy whites pulled up next to them and yelled out racial epithets. The Robesons were offended and annoyed, but not stunned or stymied by the incident.[50]

When Paul's tour ended in March 1926, the couple returned to New York City exhausted and ready to once again put a little distance between them. They took separate vacations. According to Essie's diary, Paul went to Atlantic City alone, with her blessing, and she went with her friend Minnie Sumner to the luxuriously decadent villa of beauty magnate A'Leila Walker, daughter and heir to the fortune of the famed cosmetics tycoon Madame C. J. Walker. Lewaro, her famed Hudson Valley estate, was a weekend retreat for many of Harlem's elite.[51] For two days, Essie enjoyed a beautiful suite overlooking the river, ate well, relaxed, and then packed up and took the train home. Paul was waiting to greet her upon her arrival, and it was back to business for both of them. But things were still up and down. They sometimes argued over money, which was still tight. In May, they fought after Paul spent money on something Essie deemed frivolous. A month later, he came home drunk, "again," at 3:30 in the morning. Essie wrote in her diary that she "was disgusted" by Paul's behavior. Out of spite, or perhaps frustration, Essie went out and got drunk with her friend Minnie a week later, guiltlessly admitting she had had "great fun" in doing so. Around this time, Paul also seemed to be becoming interested in other women, which caused Essie to be concerned but not worried.[52]

By June 14, however, presumably after some talk and reflection, Essie felt that she and Paul were on a better footing. "We sort of started life all over again," she wrote.[53] Essie was not only still working to promote Paul and Larry's careers when they came back to the States; she was also still trying to jumpstart her own new career. She was trying to find a producer for the play she had written in France. She had titled it "Aunt Hagar's Children," after an Old Testament character: the Black female slave who bore children for Abraham. Thus, in Black folklore Hagar's children are sometimes referred to as the children of Africa, presumably including those in the Diaspora. In any case, Essie's play followed in the footsteps of many Harlem Renaissance works of fiction by including and addressing the liveliness of Negro folk traditions, the differences between the Black North and the Black South, and the role of music and dancing as the centers of Black cultural life. Essie's play begins at a church picnic in rural Georgia with characters speaking in a heavy, almost exaggerated, Black Southern vernacular. Against a background of hog roasting, banjo playing, and dreams of a better life, Essie describes the migration of a Southern Black man, "WC," from the fields of Georgia to the throbbing nightlife of Harlem. After the heartache of leaving his lover, Sally, behind, the humiliation of racism on a Jim Crow train, and his confusion about how to fit in and get ahead in the North, he finally settles in, finds happiness (with his Southern girlfriend joining him), and at long last feels as at home with his people in the North, just as he had in the South. The message seems to underscore the importance of perseverance, acceptance, and community as bulwarks against societal racism. The play is short, rough around the edges, and has a sense of incompleteness about it. Essie even described it as an "outline" but nevertheless had it copyrighted on May 1, 1926, with the hope and expectation of publication—though that never did happen.[54]

At one end of the spectrum, the Robesons' social calendar included elegant parties with the likes of New Zealand–born opera singer Frances Alda, the Guggenheims, and writer H. L. Mencken.[55] They even made a trip to California to meet with filmmaker Cecil B. DeMille about a possible movie deal, which Paul signed a contract for, but because of scheduling conflicts, never resulted in a movie. Essie attended dozens of theater and concert performances, sometimes going to three or four shows a week, and occasionally attending one production two or three times. She surveyed the cultural landscape with great thoroughness and precision. Paul sometimes accompanied her, but more often did not. Still, Paul and Essie continued to see and enjoy the company of their old Harlem crowd, both those inside and outside of show business. Essie also attended sorority meetings, went to the NAACP's various social events, and spent a lot of time with her old friend Minnie Sumner, who was like a sister to her. They shopped, talked, and went to dinners and parties together.

In 1926 Minnie had her own personal trauma and perhaps in some ways Essie was helping her to get through it. Minnie was married to Essie and Paul's friend William Patterson (Pat), a lawyer who would later become a leading figure in the Communist Party. In the fall of 1926, however, Pat was embroiled in a tabloid sex scandal—after having been literally caught (by private detectives) with his pants down in a Harlem hotel room with another woman. That incident, which was splashed across the front pages of traditionally Black newspapers, publicly humiliated Minnie and contributed to the unraveling of their short, tumultuous marriage.[56] Essie was there for her.

While Minnie's marriage was falling apart, Essie's relationship with

Paul was good again: not perfect, but relatively stable. In early 1927, Essie became pregnant with the couple's first child. While she had gotten pregnant once before they were married, this time Essie was not only ready for motherhood, she was thrilled at the news of her pregnancy. Essie had feared that she might not be able to have children because of her medical history (and possibly, her 1921 abortion), so this pregnancy felt fragile and important. There is even some evidence to suggest that she saw a fertility doctor to try to help her to conceive.[57] Once the baby was on the way she was careful to take all the necessary precautions, such as eating healthily, taking long naps, and cutting back on her travel. Even though she knew she would not be able to join them, she made plans for Paul and Larry Brown to do a concert tour in France and England in the late fall of 1927, when she would be seven and eight months pregnant. Paul expressed concern about Essie's health, but they both agreed that the concert tour was too important to miss.

Paul and Larry boarded the ship bound for Europe on October 15, 1927. The two men had carved out a niche for themselves over the previous two years, singing their own versions of Negro spirituals that were impressing audiences throughout New York City and beyond. To showcase this rediscovered and reconfigured genre and promote Paul's reputation as a singer as well as an actor, Essie had arranged for the duo to appear in a series of concerts in France and England.[58] Aboard the ship, still worried about leaving Essie given her condition, Paul wrote to her expressing his love and gratitude. "I love you more than I love my very self," he professed. "I almost melt away with happiness when I think of the beautiful days we have before us." A few weeks later, Paul gushed in another letter, "I have grown in these two months of separation to love you with a love that seems unbelievable to me. Nothing matters but you—I don't matter—the world doesn't matter and I am so anxious to see you to show you a new love."[59] The days ahead would not be as purely happy or loving as Paul promised. But at that moment, with his career on an upward trajectory and a new baby on the way, Paul recognized that the one other person most responsible for his success and happiness was Essie. For her part, Essie must have also felt very secure in her relationship and confident about her future with Paul and the life and family they were building together.

four

REMAPPING A MARRIAGE, CAREER, AND WORLDVIEW, 1927–1933

I realize that people are not going to live my life for me.
I am going to have to live it myself.
Eslanda Robeson

In the fall of 1927, Paul Robeson was in Europe, preparing for his debut concert in Paris set for October 29 at the opulent Salle Gaveau Theatre. Built in 1905, the Salle Gaveau was a gilded masterpiece by architect Jacques Hermant and one of the most desirable concert venues in Paris. The night of Paul's concert, the 1,700-seat concert hall was filled to capacity, with a glittering array of notable people in attendance, and the reviews were magnificent.[1] Meanwhile, Essie was in New York, nine months pregnant and struggling physically. In letters home, Paul thanked Essie profusely for her selflessness. "So many thanks, darling, for all you have done for me—for my career, for your patience and care and devoted love. And know whatever I achieve shall have been due in great part to your unselfish interest and devotion."[2]

Four days after the Paris concert, Essie gave birth to the couple's first and only child, Paul Jr. And once again, she was alone and in pain at a critical moment in her life. She successfully delivered a healthy—and enormous—eleven-pound baby, but she did not recover quickly. A few weeks after Paul Jr.'s birth, Essie developed phlebitis and an abscess in her breast.[3] She was bedridden, but reluctant to interrupt Paul's concert tour by telling him, especially since he was receiving such rave reviews. A similar scenario had occurred five years earlier, during his first trip to Europe in 1922. But this time, after weeks of watching Essie suffer, her mother intervened and sent Paul a cable telling him how sick his wife was. Feeling anxious about Essie's condition, and perhaps a little guilty for having been away so long, Paul returned to the States on December 26 to see Essie and meet his two-month-old son and namesake.

Essie's full recuperation would take months. It was not until January that she began "to feel human again."[4] She did manage, however, to send a few cards and letters to friends, gleefully announcing the birth of their son. In a note to the Van Vechtens, she described the baby as "beautiful," with "black velvet eyes and black satin hair — lots of it."[5] In another letter, Essie wrote that she used to cry as a result of "nervous exhaustion," but the exhaustion of motherhood made her "grin at the slightest provocation."[6]

The birth of her son was indeed a happy time for Essie. Relieved to have delivered a healthy child, even if her own health was still fragile, Essie finally allowed herself to relax. The last months of her pregnancy had been difficult, not only physically, but emotionally as well. In October, Essie had received the devastating news that her young friend, the newly married Clarissa Scott Delaney, had died tragically of kidney disease after a short six-month illness.[7] Clarissa (Clare, as she was known to family and friends) had visited Essie and Paul when they were in London in August of 1925. She had stayed with them at their flat in Chelsea, and had dined, shopped, and gone sightseeing all over London with them. Essie fondly recalled "many jolly evenings" with "young beautiful" Clare. There were "long evenings in our charming drawing room lounging about[,] discussing Art and Love and Life." Clare Scott Delaney had been a budding poet of the Harlem Renaissance who had worked briefly as a teacher and social worker before marrying lawyer Hubert Delaney. A graduate of Wellesley College and daughter of educator Emmet Scott, Clare, like Essie, had been a member of the Delta Sigma Theta sorority. Clare had been so full of life and verve and ambition, planning a long and happy life. Essie must have been struck by the sad irony of losing Clare only three short weeks before she gave birth. Memories of "lovely Clare" stayed with Essie for some time, tempered only by the happiness of her new baby.[8]

By April Essie had recovered from her post-childbirth complications and slowly resumed her various managerial duties. Paul returned to Europe to work. He was already committed to performing in a new production of the musical *Show Boat* at the Theatre Royal, Drury Lane, in London, as well as a series of matinee concerts with Larry Brown at the same theater. The plan was for Essie to join him as soon as possible. In May 1928, she left her six-month-old baby in the care of her mother and sailed to London. Essie had made arrangements for Paul Jr. and her mother to spend the summer at a vacation house in Oak Bluffs on Martha's Vineyard while she got things set up for them all to be together in London.

Also on board the ship to England was Essie's Greenwich Village friend Naomi Bercovici, a Romanian sculptor married to the Jewish writer Konrad Bercovici, known for his sympathetic treatment of Roma (Gypsy) culture. After the fanfare of her departure—with a lively "bon voyage party" on the ship—Essie settled in to a series of long, rambling, and sobering conversations with Naomi as they glided across the great expanse of the Atlantic. They talked not only about their common friends in New York but also about the radical activist-intellectuals Emma Goldman and Alexander Berkman, and the French writer Émile Zola. It was the first time that Essie had heard details of the Russian pogroms, which had begun in the 1800s and continued into the twentieth century, and she was shocked. Bercovici, herself associated with anarchism, told Essie about "the worldwide persecution of the Jews." Essie was so overwhelmed that she wrote in her diary: "Lynching and burning at the stake seemed a little tame after listening to the horrible details of the pogroms."[9] Her conversations with Bercovici were a part of her deepening political awareness of global injustices.

Paul met Essie at London's Waterloo Station and took her back to a small flat he had rented near the theater and bustling Regent's Park. Essie was thrilled to be reunited with Paul. Soon after her arrival in London, Essie sat in the audience of the cavernous Theatre Royal, Drury Lane, proudly watching Paul perform what would become his signature ballad, "Old Man River." He was in top form. As his powerful voice filled the theater, Essie studied the audience's reaction. They went wild with "stomps and cheers,"[10] she reported with approval. The critics agreed. A review article in the *Daily Express* exclaimed, "We sat there in a trance of noiseless ecstasy as he touched our heart-strings with his marvelous voice."[11] As for his acting performance in *Show Boat*, it was such a hit that the Queen of England and the Prince of Wales attended performances, as did many other famous Europeans and Americans. Essie was ecstatic about Paul's dual musical and theatrical triumphs.[12] In her words, she was "seething with ambition for him."[13] Essie wrote to friends in New York expressing joy at the new life they were making in England.[14]

Some months after Essie arrived in England she sent for her mother and baby. Even though Paul Jr. was by all indications an affable, delightful child, Essie was far too busy for full-time motherhood. She made the arrangements for her mother—Ma Goode, as she was then called by the family—to move in with them and be Paul Jr.'s full-time caregiver, a role she would fill for well over a decade. Stern and no-nonsense, the elder Eslanda was not a traditional cookie-baking grandmother, but she enjoyed taking care of her only grandson and, when he was older, she charmed and entertained him with her wonderful talent for storytelling.[15] This arrangement freed Essie to travel with Paul, attend meetings and performances, and fulfill her increasingly demanding managerial duties.[16]

By 1928, Paul was receiving more offers to perform than he could possibly accept. On the table were a film role and plans for a two-month concert series in the United States that would include a booking at Carnegie Hall, where he would appear in white tie and tails and sing to a captivated audience of four thousand. To top it all off, Paul signed a contract to perform the powerful lead role in Shakespeare's *Othello*, to be staged at London's Savoy Theatre in the spring of 1930. This would be a high point in his ascendant career. He would be only the second Black actor to play the part. While Paul's work on stage was glamorous, Essie's backstage work was gritty and thankless. She minimized negative publicity, dealt with thorny business problems, and tried to keep their domestic lives organized and on stable ground.

In January 1930, before rehearsals for *Othello* began, Paul and Larry Brown began another concert tour, this time through Central and Eastern Europe. Essie went along and chronicled the trip in her diaries. They went to Prague, Bucharest, Dresden, Düsseldorf, Cologne, Brno, Czernowitz, and Vienna. Essie traipsed through museums in most of these cities and always made a point to look for whatever African art or artifacts they had on display. In Vienna she met up with Percy Julian, a young African American chemist—a friend of a friend—studying for his doctorate at the University of Vienna (Julian would later become a pioneer in the field of medicinal chemistry). While Paul and Larry rehearsed, she and Julian toured the campus and the city.[17]

In Brno, Czechoslovakia, Essie, Paul, and Larry danced the night away in the city's lively cabarets. Poland was a different matter. Still cognizant of the stories of pogroms that Naomi Bercovici had told her, Essie met an Austrian Jew whom she did not name in her diary, but who told her of rampant anti-Semitism and the horrible treatment of Jews there by both civilians and the military.[18] This was a sobering encounter that would have an even more significant effect on Essie later, as the fascist movement in Europe unfolded.

In March the Robesons were off for ten days to the small picturesque mountain town of Territet, Switzerland, to work on an edgy experimental silent film called *Borderline*. It was a film in which Paul played the character of Pete, a Black man living quietly in a Swiss border town until his girlfriend (or wife, it is unclear which) arrives and everything changes. Essie herself took the role of Paul's troubled love interest and partner, Adah, who is at the center of the controversy. The plot of the hour-long film is barely decipherable with its montage of scenes connected ever so slightly to one another. Still it was Essie's cinematic debut, and she enjoyed being in the spotlight.

The film revolves around Adah's taboo affair with a local white man, Thorne, and the confusion, chaos, and racial animus that the affair unleashes. When the illicit relationship is discovered, the man's wife goes mad and is accidentally killed in a scuffle with him. The local people are furious, and first Adah, then Pete, are seemingly blamed and ultimately forced to leave town. Essie's character is a sultry seductress who peers over her shoulder or from beneath a sexy hat with an air of mystery. Even though she had no training and no acting experience, and despite a rather jumbled script, Essie's performance was compelling. Absent any dialogue, facial expressions and body language were key. In that respect the *Borderline* director demanded more of Essie than of Paul, who stood still with a sad, pensive look for most of his on-screen time. Essie, meanwhile, fought with her white lover, offered a look of curious anticipation at the prospect of reuniting with Pete, and finally, suitcase in hand, turned her back on the troubled little town and walked away. In the end hers was a tragic character who loses her husband, her lover, and her reputation. The role allowed Essie to be expressive and to showcase her natural talent. Kenneth MacPherson, the producer and director, praised her acting ability. One reviewer years later described *Borderline* as "both of its time and decades ahead of it. Its fusion of racism and sexuality would not be seen again until well into the postwar era."[19] Others cite the film's modernist and even feminist sensibilities.[20] Essie described the avant-garde film as vague, "futuristic," and very "high brow," but she delighted in having had the experience.[21] She sent letters home jokingly boasting of her big film debut.[22]

The *Borderline* project involved some eccentric British and American artists, most notably the Bohemian poet, novelist, and expatriate Hilda

Doolittle (H.D.), and her friends and lovers Kenneth MacPherson and Bryher (Annie Winifred Ellerman Bryher), whose small production company, POOL, bankrolled the low-budget film.[23] Essie and Paul were only on the set for a little over a week, but Essie enjoyed the lively and fun-loving crowd of actors and filmmakers that they were working with, and she kept in touch with H.D. and Bryher for some time after the filming ended. Essie harbored fond memories of the filming of *Borderline*, and the singing, dancing, drinking, and wild conversations that accompanied it. The town of Territet was so lovely that she would later send her mother and son there for an extended stay, and would return many times herself. When their contributions to *Borderline* were finished, Paul and Essie packed up and moved on to their next project. The film would open in November to tepid reviews. It was "stopped at U.S. Customs because of its frank treatment of racial discrimination and interracial sex."[24]

A concert tour through Scotland in late March of 1930 was a different experience altogether.[25] Everywhere they went they encountered African and Afro Caribbean students and workers. Nigerian and West Indian students provided Paul and Essie with an opportunity to talk and hear about the experiences of racism that the Black students endured as well as their memories of home. After Paul's concert they met with small groups of young Africans who sought them out. In particular, a young Nigerian named Ornwu offered a vivid description of the discriminatory treatment that Blacks were facing in Scotland, where interestingly, Essie's grandfather had obtained his college education (in Edinburgh) more than a half-century earlier.[26] Paul and Essie had both already begun to take a greater interest in Africa and the African Diaspora through books, art, and the broad international community that they encountered in their travels.

Having won rave reviews on the New York stage since 1923, Paul was already a rising celebrity when they settled in England in 1928. But after his London performances and European concert tours, he was as close to being an international superstar as a Black man could get in those days. Essie and Paul enjoyed professional success, a deluge of social engagements, and newfound prominence. But even as Paul's artistic status soared, his and Essie's marriage began to unravel.

Paul Robeson was a complicated man: enormously talented, intellectually intense, and deeply passionate about art, world cultures, and language (his political passions would come later). He was also gentle, charming, seductive, and physically beautiful, and many women gravitated toward him. Paul, like Essie, had an insatiable desire for new experiences and relationships. For Essie, those relationships were largely platonic. For Paul, many were not. Paul had enjoyed affairs with other women since the early years of his marriage to Essie, but he had always treated Essie as his primary partner. And he had always been discreet; it was understood that as Mrs. Robeson, Essie would be afforded some respect and deference.[27]

In 1930, however, Paul began a relationship with a young British woman named Yolande Jackson that would prove quite different than his usual affairs. Paul was not only sexually involved with Yolande; he became deeply involved emotionally as well. In the book Essie wrote with Pearl Buck years later, she commented that Americans had "immature" attitudes about sex and that "there was nothing sacred about sex—it was just an urge like other normal urges."[28] Presumably then, if this affair had simply been about sex, or sex and friendship, Essie might have been able to once again look the other way. But it was more than that.

Yolande Jackson was a British actress from a wealthy family with a sharp wit, a hearty laugh, a carefree spirit, and a flair for the extravagant. She was not much of an intellectual, was a mediocre performer, and was more often described as "attractive" rather than beautiful, but Paul was captivated. The situation was further complicated when Essie discovered yet another intimate relationship Paul was having, with the young actress Peggy Ashcroft. Knowledge of this second relationship threw Essie into a complete tailspin. Ashcroft, newly married herself, had just played opposite Paul in the London production of *Othello*. Essie had befriended Peggy and supported her nascent career, so she felt doubly betrayed.[29]

Essie confronted Paul about Ashcroft in what, by all indications, was a blunt and emotional letter. The confrontation occurred after Essie discovered and opened a love letter from Peggy to Paul. Although there are no extant copies of Essie's letter (it is referenced in Paul's reply), judging by his response, she was both devastated and furious. But instead of being contrite, as Essie might have expected, Paul was angry at her for opening his mail and violating his privacy.

By the end of September, Paul and Peggy had ended their affair but he had decided he wanted a divorce from Essie so he could marry Yolande. Essie and others warned him that an open affair and possible marriage to a white woman would do terrific damage to his career, but Paul was undeterred. He did not care about the consequences, he insisted; he wanted to be with Yolande and he was determined to do just that.[30] Essie was at first devastated, then confused and frustrated, and finally angry but accepting. She wrote in her diary with a tone of hard-edged resignation: "I am surely a jackass if ever there was one. I should have seen the handwriting on the wall. Fancy believing his lies right up 'til the last. He was a smooth one though. He must have been lying to me for five years steadily. Well, I'll never let another man know what goes on in my mind and heart. Paul has told me I refuse to face things etc. But now I know, and now I shall face things squarely. We will begin from here."[31]

After the Ashcroft revelation, and with the knowledge that the even more serious relationship with Yolande was ongoing, Essie sent her mother and young son to Switzerland and then Austria for an extended stay so that she could try to sort things out with Paul. They would remain there for some time, joined for several months by Essie's brother John, who had come over to be with family after some health problems.[32] No quick progress was made toward mending the rift between Paul and Essie, but they did travel together to visit Paul Jr. a week before Christmas 1930. After that, Paul traveled back to the States alone on business. In late December, Essie wrote calmly to the Van Vechtens that Paul had fallen in love with another woman and, while she was initially devastated that he had "not only strayed but gone on a hike," she had resigned herself to the situation. "Be nice to Paul," she urged, generously. "His life is rather complicated just now."[33] Essie was not being disingenuous. She did want friends to know her side of the story and she was not prepared to be a silent victim. Paul had left her and she was understandably angry. Still, she had not closed the door on the possibility of their getting back together. And in a sense she was acting in her usual fashion, that is, worrying and taking care of Paul. Even when they were no longer living together as a married couple, her protective reflex endured.

Calm, but heartbroken and with trepidation about what would come next, Essie began searching for ways to fill the void. After all, Paul had been everything to her: friend, lover, business partner, and more. Several times she put her scientific sensibilities aside and, on the advice of her friend Cecil Gillot, paid visits to a clairvoyant, a psychic, and a palm reader. The future must have seemed uncertain indeed. The floorboards beneath her had given way and she was grasping for something to hold on to. So there Essie sat, in a cluttered little room at 24 Harrington Street in London's Kensington neighborhood, holding a crystal in her hand and listening to Miss Nell St. John Irvine predict her future, telling her she would divorce, remarry, achieve financial security, and enjoy great success from her "own creative work." Her real future would unfold quite a bit differently.[34]

The years between 1930 and 1932 were extremely difficult for Essie, and there were times she felt as if she were losing control of everything she had built and come to rely on. She was hospitalized more than once.[35] But determined and ever resilient, she began to see her new situation as an opportunity for growth. She began actively cultivating her expanding interests in writing and in Africa. Essie had already worked on a number of writing projects, most of which had yielded incomplete or unpublishable results. But she persevered. A few months after things with Paul came to a head, she traveled back to the U.S., to her mother's home state of South Carolina to research a new novel, a fictionalized account of her mother's and grandmother's lives. With this writing project, and many others to come, Essie took a special interest in women—how they managed life's obstacles and how they negotiated with and navigated the world around them.[36] During her time in South Carolina, she stayed with Marian Paul, a southern civil rights activist and friend of the Cardozo family. She also went to a talk by the educator and civil rights leader Mary McLeod Bethune.[37] Essie never completed the book project, which she had titled *The Three Eslandas*, but the trip left her inspired to pursue her career as a writer in earnest.

In addition to pursuing new interests and career options, Essie also began to establish an independent social life: she wanted new and exciting experiences and new relationships. Some of the connections she made in this period would be deeply meaningful, and others more fleeting. She developed, for example, a complex albeit short-term relationship with the British stage actor and screenwriter Noel Coward. They dined together regularly, celebrated their December birthdays together (first at her flat, then at his), and enjoyed many shared evenings at the theater. They spent so much time together in the fall of 1930 and spring of 1931 that Paul became convinced they were lovers, a suspicion reinforced when Essie became unexpectedly pregnant and had a second illegal abortion in March 1931.[38] In a cryptic letter from New York soon after the abortion, Paul chastised Essie, telling her to be more careful. He wrote that her relationship with Coward was her business, but he insisted on discretion, even with the divorce pending. It was around this time that Essie also reconnected with her old boyfriend, Grant Lucas. It is unclear the precise nature of their renewed relationship, but Essie was reaching out for emotional support and affirmations. Grant had been very special to her at one time. In the spring of 1931, after she had made another brief return visit to the States, she confided to her diary that the two of them had "become much more than reacquainted."[39] Essie went on to note that Lucas "has done a great deal for me in this last week, has helped me find myself in many, many ways. I shall always be grateful to him for that."[40] Back in London Essie had also been dating a man named Michael Harrison whose company she enjoyed very much, but her diaries and letters tell us very little more about him.[41]

The previous December (1930), Essie and Paul, having arrived at a brief rapprochement, went to Paris together "as friends" to take in some stage performances. Paul left Essie alone in Paris after a couple of days, possibly to rendezvous with Yolande. The next day, perhaps as a way to boost her deflated ego, Essie enjoyed an anonymous tryst with a "very attractive Frenchman" in a Paris theater. She described the experience in a rather salacious entry in her diary: "He caressed my hand for fully half an hour, then placed my hand on his thigh and held my hand in both of his, caressing it ever so gently, but rather beautifully. Then he began to move, his breath came in quiet gusts, and finally he seemed to have an emission—all very quietly. Then he gave a great sigh of pleasure and delight, dropped his program on the floor, reached down to pick it up, and kissed my hand passionately, before releasing it. All the while, my hand had been near his knee, and nowhere near his person. . . . It was remarkable," she concluded.[42] Some time later she relayed this titillating encounter to a friend who told her casually and playfully that all the Frenchmen go the cinema to flirt and fondle, never to watch the films. This was the brazen and uninhibited Essie, determined to have her own fun and adventures just as Paul was going to have his.[43]

Even as divorce seemed increasingly likely, Essie tried to keep up appearances to the contrary. In the fall of 1931, while in Tirol, Austria, for two months with her son and her mother, Essie wrote to her friend Grace Nail Johnson (wife of James Weldon Johnson) telling her how lovely it was in Austria, how handsome, smart, and friendly Paul Jr. was (Essie referred to him by the German diminutive version of his name, "Pauli"), and how she and the entire family had spent the previous Christmas in Switzerland and would spend Christmas 1931 in Austria. "A different country each year" for the Robeson clan, she predicted. But in fact she was not at all sure what future holidays would be like or whether her family would in fact be together.[44]

Essie and Paul's marriage continued to be unsettled. By March of

1932, feeling insecure and desperate, Essie reached out to her old friend Larry Brown to help her figure out what was going on with Paul and to surreptitiously help her obtain information about his relationship with Yolande—in other words, to spy on him. Writing to Larry under the name Cardozo, rather than Robeson, so as not to arouse the curiosity of the casual reader in the post office (as she explained it), Essie pleaded with Larry, who was then on tour with Paul, to do some "harmless" personal reconnaissance. "If by chance," she wrote slyly, "you come across some letters in a bold free hand, stamped from London, in his pockets, or luggage, and they find their way to me, no one will ever be the wiser, that I swear, and no one will ever know how I got them."[45] Essie was grasping at straws in trying to get her hands on letters that Yolande might have sent to Paul on the road. Her note to Larry asked for any shred of information: "What does he say of me? Of Yolande? Of Pauli?" Her anxiety was apparent. It was unclear whether Essie wanted evidence to strengthen her hand in the divorce proceedings or merely to better assess what Paul was thinking, feeling, and planning. "This is not for sentimental purposes," she assured Larry in describing her request, "but so I can plan some reasonable course of action."[46] Even though he was fond of Essie, there is no evidence that Larry provided her with any information.

By late spring, Essie had conceded to Paul's request for a divorce. Their marital woes had hit the newspapers and the end of the marriage seemed inevitable. "I put off the evil day [divorce] as long as I could," she confided to a friend, "hoping something would happen, but he insisted he must have his freedom, and that I just had to give it to him, so I felt I must."[47] In June 1932, Essie spent several weeks in Paris. She had a few different reasons for going there. First, she had agreed with Paul to obtain evidence for the divorce proceedings. Second, to advance her writing career, she planned to do a series of interviews with Black artists, writers, and expatriates living in Paris, as the basis for a series of articles she planned to write. Finally, she simply wanted to shop, eat, drink, dance, and enjoy the Parisian summer.[48] Having moved back from Switzerland, Ma Goode and Paul Jr. were now living with Essie in London, where her mother was continuing to look after the young Pauli. This gave Essie greater freedom to travel and explore because she did not have to worry about managing a second household.

The colorful streets of Paris were just the place to get her mind off Paul, but the trip would also prove to be deeply meaningful for her in other ways. Her primary escort, companion, and confidante in Paris that summer was Kojo Touvalou Houénou, the Dahomean royal and anti-colonial agitator. He and Essie had met at a dinner party eight years earlier and had spent time together on a number of occasions over the years.[49] While there appears to have been no romance between them, he was the one who met her at Gare du Nord station at 10 A.M. on June 3 and took her to the Helios Hotel on Rue de la Victoire, where she always stayed.[50] Then they went out to Delmonico's restaurant for cheese and wine, and had a long, meandering conversation. Essie noticed that the usually well-dressed African aristocrat looked "a bit shabby" this time, but she nevertheless found him as "charming as ever."[51] She described him as "something of a philosopher"—"worldly, brilliant" with qualities that "made him extremely attractive to women."[52]

Kojo was a well-known personality around Paris in the 1920s and 1930s. Descended from African royalty, he was widely referred to as Prince Touvalou. He was born in Dahomey (later Benin), but his father had sent Kojo and his brother to be educated in France in the 1910s. After studying law at the University of Bordeaux, and fighting in World War I, Kojo returned to Dahomey before relocating to Paris. A complex man by all accounts, Kojo was as much French as he was African in his dress, manner, and sensibilities. But after witnessing riots against colonial tax policies, he became political and formed the Amitié Franco-Dahoméenne, an association that advocated for fairer treatment of French colonial subjects. His views would later evolve from a demand for better treatment for Africans within the French Colonial structure to an insistence that colonialism end altogether.[53]

An erudite Black socialite who knew everyone worth knowing in Paris, Kojo seemed to Essie to be "intelligent, very well informed, (and savvy) . . . in the French gallant style. He knows and is known in nearly every inch of Paris."[54] He had earned a reputation for himself years before by successfully suing a local café, El Garon, for discriminatory treatment. In 1924, Kojo had been physically assaulted by a white American patron who was outraged that Kojo, a fellow customer, had expected to be treated as an equal. The resulting lawsuit garnered quite a bit of attention in the French press and led to changes in French law to bolster the rights of Black colonial subjects in France.[55]

Kojo also became a strong supporter of the Black Nationalist leader Marcus Garvey, and a vocal critic of colonial rule. Unlike most Black French elites, who declined to champion Garvey's "Africa for the Africans" slogan, Kojo admired Garvey, and had traveled to the United States in 1924 as a guest of Garvey's organization, the United Negro

Improvement Association (UNIA). Kojo was later appointed to a high position within the UNIA hierarchy, although it's unclear whether the appointment was anything more than symbolic.[56] He also co-founded the journal *Les Continents* with noted French Guyanese writer and intellectual René Maran, who at the time was living in Paris as well.[57] The two men also launched the Ligue Universelle pour la Défense de la Race Noire (LUDRN) to advance land rights for Africans along with full citizenship rights for all subjects under French rule.[58]

Kojo was both a patron and a guide to the city for many Black American writers and artists who came to Paris for short and extended stays. He befriended them, mentored them, showed them the town, and published many of their poems and essays in *Les Continents*, alongside the speeches of Garvey and others. He was also the inspiration for a character in Claude McKay's novel *Banjo*.[59] While some observers of the era regarded Kojo as a "bogus prince," a "brazen social climber," and even a "megalomaniac," historian Christopher Miller writes that he was an influential and "enigmatic figure. . . . and part of a fractious vanguard of black intellectuals" living in Paris in the 1920s and 1930s.[60]

The first order of business after Essie arrived in Paris in the summer of 1932 was to document Paul and Yolande's Parisian trysts. No-fault divorces did not exist in those days: one party had to demonstrate that the marriage vows had been broken. Paul had suggested in a letter that Essie obtain proof of adultery to support the divorce petition and lessen the possibility of any glitches or complications. This left Essie with the awkward task of proving her husband's infidelity. She had to go from hotel to hotel and get documentation that "Mr. and Mrs. Paul Robeson" had checked in as guests on dates when she was demonstrably elsewhere. Kojo went with her on these detective missions as moral support, witness, and translator if Essie's quite serviceable French faltered.

She went to the Hotel Lancaster first. To lighten the mood, Kojo joked that she might have difficulty getting information out of staff at the Lancaster since illicit affairs were such a good source of business for them. But she was armed with a letter from Paul, and secured the hotel documents without a hitch. Yolande had registered as Mrs. Robeson, brazenly providing her own London address. Essie had the evidence notarized the next day.[61] Judging from her diary entries, she carried out this presumably emotion-laden task in a businesslike manner. She wrote much more about the clothes she bought, shows she saw, and restaurants she dined at than about the impending dissolution of her eleven-year marriage. Perhaps it was too painful to write about, or perhaps, after two years of drama, Essie was just numb, ready to put the whole episode behind her.

Kojo was a wonderful distraction. They lunched together and he took her to dinner and the opera, managing to secure excellent seats on very short notice. He even tagged along on shopping trips. And he made her laugh. He shuttled Essie all over Paris, and they visited cafés, flats, and nightclubs, where Kojo introduced her to prominent French-speaking Africans and Afro-Caribbeans, as well as members of his wide and eclectic social network—including Kojo's close friend and collaborator René Maran, whose novel *Batouala* had won wide acclaim.[62] Essie found Maran to be "shy, scholarly, charming, frank, honest, sincere and idealistic."[63] On June 13, Kojo introduced her to Gratien Candace, a member of the French Chamber of Deputies, Pan-Africanist, associate of Du Bois, critic of Garvey, and native of Guadeloupe whom Essie also found very interesting.[64] The nearly one dozen interviews she conducted in Paris that summer became the basis for a series of essays she later wrote entitled "Black Paris," which were published in 1936 in Dorothy West's journal, *Challenge*.[65]

One special evening, Kojo took Essie to meet the renowned Sudanese dancer and actor Habib Benglia, who welcomed her warmly. Essie had seen him perform in 1925 on her first trip to Paris with her friend Bert McGhee and again with Paul later that year, and had been impressed with his talent.[66] Benglia talked to Essie at length about his small village in French Sudan and his dreams of a global Black dance theater company that would perform on both sides of the Atlantic and in Africa. He was a dark-skinned, middle-aged man who spoke with "colorful" and dramatic expressions. Essie did not fail to notice that he also "had the body of a Greek God."[67] Described by one writer as "a magnificent-looking Senegalese," he once danced in the Folies Bergère wearing a G-string and surrounded by white female dancers.[68] Benglia also appeared in more than thirty French-language films over the course of his career, including Jean Grémillon's *Daïnah la métisse*.[69] He was bold, irreverent, and politically aware, and Essie found him utterly fascinating. Even though Benglia had decided to make Paris his home and enjoyed many European fans, he did not hesitate to level biting criticisms against the injustice of colonialism. The "only troubles Africa has," he told Essie wryly, "are the sickness, the beasts, and the white man, and the white man is all three."[70]

Another person who caught Essie's attention was a sharp-witted and lively Martinican named Paulette Nardal, who was editor of the journal

La Revue du Monde Noir (A Review of the Black world), which strove to break down the "great barriers of isolation" that divided the African Diaspora.[71] Kojo introduced Essie to Nardal, whom Essie described as a "handsome bronze-black goddess," intelligent, talented, and creative. They spent hours talking about culture and politics in the Black world. Nardal and her sister, Jane, had hosted a much-celebrated literary salon, "cercles d'amis" as Nardal called them, outside Paris in the 1920s. The "cercles" were frequented by numerous Harlem Renaissance writers and Francophone African and Caribbean intellectuals, from Claude McKay and Langston Hughes to Leopold Senghor and Aimé Césaire. "With her fluent English, Paulette Nardal became the most important connection between 'the Harlem Renaissance' writers and the Franco-phone university students who would become the core of the Negritude movement," wrote literary scholar Brent Hayes Edwards.[72] Nardal was also very sensitive to gender issues and the representation of women in literature and politics.[73] Essie found the ideas and stories of these Black Parisians engaging, exciting, and compelling. Her exchanges with them contributed importantly to her growing sense of a diverse and complex African Diaspora, of which American Blacks were only one part. Her worldview was widening.

Essie also became very friendly that summer with the former vaude-ville performer turned saloon owner Ada Beatrice Queen Victoria Louise Virginia (Bricktop) Smith. A tough-talking, hard-working woman who had made her way from the poverty of the Black American South to the bright lights of Paris, Bricktop ran a legendary club in the Montmartre neighborhood that bore her name. She went on to open similar clubs in Rome and Mexico City.[74] During the 1920s and 1930s, Bricktop was well known and widely celebrated in Paris. Essie Robeson described their meeting this way: "She is a big thick woman, light yel-low with freckles, good carriage, aggression, hair combed straight back from a strong face. . . . She told me she had not expected to like me, but was crazy about me. Said she heard I didn't bother with niggers [ordi-nary Black folk], and was high hat [a bit of a snob]." But Essie quickly dispelled these notions and the two women became as "thick as thieves" by the end of the summer.[75]

Bricktop, so nicknamed for her distinctive red hair, was a lively, ram-bunctious woman, and Essie had much fun with her during the few weeks she was in Paris and upon subsequent visits. Many of Bricktop's acquaintances were only able to see one side of her—the spirited night-club hostess—but Essie got to see more. One evening, Essie was invited to dinner at her new friend's home, and was driven there by Bricktop's personal chauffeur.[76] Bricktop lived with her mother and husband (at the time), and they maintained a lovely little place in the Parisian suburb of St. Cloud, surrounded by well-maintained gardens and far removed from the colorful, rowdy nightlife over which Bricktop presided most evenings. Essie enjoyed a quiet meal with the family and afterward went for a walk in the garden with Bricktop. They shared their thoughts and feelings about life and family. "She is a good fellow—strong, friendly and no nonsense," Essie concluded.[77] In her own autobiography decades later, Bricktop remembered Essie fondly and even claimed to have "saved" Essie's marriage by persuading Paul not to go ahead with the divorce. There is no corroborating evidence for the claim, but the impending divorce was definitely weighing on Essie's mind that summer, and she undoubtedly shared some of her thoughts and feelings on the subject with Bricktop.

During this trip, Essie indulged herself intellectually, socially, and sensually. She described one night when she and a man named Bill White "danced to our hearts' content," leaving Bricktop's in the wee hours of the morning to go to the Melody Bar and not returning to her hotel until 9:00 A.M., long after the sun had come up.[78] "He is wholly charming, a delightful companion, and we have had some fun together," Essie wrote in her diary.[79] She also described an afternoon spent at Jim Newell's charming flat, sipping absinthe instead of the tea that she was promised.[80]

Even as Essie was allowing herself to cut loose a bit, there were sobering aspects of the trip. The child of her friend Maurine Browning was hospitalized in Paris with typhoid fever and was near death. Essie went to visit every other day and empathized that it could just as easily have been her own child in that bed. Another friend—who remained unnamed in Essie's diary—told her of her sister's recent suicide, perhaps underscoring the fragility of life in Essie's mind.[81]

Essie left Paris on June 21, 1932, and returned to England to write, check on her young son and her mother, and ponder her personal and professional future. After her conversations with Kojo and his friends in Paris, she was more certain than ever that Africa would somehow be a part of that future. On July 31, Essie accepted an invitation to visit her friends Leonard and Beatrice Barnes at their country house in Burford, England, near Oxford. Leonard Barnes was a Brit who had spent many years in South Africa as a farmer and itinerant traveler and who had written extensively about his experiences there. It is not clear how they met initially, but Essie had become curious about Barnes's personal history after reading his book *Caliban in Africa*. (Barnes wrote several books on Africa, including a text recognized as the first serious indictment of the South African system of white rule.) Essie traveled to Burford alone by bus. As she left London, she noted the passing countryside, the drab stucco houses, and the velvety green fields off in the distance. Curious and engaging, Essie always took an interest in her fellow travelers—in this case, a Catholic nun who recounted fascinating stories to Essie of her work in a hospital in India—all of which both made the travel time pass quickly and whetted Essie's growing appetite to see the world beyond Europe and the United States.[82]

Leonard Barnes met Essie at the bus station to drive her to the house. After lunch, the couple entertained Essie with stories about South Africa and their experiences there. Having been an officer in the British military and in civil service after the war, Barnes had decided to leave that life behind and travel to the southern tip of Africa to farm. He told Essie of camping in the bush and going on a dangerous lion hunt. He described the beauty of the landscape and the kindness of the people in Bechuanaland. Over time, what started as a personal adventure for Barnes evolved into a strong political and cultural connection and commitment to the Cape region of southern Africa.[83]

Leonard and Beatrice had shared the adventure, and both of them talked to Essie about the history of southern Africa, including Shaka Zulu, the nineteenth-century warrior king who dominated the region, and the myths and legends that surrounded him. "I saw their album, with many fascinating pictures . . . one very interesting one of a native, a fine type." The figure impressed Essie so much that Barnes gave her the photograph to keep. She treasured the gift.[84] In 1945, Essie would cite one of Barnes's books in her own monograph on Africa, and Barnes would serve on the board of the Council on African Affairs with Essie in the 1950s.[85]

Anna Melissa Graves, an American Quaker who spent time in London, was another person Essie met in 1932 who further piqued her curiosity about the African continent. Graves "was a writer, teacher, world traveler, and internationalist, [who] from the 1920s to the 1940s . . . traveled through Africa, Central and South America, China, Europe, and the Middle East." Graves was also active in the Women's International League for Peace and Freedom, a group Essie would later support as well.[86] In May 1932 Essie attended a lecture by Graves at 72 Gower Street, then arranged to have lunch and spend an evening with the fascinating woman, who was twenty years her senior. They had breakfast together the next morning, still talking about Africa and the world. Essie was impressed with Graves's work and ideas, describing her as having "set out to prove that all peoples are equal; the same characteristically, psychologically, fundamentally, all over the world, and not different racially and nationally."[87]

It would be four years before Essie would finally set foot on the continent of Africa herself, but she was already mapping her itinerary and thinking through the logistics of such a journey.[88] She even applied for a Guggenheim fellowship to help cover her expenses, noting in a letter to a friend that if she did not get the Guggenheim, Paul had agreed to underwrite the trip. The Guggenheim application, which included a "plan of study" and short personal statement, offers some insight into how Essie viewed "the idea" of Africa and her relationship to it in the early 1930s. She applied for the one-year fellowship in order to "travel in Africa, especially the interior," in the hopes of learning "to how great an extent our [American Negroes'] original racial characteristics have been submerged by western culture and transplantations." She planned to use her research findings to write a Negro-African play and novel. In her written "plan of study" Essie talks about her own insularity from the harshest aspects of racism because of her light skin color. She then writes about Paul as having, on the one hand, immersed himself in many aspects of Western culture, and on the other hand, as having "retained most of his 'typical racial characteristics'"—citing his Bantu origins and making the assertion that his "features, physique and temperament are definitely African." Her goal, as she awkwardly stated it, was to draw parallels between "ultra Modern" Negroes in places like Harlem with those living in "remote jungle settings." In a somewhat naïve way, Essie was rejecting notions of Africans as a primitive people distinct from either Europeans or Africans in the Diaspora. At the same time, in referencing Paul, she alludes to some presumably "essential" African qualities and characteristics, an assertion that she would later realize belies the diversity and vastness of the African continent and its many peoples, and ignores the myriad of historical changes that have occurred over time and across generations. It is significant to note that although Essie and Paul came to share a deep and abiding interest in Africa, many of Essie's early investigations into Africa were conducted during their separation in the early 1930s. Her interest in Africa and the world was independent and longstanding.[89]

In 1932 Essie's personal life was still very much in limbo. The issue of whether and how the Robesons would divorce dragged on for two long years. August 17, 1932, marked Essie and Paul's eleventh wedding anniversary. "It seems incredible!" she mused in her diary. "Here Paul and I are arranging the final agreements for [our] divorce." That night Essie saw a mediocre play by herself and took a leisurely stroll home to her flat. While admiring the moonlit silhouetted statues in Regent's Park and the Piccadilly Circus "aglow in white lights," she wondered what the future might hold.[90]

Essie and Paul's personal turmoil played out amid a swirl of public rumor and innuendo.[91] Some newspaper gossip columnists condemned Paul for abandoning the loyal wife who had helped to build his career. Others hinted that Essie was partly to blame. A snippy *Amsterdam News* columnist offered her opinion of the breakup: "Mrs. Robeson's desire for a career is an important element. Still, it is possible to have that career and hold her family intact. Even though it may be a breach to voice this sentiment, it does seem to me that a mother's selfishness plays some part in the rift." Ironically, the column was titled "The Feminist Viewpoint."[92] Although wrong about the origins of the Robesons' marital troubles, the column was likely inspired by Essie's own public statements about divorce and a woman's right to work.

In the summer of 1932, Essie wrote an essay entitled "I Believe in Divorce," in which she laid out her thoughts on marriage and monogamy, seemingly using the column to sort out her feelings and perhaps talk herself into certain beliefs as much as to persuade her readers.[93] Essie complained that marriage was overrated and outdated. "This marriage business is a hangover from the cave man era," she wrote. "Where is women's place today? In the office, in politics, in the fields of artistic, literary, intellectual, and internationalist endeavors?"[94] In an interview with J. A. Rogers of the *Amsterdam News*, Essie revealed a rare tinge of bitterness when she commented, "Paul has arrived. He doesn't need me any more." But then she went on to profess that she was done with the whole institution of marriage, harbored no hard feelings toward Paul, and intended now to focus her energies on her own career and on raising her son.[95]

In trying to neatly sum up her own messy marital situation in the 1932 article, Essie wrote, "I have been married for eleven years now to one of the most charming intelligent gifted men in the world. . . . My husband and I have been exceedingly happy. I think we are happier now than we have ever been. But we no longer wish to be married."[96] Paul's letters to Essie echoed the same civil but loving tone. "I would love to see you and talk to you," he wrote in August 1932, to benefit from what he termed "that common-sense approach of yours."[97] In another version of her "divorce" essay, Essie wrote that she had no regrets and that she had "found self expression on a grand scale in building his career."[98] But, she concluded, "the friendship we are now building has nothing to do with marriage." It sounded logical, calm, and mature, but not surprisingly many unresolved feelings lay just beneath the surface.

Over a decade later, while still legally married, Essie would offer even stronger, but slightly altered, views on the subject. "I think the darkest part of [marriage] is that we insist we're something we are not. We insist we are monogamous, but we are not. And the dangerous thing is that we build our social structure upon this false base, and so we have confusion, the double standard, resentment, and dishonesty between the sexes. I think it absolutely essential for women as well as men, to be able to find interest, companionship, and joy in other human beings. Very few individuals are many faceted enough, complete enough, to satisfy all the needs of another individual. In marriage one settles for the greatest common area of mutual affinity, and then one picks up the bits and pieces elsewhere. And by bits and pieces I don't necessarily mean sex relationships. For myself it would mean good talk, a good bridge player, a good dance partner."[99]

Essie's evolving views on marriage and monogamy were informed by her upbringing as well as her relationship with Paul. She was always a strong and independent woman. Her mother, who raised three children without a husband, had been the same way. Essie had not grown up with rosy or conventional notions about love, marriage, and family. Moreover, in the social circles in which she and Paul traveled, traditional and conservative conventions about sex and marriage were constantly being questioned and transgressed. It is then not surprising that Essie would articulate a critique of monogamy and a defense of the right to divorce.[100]

As the divorce proceedings rolled on, however, and as Paul and Essie continued to talk, write letters, and spend time together, Essie's ambivalence about her own divorce grew. She was sure that women in general had a right to divorce; she was just not sure if she wanted one at that particular moment and on the terms she was being offered. Adding to her discomfort and resentment was her sense that Yolande was overly impetuous and demanding: she would often call Paul on the telephone when she knew he was with his family and spending time with his son. What finally caused Essie to refuse Paul the divorce, however, was money. Essie heard from a mutual friend that Paul was making

$1,500 a week in *Showboat*, and had received offers for radio contracts that would double that, while Essie, by her account, was struggling on $100 a week from Paul that she complained was always late in arriving.[101] Her professed poverty was exaggerated, but her feeling that she was being treated unfairly was very real. "Well, that settles it," Essie wrote in her diary. "I called Mr. Crane [her lawyer] at once, cancelled the divorce, am suing now for separate maintenance. . . . was so angry I couldn't sleep, thinking about it all. The swine!" she fumed. Having just published an essay in which she referred to Paul as essentially one of the most amazing men on the planet, it is clear that Essie's feelings were conflicted at best.[102]

September 1932, the same month that Essie decided not to cooperate with the divorce, Yolande and Paul called off their wedding plans. There are competing accounts of their breakup. Martin Duberman, one of Paul Robeson's biographers, concluded that when Yolande broke things off, Paul was utterly "devastated" and even contemplated suicide. But Paul Robeson Jr. and Essie, in her diary at the time, indicate that when Yolande finally succumbed to pressure from her friends and family and decided not to marry Paul, he had already decided that he preferred to be free. Regardless of the causes of the breakup, by December, Yolande was pursuing Paul again. By this time, however, Paul was spending more time with Paul Jr. and Essie, who was advising him on how to get Yolande "off his neck."[103] Given Essie's typical candor, and what she likely thought of Yolande Jackson, we can only imagine what that advice to Paul might have sounded like.[104]

Through all of the highs and lows with Paul, Essie had not put her own personal life or amorous desires entirely on hold. In the fall of 1932, she spent nine glorious days in Paris, where she carried on a brief flirtatious liaison with the handsome French artist and intellectual Marcel Duchamp, whom she had met through her friend, actress Rita Romilly. Duchamp was a captivating personality. An avant-garde artist closely associated with surrealism, kinetic art, and the Dadaist radical cultural movement in Europe, Duchamp spent several afternoons and evenings with Essie dining, drinking, and talking. "Marcel definitely showed his leaning toward me, but we couldn't 'arrange' it somehow," Essie wrote in her diary with a tinge of wistful regret.[105]

As the year wound down, Essie and Paul's relationship was surprisingly strong given all they had been through. Eventually Yolande stopped calling and Paul moved back in with Essie. "We are very happy," she pronounced. This over-simplification may have reflected

Essie's hope that life could still return to some semblance of normalcy more than it described the reality of the situation. Nevertheless, they traveled to Holland together, spent time in the London flat, and rekindled their friendship. "I am 36 years-old," she wrote on her birthday in December 1932, "and I am happier than I have ever been in my life. . . . Paul and I understand each other." This was, she felt, "the beginning of a new [phase of] life."[106]

Indeed, by the close of 1932, Essie and Paul had reached an understanding about their relationship and their marriage. They would remain together for the rest of their lives. Yolande was out of the picture: there would be no more Yolandes. There would be intimate colleagues, friends, and lovers, but no more threats of divorce or newspaper headlines of marital strife.[107] In February 1933, the front page of the *Chicago Defender* featured a photo of all three Robesons with the headline "Singing in Harmony Again," and quoted Essie as saying, "There is nothing to that rumor that we are getting a divorce." They remade their public image as a solid and stable nuclear family.[108]

Appearances aside, their family arrangement was distinctly nontraditional. Essie would remain Mrs. Paul Robeson. But more often than not, she and Paul slept in separate beds and agreed not to probe too deeply into one another's sexual lives. This was perhaps a less than ideal situation from Essie's point of view, but she accepted it and adjusted to it. A practical woman, Essie did not intend to lose everything she had invested in their relationship and in his career by being intransigent about Paul's desire for sexual independence. She realized, too, that she was free to pursue other relationships if she wanted to. She also felt that Paul needed her. She was his emotional anchor, career adviser, confidante, and most importantly, his loyal friend. And in many respects and for perhaps complex reasons, she wanted to be those things for him. They had a history together and a son. They were, after all the storms they had endured, still a team.

At some point, Essie even stopped worrying about how the world viewed her marriage and family. By 1949, she would write, "Americans are too much concerned with appearances. If husband and wife go out separately, what will so and so think, what will the neighbours say? I've got to the point where I really don't care what people think about me. I realize that people are not going to live my life for me. I am going to have to live it myself. . . . We manage to have a lot of fun in our home because we live our own lives the way we want to live them."[109]

Eslanda in front of a map of Africa, January 1, 1950. Photo by Ann Rosener/Pix Inc./Time Life Pictures/Getty Images.

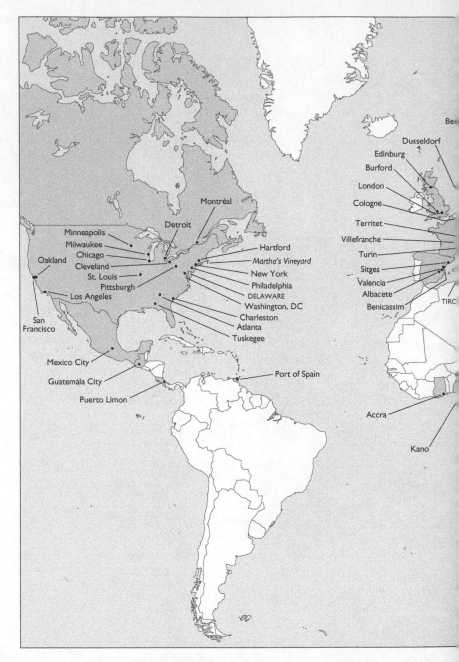

A Select Mapping of Eslanda Robeson's Travels. © Bill Nelson Maps.

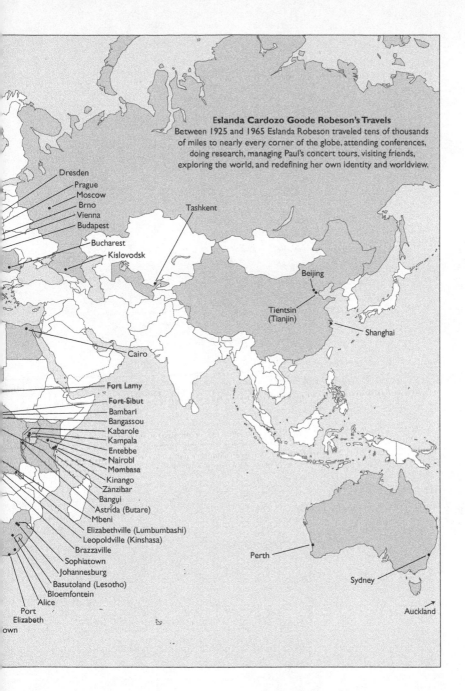

Eslanda Cardozo Goode Robeson's Travels
Between 1925 and 1965 Eslanda Robeson traveled tens of thousands
of miles to nearly every corner of the globe, attending conferences,
doing research, managing Paul's concert tours, visiting friends,
exploring the world, and redefining her own identity and worldview.

Dresden
Prague
Moscow
Brno
Vienna
Budapest
Bucharest
Kislovodsk
Tashkent
Beijing
Tientsin
(Tianjin)
Shanghai
Cairo
Fort Lamy
Fort-Sibut
Bambari
Bangassou
Kabarole
Kampala
Entebbe
Nairobi
Mombasa
Kinango
Zanzibar
Bangui
Astrida (Butare)
Mbeni
Elizabethville (Lumbumbashi)
Leopoldville (Kinshasa)
Brazzaville
Sophiatown
Johannesburg
Basutoland (Lesotho)
Bloemfontein
Alice
Port
Elizabeth
own
Perth
Sydney
Auckland

CERTIFICATION OF VITAL RECORD

GOVERNMENT OF THE DISTRICT OF COLUMBIA
DEPARTMENT OF HEALTH
CERTIFICATE OF LIVE BIRTH

ALWAYS WRITE WITH INK.

RETURN OF A BIRTH.

84458

To THE HEALTH OFFICER, 503 D STREET, N. W.,

WASHINGTON, D. C.

SPECIAL NOTICE TO MIDWIVES: (This Birth Return is to be used ONLY in case the child Breathes. In case of STILL-BIRTH the Midwife must report IMMEDIATELY to the Physician to the Poor in the District in which the birth occurred.

1. Date of Birth, *Dec. 15th* 1895.
2. Place of Birth, (Street and Number,) *2216 - 13th St. N. W.*
3. Was it a Male or Female? *female*
4. Was it White or Colored? *Colored*
5. If Twins or Triplets state their Sex and Color, —
6. Full Name of Mother, *Mrs. Eslanda Goode*
7. Mother's Maiden Name, *Eslanda Cardoza*
8. Mother's Birthplace, (State or Country) *South Carolina*
9. Full Name of Father, *J. J. Goode*
10. Father's Occupation, *Clerk* 11. Father's Birthplace, *Ecc.*
12. Number of Children Mother has given birth to, including present birth, *three*

Signature of Medical Attendant, *H. Kogster M.D.*
Address, *915 - 16th St. N.W.*
Signature of Midwife,
Address.

DC136164

This is to certify that this is a true and correct reproduction or abstract of the official record filed with the Vital Records Division, Department of Health, District of Columbia.

DATE ISSUED **NOVEMBER 16, 2011**

Willis R. Bradwell

Willis R. Bradwell Jr., Registrar

WARNING: IT IS UNLAWFUL TO MAKE COPIES OF THIS DOCUMENT AND PRESENT THEM AS AN OFFICIAL COPY OF AN ORIGINAL CERTIFICATE.

ANY ALTERATION OR ERASURE VOIDS THIS CERTIFICATE

Eslanda Goode's birth certificate, 1895. Some documents and publications erroneously list her birth year as 1896. Washington, D.C., Vital Records.

(*top left*): Francis Lewis Cardozo, Eslanda's maternal grandfather. From the personal collection of Paul Robeson Jr.

(*top right*): Catharine Romena Howell, Eslanda's maternal grandmother. From the personal collection of Paul Robeson Jr.

Lydia Cardozo, Eslanda's maternal great grandmother, circa early 1800s. C. O. Gott/Library of Congress.

Eslanda, circa 1916. From the personal collection of Paul Robeson Jr.

Eslanda C. Goode, Eslanda Robeson's mother, circa 1935. Yale Collection of American Literature, Beinecke Rare Book and Manuscript Library/ Carl Van Vechten. Courtesy Van Vechten Trust.

John J. Goode Sr., Eslanda Robeson's father, circa 1900. Paul and Eslanda Goode Robeson Collection, Howard University, Moorland-Spingarn Research Center, Manuscript Division.

Eslanda's brother Frank Goode. Paul and Eslanda Goode Robeson Collection, Howard University, Moorland-Spingarn Research Center, Manuscript Division.

John Goode Jr., Eslanda's eldest brother, circa 1914. From the personal collection of Paul Robeson Jr.

Eslanda (*center front*) with her Delta Sigma Theta sorority sisters at
the University of Illinois, Urbana, 1915. From the personal
collection of Paul Robeson Jr.

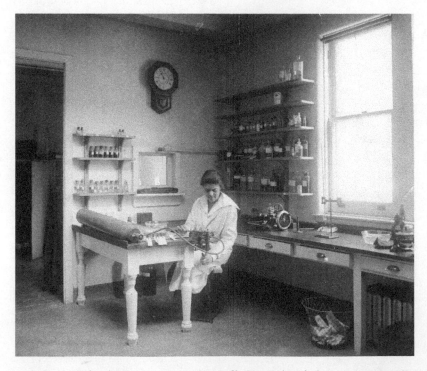

Eslanda in Columbia Presbyterian Hospital's Surgical Pathology Laboratory in
New York City, circa 1921. From the personal collection of Paul Robeson Jr.

(*top*): Eslanda in London, 1932. From the personal collection of Paul Robeson Jr.

Eslanda and Paul en route to New York to film *Emperor Jones*, London, March 5, 1933. Special Collections and University Archives, Rutgers University Libraries, Julius Lazarus Collection/H. L. Davis.

Eslanda with baby Paul Jr., Christmas, 1928. From the personal collection of Paul Robeson Jr.

Eslanda as "Adah" in the film *Borderline*, 1930. Yale Collection of American Literature, Beinecke Rare Book and Manuscript Library, Hilda Doolittle Papers.

Eslanda with Paul and American playwright Eugene O'Neill (*center*) in Provincetown, Massachusetts, circa 1925. From the personal collection of Paul Robeson Jr.

Marcus Garvey (*right*) with Prince Kojo Touvalou Houénou (*center*), Eslanda's friend and confidante, and George O. Marke (*left*) in 1924. James VanDerZee © Donna Mussenden VanDerZee.

(*top*): Eslanda (*front row left*) and Paul with Indian friends in London, 1936.
From the personal collection of Paul Robeson Jr.

Paul and Eslanda become honorary members of the London-based West African
Students' Union, 1936. From the personal collection of Paul Robeson Jr.

(*top*): Eslanda and Paul in the motion picture *Big Fella*, 1937, England.
From the personal collection of Paul Robeson Jr.

Eslanda and Paul with Paul's African Studies language tutor, Charles Johnson, on
the set of the film *King Solomon's Mines*, 1936. Akademie der Künste, Berlin,
Paul Robeson Archives/photo by Gaumont-British Pictures.

Eslanda (*seated, second from right*) with Charles S. Johnson (*seated, center*), publisher of *Opportunity* magazine and prominent sociologist, and poets Langston Hughes (*standing, first from left*), Arna Bontemps (*standing, second from right*), Owen Dodson (*standing, first from right*), Ira Reid (*standing, third from left*), and anthropologist Melville Herskovits (*front row, right*), circa early 1940s. Paul and Eslanda Goode Robeson Collection, Howard University, Moorland-Spingarn Research Center, Manuscript Division.

(*top*): Eslanda and Paul arrive in Manhattan from England aboard the
S.S. Majestic en route to Hollywood for the screening of *Showboat*,
October 1, 1935. © Bettmann/CORBIS.

Eslanda and Paul in Barcelona, Spain, on February 3, 1938 to support
the Republican cause. Associated Press.

(*top*): Eslanda (*standing, left*) with three Toro women in Uganda, 1936. From the personal collection of Paul Robeson Jr.

A Toro herdsman in Kabarole, Uganda, 1936. From the personal collection of Paul Robeson Jr. Photo by Eslanda Robeson.

(*top*): Eslanda and Paul Robeson Jr., with the chief justice of Buganda, and a local child in Kampala, Uganda, 1936. From the personal collection of Paul Robeson Jr.

Paul Jr. (*farthest left*) with African National Congress leader Z. K. Matthews, his wife, Frieda, and their children, in Alice, South Africa, 1936. From the personal collection of Paul Robeson Jr.

(*top*): Eslanda (*second from right*) is greeted by friends in San Francisco in 1945 as she arrives for the founding meeting of the United Nations. *California Eagle* publisher, and Council on African Affairs member, Charlotta Bass, is second from left. Southern California Library for Social Sciences and Research. Photo by Irving C. Smith.

Eslanda being interviewed by reporters in Peking (Beijing), 1950. From the personal collection of Paul Robeson Jr.

five

BECOMING A WRITER AND
ANTHROPOLOGIST, 1930s

> *I began to get my intellectual feet wet.*
> Eslanda Robeson

By the mid-1930s, Essie had been a writer for some years. While she had not made a living from her writing and regarded herself as a somewhat accidental writer ("all of my books occurred somewhat inadvertently," she once said), she was a prolific diarist, novelist, playwright, and now an aspiring journalist. And it was as a writer and anthropologist, and as a part of London's vibrant international and African Diasporic intellectual community, that her growing interest in the vast, diverse, and dynamic region known as sub-Saharan Africa came into sharper focus.

In some respects Essie's path to Africa ran through many other places: meetings with African students in Edinburgh; visits to African art collections in Düsseldorf; conversations with South African and Kenyan students in her anthropology seminars in London; her friendship with Leonard Barnes, Kojo Touvolou Houénou, and Anna Graves; and her interviews with Afro-Caribbeans and Francophone West Africans in Paris. As for Essie's writing career, it too was slow to get off the ground, with a number of false starts. Her first book was one such false start. After years of trying with limited success to get much of her fiction work published, Essie was excited when Victor Gollancz agreed to publish *Paul Robeson, Negro*, in 1930. Gollancz was a new publishing house and its founder and namesake had left-wing sympathies and anti-racist sensibilities. The idea of publishing a biography of a great Negro artist like Robeson was undoubtedly appealing to him.[1] The book, a mere 178 pages, was written in the third person to give a veneer of objectivity. It was published just before Essie discovered the devastating letter from Peggy Ashcroft but after she had learned about the seriousness of Paul's affair with Yolande Jackson.[2] Befitting the delicacy of the situation, and the uncertainty of the moment, Essie's narrative was a deliberately crafted (and consciously altered) story of their lives. She portrayed their marriage as solid, Paul as devoted to her (despite amorous distractions), and herself as indispensable to Paul and their partnership. According to Paul Robeson Jr., the book was "her way of publicly defending what she felt were her irrevocable rights as Mrs. Robeson."[3]

Publicly, Essie presented the book as her tribute to Paul, but she certainly could not be accused of hagiography. Laden with praise for his brilliance and accomplishments, Essie offered a good dose of subtle and not so subtle criticisms as well, mostly about his work habits and hypothetical infidelities, ones that she felt were all too real. The book chronicled Paul's early family life, his football career, legal studies, and rise to a position of great stature as an artist. But then, as if to bring him down a notch or two, Essie described Paul as sometimes "lazy, with a capital L" and even childlike. She even suggested he was disinterested in his own son, or at least less involved than she thought he should be. These negative comments were couched in a much longer narrative about his many amazing talents, but still she made her point.[4]

In terms of their marriage, Essie depicted Paul as a mischievous flirt, but a husband lovingly devoted to the wife who had worked so hard on his behalf. In her scenario, "if" Paul had been unfaithful to her, "surely" he was contrite and she was confident he would never leave her. In essence, Essie scripted a fictional marital dynamic and played out her desired outcome. If she did feel vulnerable, perhaps the narrative she created was her insurance policy against abandonment. If she felt a bit powerless over her life and future, perhaps it was her way of flexing her muscle. Regardless of the complex emotions behind Essie's depiction of their marriage, Paul viewed the critical and contrived passages as deceptive and disparaging, and he resented them.[5] This took yet another toll on their relationship.

Even though *Paul Robeson, Negro* was about Essie's famous husband, it was not only about him. A good portion of the book offered Essie's own reflections on a range of issues that informed Paul's life, but were not "about" Paul per se. She included commentary on Harlem as a Mecca for Black people seeking greater freedom of expression. She inserted a short history lesson on Reconstruction, no doubt drawn from her own family history. And she wrote several passages about the nature and prevalence of American racism and discrimination. Essie did not fail to talk about a subject she wrote about often in her fiction, the color biases within the Black community and the divisions within the larger African Diaspora.[6] These passages offer insights into Essie's views of the larger world in 1930, some of which would change as time went by and her own horizons broadened. Perhaps most striking are her views on race, Africa, and African culture, which both challenged some prevailing stereotypes and reinforced others. For example, Essie talked about Black people as "naturally humorous," and Paul as having "typical Negro qualities."[7] These generalizations belie the deeper understanding of culture and race that would be reflected in her later writings, and they were insignificant relative to the larger profile she offered of Paul Robeson himself.

Essie had her own professional objectives in writing the book about Paul. As an aspiring writer, she very much wanted a respected book publication to her credit, and she had hoped that *Paul Robeson, Negro* would be that feather in her cap. Unfortunately, it received only a luke-warm response from critics, who felt it was slim in content and predictably biased in Paul's favor. In a lengthy and mainly positive *Herald Tribune* review, her friend, Harlem Renaissance poet Langston Hughes, described the book as "chatty, informing, and naively intimate."[8] Essie had hoped for other adjectives to describe the publication, I am sure. Even if she was disappointed by the book's reception overall, she was not deterred from a writing career, though she did briefly retreat to what may have felt like the "safer" world of fiction writing. Throughout the fall and winter of 1930, she labored tirelessly on a novel entitled "Black Progress," which she finished in January 1931. She hoped that the book, a semi-autobiographical story about the plight of a middle-class Black family, would be published and later become a full-blown stage production. Neither event would come to pass. But "Black Progress," as well as another play Essie was working on called "Uncle Tom's Cabin" (with the title borrowed from Harriet Beecher Stowe's book), provide insight into some of the issues that were on her mind and the kinds of characters who most resonated with her.

Essie's version of "Uncle Tom's Cabin" was a musical comedy, a "parody" of Stowe's 1852 fictional account of slavery, set in a series of nightclubs in New York, Paris, Berlin, and Leningrad. The characters were dancers, agents, nightclub owners, blues singers, and musicians who were all scheming in various ways to climb the ladder of success.[9] Essie's characters were composites of people she knew and some of the story lines mirrored dramas that had played out in her own family and among her eclectic and international circle of friends. For instance, some of the middle-class characters in Essie's novels grappled with the implications of their privilege, while others were relatively oblivious, and still others were consumed with guilt. She created light-skinned Negro characters who wrestled with the consequences of passing for white or the temptation to do so, and interracial couples who confronted the danger of crossing the color line. A rough draft of another play Essie wrote centered on an aristocratic British family living in London whose adult son, Michael, is gay. His family suspects he and his longtime friend, Freddy, have become lovers. The play, titled "Leave Them Alone," was perhaps Essie's veiled statement against the homophobia of her day.[10]

Essie wrote a third novel, "Color" (re-titled from the original "Your Color is Showing"). Set in the 1930s, the novel was again a loose composite narrative involving versions of her family, friends, and acquaintances, and dealt with the issues of racial passing, racial injustice, and the compromises and sacrifices that Black people had made in order to navigate the color line and make decent lives for themselves. The novel, 170 or so pages long, revolves around the lives of three young college students as they begin their careers after graduating from a large Midwestern college outside Chicago, possibly the University of Illinois. The two men, A.B. and Tom, are serious musicians and set out to make their artistic dreams a reality. The third student, Antoinette (Toni) Napier, is a smart and beautiful economics major who ends up working for a real estate firm on Wall Street. The primary difference between the three is that Toni has passed for white during her years at college, living in a selective women's dormitory and dating a popular and wealthy white football star on campus. Toni's slightly darker-skinned mother had declined to attend her own daughter's graduation for fear of revealing her secret and compromising her future opportunities. Toni continues the charade when she lands a job on Wall Street.

Interspersed with the stories of Tom, A.B., and Toni are other stories that give a larger sense of the hostile racial landscape of 1930s America. The Napier family maid, a Southern-born Black woman, confides in Toni that she had "accidentally" set fire to her previous employer's house just as he was about to mobilize a lynch mob to go after a local Black man deemed too uppity. The lynching was averted due to the maid's savvy and brazen intervention, and she vowed never to work for white folks again.

As the three young protagonists struggle to fulfill their dreams, they also work, in different ways, to defy conventional expectations. In the process they are thwarted, humiliated, and forced to make difficult choices. Toni, who initially "passes" for white for practical reasons, still loves her Black family, and once back in New York, goes home to Harlem every weekend. She eventually succumbs to the advances of a white suitor and chooses to hide her racial identity in order to marry him. "I didn't exactly disown you," she tells the sister she supposedly adores, explaining she simply failed to mention to her new husband that she had either a sister or a mother who was living. To make amends and redeem herself, she promises to funnel money back to her Black family once she is secure in her new life. Meanwhile the two aspiring young musicians, Tom and A.B., are making tough choices of their own. They agree to perform in a degrading minstrel-type cabaret until they can leave for Paris (where they can play music that is meaningful and serious), which they eventually do.

"Color" was not a literary masterpiece, but it did offer a serious social commentary. In it Essie crafted complex and talented characters living in a world with racism and injustice all around. They were not trying to change the world but simply to plot a course as best they could. None of the characters was perfect, but neither were they villains. Essie's novel conveyed both the sense of limited possibilities as well as the resilience of educated Black people living in the 1930s. It is interesting that the theme of crossing the color line comes up frequently in Essie's nonfiction writing. She seems nonjudgmental of those Black people who chose to claim white privileges. Yet this is precisely the opposite of the path Essie herself chose to take. She married a brown-skinned man, expressed pride in her African heritage, and if there was ever an instance in which her racial status was ambiguous, she quickly clarified things.

Several publishers and producers rejected all three novels outright, and even Essie's friends were less than enthusiastic.[11] Ever resilient, Essie decided that if fiction was not going to be her medium, then perhaps journalism would be a better outlet. She had started taking a deeper interest in politics and world affairs, which her fictional characters had rarely delved into, and she began to look for serious nonfiction subjects to write about. Real-life narratives proved as interesting to Essie as the fictional characters she had been constructing for her plays and novels. For example, she wrote a lengthy biographical sketch of Oliver Golden, a Black American born in 1891 in Yazoo, Mississippi, who relocated to the Soviet Union in 1925.[12] She would later draft biographical sketches of the French African leader Félix Éboué and others.

In October 1931, Essie landed an interview with the legendary

Indian spiritual and political leader Mahatma Gandhi. The meeting was arranged by a mutual friend, an Indian journalist identified only as Mr. Lal. At the time, Gandhi's movement had not yet borne fruit, but he was already known worldwide. Gandhi was in London for several months, giving lectures and meeting with supporters. He had recently been released from prison after serving an eight-month sentence for nonviolent resistance to British colonialism. Gandhi had chosen to live in one of London's slums during his visit, but Essie met him at an office on Knightsbridge Street. "I found [him] sitting on the floor, spinning; using a flat instrument . . . turning the small handle with his right hand, and pulling the thread with his left," she wrote. Gandhi reasoned that the expansion of Indian-produced textiles was one step toward economic independence. So he sat on a bare floor in a London office building practicing what he preached. Essie wrote: "He has no teeth in front, is very thin, dressed in rough whitish cloth, legs bare, but with a white cloth thrown over him for warmth: [and] big spectacles."[13]

Essie was wholly impressed with this tiny, seemingly fragile man who had such a large and powerful intellect and commanding presence. As she probed Gandhi's views about empire and potential solidarity among oppressed peoples, she asked whether there might ever be "brown supremacy" in the world, a unity of the dark colonies to counter white domination. "He said quite simply," she wrote, that he was not "working for, or interested in, any supremacy, but for equality." His answer impressed Essie. He exuded, in her view, "truthful, commonsense" views and "the utmost simplicity and dignity."[14] Like her novels, this first major interview went unpublished. But in the years that followed, as Essie's understanding of colonialism deepened, she would write dozens of articles on the subject. It is also perhaps this 1931 meeting with Gandhi that ignited an interest in India that Essie would find compelling for the rest of her life. Essie was not the only African American with deep interests in and solidarity with the Indian freedom struggle in this period. From publications like *The Negro World* and *The Pittsburgh Courier* to *The Bombay Chronicle* and *Independent India*, expressions of solidarity and support flowed both ways between African Americans and Indians living under British rule.[15]

Prior to the 1930s, Essie had been curious about social issues and keenly sensitive to issues of racism and the color caste system within the Black community, but she had not tried to forge any sophisticated political analysis. Her friends in Harlem were a savvy group, but the American, European, African, Afro-Caribbean, and Asian intellectuals and artists whom she came to know in London were far more worldly.

The international network of relationships that she formed in London and later in Africa in the 1930s was pivotal in helping Essie to form a more complex global perspective. She took every opportunity that presented itself to exchange ideas with these new international friends, in settings both with and without Paul. During this time Essie's curiosities were expanding in all directions.

In the early 1930s, Essie and Paul shared a growing interest in the world, and especially in Africa. They read voraciously and frequently invited young African students to their apartment at 19 Buckingham Street in London's Adelphi neighborhood—among them some of the future leaders of Nigeria, Ghana, and Kenya—where they talked about politics, culture, and life.[16] Around this time Paul undertook an in-depth study of African languages as his entrée to the continent and its many cultures. The Robesons were so immersed in the lives of African expatriates and students in the 1930s that they were made honorary members of the London-based West African Students' Union (WASU), which was itself much more than a social and cultural organization.[17] According to historian Marc Matera, London-based "organizations like WASU . . . were, at once, essential to, and the most visible by-products of, the making of black internationalists."[18] WASU gatherings were the sites of debates, exchanges, and network building that would bear fruit as Pan-African initiatives and African independence struggles unfolded. People like the legendary Caribbean-born intellectuals George Padmore and C.L.R. James were a part of the WASU circle, just as Essie was. The conversations, reflections, and memories of her African friends in London fueled and animated Essie's imaginings about the vast continent, and whetted her appetite to not only know more, but also, more importantly, go to Africa herself.[19]

Determined to expand her knowledge of the continent, Essie enrolled at the prestigious London School of Economics (LSE) in 1933 on what was called an "occasional" or "visiting" basis to study anthropology and African societies. Having abandoned her medical school ambitions long before, she turned her intellectual curiosity toward understanding the human condition in order to improve it. Why were oppression and injustice tolerated? Why were racial hierarchies so entrenched and well maintained? What were the history and likely future of Africa, India, and the rest of the colonized world? What was the role of culture in the fight for equality? What was the relationship between Africans and Black Americans? Answering these core questions became one of Essie's life's ambitions.

In pursuit of answers, Essie took a range of courses that required her to engage in a rigorous study of African cultures and traditions, the topography and natural resources of the continent, and Africans' early encounters with Europeans.[20] Essie thought that many of the anthropologists whom she encountered at LSE still viewed Africans through a racist lens. Anthropology as a field certainly had racist tendencies, and many scholars brought to their research notions of African inferiority. Essie was frustrated at times by professors and fellow students who arrogantly and condescendingly described Africans as uncivilized "primitives."

Still LSE, with its large population of foreign students (including many from Africa and India) and international faculty, was a site of lively intellectual debate around issues of colonialism, fascism, and world politics. Essie's courses at LSE and the wider milieu of 1930s London provoked her to think in new ways, to ask bigger and deeper questions about the world, and to imagine anew her own future career as a writer, scholar, researcher, and eventually, activist.[21]

One of Essie's professors at LSE was the famous Polish cultural anthropologist Bronislaw Malinowski, who pioneered participant observation as a cornerstone of social anthropology and is described by some as one of the founders of the field. Born in 1884 in Krakow, Malinowski was an early and ardent critic of Nazism. He mentored a whole coterie of LSE students, including dozens of African students who were studying in England thanks to scholarships specifically designated for colonial subjects. His seminars on Africa were the place for heated and deeply relevant debates involving thinkers and activists who had first-hand knowledge of the subject.

Malinowski, who went on to teach in the United States at Cornell, Harvard, and Yale, was a rigorous teacher. Essie, however, was far from intimidated. While she respected Malinowski's keen mind and the path-breaking work he had done in Papua, New Guinea, she did not hesitate to challenge him in class and remained skeptical about whether a white anthropologist could do bias-free research on people of color. She viewed some of what she heard in Malinowski's classes as blatantly racist and offensive. Malinowski's own list of scholarly publications included titles like "Sex and Repression in Savage Society," "Crime and Custom in Savage Society," and "Myth in Primitive Society."[22] Even though such terminology was common in the 1920s and 1930s, Essie took issue with descriptions of dark-skinned peoples as backward, primitive, and savage, and she did not hesitate to express these views inside and outside of class.

According to biographers and his own published diaries, Malinowski was a complicated man plagued by anxieties, phobias, and character flaws. While he broke with early twentieth-century European scholars who saw Black and Brown people of the world as representing some lower form of humanity, Malinowski himself was not free from racist or elitist views, some of which Essie must have detected in class. The publication of his New Guinea fieldwork diaries in 1967 created a sharp debate between his defenders and critics, with the critics alleging that he was a narcissistic hypochondriac, prone to violent outbursts, who harbored racist and condescending views toward the "native" people with whom he lived while doing his research. The diaries were published posthumously so Malinowski could not respond to the reviews, and we will never know Essie's reaction since she also did not live to read the revelatory publications.[23]

Essie was one of the few Black American students in Malinowski's seminars, although Ralph Bunche would study briefly with him a few years later. Essie's intellectual interests included both the African and the Black American experience. After one class discussion about segregation in the United States, she wrote Malinowski, on her own initiative, a ten-page reflection. "My Dear Professor Malinowski," she began. "Last week we talked about the idea of Segregation as a possible solution to the Negro Problem in America. There was so much I wanted to tell you about the idea, that I have put it down on paper. . . . I would be glad to discuss it with you someday."[24] She then carefully described the political and economic roots of American racism and the pathology of anti-Black sentiment among white Americans. It is unclear what his reply was to Essie's letter but to his credit, Malinowski was the one who first suggested that Essie pursue a Ph.D. in anthropology. She was resistant at first, saying it was too "high brow" for her, but Malinowski insisted she would be good at it. "It is what you have been doing," he told her referring to her interest in people, cultures, and diverse ways of doing things.[25] Years later Essie decided to pursue a graduate degree in anthropology (a degree she would never finish), and from the start she was determined to do her fieldwork somewhere in Africa.[26]

On her own, Essie was grappling with issues of race, culture, and assimilation, themes that appeared repeatedly in her fiction. It was also around this time that she became acquainted with the young African American anthropologist Allison Davis, who was also at LSE for a short time, and who would go on to have a distinguished and pioneering career in the field of race and anthropology.[27] A committed "race woman"—meaning a Black woman proud of her African ancestry and committed to the progress and plight of Black people—Essie was increasingly impatient with Blacks who looked to Europe and the West instead of Africa for insights and inspiration. She expressed both a leftist Pan-Africanism and an internationalist view of Black identity and politics. Interestingly, in 1934, when Dr. Harold Moody, a Jamaican living in London, asked Essie and Paul to support the newly formed League of Colored Peoples (LCP), a group that advocated for the rights of people of African descent living in Europe and throughout the African Diaspora, Essie bluntly, perhaps rashly, refused. She said that people of African descent in Britain had turned their backs on Africa and were "trying hard to fit into a white world and a white future. That is their affair, not ours."[28] In a harsh way, she seemed to be making a distinction between Black Britains who had settled there permanently and her student friends who had the view of returning to Africa after their studies. The line between the two was thinner than Essie was prepared to acknowledge, and Moody's work and ideas were closer to her own than she seemed to appreciate. Essie also presumed to speak for Paul on this matter when it was not at all clear that he shared her view. In fact, he would later lend his support to Moody and the LCP.

In terms of Essie's Pan-Africanist views, she was a supporter of African and Third World unity as a strategy against colonialism and imperialism. She was a "race conscious woman" with a focus on Africa and peoples of African descent. Her support for African leaders, however, was never unconditional and would always be framed within a larger understanding of geopolitical dynamics. That is, her Pan-Africanism, in the tradition of W. E. B. Du Bois more than Marcus Garvey, was still deeply international. Essie articulated the links between the colonized peoples of the world and never saw her allegiances or her analysis in narrowly racial or nationalist terms.[29] She was deeply influenced by the Indian activists and intellectuals whom she met in London—such as law student Rajni Patel and aspiring filmmaker D. G. Tendulkar—and saw important links between the Indian and the Black American experience. She made a point of connecting not only the ideas, but also the people. She introduced poet Langston Hughes to Jawaharlal Nehru in the 1930s and made other similar introductions as well.[30]

Around this time Essie was in touch with the Black novelist and anthropologist Zora Neale Hurston, whom she and Paul had known in New York in the 1920s. Hurston encouraged Essie in her study of African cultures and societies. "What you tell me about your studies is thrilling," she wrote to Essie in 1934. "You know that we do not know anything about ourselves. You realize every day how silly our 'leaders' sound—talking what they don't know." Referring to the importance of studying indigenous African cultures, Hurston concluded, "This means you are going to Africa to study at [*sic*] first hand. That is glorious." She then harshly criticized a number of Harlem writers and activists who had recently disparaged Black "folk" sources. Hurston wrote, "I have steadily maintained that the real us was infinitely superior to the sympathetic minstrel version." Hurston stressed the importance of a kind of authenticity and complexity when dealing with Black subjects. In telling Essie about her debut novel published in 1934, *Jonah's Gourd Vine*, the story of a Black minister in a small U.S. southern town, Hurston wrote: "I tried to be natural and not pander to the folks who expect a clown or a villain in every Negro."[31] Essie's communications with Hurston may have influenced both her reaction to Harold Moody and her interactions with not only Malinowski (whom Hurston also knew), but her other LSE teachers and classmates as well.[32]

While Essie was influenced by Malinowski, and developed a collegial but sometimes contentious intellectual relationship with him, she developed a much closer and more personal relationship with one of his younger colleagues, economic anthropologist Raymond Firth. A native of New Zealand, Firth came to the LSE with his wife, Rosemary, who was also an anthropologist. He became a legendary figure at the school and would live to the ripe old age of one hundred. During the 1930s, Firth was a young professor at LSE and he and Rosemary became close friends of Essie's. Essie wrote him long, rambling, personal letters during her travels to Glasgow, California, and Leningrad, addressing him as "Raymond, Dear," and signing her letters, "Landa," a nickname she apparently only used during her student days at LSE.[33] In one letter, she lamented that her travels and family obligations took her away from her studies at LSE and her informal discussions with Firth. "Raymond, Dear: I do enjoy my evenings with you so very much, that I am furious about having so few. The more I see you, the more I like you."[34]

Essie's family obligations and work on behalf of Paul's career often kept her from focusing on her studies as she might have wanted to. She made her own decisions, to be sure, but she often felt torn between two callings. She would write to her professors apologizing for not being able to be more of an active participant in some of her classes because she was on the road with her husband.[35]

During this period, Essie and Paul's mutual interests in Africa continued to deepen. It was a growing passion that they pursued independently and together. More than anything else, Paul and Essie had an intellectual relationship. They talked about ideas and history, culture and politics. They talked about the interesting people they met and the books they read. So as Essie's interest in, and knowledge of, Africa grew stronger over the early 1930s, she undoubtedly influenced Paul's thinking and vice versa. It was Essie, however, who would eventually make Africa and its liberation the central focus of her life's work. It was Essie who first introduced Paul to Jomo Kenyatta. And it was Essie who interviewed African expatriates and applied for a Guggenheim to travel to Africa.

In the winter of 1934 Paul received a most appealing invitation. He was asked to participate in a film about the Haitian revolutionary Toussaint L'Ouverture that was to be made in the Soviet Union. It was to be directed by the preeminent Soviet filmmaker Sergei Eisenstein, director of *Battleship Potemkin* and other Russian classic films. The British writer Marie Seton, an acquaintance of Eisenstein, came to dinner at the Robesons' apartment at 19 Buckingham Street one evening to discuss the project. Essie made duck, one of her culinary specialties, and Marie climbed the narrow, creaky stairs to their place with a personal letter from Eisenstein inviting Paul to come to Russia to make the film.[36] The three enjoyed a lovely dinner, a lively conversation ensued, and by the end of the evening the Robesons had accepted the offer. They were both excited to go.

Essie wanted to visit the Soviet Union for many reasons. First, in the circles she and Paul traveled in there was a buzz about the place. Two years before the Robesons made their trek, a group of twenty-one American Negroes had landed in Moscow to make a film called *Black and White*, which was to be about race relations in the United States. The film was never completed, but the trip was historic and transformative. Louise Thompson, who would later marry the Robesons' friend William Patterson, was forever changed by all that she saw, learned, and experienced. The Black film cast was made up of artists, writers, leftist intellectuals, and ordinary workers, all curious and eager for a chance to see the world, especially a part of the world that claimed to stand in opposition to racism and imperialism.[37] Even though Essie did not know many of the artists well, she did know Langston Hughes, who wrote and spoke about the experience widely and undoubtedly piqued Essie's curiosity even more. A second reason that Essie wanted to travel to the Soviet Union had to do with her familial ties to the region. The precise reason that her two brothers chose to migrate to the socialist country is unclear, but we do know that they were in search of work and new opportunities and that by the time Essie and Paul headed to the Soviet Union, Frank and John Goode were already there.

In December of 1934, then, with Marie Seton in tow, Essie and Paul took a train from London and headed east toward Russia. It was a long distance to cover. Along the way, they had a daylong layover in Berlin just a few days before Christmas. The ugly face of fascism could be seen everywhere. Hitler was already firmly in power, but the world did not yet know the full extent of the Nazi atrocities. Essie and Paul both knew that Jews and communists were being rounded up and that some of their German friends were being targeted. During their stay in Berlin, rather than stand around the train station for hours, they booked a hotel room for the day to relax in private. While they were at the hotel Essie called up one Jewish friend who came by to visit with them. He was in a terrible state, and told them some of the details of the brutality and vicious persecution that was under way. Paul and Essie were both shaken by the news.[38]

A few hours later, in the Berlin train station, another disturbing event occurred. As they were preparing to depart, Paul and Marie were surrounded by a group of hostile German soldiers with menacing looks and loaded guns, who spat out racial epithets in German (which Paul understood). Paul thought an attack was imminent. The soldiers moved in closer and the situation grew tense. Essie had gone to check on their luggage, but returned just as the train to Moscow arrived at the station, so the three were able to board quickly before any physical confrontation could occur. As their train pulled out of Berlin, Essie was haunted by the thought of what was unfolding there. Essie was chilled to the bone by what she heard and what she observed, by the fear she felt with every breath. Later recounting in her diary an amalgam of her feelings, including those expressed to her by Paul and Marie, Essie wrote that it was "a terrible feeling of wolves waiting to spring." "Uniforms, brown shirts, swastikas everywhere . . . no one looks left or right." Essie imagined the feelings were akin to those of a "Negro in Mississippi" waiting to be lynched: "I suddenly understand for the first time. . . . Terror. Fear. Horror. Tension."[39] Their train crossed the German border into Poland and chugged on toward Moscow. As Berlin faded from view and memory, Essie's mood lifted. It was December 22, and holiday celebrations had begun early in the dining car. "We had vodka and champagne with dinner," she recalled, and "wine with lunch." They literally washed away the fear and angst they had felt at coming face to face with fascism. It was such a different Germany than Essie remembered from years past. By the time they reached their destination, they had made new friends on the train and all were in good spirits.

In addition to working with Eisenstein on the film about Haiti, the Robesons had also come to the Soviet Union to see for themselves what other friends and acquaintances had encountered there. In the 1930s, many Black leftists and artists looked to Russia as a hopeful political model, a socialist country that had condemned colonialism and formally rejected racial hierarchy.[40] W. E. B. Du Bois had visited the country in 1926, less than a decade after the Bolshevik Revolution, and spoke positively about what he saw.[41] In the 1930s, the Communist Party USA, a loyal ally of the Soviet Union, was at the height of its popularity among Black artists and intellectuals, including some friends of the Robesons from Harlem. Essie and Paul were curious about the country, and felt especially drawn by reports that there was little or no racial prejudice there. They had listened with great interest to the tales and critiques of Max Eastman, Claude McKay, as well as the negative views of Emma Goldman. Now they had come to evaluate the situation for themselves. After they arrived, Essie wrote to Carl Van Vechten and Fania Marinoff, "We love it here, and we are profoundly interested in what they are doing."[42]

Essie and Paul were not the only members of the family drawn to, and curious about, the Soviet Union in the 1930s. Essie's mother had been fascinated by Russian culture since childhood, and Essie's two brothers had migrated there with great hopefulness. Frank Goode, the most adventurous of the three siblings, had attended Columbia University before leaving for Europe to fight in World War I. Years after the war, he left the United States for good, landing in the Soviet Union in 1934 at the age of forty-one, only a few days before the Robesons' arrival.[43] He eventually joined the Russian circus as a member of a celebrated Greco-Roman wrestling team and traveled around the vast country performing for urban and rural audiences.[44] A few years later he would settle in the city of Gorky; marry a Russian woman, Shura; claim Soviet citizenship; and have a daughter, whom he would name Eslanda.[45] Essie's brother John had arrived in the Soviet Union the previous spring, but his stay would be temporary.

On their 1934–1935 trip, Essie and Paul also met or became reacquainted with a number of African Americans who were living in the Soviet Union, a small delegation of whom met them at their hotel upon their arrival. They spent time with their old Harlem friend William (Pat) Patterson, who was in Moscow recovering from a bout of tuberculosis. Although Essie had likely not fully forgiven "Pat" for what he had done to her old friend Minnie, she and Paul both made a point to see him and talk to him while they were there. (Paul spent more time with him than Essie did.) They also met and socialized with the famed African American singer Marian Anderson, who had just performed a historic concert in Leningrad. The Robesons had met Anderson in London in 1928 when Paul was doing *Showboat*, introduced by none other than Alberta Hunter. They liked her immediately. Both Essie and Paul were in the audience at Anderson's debut London concert that same year, and they would spend considerable time together on many occasions after that. But while in Russia in 1935, the shy and less politically engaged Anderson kept a relatively low profile, unlike the Robesons, who were the toasts of the town.[46]

During their visit, Essie and Paul were treated like dignitaries by Soviet officials. While they were technically guests of Sergei Eisenstein, who himself was a bit out of favor with the Russian leadership, city officials in Moscow quite literally rolled out the red carpet for Essie and Paul.[47] They were shown the best of the Soviet system: model schools, state-of-the-art hospitals, and not a hint of Jim Crow segregation. They were impressed. "The Soviet people have embarked on a great social experiment," Essie wrote in the Black New York newspaper the *Amsterdam News*. They "have built a society where a Negro is not treated like a Negro, but is treated like a man." Her comments echo almost identical statements made by Paul and later by her brothers. What attracted her, and Paul, to the Soviet Union, she said later, was the absence of racism, pure and simple. The appeal for Paul was more multifaceted, since he also had a special interest in Russian languages and culture. In an interview with the *Chicago Defender* during his stay, he proclaimed Soviet theater "the most interesting in the world."[48] To be sure, Paul and Essie's whirlwind tour in 1934 and early 1935 exposed them only to a showcase of socialist ideals and achievements. They did not witness or perceive any of the many problems already brewing in Soviet society. Indeed, Essie's only complaint was the weather. She wrote to a friend back home, "It is 33 degrees below zero, and the Russians hold their noses in the streets to keep them from freezing." Still, she deemed the whole trip "an ideal holiday, I must say, the most interesting we have had."[49]

Essie, despite being the younger sibling, had been a kind of surrogate mother to her two older brothers as they grew up. She was the dutiful daughter who kept things together at home while her mother worked, who thwarted the insults of playground bullies with her sharp tongue, and who provided money and resources to both brothers at different times when they were down and out. By 1935 she and Paul had decided not to divorce and their finances were in good shape. Essie was pleased to be able to share some of that good fortune with her brothers as a way to help them get settled in Russia. "I left the boys really better fixed than they have ever been," she wrote reassuringly to her mother in January of 1935. "They have everything they could possibly need."[50]

After the Robesons returned to London from the Soviet Union, Essie and Paul made plans for an extended stay in the United States beginning in September. After spending some time on the East Coast with family and friends, and after a short concert tour for Paul and Larry, Essie and Paul flew out to California for the filming of a remake of the movie version of *Showboat*. They stayed there several months and Essie was fascinated by the place. These were the early days of Hollywood and the new medium of film represented an exciting new departure.

In stark contrast to the glamour and excitement of Hollywood were the disturbing social and economic realities of the Great Depression, which Essie and Paul saw all around them. Bread lines, evictions, and massive unemployment were signs of the times, and all of this devastation hit Black America especially hard. An acquaintance of Essie's in Harlem, journalist Marvel Cook, who interviewed Essie during her 1935 visit to the States, also was co-author of an article for *Crisis* magazine that same year that dramatized the brutal effects the Depression was having on Negro women. The article, "Bronx Slave Market," was co-written with activist Ella Baker and documented the slave-like conditions of Black domestic workers in New York in the 1930s. Given the blunt trauma of the Depression on the communities and people that Essie loved, the success that she and Paul were experiencing must have been bittersweet.

In addition to large and troubling social issues, Essie had her hands full personally and professionally. She had always been busy, but in the mid-1930s—as she fought to advance Paul's career, triage the deluge of offers and requests that were coming his way, pursue her own fledgling career as a writer, manage the family finances, and oversee the care of her young son—she sometimes felt overwhelmed, although externally she remained calm. When the Robesons' old friend Walter White complained in November of 1935 that they had not responded quickly enough to his request for Paul to do a benefit concert for the NAACP while they were in the States, Essie lost her patience. White had hinted that Paul and Essie were being elusive. "Elusive, hell," she wrote. "We are hard-working people, you mean." She went on to explain that she had tried to respond to his request but was unable to reach him; further, they were already overbooked and stretched to the limit, and the benefit would have to wait until another time.[51]

After Paul finished his scenes from *Showboat*, the couple headed home. On their way back to London by way of New York, Essie stopped off in Chicago to snag an interview with the rising star athlete Joe Louis, who was soon to become the next heavyweight-boxing champion of the world, and was already a great source of pride for the Negro American community. Essie was building her portfolio as a journalist bit by bit; even when pieces did not get published, as was the case with this one, she welcomed the opportunity to get more experience under her belt. During their stay in Chicago Essie was not only wearing her journalist's hat; she was thinking of her interest in anthropology as well. She wrote back to her professor Ray Firth in London, "I had a long fascinating visit with the Herskovitses [noted anthropologist Melville Herskovits and his wife] in Chicago. Paul went with me, and we enjoyed them immensely."[52] The Robesons had first met Herskovits in New York in 1924 when he was conducting research and teaching at Columbia University.[53] He and Essie exchanged letters about shared intellectual interests.

Melville Herskovits's research focused on the importance of Africa for African Americans, and he was a strong advocate of African independence in the post–World War II years. Essie clearly found their exchanges very stimulating, and Herskovits went to great lengths to share information with Essie that he thought would be of particular interest to her as a budding anthropologist. We can only speculate about their conversations about Malinowski, whom they both knew and were critical of. Herskovits was pretty open about his disdain for Malinowski. One historian reported, "Herskovits abhorred European scholars who worked for the state, particularly anthropologists like Bronislaw Malinowski, whom he believed acted in service to imperialist governments and not a search for truth. In 1936 Herskovits expressed his irritation at Malinowski's 'prescription for running the lives of the East Africans!'"[54] As an aside, Herskovits had his own critics. Some Negro scholars like Rayford Logan thought that he was overly controlling and condescending in his relations with Black colleagues and students.[55] Essie and Paul did not view or experience him that way.

In April of 1935, a new film about Africa, *Sanders of the River*, starring Paul Robeson, opened in London. In it Paul played a local African chief, often clad in leopard skin and loincloth, who was loyal to the British commissioner. Essie had negotiated a lucrative contract for Paul, but she had been unable to secure rights to approve the final version of the film. As a result, the final cut of the film had an unapologetically pro-colonial message that pained the Robesons deeply. *Sanders* premiered with great fanfare at a time when the couple was deepening their knowledge of and commitment to the plight of Africa and the cause of African freedom. Their friend Jomo Kenyatta, the future president of Kenya, had even accepted a small part in the movie. But the success that *Sanders* enjoyed among American and British audiences and the boost it represented for Paul's career were bittersweet—and more bitter than sweet.

Another negative association with the film for Essie was her suspicion that Paul was romantically involved with his young and lovely costar Nina Mae McKinney, a twenty-three-year-old beauty who had performed on Broadway, in Paris cabarets, and as a lead in the all-Black Hollywood movie *Hallelujah*.[56] Essie felt awkwardly in competition with Nina for Paul's affections, to the extent of putting on a sexy dress one evening to try to entice Paul to stay with her rather than go off for a suspected rendezvous with McKinney. At the same time, however, Essie enjoyed her own innocent flirtation with a married but handsome British actor named Richard Donat.[57]

Paul was extremely distraught over the ideas championed by *Sanders of the River*, so much so that he walked out of the Leicester Square Theatre during the London premiere. Essie followed him outside, intercepted him, and convinced him to return. Marcus Garvey was one of a number of Black critics of *Sanders*. He excoriated not only the anti-African messages in the film, but also Paul Robeson for participating in it. "Why should we have a Negro of ability playing the part that will assist others to dishonor and discredit the Black Race?" he demanded to know.[58] For practical reasons, Essie and Paul had to ride out the publicity surrounding the film and temporarily suppress their own criticisms of it. But Essie too was painfully disappointed and embarrassed by their association with the production. She became determined that neither she nor Paul would ever support another film like *Sanders*.[59]

The experience of the *Sanders* movie convinced Essie that in order to understand the tangle of complex social and political issues represented by colonialism, to speak and write effectively about them, and to debate with her colleagues more effectively, she had to visit Africa herself. Yet

Essie's first African journey, in 1936, was not only a scholarly expedition, but also a personal quest. She had long harbored a desire to make the trip, ever since her conversations with Leonard Barnes and Kojo Touvalou Houénou in the summer of 1932. Like many Black Americans who visited the continent in the early 1900s, Essie was on a "pilgrimage" as much as anything else.[60] Essie wanted to discover Africa, but she also admittedly wanted to discover herself, in some nearly ineffable way. Africa represented the land of her ancestors; it was her "old country," as she put it, borrowing the phrase European immigrants commonly used to refer to their roots in Italy, Poland, Russia, or Ireland. And myths and stereotypes about Africa had fueled the anti-Black racism she had witnessed firsthand her whole life. So for her, the desire to visit Africa was very personal.

Essie had very high hopes for this trip. She planned to collect data for her anthropological research, learn more about the political landscape of the vast continent, and have "a high adventure" with Paul Jr., who, she had decided, would be her very special travel companion.[61] The decision to take her eight-year-old son along must have been a difficult one, given the uncertainties and dangers of such a trip in those days. But both Essie and Paul wanted their son to experience Africa in order to better appreciate his African ancestry. The Robesons had left the Black enclave of Harlem when Paul Jr. was just a baby. Since then, he had lived primarily in England and continental Europe, except for a year-and-a-half stint with his grandmother in the United States and Canada. For the most part, he had white British friends, wore short pants like his classmates, spoke with a British accent, and had very little knowledge of the larger Black world, except through books. Moreover, he had been surrounded his entire life by considerable comfort and privilege. In his own words, he was "a black rich kid in an almost entirely white environment."[62]

The year 1935, though, had been an eventful year for young Paul, and a trying year for Essie as a parent. He and his grandmother had been sent back across the Atlantic—partly because Essie's mother wanted to return and partly because Essie and Paul wanted to test the culture and educational waters for Paul Jr. They relocated first to Greenwich Village, then to Montreal, and eventually to a country house in western Massachusetts. It was a tumultuous year for the boy: he changed schools twice in only a few months, was called a "nigger" and shoved into a swimming pool by the school bully, and was treated harshly by his third-grade teacher. Essie was furious and frustrated when she heard the news from her mother about what Paul Jr. was going through. She was more concerned at his "spirit" being suppressed than anything else.[63] Paul Jr. himself later reflected on the difficulties of that year, describing himself as a "depressed and angry" child, fed up with his grandmother's rigid rules, and explaining "the unrelenting racism" he encountered in the United States.[64] Essie wrote long and anguish-filled letters to her mother in New York, asking questions, making suggestions, and expressing her own indecision about what was best for her son. After all that, a major trip to Africa would be the perfect tonic, Essie must have reasoned. Africa would show him starkly different cultures and material realities, bolster his confidence, and broaden his horizon. It would also allow him to share a special summer adventure with his mother.[65]

In the American and European imagination of 1936, Africa was the place of Tarzan comic books and stories about cannibalism. Negative images and racist myths about Africa were ubiquitous, including in liberal academic and social circles. Even many Black Americans shunned any association with the land of their ancestors, viewing it as backward and an embarrassment. Essie wanted to inoculate her son against these biases and misperceptions. Put bluntly, Essie wanted to "acquaint him with his Black people."[66]

Traveling to Africa in the 1930s was arduous for anyone, but for a Black woman there were unique emotional, psychological, and even logistical challenges. European colonialism still dominated the continent. Making arrangements and securing visas was so difficult, in fact, that Essie left England without proper paperwork for all the places she intended to visit, unsure about whether she would be able to enter those areas when she arrived. Since Blacks and white colonials lived in segregated worlds, orchestrating her lodging and transportation was not at all straightforward. Essie had made arrangements to do some of her primary fieldwork in Uganda, but she intended to visit Kenya, Basutoland, Swaziland, and South Africa along the way. It was an ambitious itinerary, from Madeira to the Cape of Good Hope, up the east coast to Kenya and Zanzibar, followed by an extended stay in Uganda. On their return trip they would briefly stop over in Egypt and Sudan, then finally return home. She was determined to see more than the tourists' or missionary's view of the African continent.

Essie encountered her first obstacle even before she left England. She had purchased her tickets, obtained the necessary vaccines, and sent letters to friends and friends of friends whom she hoped to meet while she was in Africa. But the South Africans refused to give her a visa. They did not say "no" outright; they just kept putting her off—in her mind, because they were hoping to deter her. "The visas were a real problem," Essie recalled, "it seems if you are Negro, you can't make up your mind to go to Africa, and just go. Oh no. Not unless you are a missionary. The white people of Africa do not want educated Negroes traveling around seeing how their brothers live."[67] Refusing to have her plans thwarted, Essie told Paul she was going to go, visa or not. If she were declined entry when she got off the ship, she would put up a fuss and he should do the same on her behalf from London. "Angry, frustrated," a little nervous, but still determined, Essie moved forward with her plans.[68]

Against this backdrop, to help ensure a successful trip Essie enlisted the help of a family acquaintance, J. D. Rheinallt Jones, the Welsh-born founder of the South African Institute for Race Relations whom she had met in London but who now lived and worked in South Africa. She asked Jones to provide her with a letter of introduction to smooth the way with colonial officials in South Africa when she arrived. He advised her to be careful about what she said publicly given her absence of an official South African visa.[69]

Essie knew that the social dynamics would be complicated. She was an American woman and a Negro; she had the privilege of a U.S. passport, but shared a common ancestry with the subjugated masses. She had a personal and political desire to bond with Africa's oppressed people, but many of her contacts and connections were among the political, religious, and intellectual elite, both white and Black. Still off she went—the wife of a celebrity, with her fine luggage, good clothes, and sophisticated taste, determined in some awkward, ill-defined, but still thoroughly genuine way to "reclaim Africa." Her view of the continent and its people, and how she saw her relationship to both, would deepen and mature quickly and profoundly.

It was the eve of World War II in Europe. The aggression and atrocities of Hitler were in the news daily, and the Great Depression in the United States showed no signs of easing. In the spring of 1936, the Italian army under the command of fascist Benito Mussolini made its first imperialist forays into the African continent, pushing troops, tanks, and warplanes into previously independent Ethiopia and launching what would become a heinous five-year occupation.[70] Back in Harlem, people were protesting the invasion in the streets. A few weeks later, against the backdrop of war and strife on both sides of the Atlantic, Essie, with her eight-year-old son in tow, would set sail for southern and eastern Africa on a long-awaited trip that would truly change her life.

six

AFRICA AT LAST, 1936

Big talk, challenging ideas, enthralling discussions. The walls of our world
moved outward and we caught a glimpse of things in the large.

Eslanda Robeson

Essie and Paul Jr. departed for the African continent on May 29, 1936. After Paul saw them off from Waterloo Station in London, they took a train to Southampton, then the giant ship *Winchester Castle* bound for the so-called dark continent.[1] The three months Essie would spend in South Africa and Uganda would become a defining experience in her life. "Pauli is wide eyed and eager about everything," she wrote to friends as they began their journey, adding, "I'm pretty thrilled myself."[2]

Ironically, but not surprisingly, the Robesons were the only Black passengers on board. There were Australians on holiday, Brits on business, and a few Christian missionaries among the other passengers, but not a single dark face among them. Essie wrote in her journal that their fellow passengers were civil but that during the first few days of the trip, she and Paul Jr. had minimal contact with their shipmates by choice. They stayed in their large and stately first-class cabin, playing cards and board games that Essie had brought along precisely for this purpose. Eventually, however, they did come out and mingle.

Paul Jr. was a smart and engaging little boy, with his father's charm, and he made friends easily. Before long, Essie too found herself in conversation with other passengers on the ship. As she interacted and socialized with her fellow travelers, she took note of the class dynamics on board the vessel. She was appalled that the less affluent second- and third-class passengers who traveled in the dark bowels of the ship were allowed to come up to the first-class deck only on Sundays to worship at weekly church services but never to enjoy the pool or other comforts. "They may come up and pay their respects to God first class," Essie wrote sarcastically.[3] She abhorred the crude disparity but still enjoyed being on the privileged side of the divide—another contradiction.

Trans-Atlantic sea travel was slow and boring. Several days after they departed from England, Essie and Paul were happy to set foot on land again. They docked and spent an entire morning exploring the island of Madeira, a former Portuguese colony off the coast of Morocco and a favored, though isolated, tourist destination. "An extraordinary island," Essie wrote, "rising 3,000 feet straight up out of the sea, sheer and green and beautiful."[4] After a brief half-day excursion they were back on the ship and back at sea. Two days later, they reached the coast of Senegal. Essie had a very emotional reaction to her first glimpse of sub-Saharan Africa off in the distance. "It is a gray and heavy thought," she wrote, "that between 1666 and 1800 more than five and a half million kidnapped Africans, my ancestors, began the dreadful journey across the Atlantic from this very stretch of coast, to be sold as slaves in the 'new world.' . . . No wonder the sea and sky and very air of this whole area seem sinister to me."[5]

Even as the legacy of Africa's tortured past loomed large, Essie was curious about how her white shipmates viewed the continent and their relationships to it. Ever the ethnographer, she queried the White South Africans and Rhodesians aboard, most of whom were quite civil and eager to talk about their lives in Africa. Without seeming to render judgment, or to express offense at the obvious racism and injustice in their accounts, Essie listened as they told their stories. One seventy-year-old woman, whom Essie referred to as "Mrs. G.," told her that her late husband had been close friends with Cecil Rhodes, the famed white colonizer after whom Rhodesia was named. She went on to tell Essie all about her wonderful "native servants," how fond she was of them and vice versa. Essie wrote in her diary that she felt as though she was "listening to a White Southerner from our own Deep South with their patriarchal" attitudes.[6] Another young white tobacco farmer told of his adventures in "the bush" with baboons, leopards, lions, and "frightened natives"—an account that seemed straight out of a Tarzan safari story.[7] Essie drew another parallel to the U.S. context: "'Native' seems to be their word for 'nigger,'" she observed dryly. She would later learn about the even more insulting term "kaffir."[8]

Finally, after more than two weeks at sea, Essie and Paul Jr. arrived in Capetown, South Africa, at 7:00 in the morning on June 15, 1936. It was pouring rain when the ship docked. Essie was immediately met in the ship's lounge by local reporters asking a barrage of questions about her famous husband. Why had he not made the trip with her? What did she and he think of the so-called native situation in South Africa? What was the true purpose of her trip? They wanted to know what she thought of "the primitive mind," how much "European blood" she had, and even her predictions about the impending world heavyweight boxing match between the Negro fighter Joe Louis and the white contender Max Schmeling. Essie felt overwhelmed and uncharacteristically vulnerable. She had arrived without a proper visa and was trying to maneuver her safe entrance and a visit to Swaziland. She did not want to say anything in the press that would jeopardize her stay. "Newspapermen are the same the world over," Essie thought to herself and later confided to the pages of her diary. "They can ask some very ticklish questions, and corner you into making some rash statements if you are not very careful."[9] Her initial answers to the pushy herd of reporters were coy and vague, but she still found herself quoted in the press in ways that did not convey her true feelings. "My husband has never been interested in politics," she was quoted as saying in one article. It went on to quote Essie as observing that Paul "had no fanciful ideas about Africa for the Africans."[10] There is no simple way to explain these published comments. Either Essie chose to handle what she perceived as a hostile situation by depicting herself and Paul as harmless and apolitical, or she was simply misquoted by a biased press determined to print what they wanted to hear. In either case, Essie felt bruised by the encounter and was relieved to put it behind her.

Essie and Paul Jr. were also met at the dock in Capetown by Professor Isaac Schapera and one of his faculty colleagues at University of Capetown. Schapera, a young white South African from a small village, had, like Essie, been a student of Malinowski's at the London School of Economics and would go on to become an expert on the Tswana people of what is now Botswana.[11] Schapera made his way through the crowds and the rain to greet Essie and her son. He took them directly to an office on the campus so that she could make an overseas call to Paul to let him know that they had arrived safely. After that, she and Paul Jr. went to visit some contacts in the "colored" community. They had a wonderful dinner at the home of Louise Ballou Gow, a childhood friend of Essie's Harlem pal Hattie Bolling. Gow, a Black American, had married Francis Gow, a South African AME minister and missionary in Capetown, and the couple had settled in an area called Woodstock. A talented violinist, devoted educator, and mother, Louise lived and worked in South Africa for nearly fifty years.[12] She took Essie and Paul Jr. on a little tour of the area, including a stop in the area called District Six, the site of an intense struggle some years later over the government's forced removal of the colored population to make way for new white settlements.[13] Essie was touched by the generosity of the local people, like the Gows, who had taken "perfect strangers, immediately, into their homes, hearts and lives."[14]

Essie and Paul Jr. spent three eventful weeks in South Africa, and she savored every moment of the experience. Capetown is one of the world's most beautiful cities. The magnificent Table Mountain towers over the blue green waters of the Atlantic and Indian Oceans. Lush green carpets of land contrast with dry dusty stretches, which have their own simple beauty. The whole city is adorned with the bright red spindly blossoms of the indigenous Protea plant. But as Essie discovered, Capetown's physical beauty has for centuries been a backdrop to poverty and brutal racial hierarchy. Essie wrote in her diary each day about the gross injustices of the South African system, which she would later research and elaborate on in her published works. "No African may be in any public place in the Union of South Africa after curfew, except by special permit," Essie recounted.[15] In addition, "Africans are required by law to live in [sequestered] native reserves" and carry the equivalent of passports in their own country.[16]

Soon after arriving, Essie visited the "reserve" of Langa, several miles outside the city. Reserves, also called "locations," were essentially all-Black ghettos where poverty was rampant. Essie learned how it was illegal for Blacks to live in white areas and how the strictly enforced pass system kept the majority Black population subjugated, corralled, and controlled.[17] Langa was the first place Essie visited where she felt she saw how ordinary African people lived. Langa was considered "one of the better locations," but there were "no baths, no toilets, no water of any kind in the houses in Langa. There are community taps and toilets at the back, serving larger groups of houses."[18] The Robesons were initially taken around by the white superintendent of Langa, who showed them the local hospital and its environs. They were then "turned over" to a local Black teacher, Mr. Mama, who greeted them warmly and brought out local children to welcome them with songs and engage them in conversation in English. He reminded Essie of the Negro teachers she had known from schools like Tuskegee and Hampton in the United States.

They then visited Capetown's diverse "colored" community, which included people of Chinese, Indian, and Malay backgrounds.[19]

The similarities between South Africa and the U.S. South were apparent to Essie right away. She was particularly interested in the condition of the country's workers and the way in which race and economics were linked. The contradiction of having Black domestic workers in intimate contact with white families while racial segregation laws were in force was not lost on her. "The white folks want the Negroes to work for them," she wrote. "While they proclaim a fear and horror of Negroes in general living near by, they seem quite comfortable when the Negroes who work for them live within call—or indeed live right in their homes."[20] This was as true in South Africa as it was back home.

Essie was struck by the image of Black laborers and unemployed job seekers "trudging" on the dusty and ditch-riddled roads outside Capetown as they made their way from the reserves to the white areas, where the jobs were, and back again.[21] Essie saw miners winding their way home, weary, dirty, and bedraggled, with government-run "pick up vans" stopping them randomly. Any Black person without a "pass" (a special identification card that only Black people were required to carry) was carted off to jail.[22] The pick up vans reminded Essie of "dog-catcher's" wagons, and the powerful and disturbing scene of Black people publicly humiliated and rounded up like animals on the street, which she was able to capture some images of with her camera, almost brought her to tears. Her sadness was tempered only by her rage. She resolved to take it all in and use it later as ammunition in her war of words against South Africa's brutal regime, a regime that would only grow worse with the formal advent of the Apartheid system some twelve years later.

If Essie had arrived in South Africa with a slightly muted voice, afraid of whether she would be allowed to complete her itinerary if she spoke her mind, she certainly left on a very different note. Essie boldly indicted the racism she had witnessed, and even commented on the unwarranted divisions and tensions between Blacks and so-called Colored or mixed-race people who had a distinct social, yet still subjugated, status in South Africa relative to whites. "A person with the slightest tinge of Negro blood in his veins is a 'Nigger' the world over," she proclaimed, suggesting that unity among the darker races was needed—and condemning lighter-skinned Blacks in the United States and South Africa for feeling a sense of superiority vis-à-vis their darker counterparts.[23]

On June 16, 1936, Essie and young Paul boarded yet another ship, and sailed past the point where the Indian and Atlantic Oceans meet, heading up the eastern edge of the country to Port Elizabeth. On the short boat ride from the Cape to Port Elizabeth, Essie befriended a young Black nanny who was "in charge of some white children."[24] The woman told Essie about her life and described the discrimination and abuses that she and her family had suffered. "The nursemaid told me many stories about the brutality of the Boars [white South Africans, Afrikaners, of Dutch ancestry] . . . so savage, so barbarous," a stark contrast to the "native stories" told to Essie by her white shipmates on the first leg of her trip.[25] The woman also had views and knowledge of the larger issues that surrounded her, explaining to Essie "how the South Africans keep trying to pit the Cape Colored against the Natives, impressing the former with the idea that they are better than the blacks—more European—keeping them in separate schools, in separate living areas." Essie's "colored" phenotype may have prompted the candid discussion. The woman added, however, that things were changing and the so-called colored people were realizing that their fate was linked more to their Black counterparts than to the white elites, offering personal examples from her own family to underscore the point.[26] Essie nodded and took it all in. In fact, the experience may well mark the beginning of Essie's appreciation of the wisdom of the common people of South Africa, an appreciation that became part of her writings about the area and conditions there.

Upon their arrival in Port Elizabeth on June 19, the Robesons were met by Essie's old friend from London, a young physician named Rosebery Bokwe. His sister, Frieda, was married to Z. K. Matthews, who would become a legendary leader of the African National Congress (ANC). Matthews too had studied with Malinowski at the London School of Economics and Essie had known him there as a part of a larger circle of African students and intellectuals. She would come to know him much better, however, in the years to follow.[27] Matthews would be jailed for his political activities in the famous Treason Trials of 1956, along with two men who would become icons of the South African freedom struggle: Nelson Mandela and Walter Sisulu.[28] Matthews died before the end of Apartheid, but his contributions to the cause are still widely celebrated. As for her old friend Bowke, Essie felt close to the staid and unassuming doctor and was happy to see him relaxed and at home in South Africa. She wrote to Paul, "You would be amazed at Bokwe. He looked so quiet in London. He is really brilliant, quite fun, enormously popular."[29]

Bokwe was accompanied by Max Yergan, whom Essie would later

work closely with in the Council on African Affairs (CAA). Paul had met Max before, but Essie met him for the first time in South Africa and liked him "on sight."[30] Max Yergan was an enigmatic figure. A learned man with deeply held beliefs, Yergan had first come to South Africa in 1920 as a missionary working with the YMCA, but had been transformed and radicalized by his experience there. By 1931 he was considering himself a "revolutionist" who favored transformative social change and was harshly critical of both colonialism and capitalism. He would later return to the United States, embrace communism and work with not only the CAA but also the National Negro Congress and other left-wing organizations, only to eventually betray his comrades and testify against them during the anti-communist McCarthy period. But when Essie met him in 1936, he was a different man. He had just returned from India, where he had met with Nehru, and was still digesting the experience of a trip to the Soviet Union. They had many things in common, enjoyed many long conversations, and the rapport established between them was genuine.[31] After collecting Essie and Paul Jr. at the docks in Port Elizabeth, Bokwe and Yergan took the two to lunch and then to an African reserve called New Brighton.

In New Brighton, Essie observed "pathetic" shack homes as well as living conditions even more deplorable than what she had encountered outside Capetown. Yet despite the poverty and suffering she witnessed everywhere, Essie was impressed and inspired by the richness of the intellectual and political exchanges she had not only with Yergen and Bowke, but also with the people they met in the dusty villages and ramshackle little dwellings of South Africa. "Big talk, challenging ideas, enthralling discussions. The walls of our world moved outward, and we caught a glimpse of things in the large. Maybe we didn't solve anything. Maybe we couldn't. But at least we could know what was going on. To be aware was to be alive," she concluded. "And I thought as I listened, these Africans, these 'primitives,' make me feel humble and respectful. I blush with shame for the mental picture my fellow Negroes in America have of our African brothers. . . . I am surprised and delighted to find these Africans far more politically aware than my fellow Negroes in America. They understand their situation and the causes of the terrible conditions under which they live, and are continually seeking—and are firmly resolved to find—a way to improve their lot."[32] If she was not clear about the connections among colonialism, racism, and exploitation before her trip to Africa in 1936, Essie certainly came away from the experience with a vivid sense of this relationship. In addition, she encountered in Africa a distinctly different picture of the diverse peoples of the continent from those mostly negative depictions that she had known from her time in the United States and Britain.

While in South Africa, Essie talked with her hosts and others about culture, economics, politics, history, and the future of Africa and the world. "The conversations ranged widely," she recalled in her book *African Journey*, from problems with "African education," to the "conditions in India," to "Italy's activities in Ethiopia." She savored these opportunities to learn and debate, but was disturbed by the absence of African women. She noticed that women often ate separately and did not partake in the lively after-dinner discussions about politics and public life. Still, Essie participated in those conversations with confidence and determination.[33]

After leaving New Brighton, Essie, Paul Jr., and their two companions proceeded northwest to Yergan's home in the tiny mission town of Alice, where he lived with his wife, Susie, and their three children, and where Essie would stay during much of her time in South Africa. There was another reason for heading that direction. In nearby Grahamstown on June 22, 1936, Rosebery Bokwe married his longtime sweetheart, Irene, in an elaborate ceremony that involved a large extended family, spanned several days and two villages, and entailed much dancing, eating, and drinking. Essie was thrilled that she and Paul Jr. could be a part of the festivities.[34]

After Bokwe's wedding celebration, Essie visited the African reserve of Ntselamanzi, set on a depressed and "barren bit of ground." It was another sobering and eye-opening experience. At the same time, Essie was struck by the generous hospitality she encountered there. Though they had very little themselves, people opened their homes and pulled up extra chairs at their tables for unexpected guests whose names they barely knew.[35] The local poverty was gut-wrenching. Essie and Paul Jr. were so moved and disturbed, they began giving coins away to destitute families along the roadside. They tried to be careful though, understanding that such charity had to be offered in just the right way so that local people would not take offense. "We changed a lot of notes into silver and, thus armed, took to the roads again," Essie recounted. "We gave one charming Basuto family two half-crowns, and the man thanked us with such dignity I could have cried."[36] This was Essie's awkward but genuine way of trying to make a small difference.

One of their hosts during their stay in the area was Dr. James Moroka, a medical doctor and professor trained in Scotland, as well as a member of the ANC who had been jailed for his activities as a young man.[37] Moroka, whom Essie found interesting and "very attractive," was by this time among the more privileged Black South Africans.[38] He lived in a fine house in a designated native area outside of Bloemfontein and drove a brand new Hudson Terraplane automobile.[39] He took Essie on a one-day visit to Basutoland, where the local people wore distinctive shawls and traveled almost exclusively on horseback.[40] Later that evening, Essie enjoyed the intergenerational conversations around Dr. Moroka's dinner table, which included many of his students. After dinner they all sat by an open fire in the drawing room and continued their exchange. The discussions covered the plight and future of Africa, but also gave the young Africans an opportunity to ask Essie about conditions in America and England.[41]

On July 2, Essie and Paul Jr. joined Dr. Alfred Bitini Xuma in Sofiatown.[42] Essie did not mind at all being "passed off" from Dr. Moroka to Dr. Xuma. "This traveling about Africa reminds me of traveling in the Deep South in America: you are passed from friend to friend, from car to car, from home to home, often covering thousands of miles without enduring the inconveniences and humiliations of the incredibly bad Jim Crow train accommodations and the lack of hotel facilities for Negroes."[43] Through it all, Essie felt she was in good and capable hands. She regarded Max Yergan, who coordinated the South Africa leg of her trip, as their "guardian angel, he took such good care" of Paul Jr. and herself.[44] In Sofiatown they were received warmly, and Essie spoke before a local group about the racial politics back in the United States.[45]

At one point, they passed briefly through the outskirts of Johannesburg, South Africa's largest city. South Africa was a resource-rich country and Black labor had been brutally harnessed by the colonial system so that the British and later the Dutch-descended Afrikaners could profit from the extraction of diamonds, gold, and other minerals. Essie and Paul Jr. were able to get an insider's view of life inside one of South Africa's notorious mining compounds. Since it was Sunday and the white overseer was away, they were given a tour of the facilities at the Robinson Deep compound by the workers who lived and labored there. Describing herself as normally "shockproof," Essie was stunned by the deplorable conditions the resident miners showed them. The mines were gloomy and treacherous, and the barracks where workers slept at night were cramped and depressing. Their huts reminded Essie of "dog kennels."[46] While in Johannesburg, Essie was again honored at a reception and invited to offer her views on the Black American experience as it related to Africa. Then as they left Johannesburg and traveled further afield, Essie met another group of miners on extended migratory labor duty far away from their families, passed through an isolated leper colony, and visited ramshackle rural schools.[47]

During her trip to South Africa, Essie not only witnessed suffering; she also noticed a growing spirit of resistance. Quite fortuitously, a historic political conference was being held in the town of Bloemfontein in the Orange Free State region while they were there, and because several of their hosts were slated to participate, Essie and Paul Jr. were invited to observe. Essie was thrilled to be going to the gathering, which she described accurately as "the biggest African convention to date. . . . [South] Africans from all parts will be there. . . . to discuss the new land acts and voting rights. . . . It is pure luck that I can be there."[48] Essie's participation in the All-African National Convention in Bloemfontein was a highlight of her trip. The conference included four hundred delegates from all over the country and was organized in specific response to the Herzog bill, new legislation that had been designed to disenfranchise the handful of Black Africans who were allowed to vote in South Africa at that time.[49] While the system of "white rule" called Apartheid would not be formally established for more than a decade, by 1936, when Essie was visiting, white colonial rule was the order of the day and the building blocks of Apartheid were already being put in place. Historians now cite the gathering in Bloemfontein as a defining moment for the nascent liberation movement that would eventually topple the Apartheid regime sixty years later. Essie was especially interested to meet and talk with the women delegates to the convention about problems and challenges facing women in South Africa. They were, in turn, curious to hear about the progress of women in the United States.

Soon after the Bloemfontein meeting, Essie and Paul Jr. boarded yet another boat and started making their way north toward Uganda. There would be many fascinating stops along the way. One was in Zanzibar, an eclectic and colorful island off the coast of Tanzania that enthralled Essie and Paul Jr. with its sights, sounds, and smells. A mixture of languages and smells mingled on the crowded, narrow streets. Essie hired a car to take them around the "fairytale island," with its aromatic "clove and coconut groves" and impressive Arab architecture, including "large stone houses" adorned with "heavy wood carvings." They also visited the local museum, markets, and a Swahili village before reboarding their ship to continue their journey.[50] Zanzibar's mélange of cultures reflected the waves of migration, trade, and colonial domination by one group then another that marked the island's history.

They arrived in the port city of Mombasa, Kenya, on July 15. Essie looked around and soaked up the sights. She could see Mount Kilimanjaro in the distance and the hauntingly beautiful baobab trees, and she immediately noticed the Arab and Asian influences mixed in with the African. They stayed overnight at the Manor Hotel before boarding a train the next day, heading northwest toward Kampala. In one of many small indications of the extent of Paul Robeson's fame in 1936, the European owner of the hotel was a devoted Robeson fan, and treated Essie and Paul Jr. with exceptional care and deference after realizing who they were.[51] Indeed, Paul had a worldwide fan base; he was well known as a pioneering Black artist not only in Europe and the United States, but also throughout Asia, Africa, and Latin America.

Essie and Paul Jr. left Mombasa and traveled high into the Kikuyu countryside, past the sugar cane and coffee plantations, through Nairobi, and around the northern end of mighty Lake Victoria. They then left Kenya and entered the British Protectorate of Uganda.[52] "All along the way the scenery was extraordinary," Essie wrote, and her son was mesmerized by the gazelles, zebra, wildebeests, and ostriches running just outside the train window.[53] Essie wrote to Paul that travel was difficult, but she dared not complain because "every moment of [it] was interesting."[54] Instead of being met upon their arrival in Kampala by their friend from London, Akiki Nyabongo, cousin to the King of Toro, the Robesons were greeted by two of his surrogates, a "kindly" English couple, the Bowers. Nyabongo had been delayed, so he had called upon the Bowers to meet Essie and take care of his guests for the night.[55] Many things could disrupt or delay an otherwise well-planned itinerary in sub-Saharan Africa, where roads and communications systems were notoriously bad. As was her way, Essie regarded this unexpected change of plans as an opportunity to learn something new and thus she proceeded to query her hosts about their views on Africa and colonialism. Mr. Bowers, who ran a local girls school under the auspices of the Anglican Church, was a talkative and opinionated fellow. He told Essie about taxes, colonial policy, education, and salary differentials between whites and African workers. When Essie pressed the affable old man on the injustice of unequal pay, a semi-polite disagreement ensued. It was likely a relief to everyone that Essie and Paul Jr. only stayed with the Bowers for one night.[56]

Nyabongo, whom Essie had befriended when he was an anthropology student at Oxford, arrived early the next day to rescue them, and they began the half-day drive from Kampala to Kabarole.[57] The sun was hot, and the roads were so dusty and rugged that they had to stop several times along the route for refreshments and relief. Nyabongo's family was royalty in this part of Uganda, so he and his guests were given special treatment everywhere they went. For example, when they pulled off the road for lunch in the tiny village of Butoke-Butotano, a group of men and boys dressed immaculately in white came out to the roadway to greet them. "Odd that there are no women," Essie thought to herself.[58] As was the custom, the women were waiting just out of sight.[59] Essie noted the gender divide and women's relegation to peripheral spaces on many occasions. During this stop, Nyabongo and Paul Jr. were taken to private quarters where they were stripped, bathed, and dressed in fresh clothes. Essie graciously declined the same treatment. She was later told that women would have quickly appeared if she had accepted the offer.[60]

Nyabongo would accompany and help to guide Essie and Paul Jr. for the duration of their trip. He had also agreed to aid Essie in her research and made all the logistical arrangements for her stay. Essie found him "intelligent, friendly and efficient," and felt she was in very good hands.[61] She was indeed. Whatever Nyabongo's itinerary planning skills, his intellectual acumen and creative talents alone would have made him a perfect travel companion for Essie. The same year as Essie's visit to Uganda, Nyabongo published a book, part autobiography, part history, and part fiction, entitled *Africa Answers Back.* Set in a mythical Uganda, the book was described by one applauding reviewer as a textured "narrative of African empowerment and emancipation." We can only imagine the animated conversations that Essie and the thirty-two-year-old Toro prince had during her African journey.[62]

In order to grasp the complexity of Essie's navigations in sub-Saharan Africa in 1936, one needs to look closely at the colonial realities in the region, some of which she was aware of, but some of which she undoubtedly was not. The land mass that came to be known as Uganda had been a hotly contested area because of its mineral wealth. The British, Belgians, and Germans had squabbled over the borders of the protectorate. Africans themselves had fought one another over those borders and others, then employed widely varying and conflicting strategies of resistance to European rule. One strategy was accommodation. Some colonial subjects were sent off to England to receive university training with the idea that they would return and be intermediaries between the Brits and the indigenous population. England's strategy of indirect rule meant that agreeable local chiefs and later Black Western-trained intellectuals were viewed as the desirable colonial and neo-colonial operatives. But while some African elites openly collaborated with colonial powers, others used their Western education to turn the tables: they argued for African rights in British courts and made a moral case against white domination, first in Christian churches and organizations, and later in the international arena after the establishment of the United Nations. Moreover, there were African resistance movements, in the Uganda area and beyond, that refused to compromise or negotiate. The woman-centered Nyabingi Movement, based in southwest Uganda from 1910 through the 1930s, was one of these.[63] Thus there were all kinds of resistance going on in Uganda around the time of Essie's trip. Even though she met with a wide array of people, unlike her time in South Africa, she still did not encounter the most radical forces on the ground at the time. Her trip to Uganda occurred under controlled circumstances and under the watchful eye of British colonial authorities and British intelligence. Nevertheless, those she did meet opened her eyes in ways she could not have imagined.[64]

The village of Kabarole was Essie and Paul Jr.'s home for their four-week stay in Uganda. Nyabongo had arranged for them to have a small guesthouse to themselves with a corrugated metal roof, mud-clay walls, outdoor bath and lavatories, and a small patio area. The entire compound was surrounded by a tall reed fence for privacy and for protection from local wildlife.[65] They were the official guests of the local leader, Chief Kaboha, so they were well taken care of by rural Ugandan standards. When they arrived, Essie was not only exhausted from the heat; she had also managed to contract a "bug" that gave her a "roaring fever," chills, nausea, and the sensation of her "head bursting, eyes bulging, back broken in two at the waistline." Paul Jr. was quite concerned, and so were their hosts. The chief sent someone to check on her every morning. Essie recovered in a few days, however, and was soon ready and eager to take in her new surroundings.[66]

Essie felt very welcomed in their little village. People came to visit, sent their children to play with Paul Jr., and delivered presents at their doorstep, including fresh eggs, birds, and on one occasion, a live goat. Essie did not know quite what to do with the goat, but she accepted it, and all the gifts she received, with gracious appreciation. The goat was retrieved by one of the locals only to reappear as stew the next day.[67]

The Kingdom of Toro, according to some observers, had "some of the most beautiful and most fertile land in one of the richest regions to be found in Africa."[68] The area had an almost mythic natural beauty; the misty snow-capped peaks of the Rwenzori Mountains are sometimes referred to as "mountains of the moon."[69] It was a "paradise for pastoralists," and herdsmen had thrived in the region for generations, even withstanding a rinderpest epidemic in the late nineteenth century that nearly wiped out Toro's cattle population. The area would later become known for its rich Kilembe copper mines. The Toro Kingdom contained multiple ethnic groups, including the Bakonjo, Baamba (Amba), and dominant Toro (Batooro), and bordered the mineral-rich and turbulent Congo. Because Uganda was made a British protectorate in 1894, rather than a colony per se, the local provinces enjoyed slightly more autonomy than their counterparts in the neighboring colony of Kenya.[70] The Toro people, by the way, were the favored group of the British. And their strength, aggression, and powerful allies aided them in securing dominance over smaller groups in the area that also sought greater autonomy. But Essie would not tell this part of the story in her ethnographic travel diary *African Journey*, which was published a decade after her trip was completed.

Essie's research focused specifically on the herdspeople in Toro. Determined to plunge in and experience the details of their daily lives as much as possible, Essie donned tall rubber boots and a mosquito veil and traipsed through mud and eight-foot-tall elephant grass to tend cattle and talk with local women and men about their lives, their work, and their culture. Some came to trust her enough to allow her to photograph them, and to share with her intimate details of their lives.[71]

Perhaps most interesting to Essie was the unique status of Toro women. They did not enjoy full equality with men, but upper-class Toro women were among the first in East Africa to receive formal education and they enjoyed significant property rights. Legal changes in the 1930s granted unmarried Toro women additional rights and greater economic independence, which meant there was less pressure to marry. Much of the women's economic security came from their participation in the cattle industry.[72]

Essie studied the Toro's herding and milking practices carefully, and took note of the strict division of labor between men and women. Women participated in the dairy farming, but they never milked the cows. The cattle kraal, an open area where milking occurred, was a male domain, and Essie had to get special permission to enter. She was unique in her ability to observe work on both sides of the gender divide. "I have been working with the herdswomen in the dairy, learning a lot about custom and tradition," she wrote in her notebook. "Everything connected with the handling of the milk after it is collected from the cattle is called 'bisahi' and is women's business. Bisahi is considered elegant work for ladies, and they take great pride in their knowledge and expertness. Experience in any branch of bisahi is definitely an accomplishment." The hut where the women worked was "beautifully built and immaculately kept."[73]

In addition to studying the herding practices, Essie also learned a little bit of the Rotoro language spoken by the locals. She grew quite familiar with the women, as they laughed and teased one another during the workday.[74] In an obscure little African community filled with women whose lives could not have been more different than her own, Essie managed to make friends. Through an interpreter, she sat and talked with the women late at night about their lives and hers. They were curious to know "what kind of work women did 'outside' [of their village and region], how they brought up their children, how their men treated them, how they dressed, whether they went to school with men. They wanted to know if I thought our Black children will have a place in the world, a real place, or will they only be told what to do?" They said to Essie, as she later recounted it, "We are tired of being told what to do. Our children will be more tired of it."[75] Essie relished these candid exchanges. She befriended people at all levels of Toro society, including the group's king and his wife—a tall, dignified, statuesque woman who made quite an impression on Essie.[76]

Essie had come to Kabarole to study the "cattle culture," but she was interested in more than the local economy and work practices: she wanted to learn about the ebb and flow of daily life, including the villagers' customs, diet, and architecture. Day by day, she slowly immersed herself more and more in the village's routine of work, meals, and social obligations. She took photographs and copious notes, documenting details about how the beds were crafted; how beer and banana wine were made; what types of jewelry, dresses, shoes, and head wraps the local women wore; and how food was prepared.[77]

Essie also documented the many inconveniences she experienced, writing about them with a tone of humility and acceptance. The toilet situation in rural Africa in the 1930s, for example, was radically different from what she was used to. On one of their early stops, Essie noted, "I had my hands full negotiating the lavatory." The facilities were rudimentary, made of thatched walls, an open ceiling, a pile of soft leaves, and a hole in the ground. She did notice that the lavatories were always neat and clean, despite the lack of modern fixtures or plumbing.[78] Inconveniences notwithstanding, Essie embraced the whole experience and felt "lucky" to have the "opportunity" to live in a village where no Europeans had ever stayed, and to be welcomed so warmly by the local people. Essie delighted in the newness of certain daily routines. "It is fascinating taking one's morning bath in the sun, protected only by a high reed enclosure," she wrote, and "evening bath[s] under the stars!!"[79]

On August 5, Essie, Paul Jr., and several of their new friends from the Kabarole village took a spontaneous excursion into the Congo, hoping to enjoy an impromptu safari. They drove northwest, crossed the Semliki River by pontoon ferry, passed the salt mines and Lake Dweru in Katwe, and finally reached the Congolese border.[80] Navigating the racial dynamics, language barriers, and politics in colonial Africa was no small feat. There was obviously a huge gulf between the rights of native Blacks and white colonials even if customs varied from place to place, and few people knew precisely what to make of Essie. Some practices were enshrined in law, while others were simply customs imposed by those with the guns and the power at the local level. Because customs and colonial law varied from region to region and even within a single colony, Essie never knew what to expect when she ventured off the beaten path, or how her own role as a light-skinned Black American would be perceived.

One race-related incident occurred when she and her group arrived at the Congolese town of Mbeni and attempted to check into a tiny Belgian-owned hotel. The white hotel owner refused to give them rooms, saying that if he accommodated Blacks, his white patrons would leave. There were not too many prospective white patrons as far as Essie could see, but the innkeeper was adamant. Fortunately, Essie had strategically befriended the local Belgian district commissioner when they crossed the border, impressing him with her French, and thereby easing their passage. The commissioner happened along during their negotiation with the innkeeper and intervened on their behalf. Essie and her companions were finally given two rooms, but their two Toro porters were refused service and were forced to eat and sleep in the car, in yet another example of the differing class privileges even among Black colonial subjects. To add insult to injury, two Belgians in a room next to Essie's came in drunk in the middle of the night with two local prostitutes and proceeded to make a raunchy ruckus.[81] Essie and her group could not wait to get out of there. They left first thing the next morning.

One of the highlights of their trip to the Congo was a visit to the famous "Bakonjo-pygmy village," Ngite, located deep in the Ituri

Rainforest. Essie and her little entourage hired a local "headman" to guide them to the village, which involved a one-hour drive and long walk through thick jungle foliage. The village was "built among the sunny shadows and immense tree trunks in a small clearing." The Ngite people averaged a little over four feet tall, a few inches shorter than Paul Jr., who was only nine years old. There were about ten thousand Ngite people in the forest, living in bands of twenty-five to fifty.[82] Essie's group spent several hours there. They asked the villagers questions through a translator, exchanged smiles and nods, and took photographs.

Essie's last week in Uganda was hectic because Nyabongo insisted on taking her to all of the five provinces before her scheduled departure. During a one-day trip to the hilly and mineral-rich province of Nkole, Essie met with some local chiefs who had hosted anthropology colleagues of hers from London some years back. Understandably skeptical of white researchers, these chiefs had been both amused and offended that the men had come to study their history and culture without first bothering to learn any of the indigenous languages. They said to Essie, "White people are not interested in us. They only want to take away our land and our cattle, and make us pay taxes."[83]

Passing through Kampala on one of their last excursions, Essie and Paul Jr. spent the night with the Kalibala family, friends of Nyabongo. Mr. Kalibala had been educated in the United States at Tuskegee Institute, the Alabama school founded by Booker T. Washington, and he had later attended Columbia University. His wife was a Black American from Boston, the daughter of a Baptist preacher. The Kalibalas hosted a fancy party for Essie and Paul Jr. where they were introduced to other local residents who had been educated in the United States or Britain. They were "all dressed in European clothes, and all argumentative," Essie noted, wholly unimpressed with the lot of them.[84]

On the very last leg of the trip, Essie and Paul Jr. had an even more awkward and unpleasant experience. Nyabongo drove them to Entebbe, twenty miles outside of Kampala, where they would be overnight guests of the British governor, Sir Philip Euen Mitchell, and his white South African wife. They had met the Mitchells at the King of Buganda's annual Birthday Tea the previous week, and the governor had insisted on hosting the Robesons in Entebbe, the headquarters of the British administration—in other words, the capital of colonial rule—before they left.[85] Even though she was quite uncomfortable with the invitation, Essie felt she had no choice but to accept. After having seen the want and poverty, the hard living conditions, poor roads, and makeshift housing that everyday Africans endured, it seemed wrong and unfair to enjoy the modern conveniences of a colonial mansion and be waited on by its army of Black servants. "Coming to Entebbe was like coming into another world," Essie wrote disturbingly, "a European world in the very heart of Africa."[86]

After putting Paul Jr. to bed, Essie joined the adult guests who had assembled for dinner. On her last night in Uganda, she found herself oddly and uncomfortably surrounded by white colonial elites. They were all quite cordial and solicitous of her opinions on Africa and Africans. She did the best she could to offer insights without offending her hosts. Seated next to the governor himself at dinner, Essie was prodded by him to report on what she had learned during her stay in Uganda and what she thought the colonial administration could do to improve the condition of the local people. Her reply, restrained but strategic, was that Britain should prioritize African education, senior administrators should not take the reports of low-level colonial appointees at face value, and anyone spending a significant amount of time in Africa should try to learn at least one of the indigenous languages.[87] She was thinking on her feet and was quick to remember what the local people she had met told her about whites coming into the region without bothering to learn the language. Those were three modest points she decided to put on the table. It was, of course, not all she could have said or what was really on her mind and in her heart.

After she retired to her room that night, Essie literally tossed and turned all night, unable to sleep, thinking about whether she had chosen her words carefully enough when she had spoken to the governor at dinner. She had found herself in the unique situation of being able to speak truth to power, and she feared that she had failed to take full advantage of the opportunity. Her gut instinct had been to tell the white colonials to pack up, go back to Europe, and give the Africans their lands back. But she had opted for a more tempered response in the hopes that her words might have some small influence. She had seen Africa close up. "Savages, my eye!" she wrote to Carlo and Fania, "Look at this beauty. Aristocratic, beautiful, charming, and intelligent, are typical."[88] She had seen beyond the caricatures and cartoon depictions and even beyond the stories of her African friends and colleagues in London. She had seen past the one-dimensional view of Africans as either victims or brutes. She had met real people—smart, hard-working, resourceful, and hopeful individuals. What was she going to do with this new knowledge? This question was at the forefront of her mind as she prepared to leave the continent.

On August 17, 1936, Essie and Paul Jr. were driven from the governor's estate in Entebbe to the airfield in an official state car with the British flag appended to the hood.[89] There they took off in a small propeller plane, leaving Uganda behind. It was Paul Jr.'s first flight, and although Essie was suffering from a terrible bout of dysentery, as the plane soared above the African landscape, she pulled herself together enough to marvel at sights below: the giraffes and elephants and the vast, sometimes desolate stretches of arid land. They made several stops in Sudan, including in the town of Juba, where they had dinner and spent the night before taking off again; Malakal, where they enjoyed lunch; Khartoum, for another overnight stay; and Kosti, where they had tea. Once they had arrived in Alexandria, Egypt, where they were to change planes, they stayed in a "magnificent hotel" in Luxor with a balcony overlooking a grove of date palm trees.[90] By this point, however, Essie was having trouble fully appreciating the vistas because she was terribly sick. Her symptoms became so severe that she feared she might actually have to contact her husband to come "collect" her, underscoring, in her written account of the experience some years later, that she was "definitely not the kind of person who [normally] has to be collected." In the end, she suffered through and did not call for a rescue. "I always like to finish everything I do," she said.[91]

On one of the final legs of the trip, Essie and Paul Jr. were on board a shiny Scipio airplane heading homeward, and Essie was feeling proud of her son, who had been a steadfast companion, caretaker, and fellow explorer. Most of the other passengers were friendly enough, but one was not: a crude, aging colonial administrator who had recently retired and was returning to England after making his fortune in the colonies. He was, in Essie's assessment, "red-faced, choleric, and given to asserting himself." When he set eyes on young Paul Jr. and overheard him speaking the "King's English," the administrator could not contain his astonishment at how articulate the boy was. "Pity he's got that handicap. . . . Pity he's Black," he bluntly remarked to Essie, seemingly oblivious to the possibility that she would find the remark insulting. Essie didn't hesitate to offer a sharp retort. "His color, his background, his rich history are a part of his wealth," she snapped. "We consider it an asset, not a handicap." She left the rough-speaking Englishman bewildered but checked.[92]

She continued the conversation in her own head as she wrestled with the pathology of racism and white supremacy. "Soaring in the clouds," she wrote, "with the strange distant toy world spread out below, I felt removed from earth-bound things. Why am I really glad and proud to be Negro? Why am I sorry for this pitiful 'superior' European? Why do I actually feel superior to him?" Essie felt sorry, in a way, for the "pathetic" and "weak" old man because he was so ignorantly tethered to the past and trapped in his narrow and insular worldview. He had "arbitrarily walled himself off from more than two-thirds of his fellow men, the non-white peoples of the world. . . . Only fear can explain such irrational behavior," she concluded.[93] Ten years later, the implications of this exchange still relevant and fresh, Essie published an article in *Negro Digest* entitled "Is Black a Handicap?" The epigraph read: "Color an asset, not a handicap."[94]

On August 25, eight days after they had taken off from Entebbe and three months after their original departure from London, Essie and Paul Jr. returned to England. Essie was so sick by the time they arrived home she had to be taken off the plane on a stretcher and taken directly to the hospital for tests and treatment (she was released a few days later).[95] Even though the trip had wreaked havoc on Essie's body, its influence on her thinking and on her psyche cannot be overstated. Essie had been seduced by the beauty and complexity of the African landscape. She also had been captivated and inspired by the generous, hardworking, long-suffering, but hopeful people she had met, from the herdswomen of Toro to the miners of Robinson Deep, to the intellectuals and activists she encountered in Bloemfontein. Memories of her "African journey" would always remain with her. Because of this transformative experience, Essie's arrival home was at the same time a new departure—on a journey toward becoming an anti-colonial writer and activist.

seven

MADRID TO MOSCOW, POLITICAL COMMITMENTS DEEPEN, 1936–1939

Ruins of homes are everywhere — naked in the sun;
some completely demolished, lying in heaps of debris on the
ground, telling a grim story of the lives crushed.
Eslanda Robeson

While Essie and Paul Jr. were in Africa, Paul had taken a second short trip to Moscow, where he spent time with filmmaker Sergei Eisenstein and practiced his Russian. He had agreed to return for a highly touted concert tour to four Russian cities beginning in October. So shortly after their return from Uganda, Essie and Paul Jr. joined Paul for what was Essie's second trip to the Soviet Union. It was a precarious time in Soviet history. Joseph Stalin was firmly in power, preparing to roll out a new constitution for the country. Far-reaching and aggressive economic changes were in motion, even as Stalin was beginning to systematically suppress those opposed to his plans and his leadership. His notorious purges were already under way. Still, outsiders, including a number of Black Americans, continued to migrate to the Soviet Union. Soviet society, particularly its claim to be an oasis of racial justice and its role as a staunch opponent of colonialism, had a unique appeal.[1]

Before their visit, Essie and Paul had each done their own research on the Soviet Union and had shared their findings with one another. Paul, a gifted linguist, had delved into the Russian language and culture; the politics were of great interest as well. In fact, Paul was so enthralled by the new two-volume tome by leftist writers Sidney and Beatrice Webb titled *Soviet Communism: A New Civilization?* that he had made detailed comments in the margins and spent an entire evening reading passages aloud to Essie, prompting her to begin reading the book herself.[2] For both Paul and Essie the Soviet Union's connection to Africa was key. They had talked about communism with their African friends in London so much that Paul later explained it was "through Africa that I found the Soviet Union."[3]

In addition to exploring the vast country during her second trip, Essie was anxious to see her brothers, who by 1936 had been living there for two years. John, the eldest of the Goode siblings (he was born in 1892), was a skilled auto mechanic and had found a job working in the state transportation system repairing and inspecting buses. He had worked as a chauffeur in the United States.[4] During his years in the Soviet Union he would also work as a taxi driver and foreign language instructor while in residence at the foreign workers' hostel in Moscow. Unlike his brother, Frank, he would not opt to settle permanently in the Soviet Union, but rather decided to leave in 1937. As early as 1935, John had the idea that he might not stay there indefinitely. He wrote to Essie expressing uncertainty about whether his visa would be renewed since he "had been rather sharp in [his] criticism" of his work situation and had made "suggestions" about modernization to his supervisor that were not so well received.[5] Some have suggested that when he finally did leave later in 1937 it was because he was fearful of the purges and persecution that were under way, and this is quite possible. Although both Goode brothers had initially been drawn to the Soviet Union because of opportunities to work and the promise of freedom from racial discrimination—in fact, they had conveyed to both Essie and Paul how free they felt as Black men who no longer had to endure the daily sting and stigma of racial prejudice—it was by no means a perfect situation.[6] While some freedoms were granted, others were curbed.

Even though a heavy-handed crackdown on suspected dissidents was ongoing in the Soviet Union by 1936—a crackdown that, according to Paul Jr., his parents were at least partially aware of—Essie and Paul still spoke of the communist country in positive terms.[7] They believed firmly that the anti-racist, anti-colonial policies of the Soviet Union demanded their support. Whatever bad things were taking place, they may have reasoned, were limited and simply outweighed by the good. Esther Cooper Jackson was another Black American activist, slightly younger than the Robesons, who supported the Soviet Union but never formally joined the U.S. Communist Party. When asked decades later why she and others did not speak out louder and sooner against Soviet repression, she explained that there was such rampant anti-communist propaganda during the Cold War, and such a barrage of anti-Soviet rumors, that it was difficult to sort out the truth from the fabrications. She simply did not believe much of the negative reports that were in circulation, and assumed the Robesons did not either.[8]

Perhaps the most profound evidence of Essie and Paul's confidence in the USSR was their decision to enroll their young son in a fifth-grade class at one of Moscow's model schools. Stalin's daughter was one of his classmates. In fact, Paul Jr. lived and studied in the Soviet Union for more than a year under the care of his grandmother, Essie's mother, and with the benefit of several visits from his parents. When explaining his decision regarding his son's education, Paul told reporters that he was confident that his child could receive the kind of racist-free education in the Soviet Union that he could not receive in the United States.[9]

Less than a week after they returned from the Soviet Union, Essie and Paul took off again, this time to Egypt, so that Paul could play a role in *Jericho*, a film about a Black World War I veteran, a persecuted hero who escaped the army and returned to Africa. Essie was thrilled to be back on the African continent, this time north of the Sahara. She and Paul stayed just outside Cairo and traveled each day to the desert ten miles outside the city for filming. Essie had a small part in the film, about which she was quite excited, and even though her scenes were ultimately cut during the final edits, she enjoyed the experience thoroughly.[10] Filming took about a month, and Essie was able to get out and see the sights when Paul was busy on the set and she was not. She visited the Giza Pyramids and was captivated by the serenity of the Sahara. She was also struck by the beauty and diversity of the Egyptian people.[11] *Jericho* was not a big commercial success, but it was an artistic project that Paul and Essie could be proud of: a film set in Africa that did not celebrate colonialism or denigrate Africans.

Another Robeson film produced in 1937–1938 was *Big Fella*. Essie and Larry Brown both had small parts in the movie, which was set on the French waterfront but filmed in England. It was a musical, adapted from Claude McKay's novel, *Banjo*, about an interracial community of sailors and bar patrons. Essie had a small part: she played the good-looking, no-nonsense proprietress of the Cosmo Café, where much of the drama takes place. This was the second and last film she and Paul appeared in together. One film historian points out that the film was important for its generally positive depictions of Black women as "assertive, humorous, and sassy," which was a departure from the deferential and subservient roles that were usually reserved for Black women actors at this time. The Black actress Elizabeth Welch was Paul's co-star and fictional love interest, but it was Paul and Essie's chemistry that was described as "memorable." In one scene, Essie chastises Paul for being a troublemaker in her café and warns him to settle down or she will intervene. "What have you got to laugh at, you big bozo?" she chides Paul's character, Joe. "Please ma'am, don't bring that [a previous altercation] up again," he replies. The tough-talking Essie lets Joe know that "if it's roughhousing you want, come to me, I'll give you all you want," threatening to end the next fight that he starts with other patrons.[12]

By the winter of 1937, fascism was spreading rapidly throughout Europe. What Paul and Essie had observed of the Nazis in Berlin in the winter of 1934 was only the tip of the iceberg. But as fascism advanced, popular resistance intensified from Ethiopia to Madrid. What became the Spanish Civil War, the struggle of Republican Loyalists against the fascist supporters of Francisco Franco, was the international epicenter of that resistance in the late 1930s. In the preface to the 1952 reprint of George Orwell's *Farewell to Catalonia*, about his time as a soldier in Spain during the civil war, Lionel Trilling wrote, "Everyone knows that the Spanish war was one of the decisive events of our epoch, everyone said so at the time it was being fought, and everyone was right."[13] Ernest Hemingway also took great interest in the struggle in Spain: he visited the country during the war and wrote his celebrated novel *For Whom the Bell Tolls* about the experience. And Pablo Picasso depicted the atrocities of the war in his epic painting *Guernica*. For one shining moment, Spain felt like a stronghold against encroaching fascist dictators—a stronghold that had to be defended. Volunteer militia streamed into the country from around the world to add muscle and morale to the anti-fascist forces. These international brigades, as they were called, were drawn largely from leftist and communist organizations across Europe and the United States. A unique international fighting force known as the Abraham Lincoln Brigade, named in honor of the U.S. president who signed the Emancipation Proclamation, was composed of nearly three thousand American volunteers, many of them trade unionists and communists, and at least eighty of them African Americans. In the minds of many of the Blacks who went to Spain, the struggle against Franco was an extension of the struggle against Mussolini, who had so ruthlessly occupied Ethiopia.[14] The Black Lincoln volunteers, as they were called, stepped up, according to historian Robin Kelley, "partly to revenge the pillage of Ethiopia."[15]

Essie and Paul followed the events in Spain closely and wondered what they could do to help. Even Ma Goode raised funds to support the Republican cause.[16] Indeed, by the mid-1930s Paul had come to view his art in increasingly political terms. He was a compassionate person and rigorous thinker, a world traveler and an independent scholar of world politics and world cultures. After contemplating the injustices and ominous political developments he saw around him, he became more outspoken about these injustices and the human toll they were taking. As Paul Jr. wrote later, "The seeds planted during his 1934 trip through Nazi Berlin to Soviet Moscow, when he had begun to think of himself as a citizen of the world rather than merely an artist who traveled the world, were bearing fruit."[17] In an interview in 1937, Paul Sr. himself said, "Today I am more resigned to losing my individual status as an artist; I am happy and proud to be of some little use to my people."[18] His people included Black Americans and anti-fascist Spaniards.

In the winter of 1937, Paul decided that giving concerts and speeches in England in support of the Spanish Loyalist cause was not enough. On December 27 he sang to a crowd of nine thousand in London's Royal Albert Hall in support of the anti-fascist forces in Spain. But he wanted to do more. He wanted to travel to the war zone in Spain and stand and sing alongside the freedom fighters. He wanted to express his solidarity in more concrete terms.[19] Essie was hesitant at first. She had always viewed herself as "the adventuresome member of the Robeson family," but even she had "never considered the idea of going to war."[20] It was not fear that made Essie reluctant. "Danger has always stimulated me," she wrote later, "and keyed me up to my best behavior and clearest thinking."[21] She was being practical, she reasoned. After all, what good could a singer and writer with no military training do on the front lines of a war? But Paul was determined and after several long political discussions about the spread of fascism and its significance for not only Spain but also the world, Essie was persuaded. It was important, she agreed, to stand in solidarity with those fighting in the trenches. The issue was critical and the struggle historic. And so they went, Essie armed with her pen, her writer's sensibilities, and her keen eye for details.

Accompanying the Robesons on their journey to Spain was writer and activist Charlotte Haldane, the first female war correspondent in England. Haldane was also a member of the British Communist Party, an ardent feminist, and the author of some twenty novels by the end of her career. Her own son, Ronnie, had recently served and been wounded in the Spanish Civil War, and in 1937, she was head of the International Brigade Dependants and Wounded Aid Committee in London. Charlotte was married to the world-famous British geneticist J. B. S. Haldane, who had himself just returned from Spain.[22] Like Essie, Charlotte had endured her own marital drama. She had suffered through a messy divorce from her first husband, Jack Burghes, after which she immediately married her lover, Dr. Haldane, who was almost fired from his academic post at Cambridge University on morality charges as a result of the affair.[23] Charlotte had written on the subject of divorce, agreeing with Essie that it should be easy and available for all women. The two also shared the experience of being married to famous men.[24] Years later, Charlotte said that she felt Essie's talents had never been adequately recognized, observing that Essie was "thoroughly competent, charming, and sensible," but "like most wives of famous men . . . was obliged to play second fiddle, and to perform in a minor key."[25] Charlotte may have understated Essie's independence and agency, but she proved to be an interesting travel companion for the Robesons during their trip, and her observations about Essie's strengths and talents were perceptive, if not perfectly accurate.[26]

The delegation of three left for Spain from Paris on January 21, 1938, with Spanish escorts, and specially approved visas to allow them to move through combat areas. Charlotte's bags included candy, cigarettes, and letters from the loved ones of British volunteers. They arrived in the coastal town of Benicasim and then traveled to Valencia, close to the front lines. Essie recorded their trip in her diary in vivid detail. "We eased into Spain at nightfall," she wrote in an eighty-page unpublished essay about the trip. They rode in a comfortable seven-passenger Buick sedan most of the way. "As we got closer to the front, we heard the sporadic sound of gunfire." The roads in northern Spain "were thronged with soldiers, wounded and convalescent," Essie observed. As the group moved farther south, they heard news of bombings and high casualties. They continued cautiously but steadily in the direction of the fighting.

Essie looked around her in humble amazement, observing both the ugly face of war and the humanity and tender beauty that managed to survive in its midst. She took note of the lush vegetation, tangerine groves in the background, and the beautiful but beleaguered soldiers with "sun-baked skin, weary faces, and sullen eyes." The young soldier assigned to accompany them on the trip was a Spanish lieutenant named Fernando Castillo. Essie took quite a liking to him. He was handsome, funny, knowledgeable, and brave. He shared stories of his family, including ones about the wife and young child he had left behind to join the struggle. He had not been a soldier before the Civil War, but when the conflict erupted, when Franco's troops threatened to topple the democratic government of Spain, he and his brothers felt compelled to fight. "Fernando Castillo introduced us to Spain," Essie recalled, "Paul, Fernando and I . . . and became friends after five minutes; and this friendship grew." Years later, after the defeat of the Republican forces, Fernando managed to escape Spain and showed up on the Robesons' London doorstep, seeking refuge. They took him in and helped him get resettled. He and his wife eventually ended up in Mexico. Before he left London, however, he entrusted Essie with a treasured family heirloom as a sign of gratitude: a replica of the historic 1931 Spanish Republican Constitution—his father had been one of the authors.[27]

During their stay in Spain in 1938, Essie and Paul saw remarkable scenes and met many idealistic young people, like Fernando, who were ready to die for their beliefs and their country. They were "greeted [by] everyone, with a smile of welcome, and 'Salud,' with raised, clenched fist."[28] They visited a hospital in the town of Benicasim, then a women's prison in Valencia where Franco supporters were being held.[29] The area was heavily bombed immediately after they left. Pockmarks from shelling were a familiar sight in many areas. Some buildings were entirely gutted, and others had their windows blown out. In a training camp near the town of Albacete, Paul performed a rousing concert for the volunteer soldiers.[30]

They moved on to Madrid, which was even closer to the front lines. As Essie recounted, they "passed a bit of road at a crawl with headlights out . . . windows of hotels, stores, and houses stripped with broad heavy paper to prevent them from shattering during shelling and bombing. There was some firing during the night and we could hear the guns occasionally. . . . We went up to the observation tower with a panoramic view of the front-line trenches. . . . Suddenly a shell whizzed by and hit a big white building on the right, exploding with a flash and a cloud of dust. Then a shell hit the bridge beyond the North Station. Our guns replied, followed by a bit of machine-gun fire, and all was quiet again." The city of Madrid was being evacuated, and there were instructions that no women or children be allowed to enter. Essie and Charlotte managed to get through with their special visas, which had been obtained through the Spanish ambassador to Britain, a personal acquaintance of the Robesons. Those special papers and letters of introduction came in handy: there were armed militia checkpoints along all the major roads, and their papers were inspected routinely.[31]

In Madrid, they met with officials of the besieged city and settled in at the Palace Hotel, an oasis amid the chaos of war where they enjoyed hot baths and warm meals. But they were frequently reminded of their close proximity to the fighting. The first two floors of the grand old hotel had been converted into a military hospital, where wounded soldiers and civilians were being cared for. A few blocks away was the wreckage of a school with children's artwork still visible on the walls.[32] They saw the effects of war throughout the sad, but still magnificent, city. In Essie's words, "Ruins of homes are everywhere—naked in the sun; some completely demolished, lying in heaps of debris on the ground, telling a grim story of the lives crushed beneath the heaps; some still standing with half a side torn away like a split tree, showing the steel gardens belonging to the inner structure sticking out grotesquely in midair. Everywhere in this section, the trees, which must have made the wide sidewalks very lovely, had been cut down, leaving only the bare stumps; the people had had to use them for warmth, and for cooking. There was no fuel." Life in Madrid went limping along. "Women have their washing out, children are playing in the streets, people are doing business in what shops remain."[33] Essie focused on the resilience and fundamental humanity of the people, just as she had during her visit to South Africa and Uganda.

In salute to this resilience, Paul sang to soldiers, in both Spanish and English, and sometimes in other languages. He sang in their barracks, in organized concerts, and on radio broadcasts that aired throughout the war-ravaged country. As they moved about Paul was recognized by soldiers from all over the world, and they were thrilled that he had come. Soldiers pulled out their guitars and played flamenco and folk songs, and sometimes in the evenings when things were calm, there was dancing. Paul's language skills represented a further expression of transnational solidarity, which the soldiers appreciated. These jubilant scenes amazed and delighted Essie. The music had interrupted, albeit briefly and precariously, the destructive and dispiriting effects of war. If Essie had doubted what their little delegation might accomplish by going to Spain, seeing the troops' faces during Paul's concerts and visits no doubt reassured her that the trip was worthwhile. They were essentially there to express solidarity and lift morale, to give words of encouragement and deliver not only chocolates and cigarettes, but also messages of support and gratitude from artists and activists in London. They carried out their mission and were deeply moved by the entire experience.

Essie and Paul even attended stage plays performed in one of Madrid's grand old theaters. It was a rather bizarre experience, Essie recalled, to go from fearing a bomb attack one minute to being absorbed in a first-rate theatrical performance the next. One of the plays was about the Spanish Inquisition and concluded with a rousing speech by the female lead about the contemporary situation. "The great lesson [is] that we will demand justice; the people must have justice," the impassioned actor insisted. After the applause, the entire audience stood to sing the Spanish national anthem.[34] During Essie and Paul's second night at the theater, they saw a play by Cervantes about resistance to Roman conquest. Essie felt these creative performances both reflected and reinforced Spaniards' determination to resist Franco. "The people of Madrid love this play," Essie wrote in her journal. "They say their ancestors have set a splendid example for them, and they will die rather than surrender themselves."[35] That evening Essie shared their conviction that the resistance was so strong it could not be defeated.

Essie's Spanish war journal is replete with vivid descriptions of the contradictions of war: stories of survival and destruction, resilience and despair, calm and chaos. She carefully and compassionately recorded the stories of the ordinary people she encountered. There was one "sad little family" in a hotel lounge whose brother, aged twenty-two or twenty-three, had been killed recently when a bomb on his warplane had exploded unexpectedly. The family was in mourning and still a bit in shock but they were not hopeless. And then there was Roderigo, the "Spanish Negro from Harlem," who had been wounded at Teruel, but smiled quickly when he recognized Paul Robeson. With him were soldiers "Ted Gibbs from Chicago and Claude Pringle from Ohio"— Black American soldiers there to fight against fascism in the villages and cities of Spain, presumably seeing some connection to their own fight back home. For these men and their comrades, the journey to Spain had been an arduous one. Some had to pay their own expenses while others hiked through the Pyrennes to arrive at the battlefields. For Pringle, the journey back would be equally difficult. He would spend many months in prison after the war before eventually making his way back to the United States.[36]

By their third day in Spain, Essie, Paul, and Charlotte had adjusted, as much as one can, to the realities of being in a country at war. "We hear artillery and machine gun fire," Essie writes, "but by now, like real Madrid people, we are used to it." They carried on, noticing other sights and sounds amid the clamor of war. "Driving along a coastal road from Sitges to Barcelona," Essie observed, "the olive trees were a beautiful spectacle, in the gale—the leaves were gray green on the upper side, and silvery on the under side . . . blowing in the gale, the silver caught and reflected in the sun. . . . The almond trees are now in bloom, and are beautiful."[37] Essie returned from Spain pensive but buoyed by the experience. Paul later remarked that Spain had been "a major turning point in my life." The same was true for Essie.

Despite the valiant efforts of the Republican fighters and their international allies, the fascist forces had all but won the war by the end of 1938. Barcelona fell to the fascist rebels in January. The final blow came with the capture of Madrid three months later, in March 1939. The International Brigades departed and the Spanish resistance fighters were either jailed, killed, or forced to flee. The Spanish people suffered under the Francoist regime for nearly forty years.

As Spain fell to Franco, the imperial ambitions of the Third Reich became even clearer. A full-fledged global conflict was rapidly unfolding. Most of Essie's extended family members were in generally safe areas: John Goode, Essie's brother, had already resettled in the States, and Paul Jr. and Essie's mother had come back to London the previous December. Essie's eldest brother, Frank, however, was still living in the Soviet town of Gorky and communication was difficult. In February 1939, soon after her return from Spain, Essie decided to travel to the Soviet Union alone to check on him. This proved to be a harrowing trip through war-torn Europe, especially through Nazi Germany, but she did arrive safely in Moscow. (She chose to return by way of Scandinavia.) Frank was fine when Essie arrived, but the war years would be difficult for him.[38]

Around this time, an old friendship that had been unraveling for years finally ended. Essie had reconnected with her longtime friend Emma Goldman when they moved to London in 1928. Emma was still as thoroughly infatuated with both Essie and Paul as she had been in 1925. Essie was so "vivacious," and Paul, in Emma's eyes, was an artistic "genius." Emma pleaded to spend more time with them. But over the ensuing decade—after Essie's experiences in Berlin and Spain, Africa and Russia—she was coming into her own politically, and many of her evolving views were at variance with Emma's, especially on the question of support for the Soviet Union. In 1935 Essie wrote Emma a letter describing her trip to the Soviet Union and explaining that her brothers now lived there and "loved it." Emma replied with blunt skepticism. She conceded that the Soviets had made advances when it came to the treatment of racial minorities but insisted that this was by no means the whole story, and that their record was less glowing on most other issues.[39] Still, Emma wanted to preserve her friendship with the Robesons, even if they proved to be "full fledged communist[s]," as the rumors had suggested, and she doubted. Emma ended her December 1935 letter to Essie with "Devoted love to both of you."[40]

By 1938 the gulf between the Robesons and Emma, still an avowed anarchist and staunch critic of Soviet communism, was even greater. Writing directly to Paul in 1938 after being rebuffed by him after a concert, Emma expressed her anguish: "I had hoped that you would let me see you and Essie, but evidently this is not to be. I have always held that friendship should be given only if it can be done from the fullness of one's heart. For twelve years I have been happy in the certainty of this kind of friendship from you and Essie, but during the last year it was borne in on me that you have undergone a change. . . . I am particularly sorry," she concluded, "that you permitted your new political orientation . . . to affect the free and easy camaraderie that existed between us."[41] There is no extant copy of Paul's response. It was their last known correspondence before Emma's death in the spring of 1940.

The Robesons' estrangement from Emma Goldman played out against the backdrop of Stalin's notorious Moscow trials and purges during which many Soviet leaders were arrested, tried, and some hastily executed for allegedly plotting against the state. In many cases, dissident views and criticisms of Stalin led to the persecution of those who were imprisoned or killed. It is unclear exactly how much the Robesons knew about what was going on behind the scenes, though they "followed the trials carefully" in the *Daily Worker*, the *Moscow Daily News Magazine*, and *Pravda*, the Soviet newspaper (by this time Paul was fluent in Russian).[42] Neither Paul nor Essie spoke out publicly about the trials, but privately Essie was concerned, apparently for reasons that were more personal than political. She wrote a long letter to her old friend U.S. Communist Party leader William Patterson, to express her concern about an exchange she had had with a Russian doctor friend, Ignaty Kazakov. At one time Kazakov was a favored Kremlin physician, but he was then implicated in the murder of a high-level Soviet official and in a plot to overthrow the government. It was later revealed that many of those prosecuted, including Kazakov, were likely the victims of trumped-up charges.

Essie and Paul had met and befriended Kazakov when they visited the resort area of Kislovodsk. He and Essie shared an interest in science and had discussed the idea of her possibly working in his research laboratory in Moscow. Things between Essie and Kazakov allegedly soured when he asked her to procure for him a potentially toxic chemical—tungsten—without telling her why. She initially agreed to bring some with her on her next trip to the Soviet Union from London, but she had second thoughts and decided against it. When she visited Moscow again, Kazakov was in jail. He was eventually sentenced to death and summarily executed. Paul had had an odd and disconcerting encounter with Kazakov months before he was killed, and suspected something was awry.[43]

Essie's response to Kazakov's execution requires some interpretation. Her only written reaction to the incident is in a letter she wrote in April 1938 to William Patterson. In the letter, she both explained her connection to Kazakov and simultaneously distanced herself from him. She had been "so dumb," she confessed, for naively trusting Kazakov. She implied in her letter that she believed the charges against her former friend were all true, she deemed his actions utterly "wicked," and she regretted that she had gotten mixed up with him—though she was glad she had not complied with his request to import the tungsten. "It is a very terrible thing they have done," she wrote, referring to the physicians on trial for allegedly using their medical expertise for assassinations, "and I am glad they have been punished."[44] Since Patterson was both a leader of the Communist Party, which was still a close ally of the Soviet government, and a longtime personal friend of the Robesons, it is unclear whether Essie's letter was performative or genuine. After all, her brother was still there and she had brought Paul Jr. and her mother back from Moscow to the safer environs of London. Paul Jr. reported years later that his parents had been afraid for Frank's safety, and that his retreat to London with his grandmother was due to the same fears. He also insists, based on conversations with his parents in later years, that the letter to Patterson was a well-conceived ruse to lessen Frank's vulnerability in a climate of paranoia and rampant persecutions of anyone suspected of disloyalty. Essie, in Paul Jr.'s words, "supported the purges to the hilt and denounced Kazakov" in order to protect her brother. Perhaps substantiating this view is the fact that Essie also told Patterson it was because of the spread of the war in Europe that she had brought Paul Jr. home to London until they all could go back to the States together.[45] She apparently did not want her decision to withdraw Paul Jr. from school in Moscow to be misread as a subtle criticism of the Kremlin. It is difficult to know precisely what Essie and Paul thought about the unfolding situation, but it is fair to assume that we don't know the whole story from the extant documents.[46]

By September 3, 1939, the war had officially reached England. Two days earlier, German tanks had rolled into Poland and Britain's Lord Chamberlain had declared war with Hitler. Air raid sirens pierced the mist-filled London skies, causing Essie to feel a terrible angst in the pit of her stomach. The ordinary landscape and feel of London had been replaced by the eerie and ominous signs of war. Sandbags were placed in front of major buildings, men reported for military duty with gas masks in hand, and uniformed police were everywhere. After hearing of Hitler's bombing campaigns in Warsaw and other Polish cities, Londoners were preparing for the same. The bomb attacks did not come for another year, but there were already mandated blackouts and residents were required to put black curtains over their windows to darken any prospective targets. Essie too bought dark fabric for this purpose, although she was reprimanded by neighborhood monitors about the slivers of light that escaped some windows in her flat. One day she and Paul Jr. had to abandon the taxi they were riding in and duck into a designated bomb shelter in response to an air raid siren. It was just a practice air raid, but was unsettling nonetheless.[47] Essie knew these inconveniences were minor compared to the suffering she had seen in Spain, but she knew that the situation was only going to become more dangerous for her family. It was time for them to leave.

Paul was finishing up the final scenes of *Proud Valley*, a film about a Black man who joins a Welsh mining community. He wanted to see the film to fruition, so Essie decided to wait it out with him. During the month they remained in London after the British had entered the war, Max Yergan visited them for several days. They talked of fascism, the war, and Africa. Hitler and Stalin had signed a controversial nonaggression pact a few weeks earlier, which had profoundly complicated the position of pro-Soviet organizations and individuals around the globe, and had caused major splits and schisms within the Communist Left worldwide. While this was certainly a part of their conversations, what Yergan was most interested in talking to Essie about was the International Committee on African Affairs (ICAA), an anti-colonial education and advocacy group that had been founded in London in 1937 with the Robesons' help. The group would soon evolve into the Council on African Affairs and be relocated to the United States with Paul at its helm and Essie as a strong supporter.

Essie, who had bonded with Yergan during her 1936 visit to South Africa, was the ICAA's "first contributing member." She held high hopes for the new organization when she wrote a $300 check to help get it started. Years later, after the group set up shop in New York City, she established the council's library by loaning many of her books, maps, photographs, and artifacts from her travels in Africa. Yergan himself would move sharply to the right by the late 1940s, even stooping to defend the racist South African regime at one point. But in the 1930s, he and Essie were concerned about the same issues, shared some of the same political views, and strategized together about how to launch this new and important organization.

On September 30, 1939, the Robeson clan, accompanied by Larry Brown and twenty-four pieces of luggage, started the long trek back to the United States. Several weeks and many miles later, they would begin their lives anew. For Paul and Essie, it was a homecoming: back to familiar streets, places, people, and habits. Harlem was terra firma for Paul and Essie, even though the neighborhood had changed in their absence. But for Paul Jr., now eleven, everything was new and different. He had grown up as a privileged Black child in England and had traveled widely. He was cosmopolitan and conversant in several languages. The United States had never really been his home. Essie worried about how he would adjust, but on another level, both of his parents were glad that he would now have a chance to connect with other Negro children and the Harlem they both loved.

Paul Jr.'s reintroduction to American racism (he had gotten a taste of it in 1935) came even before the family reached New York Harbor. On board the ship, the family, exhausted and seasick, went to sit down for dinner in the ship's main dining room where they were tersely informed that the ship's policy required colored passengers to take their meals in their rooms. Offended and wholly unwilling to comply, Paul and Essie, with a wide-eyed Paul Jr. in tow, walked conspicuously to the middle of the main dining room and occupied a vacant table until some acceptable arrangements could be made. They were eventually served in that dining room, the ship's racist policy notwithstanding.[48]

Essie had covered a lot of ground since she left the United States in 1928. She had been to many of the places she had once dreamed of, and had explored lands she never thought she would see. It seemed as if the whole decade she had been packing or unpacking, booking passage on ships, trains, and airplanes every month or so, obtaining visas and checking into hotels or setting up new living quarters. In coming home to New York in 1939, Essie felt a great comfort, a great sense of place and belonging that had eluded her in Europe and Russia, and even in Africa. The peace allowed her to reflect on her travels and make some broad connections between the people and places now animating her memories, and her new expanded sense of her own identity. Essie had left the United States in 1928 as a young mother, ambitious, easily impressed, and idealistic. She returned a seasoned traveler, experienced writer, emergent activist, budding anthropologist, and woman of deepening political convictions. She now saw herself as an advocate for the colonized world, an ally of the socialist (and communist) world, and in some respects a nascent feminist.[49]

eight

RETURNING HOME AND
FINDING A NEW VOICE,
1939-1945

Dipping into the business of making a NEW WORLD.
Eslanda Robeson

The Robesons received an enthusiastic welcome from their friends and family upon their return to New York City in 1939. Essie's longtime friend Hattie Bolling, who had helped Paul and Essie to elope in 1921, and who had been supportive of Paul Jr. and his grandmother during their time in the States in 1935, opened her home to them until they could get resettled. The Robesons stayed with Hattie and her husband, Buddy, for several weeks, until Essie found a lovely five-bedroom place in the Robert Morris Apartments at 555 Edgecomb Avenue in the heart of Harlem. Essie, Paul, and Paul Jr. spent over a year in that apartment together.[1] During that time, they reconnected with old friends and worked to relaunch Paul's U.S.-based career. As for Essie, she began positioning herself to become a much more vocal advocate for the causes and ideals she believed in.

Essie was excited to see her Harlem buddies again. She and Minnie Patterson immediately reconnected. Three days after Essie's arrival back in New York, the two old friends were traipsing about town together, most likely shopping, running errands, and catching up. A gossip columnist reported spotting them one Sunday afternoon catching the Fifth Avenue bus at 135th Street on their way to some unknown destination.[2] Essie adored Minnie and Hattie and the feeling was mutual. They were her sisters, her support system, and her emotional anchors, not to mention a great source of fun and laughter. She loved them dearly. Being close to them again must have made Essie feel centered in a way she had not felt for some time.

In 1939 Paul did a short stint in the play *John Henry* at Philadelphia's Erlanger Theatre, then embarked on a concert tour in 1940 with Larry Brown. Essie was pursuing her own passions and trying to find her niche. She reached out to old friends and made new ones. Essie continued to enjoy the people and the stimulation that Harlem represented, but she also longed for a spacious, quiet place to write and care for her aging mother.[3] Thus in June 1941 the extended family moved to Enfield, Connecticut, a hilly, pastoral community three hours from New York City, where Essie orchestrated the purchase and restoration of a large estate known as "The Beeches." The elegant entranceway of the house was graced with four imposing white pillars, and the lavish two-acre estate had a swimming pool, bowling alley, and several acres of land as a buffer from the outside world.[4] The purchase of the Beeches was extravagant in one sense, but Essie may have justified it as a practical decision as well, since it could accommodate her extended family. The Robesons also entertained a steady stream of visitors whom Essie enjoyed immensely. She managed to purchase the house for a very good price and even informally surveyed the neighbors before she moved in to make sure they had no problems with having a Negro family in the neighborhood.[5]

Paul, meanwhile, was traveling all over the country and around the globe, performing to sold-out crowds, offering eloquent political critiques of racism and fascism, and lending his support to the growing labor and civil rights movements. He also spoke in hopeful and glowing terms about the Soviet Union—a place, he argued, where racism had been virtually destroyed. Paul's international experiences, and his systematic study of both culture and politics, including a careful study of Marxism somewhere along the way, had led him to move steadily to the left in his thinking. He was an ally, although never an official member, of the U.S. Communist Party, and he took great interest in Socialist and Communist movements worldwide, as did Essie. It was a volatile time in world politics and what Essie made of it all is still a bit unclear. In August of 1939 the Soviets made a pragmatic pact with the Germans which ended with Hitler's invasion of the Soviet Union in June of 1941. Throughout it all Essie was both pro-Soviet and militantly anti-fascist.

Paul's public presence was much sought after during and immediately after World War II. A brilliant orator and sharp-edged intellectual, Paul was also a gifted artist who moved audiences with his portrayal of Othello and stirred them with his rendition of "Old Man River." He enjoyed an international following and a large and devoted U.S. fan base. Paul's successful segue into films in the 1930s only added to his fame. In many respects, Paul reached the pinnacle of his celebrity as a political figure and artist after the Robesons returned from England. In 1940, the widely distributed African American newspaper *The Chicago Defender* proclaimed Paul Robeson a source of hope and pride for Black America and unequivocally "the greatest of the artists we have produced."[6] That was high praise indeed and well deserved.

Because of his success and demanding travel schedule, Paul did not have much time to spend at the family's Enfield home. But he also chose not to spend much time there. Even when he was in the area, he often slept in friends' apartments in Manhattan or at the small apartment Essie rented for him in the Bollings' building in Harlem, where Larry Brown also had a flat.[7] He enjoyed the Connecticut house as a retreat but not as the place he came back to every night.

While Paul was doing his share of solo traveling after their return from England, Essie decided to do a little independent traveling of her own. The trans-Atlantic move and the task of resettling the family in New York had been stressful, and she had always wanted to visit Central America. So in the summer of 1940, she booked an adventuresome little excursion: a passage on a cargo ship that would take her to multiple countries in the region and deposit her in Mexico, where she planned to meet up with her old friend Fernando Castillo and his family. She was so excited about the trip that she wrote to her friend, Indian independence leader, Jawarhalal Nehru to tell him she was going: "I will go armed with my camera. I hope to wander around in the interesting places in the region."[8] Even though her passport application stated that the trip was for "professional work in anthropology," Essie's trip to Central America and Mexico was mostly for pleasure.[9] The planned itinerary and surprise detours are testimony to her adventuresome spirit.

Essie got as far as Panama when her little excursion took an unexpected turn. The cargo ship, on which she was the only passenger except for the crew, was diverted to a neighboring country to pick up more cargo. She was told she would have to disembark and make other arrangements for the remainder of her journey. "Well what to do?" she pondered in her notebook. The answer she came up with was to hurry off the ship and to "hotel Washington in Colón," where she was fortunate to find an available room. Essie took the disruption of itinerary in stride. She did some shopping and explored the town before booking passage on another ship, the Royal Netherlands *S.S. Crynssen*, which was scheduled to depart for Costa Rica the following day. Essie landed next in Puerto Limón, Costa Rica. There she encountered "the poorest most desolate looking people" she had seen, living in dilapidated shacks situated among coconut palms, banana trees, and coffee plantations. Curious about the variations in phenotype among the people, she learned that some were African-descended Jamaicans who had been brought over as agricultural workers. This was yet another branch of the African Diaspora that interested her. After taking a rickety train that climbed for five hours up into the hills, she arrived at the capital of San José, where she relaxed and explored for a few more days. Despite the grinding poverty, Essie described the landscape as "beautiful, unspoiled and fascinating."[10]

Essie always enjoyed meeting people when she traveled. She was open, curious, and eager to engage and informally interview her fellow travelers. It is this attitude that caused her to meet "Miss. Nina Thomas," a young woman from Washington, D.C., who like Essie was traveling alone in Costa Rica on a little holiday. They met in a local shop and struck up a conversation. Nina invited Essie to be part of a four-person tour group that was planning to get up early the next morning and visit the summit of the local volcano. Essie agreed without hesitation. This would prove to be a scary and dangerous jaunt. The group departed from their hotel with a tour guide at 1:00 A.M., well before sunrise. After being transported by a car into the mountains, they rode on horseback in the dark until they reached the mountain trail, which was "slippery from the heavy rain." The group traveled "over narrow slippery trails, rough log bridges, over chasms, [and] along a narrow trail clinging to the edge of the precipice" until they "reached the summit of the Irazu Volcano 11,322 feet up."[11] The view alone was worth what it took to get there, but Essie was relieved to get back to her hotel safely several hours later. She took a Pan American Airlines flight early the next morning to Guatemala City, where she had a wonderful leisurely and uneventful stay until moving on to Mexico.

The highlight of Essie's trip that summer was the visit she paid to her old friend Fernando Castillo, the young Spanish solider who had guaranteed her and Paul safe passage from Valencia to Madrid and back during the war and who had charmed and befriended them along the way. He and his wife, Magda, and their young child were now in exile, living in a modest house outside Mexico City. Essie enjoyed the few days she spent with them eating, recounting stories, and even going out to a local hotel to hear music and to dance. Essie returned home on September 5 exhausted, stimulated, and glad to be home.

The following year, 1941, Essie took another trip on her own that proved to be inspiring in an entirely different way. She had never spent much time in the U.S. South even though her mother's South Carolina roots were very much a part of the family lore. In November she decided to head south on her own to spend a little time with old friends and get a closer look at Black Southern life, including the notorious system of Jim Crow segregation. She first went to Atlanta, staying with Professor Ira Reid and his wife, Gladys, who was a classmate of Essie's at University of Illinois. She had known the couple in Harlem. Reid, a noted social scientist, had been recruited to teach at Atlanta University, where, for a time, he also edited the journal *Phylon.* The Reids then took Essie on a brief regional tour, passing through Mississippi, continuing to New Orleans to visit with friends at Dillard University, and finally making a stop in Tuskegee, Alabama, so Essie could see the place. Essie was impressed with the "very keen" southern Black students that she met. Ira Reid, who had previously done research on Negro workers, had recently written the study *The Negro in the American Economic System,* which may have been a topic of their dinner conversations during Essie's visit. Another likely topic of dinner conversation was the tumultuous state of the world. The Great Depression raged on. Fascism was spreading through Europe. And, even though Essie and her friends could not have known, it was the eve of the attack on Pearl Harbor and the United States' entry into World War II.[12]

As Essie moved around the country and the world, and even when she was at home in Connecticut, she became the object of government surveillance. By 1943 she was being watched by U.S. intelligence because of her increasingly outspoken political views, as well as the prominence of her equally outspoken husband. The FBI went so far as to question Essie's neighbors about her activities, her habits—even her houseguests, mail deliveries, and travel patterns. The FBI may have been a bit disappointed with the results. For the most part, Essie got along with her fellow Enfield residents. She participated in civic organizations and took part in school events. She was "a fine woman," one neighbor told undercover agents who came around snooping, adding that she was "one hundred percent American," even though she did subscribe to a communist newspaper. Others reiterated the point. Another neighbor was not so kind. She reported "the Subject and her husband, Paul Robeson, who are communists, and who are bitter against the white race."[13] All this was duly noted in a growing FBI file on both Essie and Paul.

At this juncture, in 1943, Paul was consumed with *Othello.* He was performing the coveted role on Broadway, a high point in his already stellar career. There were rehearsals and daily preparations for his appearances. He made it back to Connecticut infrequently. While an issue of *Look* magazine from the 1940s featured the Robesons as a handsome and happy "Negro" family in a beautiful home and enjoying what looked to be the perfect life, this idyllic domestic portrait was misleading. Paul was intimately involved with two other women at the time: his longtime friend Freda Diamond, and the German-born actress Uta Hagen, who was playing Desdemona opposite him in *Othello* on Broadway.

Hurtful as that was for Essie, she no longer viewed Paul's extramarital affairs as cheating per se. They had reached an agreement according to which each partner was free to do as he or she pleased with regard to sex and romance. The reality, of course, was that it was much easier for a man to exercise the privilege of free sexual expression than it was for a woman. And Paul's high-profile celebrity status, intellectual acuity, and exceptional good looks gave him even more romantic options than most men. Yet he was also constrained in a way that Essie was not: the potential threat to his reputation and career if those relationships (especially the interracial ones) became public was great. And his unabashedly militant politics meant he had plenty of critics willing to conjure up a scandal.

As their marital arrangement evolved, Essie settled for the security of knowing that Paul would never leave her and that she would continue to enjoy the respect and recognition that she had earned as Mrs. Paul Robeson. She and Paul lived parallel but gently overlapping lives in the 1940s. They were not officially separated but they moved at their own rhythms, often in different directions. They were dutiful and loyal, and sometimes affectionate, and there was an underlying time-tested friendship and familiarity between them that Essie seemed to value enough to accommodate the rest. And their deepening political convictions increasingly tied them together as well.

And they shared Paul Jr., of course. Essie devoted a great deal of her attention to her only child after the move to Connecticut. When the family first moved to the Beeches, Paul Jr. attended Enfield High School, but he later transferred to another public school just over the border in Massachusetts that focused on science and engineering and was a better fit for his evolving intellectual interests.[14] Years later, he recalled admiringly that his mother never missed a single one of his athletic or academic events during his high school years.[15] Essie took great pride in her teenage son's accomplishments. She was especially pleased when in 1943 he was accepted at Cornell University to study engineering.

As Paul Jr. matured into a young man, Essie took all the more seriously the task of building her own social, political, and professional community. In September of 1943 she accepted an invitation to widen her circle even more. The anti-racist Southern writer Lillian Smith had decided to invite an interracial group of twenty or so influential women to talk and socialize for two days at her mountain retreat in Georgia. The state's segregationist laws made the gathering wholly illegal and Smith knew she was taking a risk even convening it. Those who accepted her invitation included Fellowship of Reconciliation secretary Constance Rumbough; lawyer and advocate Thomasina Johnson; sociologist Belle Boone Beard; Sadie Mays, educator and wife of Morehouse president Benjamin Mays; the venerable activist and agitator Mary Church Terrell; and Essie Goode Robeson.

Smith's invitation read as follows: "Perhaps while we are together we shall as eighteen women of intelligence and ability and good will, work out with one another some interesting plans and projects that may be valuable to both races. I should like to think that out of this little gathering something very fine and beautiful would come. . . . I am therefore inviting from the Negro race probably its most powerful and influential women leaders," as well as a handful of courageous and forward-thinking white women.[16] Essie was intrigued by the invitation and readily accepted.

The women laughed, talked, argued, danced, and shared meals together. Perhaps some new relationships were begun and new insights obtained: we do know that the following year Smith published her controversial best-selling book *Strange Fruit* about racism and interracial sex in a small Southern town. The event at Lillian Smith's country house may not have been as transformative in the ways that Smith had hoped it would be, but for Essie, the women there became part of her growing network of friends and allies.

The events of 1943 bolstered Essie and set the stage for a more defined public role of her own. Although Essie had been engaged in intellectual and political explorations independent of Paul for some time, her activities would soon crystallize into a serious career as an anticolonial crusader and a peace and freedom activist and journalist. Three sets of developments signaled this new level of public activism: her work with the Council on African Affairs and the 1945 publication of her book *African Journey;* her second trip to Africa in 1946; and her work with the electoral campaigns of Henry Wallace and the Progressive Party beginning in 1948.

By this time, the Council on African Affairs, an outgrowth of The International Committee on Africa that Essie and Paul had helped to launch with their friend Max Yergan in 1937, had become the most prominent African American organization advocating consistently on behalf of Africa in the postwar years. The group held press conferences, issued statements, and hosted forums and meetings for Africans visiting the United States, and despite communist and left-wing members, it had a considerable mainstream following.[17] Moreover, while the council's focus was Africa, its political interests did not stop there. Yergan and others spoke out repeatedly for the need to support anti-colonial and anti-fascist struggles worldwide, especially the one ongoing in India and which Yergan knew well.[18]

Essie was not an official member of the organization at first, despite her early contribution. But even without formal recognition, she participated in meetings and public programs. She also contributed frequently to the group's main publication, the journal *New Africa*.[19] Space on the council's letterhead was reserved largely for prominent Black male leaders, including Paul Robeson, who headed the group; Alphaeus Hunton; W. E. B. Du Bois; and academics like Essie's old friend Ralph Bunche. Howard University president Mordecai Johnson and attorney Hubert Delaney, the widow of Essie's friend Clare, who later became a New York judge, were also involved for awhile.[20] Still, in terms of the actual leadership and day-to-day work of the organization, women played a significant role, and it was an eclectic group of women at that, from an aging and sometime mainstream Mary Church Terrell to the Pan-Africanist Amy Ashwood Garvey.[21] By 1943, Essie's friend Charlotta Bass, radical publisher of the *California Eagle*, a West Coast Negro newspaper, had joined the council. During the war years, mainstream Black political figures like Channing Tobias and Rayford Logan were also affiliated, as was Essie's friend and former neighbor in Harlem, sociologist E. Franklin Frazier. Rosebery Bokwe, the South African physician whose wedding Essie had attended in 1936, and Leonard Barnes, the British writer who had piqued Essie's curiosity about South Africa in 1932, also became members of the council.[22]

Initially, the council sought to influence American foreign policy on Africa by trying to persuade diplomats and government officials to change course. In 1944, a three-person council delegation met with representatives of the State Department's new Division of African Affairs to lobby for policies to benefit the colonized people of Africa. Ironically, even as the council was trying to educate government officials about Africa, the FBI had most of the leaders of the council, including Essie and Paul, under steady surveillance.[23] Historian Penny Von Eschen argues that opponents of the council frequently, and unfairly, tried to depict the group as simply an appendage of the Communist Party. In one report, the FBI deemed the council a subversive organization that was whipping up "unrest" among American Negroes by publicizing "alleged" injustices in Africa. Needless to say, the group did not make much headway at the State Department, and its members soon directed their energies elsewhere.[24] Their change in focus paralleled a shift in postwar politics. Two factors were key. One, the United States and Soviet Union became fierce adversaries, and two, Washington and Moscow began to compete for the allegiances of emerging African nations as part of the growing Cold War rivalry.

In 1945, the war ended. A quarter of a million people had died, including thousands of African Americans, and the geopolitical world was in flux. There were rumblings about decolonization and new states on the horizon, with centuries-old empires crumbling under their own weight. The balance of power in the world was shifting, and at the center of these seismic changes was the embryonic United Nations, a successor to the stillborn League of Nations that had been formed after World War I. There was promise that the United Nations would be a forum for democratic change and, with decolonization, there was hope that African and Asian people would have a place at the table. More radical actors hoped it would at least be a level battlefield for defining the postcolonial world, even if real freedom still seemed a long way off.

Many activists both inside and outside the council were eager to make sure that the interests of Africa and particularly the issue of decolonization were top on the agenda of the newly formed United Nations. They were hopeful that inroads could be made there, that the time was ripe. After all, Franklin D. Roosevelt had signed on to the Atlantic Charter, a forward-looking document that listed "self-determination" for colonized people as a postwar goal. Even though Roosevelt died two weeks before the U.N. founding conference, held in San Francisco in May 1945, council members were still cautiously hopeful that the new international body would be instrumental in the fight for African independence. Authors of editorials and columns appearing in Council on African Affairs' publications leading up to the San Francisco conference insisted that decolonization be on the U.N. agenda.

That specific demand was not realized, but the struggle continued. As historian Vijay Prashad and others have observed, the United Nations did in fact become a critical institution in the fight against colonialism and neo-colonialism, a place to garner international attention and a springboard for building solidarity among former colonies. Although rife with contradictions and clearly limited in its practical political power, the United Nations was at the center of negotiations for a better and more just future for the peoples of Africa, Asia, South and Central America, and the Caribbean.

Essie perceived the organization's importance early on and was thrilled to be one of two council representatives, along with Max Yergan, to travel to San Francisco to attend the founding conference.[25] Essie would spend the next two decades documenting the evolution of the United Nations and observing, critiquing, and prodding various U.N. bodies, committees, and officials to realize the organization's promise of promoting greater peace and justice in the world.[26]

On May 13, 1945, Essie was met at the San Francisco airport by Max and Lena Yergan. A small delegation of women, including publisher, Charlotta Bass, also welcomed her to town by displaying a four-foot banner on the side of a car that read "Welcome Mrs. Robeson."[27] They then presented her with a corsage. Essie was touched by this thoughtful recognition. Soon after arriving in the city, she stood on a hilltop with the Pacific Ocean and the Golden Gate Bridge in the distance and paused to marvel at the beauty of the city and the great sense of possibility that the birth of the United Nations represented.

After receiving a key to the council office and "observer" credentials for the U.N. meeting, Essie spent the next few days listening, debating, and absorbing all that was going on around her.[28] Even as an unofficial observer, Essie was able to actively participate in the events surrounding the conference. There were even special daily briefings for observers, so they too felt a part of the process, and nongovernmental advocacy and human rights organizations took the opportunity to meet and discuss global politics and the conference proceedings among themselves. Sessions included presentations by experts on issues ranging from the veto at the United Nations to the broader issue of human rights.[29] Essie marveled at the spectacle of it all. It was "a fantastic experience," she wrote in a very personal essay. "Alice in Wonderland couldn't have felt half so adventurous as I did. For I was a NOBODY, dipping into the business of making a NEW WORLD." She was only half-serious about being a "nobody," as she was quick to point out in the very same essay.[30] Still she deeply appreciated the historic and global significance of the founding event, its political limitations notwithstanding.

One of Essie's few criticisms of the conference came out of her nascent feminist or pro-feminist sensibilities. She complained that despite the pivotal role of women in revolutionary and anti-colonial struggles the world over, as well as in the fight to defeat fascism, they were woefully underrepresented in San Francisco. "Officialdom has a nineteenth century attitude in thinking and behavior toward women in the fast moving, radically changing twentieth century," she wrote about the conference. She added, "The men have failed in their job to date: the world has suffered war after war, each one more destructive than the preceding," and yet men were still in charge of designing a new postwar world.[31] In search of likeminded women, Essie attended an all-day forum for official and unofficial female participants entitled "Women's Share in Implementing the Peace." She was impressed by the caliber of the discussion and the company. Women from all over the globe, speaking different languages, coming from different political and cultural contexts, all sat down together to talk about common concerns and how the United Nations might contribute to finding solutions.

Essie's writing and thinking about women and gender were not always consistent. At times she was highly critical of women. For instance in an exchange with Pearl Buck in 1949 she argued that many American women brought problems on themselves, and were unnecessarily frivolous and demanding of their husbands. At other times, however, she was quite staunch in her defense of women as the real muscle behind the work of families, organizations, and social movements. She seemed to make a distinction between "American women," a term that in her exchange with Pearl Buck represents white middle-class women, and another demographic altogether that she refers to in her many observations and comments elsewhere: poor and working-class women, radical women, Black women, and women under colonialism. In these instances she talks about the toughness and political savvy of "women."[32] Reflecting on the establishment of the United Nations and its failure to fully incorporate women's leadership, Essie wrote: "Many of us thought with familiar tolerance, these men how they talk, and think they run the office, the house, the children and us; but it is we, the secretaries, wives, mothers who really know what it's all about."[33] Here, as elsewhere, Essie acknowledges the inequality between men and women and stresses the untapped leadership ability of ordinary women.

At the San Francisco meeting Essie ran into a number of old friends and acquaintances from various parts of the world, and various parts of her past. There were parties, receptions, luncheons, and plenty of opportunities for informal connections and conversations. Essie must have been especially pleased to have been invited to a cocktail party hosted by her friend Vijaya Lakshmi Pandit, an Indian activist and diplomat, and sister of future Prime Minister Nehru, who would become the first female president of the U.N. General Assembly. Pandit's distinguished political career represented the kind of leadership that Essie thought many more women were capable of at all levels.

After the U.N. gathering, Essie used what she had seen and heard there as fodder for her writing and public speaking. In June, she delivered a powerful lecture at Tufts University entitled "Background and Trends in the World." In this lecture, she underscored the centrality of Africa and the importance of African independence to establishing a lasting world peace. As she explained, "It is impossible for any reasonable person to hope for peace in the world as two-thirds of the people remain in colonial slavery."[34] She argued that the establishment of the United Nations represented significant progress toward this end, but pushed her listeners to consider the enormity of the task that lay ahead and insist that the United Nations be a catalyst for ending colonialism.

After the U.N. convention, the Council on African Affairs' leadership asked Essie to use her firsthand knowledge of Africa, her anthropological expertise, and her writing skills to create a compelling pamphlet about anti-colonial struggles and U.S.-Africa policy that would be accessible to a popular audience. "What Do the People of Africa Want?" was the result. She wrote the document in a conversational tone and directed her words at a generally uninformed or ill-informed American reader. The purpose of her twenty-three-page pamphlet was to help sway public opinion and influence policymakers at a moment when attention was still trained on creating a new balance of power. Essie wanted, first, to convince her readers of Africa's importance to the United States and the world. Second, she wanted to counter the myths that Africans were primitive and incapable of self-governance. And third, she wanted to establish the principles of independence and self-determination as being morally right and just.

The pamphlet opens by describing the great African civilizations of the past, from the Hausa and Ashanti systems of self-governance to the sophisticated artistry of the Bahima people of Uganda.[35] Essie went on to outline sub-Saharan Africa's importance as a major supplier of minerals, palm oil, cocoa, and rubber to the growing world economy, and described how all of that production had been facilitated by the injustices of colonial rule and the appropriation of Black labor.[36] Not surprisingly, she held up South Africa for particularly harsh criticism. Throughout the pamphlet, Essie made sure to avoid depicting Africans as hapless victims of oppression and to acknowledge their active resistance and efforts to determine their own fate. She also stressed the important role played by women in this regard. "African women too are organizing," she reported, listing numerous examples.[37] Essie concluded her short polemical pamphlet by arguing that thousands of African colonial subjects had fought on the side of the Allied forces in the war, and now deserved some justice and peace of their own. She further insisted that Africans were also entitled to the "four freedoms" that President Roosevelt had spoken about so eloquently in 1941: freedom of speech, freedom from want, freedom of worship, and freedom from fear. "Until the African people, along with all the peoples of the earth, achieve these simple, reasonable, dignified, human minimum essentials, this war—which includes the peace—will not be won," she wrote. "It will not be finished."[38] The Council on African Affairs distributed the pamphlet widely.

In 1946, much of Essie's work through the council focused on South Africa, where the Black, "colored," and Asian populations were still suffering from a stranglehold of racist and repressive laws and organizers were resisting by encouraging a major strike by Black miners. Still, her interests were broad and extended throughout the continent.[39] To keep up-to-date and fired up about her anti-colonial work, Essie relied on her network of contacts in southern Africa and beyond, who wrote to her regularly between 1946 and 1949. Among these contacts were her friend Newell Snow Booth, who was a Methodist minister and educator, and his wife, Esma. In 1946, the Booths traveled from Rhodesia (now Zimbabwe) into Mozambique before settling in the Congo for an extended period.

Essie also received letters regularly from Darrell and Mildred Randall, her friends in Johannesburg, who gave eyewitness accounts of the tense political situation in South Africa. They went on to become close friends of Eduardo Mondlane and supporters of the Front for the Liberation of Mozambique (FRELIMO).[40] On the eve of the 1948 election in which the all-white Afrikaner National Party consolidated power under the apartheid regime, they wrote: "More gold and diamonds have been discovered. . . . This 'glittering prosperity,' however, has been overshadowed by the increasing concern about the flow of

Africans to the cities, which has continued like a tidal wave that cannot be stopped. The housing situation for non-white people has become worse and the racial tensions of the area have continued to mount."[41] Six months later, the Randalls wrote again: "En route back to Johannesburg we visited some of the land reserved for Africans—land that is overcrowded, dry and suffering from the most serious soil erosion. It is no wonder that young Africa is surging to the cities—in despair and hope for a better life!" They went on to describe the growing "bitterness and distrust between the white and non-white peoples," and the election of a communist to the South African parliament who was then prevented from speaking to Blacks in Johannesburg for fear he would spark unrest. They concluded, "The government appears to be getting more repressive."[42]

In the winter of 1948, Essie received another set of letters from Darrell and Mildred. The conservative Afrikaner Party had just come to power. "This was a White man's election," they wrote. "Some mass meetings of protest were held, in which a few thousand Africans, Indians and Coloreds marched through the streets demanding the democratic right to vote for their own candidates. . . . Competent observers here ominously conclude that Africa is a tinderbox!"[43] Nine months later, they wrote again, "The developments which we described in our earlier letters have been more serious and far-reaching. Among these developments include the formal abolishment of the Native Representative Council without providing any alternative for the Africans to express their own voice. In the meanwhile African nationalism is surging forth! There is a growing demand for complete non-cooperation with all white people, with subsequent rejection of older African leaders 'guilty of too much patience.' At the moment, Africans are waiting for new leaders, and the type of leadership which may emerge is likely to influence the future of the entire continent."[44]

Essie received regular communication from associates and colleagues in other parts of Africa as well, including correspondence from Ruth Longstaff in Ganta, Liberia; Richard and Edith Scotti in Gombari, Congo; Lavinia Scott in Natal, South Africa; and Reverend Omar Hartzler and his wife, Eva, from Malanje, Angola.[45] She had personal and political differences with many of the missionaries she corresponded with—some of whom openly touted their soul-saving agendas—but she still relied on their firsthand accounts to keep informed about what was going on across the continent, and to provide her with valuable intelligence information from official sources that she could not have obtained otherwise.

In November 1946, the council hosted a visit to the United States by several prominent South African activists. They spoke to an overflow crowd at Harlem's historic Abyssinian Baptist Church in an event timed to memorialize the South African miners who had been killed during the 1946 strikes.[46] The keynote speaker from the African National Congress (ANC) was none other than Dr. Alfred B. Xuma, the president of the ANC from 1940 to 1949 and one of Essie's hosts in South Africa in 1936.[47] She and Paul Jr. had been well taken care of at Xuma's home in Sofiatown, and the ANC leader had impressed her greatly.[48] Essie too had made an impression on Xuma during that visit. He later wrote that when he heard her speak at the Bantu Men's Social Centre in Sofiatown about the links between the struggles of African Americans and Africans, he felt moved and inspired.[49] Xuma kept in touch with Essie after her visit.[50] In fact, she was terribly disappointed that when he came to New York, she was not able to be there to greet him. Rather she was on another African journey in 1946, this time to the Congo.

A few days after the rally at Abyssinian, dozens of council members and two hundred labor activists picketed the South African consulate in New York to protest that government's repressive and racist policies. The council also published three major papers on South Africa around this time. These efforts were geared toward not only exposing the discrimination and oppression in South Africa proper, but also preventing the racist South African government from trying to annex the adjacent territory of South West Africa (later the independent country of Namibia). They hoped to pressure U.S. politicians, embolden U.N. delegates, and rouse public interest on the subject. Essie joined this chorus of impassioned voices against the actions of the South African government. In a long speech at the Town Hall Auditorium in New York, Essie condemned moves by the South African government to take power in South West Africa (the area that would become Namibia), using her new knowledge of the growing body of international laws administered by the still embryonic United Nations to help make her case. "A mandate is a territory to be governed in the interests of its inhabitants, and of the world at large, and the mandated people are to be prepared for an eventual independence," she explained to her audience. She also used her knowledge of South African history and law to underscore her point, and to warn that an undemocratic colonial system was about to be unjustly imposed on an even larger population.[51]

In order to make the geopolitics of southern Africa as clear and relevant as possible to her American audience and to once again underscore her international view of the Black experience, Essie drew comparisons to the plight of Black Americans in the segregated South. Mocking the veracity of South African leader Jan Smuts's claim that his government had polled Blacks about the issue of annexation, Essie said, "This is comparable to saying that Bilbo [a racist senator and ardent segregationist from Mississippi] made a survey of Negro opinion in Mississippi." Essie called on the United Nations to reject not only South Africa's request concerning annexation, but also South Africa in general. Essie said the United Nations' moral credibility was on the line, arguing that the international organization had to "seriously consider the grave question of whether it would expose itself to dis-credit in the eyes of the world by harboring in its midst a nation which at the outset violates its fundamental principles of law." South Africa was not ousted, but its request to absorb South West Africa was denied.

In February 1946, Essie gave another public lecture to a crowd of a thousand at the Akron, Ohio, Jewish Center entitled "The Negro's Place in World Affairs." As had become her practice, she used the opportunity to educate her audience not only about Africa, but also about the need for racial democracy in the United States. Essie attacked Senator Bilbo for his filibuster of the Fair Employment Practices Commission and directly challenged his assertion that there was a "Negro problem" in the United States. "We Negroes believe the problem facing America is not a Negro problem but a White problem," she said. Further, "only by making America truly democratic can the problem be solved." A reporter covering the event for a local Black newspaper praised Essie's presentation as demonstrative of a "keen mind and sparkling wit."[52] She had become a polished political orator.

It took Essie more than a decade, but by the mid-1940s she had completed almost all of the requirements for a Ph.D. in anthropology. Family obligations and the war had prevented her from getting her degree at the London School of Economics in the 1930s. But once she settled into life in Connecticut, she enrolled in the nearby Hartford Seminary, a school founded in the late nineteenth century that specialized in training missionaries for work in Africa. While Essie was not particularly interested in the theological side of the curriculum, the seminary was her best option for completing the graduate degree. She completed at least a draft of her thesis, and was listed as a candidate for the doctorate in both 1943 and 1944, but for some reason never defended and was never officially awarded the degree. The experience was useful, however, because it encouraged her to read widely and gave her the tools she needed to sharpen her skills as a writer, researcher, and analyst on Africa. For instance, during her time at Hartford, Essie wrote a paper for Professor Newell Booth's "Background in Africa" course on the discriminatory practices of foreign missions. In the paper, she discussed the pervasiveness of anti-Black racism and the need for missionary groups to combat it by "sharing with," rather than "giving to," African communities.[53]

The graduate curriculum at Hartford was broad in scope and stressed rigorous in-depth readings in preparation for the comprehensive doctoral exams. Essie's reading list included Kant, Hegel, (Henry) Buckle, Nietzsche, and Marx. Essie was a mature student and not interested in being anyone's protégé. She had her own ideas and opinions and did not hesitate to make them known, just as she had done at the London School of Economics. In communicating with Essie about her upcoming exams, one of her advisers, Dr. Charles G. Chakerian, a professor of ethics, made a point to add, "In preparing for your examination, please be sure to be thorough, objective, and ever careful not to mix your own views with those of the authors studied. There will be plenty of opportunity for you to evaluate the various theories."[54] Essie was resistant to being "trained" as a traditional academic. Prof. Chakerian had likely witnessed some of that resistance, and wanted to caution her not to be too opinionated during her exam.

While much of Essie's scholarly interest had been in Africa, she settled on a thesis topic that focused on Blacks in the U.S. context. This may have been a practical decision, since she may well have hoped to complete her degree without further trans-Atlantic travel. The title of her short forty-two-page thesis was "The Negro Problem: An Approach to the Problem of Race Relations in the USA." She had originally intended for her 1936 fieldwork in Uganda to serve as the basis for her thesis, but decided to switch her topic, saving the fieldwork material for a wider audience.[55] The thesis itself was vague and generic.

Essie ultimately included the Uganda material and other data she had collected during her first trip to Africa in the book *African Journey*, published in August 1945. As mentioned earlier, the book was a major milestone in her career and her first scholarly publication. Her 1930 biography of Paul had sold reasonably well, but that was thanks to Paul's celebrity, not her skill as a writer or scholar. This book was altogether different. The result of her own arduous research and fieldwork, the book, a richly detailed, insightful narrative that combined ethnography and travel memoir, essentially chronicled every phase of her 1936 trip through South Africa and Uganda.[56] In time, it would come to be recognized as an important early anthropological text on Africa by a Black American writer, a powerful piece of travel writing, and a treatise against colonialism.

In terms of Essie's writing career, the road from *Paul Robeson, Negro* to *African Journey* was not a smooth one. Between the two projects she had tried her hand at both fiction and nonfiction projects, large and small, and while she had met with some positive responses, there were also some pretty harsh rejections. One especially blunt and insulting rebuff came from the acclaimed film and theatrical producer Herman Shumlin, who in 1944 wrote to Essie that he was extremely "disappointed" with her writing and found it uninspiring and "ponderous," concluding that he was not interested in any potential collaboration with her. Her bounce-back reply one week later was classic Essie, ever tough and resilient. "I'm a gal that can take NO for an answer," she wrote, "and go right ahead and work some more without discouragement. In fact, 'no' has always been a challenge for me."[57] She did not put her pen down or put her typewriter away. She kept on writing, almost in defiance of her critics.

Pearl Buck found *African Journey* so compelling that she encouraged her husband, publisher Richard Walsh, then head of John Day Company, to publish it, which he did. After the book was released and garnered several positive reviews, the speaking invitations started rolling in from across the country, from New York to New Mexico. Essie spoke at bookstores, union halls, and universities about Africa's history and its contemporary challenges. The publicity around Essie's book tour invariably mentioned that she was Mrs. Paul Robeson. Still, her work was increasingly discussed, debated, and praised on its own merits.

From 1945 through at least 1948 Essie was affiliated with the Harold R. Peat Management and booking agency based in New York City. They arranged her speaking engagements for fees ranging between $150 and $350 per lecture. She took more than twenty-two trips in 1947 alone, visiting such places as Johnston, Pennsylvania; Kenton, Ohio; Dallas, Texas; and Ann Arbor, Michigan.[58]

Even though Essie was recognized for her writing and was sought after as a public speaker, she never became an academic insider, never officially completed her Ph.D., and never sought a faculty appointment. In fact, much of her approach to anthropological research and ethnography was at odds with the mainstream of the field. Later, however, historians of the African Diaspora acknowledged the important intellectual and political territory that Essie had staked out. Maureen Mahon, for example, points out that her methodology itself stood in opposition to the conventional wisdom that ethnographers from "the West" had to view the cultures they observed through the lens of the "other," an other that was often deemed primitive, uncivilized, and premodern. Essie sought instead to demonstrate parallels and connections between Africans and African Americans and to document the lives of the sophisticated and capable African people that she had encountered. In her eyes she, as an American Negro, had much in common with her subjects. In addition, as Mahon points out, for Essie anthropology was a tool for liberation, rather than simply an abstract research enterprise.

In many respects the discipline of "anthropology is the child of imperialism," as Kathleen Gough so boldly proclaimed in her controversial 1968 article. From its earliest days, however, it has also uprooted old biases and sometimes inscribed new ones. Essie situated herself deliberately on the margins of the Academy and on the margins of the formal field of anthropology. Her audience was not primarily a scholarly one but a larger public. And she refused to embrace some of the basic paradigms of early anthropologists, specifically the cleavage between primitive/simple societies and complex/advanced/civilized ones.[59] After her 1936 trip Essie was eager to confront the world's racist and wrongheaded views of Africa. The book she finally published nearly ten years later was one step in that direction.

African Journey established Essie as an expert on Africa, a public recognition she had long desired and had worked hard to attain. She thus became part of a small community of Africanists who researched and wrote about the continent and frequently shared information and resources with one another. Despite her deliberate marginality to the mainstream of the field of anthropology and "African Studies," Essie did feel a part of an intellectual community, one that included, among others, Ralph Bunche, who had solicited Essie's advice about his research and his plans to visit Africa. On the eve of his trip, she loaned him her treasured Cine-Kodak camera, a special gift she had received from Paul. She also provided him with lengthy instructions regarding when and how he might use it so that he wouldn't offend the Africans he was capturing on film. Bunche was enormously grateful and eager to share his findings and photos with Essie when he returned. His itinerary in Southern Africa was very similar to hers. He visited some of the same locations, and met with some of the same people.[60]

When her book came out, Essie was especially pleased and proud to receive praise from those in her extended community whom she admired. A note of congratulations from her old friend, sociologist E. Franklin Frazier, along with the promise to attend one of her public lectures, meant a lot to Essie.[61] Also among the positive reviews was one in the *Amsterdam News* by Prince A. A. Nwafor Orizu, whose glowing praise for the book deemed it a turning point for writings about Africa and more precisely, a direct "challenge to the Negroes in America" to engage seriously and respectfully with the politics and realities on the African continent.[62]

African Journey was an important professional landmark for Essie, but it was much more than that. It also represented the payment of a debt to all the people who had opened their homes and shared their thoughts and ideas with her during her travels in 1936. A lot had transpired in the intervening decade, but Essie was pleased and relieved to finally have completed the book, which she dedicated to "the brothers and sisters who will know whom I mean."[63]

After the publication of *African Journey*, Essie was officially invited to join the Council on African Affairs. She had been a de facto member for years, but *African Journey*, and her growing visibility as a public speaker, seemed to give her a new air of legitimacy.[64] In announcing her appointment, the council's executive director, Max Yergan, issued a press release touting Essie as the author of a newly published book that had "received extremely high commendation from critics and reviewers." He went on to praise her expertise on Africa, expressing his hope that she would "contribute toward widening the influence of the Council and increasing American understanding of Africa's vital relationship to world security and peace." Of course, Yergan also mentioned that she was the "wife of Paul Robeson," president of the council.[65]

During this period, Essie strained to assert her independence from Paul, but she also continued to crave a personal connection with him. She even occasionally fantasized that she and Paul might recapture some of the romance they had once shared. In April 1945, Essie decided to travel to Chicago in the hopes of celebrating Paul's forty-seventh birthday and to toast the Chicago opening of *Othello*. The Shakespeare classic, starring Paul and Uta Hagen, had enjoyed great success on Broadway before going on tour. Essie hinted in a letter to her sister-in-law Marian Forsythe that she was hoping for a reunion of sorts. "I took off 20 pounds, exercised myself hard and flat . . . and have just had my hair done," she boasted. "What do you know? I think the big boy will be quite pleased. I'm at my best. And now is the time!!!"[66]

Essie's hopes for a reunion may not have been far-fetched. As Paul moved around the country and the world, and despite his other amorous relationships, Essie was his rock—and even with lapses in communication, she was never too far out of reach. Yes, there were others in whom he confided and to whom he pledged his affection, but Essie was the steady supporter, adviser, confidante, and ally without whom he could not live. And the tender attraction they once shared was not altogether extinguished. Paul had written to Essie from the road, calling her his "Darling Sweet," in 1943, indicating that he missed her "terribly" and concluding, "Lots of love. Write me—Love me—Hug me often. I adore you—Love you. Paul."[67] A month later, she wrote to him, "I love you, Mr. Robeson," and signed her letter, "love and kisses."[68]

Whatever Essie's hopes were when she showed up in Chicago in April 1945, the situation was more complicated than she realized. It is rumored that Bob Rockmore, Paul's lawyer and financial adviser, invited Essie to come to town for fear there might be a scene if two of the other women Paul was seeing romantically—Uta Hagen and Freda Diamond—were there at the same time. In this view, Bob thought that Essie's presence, as Paul's wife, would thwart any open conflict between the two mistresses. Regardless of others' motivations, Essie was hurt by the reception she received. Paul was friendly to Essie but he was surrounded by a coterie of other actors and admirers (although Freda Diamond, as it turns out, did not show up). When Essie later expressed her unhappiness to Paul, she did so by focusing on rather impersonal things: her shabby hotel accommodations at the Sherman Hotel (in contrast to Paul's and the Rockmores' more luxurious accommodations at another hotel), and the dismay of hotel workers when they realized that Paul's "negro wife" was being so poorly treated. While Paul had not actually made the hotel arrangements, he had not taken care of Essie properly, to her mind. She considered the whole situation an "insult," and declared that if they were to travel in tandem in the future, she would make her own arrangements.[69] It seems likely that her outrage about her hotel room had much more to do with feeling romantically spurned by her husband than anything else.

Essie's anger eventually passed. She continued with her work and travel, and she was by Paul's side just six months later when he received from the NAACP the prestigious Spingarn Medal for outstanding achievement. For his part, Paul continued to support Essie as a writer and to encourage her career aspirations. He was especially proud of the publication of *African Journey*, of which he had read several drafts. On her "big day, the day of publication," she sent him a letter filled with "love and gratitude," and soon afterward he called her from the road to relay his excitement at seeing a copy in a bookstore.[70] Paul and Essie still shared deep emotional attachments. Their relationship was never perfect and their friendship never without tensions, but in the end they took pride in one another's success, and shared many of the same values and political views.

After their return to the United States in 1939, Essie, always independent and outspoken, found her voice and her calling in a new way. She traveled. She wrote. She earned her own reputation, her own accolades, and even her own critics. The Beeches provided her with a welcome retreat, a beautiful haven where she could close herself off from the world when she chose to in order to think and work. At the same time, through her writing, relationships, research, advocacy, and travel, she was more immersed in the world than ever before—and on her own terms.

nine

INTO THE CONGO, 1946

Africa is in revolution.

Eslanda Robeson

By 1946, it had been more than a decade since Essie had first traveled to sub-Saharan Africa, and she was itching to return. Incredible changes were sweeping the continent, and she felt she would be able to speak and write with greater authority if she could see these happenings for herself and once again talk with African people on African soil. In fact, because of her increased work in the Council on African Affairs, as well as her lectures on Africa all over the country, Essie decided that it was essential that she get a firsthand view of these new developments. Through her various professional and personal contacts, she arranged to spend five months in Central Africa, in both the French- and Belgian-controlled areas of the Congo. She would keep a detailed journal to aid in the drafting of articles and lectures upon her return. She also intended to collect, for possible publication, anthropological and ethnographic data about African perceptions and experiences of colonialism.

Despite her determination, it initially seemed as though the trip would simply be too costly and too complicated. Essie did not want to rely on Paul for the money, especially if that meant negotiating with the man he had taken on as his financial manager, Bob Rockmore, whom she did not like. So she first approached her Delta sorority sisters with a promise to do a lecture series upon her return if they would subsidize the trip. Although supportive of her work, they declined.[1] Her next request for funding, to friends in the Black press, was also denied. In the end, then, she turned to Paul for some of the funding she needed, and he agreed. Minimizing costs where she could, and drawing from her royalties from *African Journey*, Essie, undeterred, finally managed to get her ticket and secure a rough itinerary. She was on her way.

Essie left her home in Enfield, Connecticut, on May 22, 1946. She took a 7:31 A.M. train to New York City, then checked luggage at the air terminal on 42nd Street in Manhattan, lunched with her friend Clara Rockmore, and dined with Paul at the Café Society uptown. Paul accompanied her back to the air terminal, where they said their goodbyes and she boarded the shuttle bus bound for La Guardia Airport. Essie and forty-three other passengers took off from La Guardia at 9:00 P.M. It had been a long day, and as she settled into her seat, she was exhausted. The plane stopped in Newfoundland; crossed the Atlantic; refueled in Portugal, Senegal, and Liberia; and finally landed in Leopoldville, Congo.[2]

Essie marveled at how much travel had changed in the decade since she'd last been to Africa. "My first trip to Africa was in 1936," she wrote, and "it took 21 days by ship. This trip to Africa, from New York, to Leopoldville, Belgian Congo, took 34 flying hours." For Essie, the journey itself—with all its ups and downs and detours—was an important and enriching part of her experience. She paused to notice people and scenes along the way, and made detailed notes about them in her journal. She noticed, for example, the type of aircraft she boarded, her fellow passengers, and the vast landscape and seascape beneath her as she moved between continents. She took in "the lights of New York . . . so lovely in the twilight" and a "huge iceberg in the sea" off the coast of Newfoundland, "a great clumsy white block, gently heaving" in the water. Her first aerial view of Africa showed a "dull brown country," but that soon that gave way to views of "a dark heavy tropical green."[3]

At the very outset of this trip Essie was reminded of the complex cultural and social dynamics surrounding her rather unique racial and class profile. Because of her husband's celebrity and her class, she was allowed access into areas of white society where ordinary Black people simply could not go. The lightness of her skin sometimes further cushioned her from the crudest forms of racial discrimination. At first glance, and in an international context, Essie might have easily been mistaken for an Italian, Greek, or Spaniard, rather than an American Negro. Essie navigated this space with awareness, angst, and conscientious care. During her layover in Liberia, for example, she and the other passengers ate dinner in a U.S. military officers' mess hall. She felt sorry for some of the young white soldiers who looked lost and lonely so far from home. She contemplated whether she should intervene and offer to organize some recreational activities, but decided against it. In her words: "I was hog-tied by the fact that this was definitely a WHITE [her emphasis] American base, and complications might arise if I, a Negro, volunteered to help. . . . That would be socializing, and probably VERBOTEN. I would also [have] been very glad indeed to have talked with some of the few Africans I saw around the base, but they were all definitely servants, obviously removed from all white contact, except to serve them. I was afraid if I were to try to talk with them it would create a dilemma for the white officer who was our host, for the other passengers all of whom were white, and for the Pan American crew, all of whom had been charming to me."[4] As if to qualify these statements, she then wrote, "Personally, I don't mind a dilemma, if it's for something important; but I was mindful of the fact that I still had a lot of journey to make with these folks, and that I might be returning home by way of this same base."[5] She had to choose her battles, so she swallowed her impulse to intervene.

Essie's dilemma at the military base was one thing, but she knew when she entered the Congo that she was entering a different kind of battlefield. The fight to impose, and later to defeat, European colonialism in the Congo region had been a bitter and bloody one. The French and the Belgians had argued over control and borders, but the struggle on the ground to subdue and exploit both the land and the people had a shockingly violent history. The only colony of the tiny nation of Belgium, Congo had been conquered in the late 1800s by the ruthless King Leopold II. Historian Adam Hochschild explains that in search of mineral wealth and to extract the country's valuable rubber resources, Leopold authorized the killing of millions of Congolese: some were worked or starved to death, while those who resisted were tortured.[6] The Congo was also the setting for Joseph Conrad's Victorian novel *The Heart of Darkness*, which not only reflected the racism and Eurocentrism of its time, but also depicted Congo as a place where untold atrocities occurred. During the 1940s, however, African resistance was building: there were abundant peasant uprisings, urban riots, and labor strikes both during and immediately after the war.[7] Essie must have known much of this history when she arrived, in part from a CAA newsletter that had covered extensively the situation in Congo.[8] Whatever research she had done beforehand, she arrived with many unanswered questions, eager to see what she could learn from observing the culture, landscape, and people of Congo.

It is unclear what Essie's original plan for lodging had been for when she arrived in Leopoldville, but one of the other passengers on her plane, Gray Russell, a fellow alumnus of the Hartford Seminary, invited her to stay at the Union Mission House when they arrived, and she agreed. She stayed there several days and dined, debated, and attended church services with her new missionary friends.[9] Essie liked Russell. He reminded her of her favorite professor at Hartford, Dr. Newell Booth; both were learned and humble men, sure of their beliefs but eager to hear what others had to say. Still the whole idea of missionary work, of saving the heathen souls of Africa, rubbed Essie the wrong way. Through her travels and studies at Hartford, she had met many missionaries who were of a different mold: tolerant, open, and respectful of the cultures and people they worked with in faraway places.[10] On this trip, unfortunately, she also met the more conservative kind of missionary: judgmental, sin-obsessed, and self-righteous. Essie wrote that two young women from the Moody Bible College in Chicago were "psalm-singing, Bible-reading, tight-lipped folks, full of all kinds of suppressions and repressions, all very sure they have been called by the Lord to do this work."[11] Essie encountered white people who were in Africa for many different reasons, and who harbored a wide range of attitudes and motives.

During her stay at Union Mission House, Essie also had some interesting encounters with Black Congolese who worked on the grounds. On her second day there, as Essie sat on the balcony of her room looking at the river and writing in her journal, a young African woman knocked on the door of her room. Essie described the encounter this way: "She could speak neither English nor French, but she made me understand that she, a Congolese, was welcoming me to the Congo. She was short, stocky, very pleasant, very black with smooth well-groomed skin, and a lovely smile. Very dignified. I showed her Paul's and Pauli's pictures, and she was most interested. She was immaculate in white." Essie delighted in the fact that, even though she was enjoying the privileges afforded almost exclusively to whites, this woman had recognized a kinship with her as an American Negro and wanted to make her feel welcome in Congo.[12]

Essie also had the opportunity to interview Samuel Lutete, the facilities manager for Union Mission House. Quiet, bespectacled, and a very reserved man, Lutete lived in a small one-room house at the back of the mission with his wife, Lini. While most of the white guests likely viewed Lutete as just another servant, Essie saw him and the other Africans she met there as individuals with stories to tell and wisdom to share. She found Lutete "intelligent" and "charming," and she was curious to know about his background. The son of a carpenter and one of five siblings, Lutete was from the Banza Manteke village near Matadi and was a member of the Bakongo ethnic group. His father had worked for European missionaries and big game hunters and had learned from them how to speak English. Lutete himself, forty-seven-years old, had been schooled by missionaries and spoke English, French, Portuguese, and several indigenous African languages. Although reticent at first, once Lutete trusted Essie he did not hesitate to share his views and ideas openly. At one point, she recounted to him an unpleasant experience she had had in the local post office, where whites had been served first, Africans served last, and she had been sandwiched in the middle — racially ambiguous in the hierarchy. "Oh yes," Lutete exploded, "always the white man first. No matter when he arrives, no matter how many Africans, always all white men first!" The way Congolese were treated under the Belgians and French, Lutete said, was like "when you see a stick trying to grow, you keep cutting it off, so it can never grow. That treatment you saw today is some of the cutting off. Always they cut us off."[13]

Essie placed a lot of confidence in the stories and experiences that Lutete shared with her. She explained her research to him and asked him to convene a meeting of local men so that she could interview them as a group. The men, all from Angola, met at Lutete's little house and Essie talked with them about their experiences and the life and conditions they had observed in the Congo. They explained about the migrant labor system in the region, unfair taxes, and exploitation. The men also described how workers were being coerced into long contracts to work on plantations and in fisheries, and how women and children were forced to do roadwork. Others sold produce to the colonials, but in lieu of payment they were given redeemable slips of paper for items they could only purchase in the store owned by those colonials.[14] The stories they told closely resembled tales of the debt peonage that Black freedpeople had faced as the sharecropping system emerged in the postbellum American South.

It was not every day that the Congolese in Leopoldville encountered an American Negro woman. Essie quickly became a source of local fascination. Soon she found herself receiving a steady stream of local visitors: "Africans come to see me, to tell me about themselves and ask me about the American Negro." There was also a feature on Essie in the local paper that heightened her visibility. "We would talk until dark," she recalled fondly, "We talked in English and French and Lingalla [one of the local African languages, also spelled Lingala], and always someone present would interpret, and someone else would confirm or correct the interpretation." Essie remembered her visitors' great emphasis on the importance of education, vast curiosity about the larger world, and lack of bitterness.[15]

Essie was eager to see all sides of the city. One day, at her request, she was given a tour by the mayor of Leopoldville, a man named Brumagne. During the tour she inquired about the women, not the elite women or the educated ones, but the women at the bottom of the social and economic hierarchy. In response, she was told about rampant, but in the words of her host, "necessary" prostitution in the city, presumably to service Black male migrant workers whose families were still in the rural areas. This gave Essie yet another angle on life in colonial Central Africa.[16] There is no indication that Essie actually met or conversed with the local sex workers, but her inquiry reflects the kind of class and gender issues that were very much on her mind in 1946.

Essie was taking everything in with her eyes wide open, but British Intelligence had its eyes on her as well. Even though she was technically a "guest" of French and Belgian colonial officials who had perhaps reluctantly authorized her visit, it was clear to everyone that Essie's loyalties were with the African masses. The British were fearful that she would migrate from Congo to the British-controlled colonies nearby, or perhaps come back to London with tales that would further inflame the demands of her African friends and colleagues living in Britain. In a memo in the files of the MI5, the British internal security agency, we can see that Essie's presence in Congo was viewed as a threat to colonial authority. The agent on the ground reported to British officials with great alarm: "Mrs. Robeson is at present in Leopoldville and her remarks leave no doubt about her *very advanced* Leftist opinions and her determination to champion the negro cause at all costs. Her indiscretions have been numerous; her crowning one was the suggestion that the native in the Congo would only get a square deal when he was governed by one of his own kin! What Mrs. Robeson's intentions are after she has finished her researches in French Equatorial Africa I do not know, but I have heard it rumoured that she wants to go to our West African Colonies. I realise it may be impolite to stop her formally but I thought you might like to know that she is, in my opinion, potentially a dangerous customer and there is no doubt about the fact that she is, ideologically at least, advance Left in her views."[17]

This intelligence report is telling on several levels. First of all, it is just one of the declassified government documents that reveal the extent of the surveillance that both of the Robesons were under as they moved around the world. The MI5 file contains communications with not only the FBI in the United States, but with Jamaican, Trinidadian, and Gold Coast intelligence agencies as well. There was a real fear by British and American authorities in particular that Black anti-colonial activists and writers like Essie were going to have a tangible influence on African independence movements. In 1946 they saw this as a threat. Second, the document illustrates that Essie was seen as a force in her own right by those on the other side of the anti-colonial struggle. She was viewed by British agents not as an appendage or extension of Paul but as a "dangerous customer" on her own.

After a few days in Leopoldville, Essie went into town to get her French Equatorial Africa (Afrique équtoriale française or AEF) visa from the French consulate and make arrangements to travel from Leopoldville in Belgian Congo to Brazzaville in French Congo. Once in Brazzaville, Essie decided to go beyond the environs of the colonial city and see the landscape that lay beyond its borders. The result was a meandering six-day trip along the mighty Congo River on a wood-burning steamer, a journey that she documented in great detail. "One way to really see the Congo," she wrote, is to "ply the Congo-Lualaba-Ubangi-Kasai River network," a three-thousand-mile waterway that snakes through Central Africa.[18] "The Congo River bed is very treacherous and dangerous, always shifting and changing, . . . so that the boats travel slowly and cautiously by daylight and tie up at the river bank at dark," Essie wrote.[19]

The full moon and roaring currents made her think about the centuries of history that flowed along those riverbanks. "Every mile of the Congo is different," she observed. "The jungle, the high grasses, the villages, the canoes; the soil on the banks now red, now brown, now light clay colored; the water now shallow and very clear, now deep and very dark, now smooth and white, now swirling with the powerful currents."[20]

The captain of Essie's steamer, a medium-sized boat called the *Baron Jacques*, was William St. John Straw, a Black Jamaican with a reputation for being one of the most skilled boatmen on the river. Essie befriended him immediately. She also noticed the various sleeping accommodations for the people on board: "The enclosed Captain's quarters and the wheel-house were on the spacious top deck. On the lower deck, which was open, were the freight, the livestock, and the many African and some Asian passengers, many of them local and traveling from village to village." There were only three sleeping cabins on the top deck, "the European deck," and although Essie, in her words, "definitely could not 'pass,' [for white] especially with my hair in that steamy heat," she had been able to secure a reservation in one of the European cabins. There was, however, some confusion with a fellow passenger who had apparently booked the same cabin, and Essie ended up sharing quarters with another woman, a European. She made the best of it, recognizing that even without total privacy, she was better off than the Africans on the lower decks. The conditions were harsh, even in the steamer's equivalent of first class. Essie did without many of the comforts she was accustomed to and, out of necessity, traveled light. She endured "the steaming heat, the heavy air, the mosquitoes, moths, flies and ants," with relatively little complaint.[21] The rainy season had just begun, "which means heat and serious rains daily."[22]

The other passengers on the top deck included a European family with six children (missionaries most likely) and a Catholic nun. As always, Africans got the worst accommodations. Not only were they relegated to the lower open deck of the boat along with the cargo and livestock, but they also had to do some of the most dangerous work. "Every time the boat prepared to tie up at the bank," Essie observed, "two Africans carrying heavy ropes made of twisted steel wires would leap into the water from the front lower deck and swim to shore, where they would climb the bank and secure these ropes around a big tree." Essie worried about the men because "the river swarms with crocodiles."[23] Thankfully, the commotion from the boat usually sent the crocodiles scurrying, giving the men a small window of opportunity to secure the boat and get out of harm's way. The boat trip ultimately took Essie to Kasai, one of the centers of diamond mining and a conflict-ridden area that would ultimately, although only briefly, secede from Congo in the 1960s.[24] Before she left the area, Essie took a tour of the Kipushi Mines. After descending twenty-five series of ladders that took her deep under the earth, she got a sense of the danger the miners faced every day, as well as the uncertainty and dark isolation that were a routine part of the job.[25]

Essie's river excursion was just one small part of her Congolese experience. One of her main reasons for going was to meet with and interview a variety of people living and working there, especially the dissidents, agitators, and African intellectuals working for reforms and changes within the colonial structure itself. One inspiring and alluring political actor whom Essie met on this trip was Gabriel d'Arboussier, "a tall, charming Deputy [Communist] from French Soudan." At the time, he had just been elected to the French National Assembly and would go on to have a distinguished career in Francophone politics and serve as an official at the United Nations.[26] He was a "coffee-colored" man with "fine features," a so-called métis, someone of mixed French and African ancestry. He dismissed this term, however, as well as the labels "evoluée" and "elite," which referred to the same population, as products of the divisive caste system within the French Union.[27] D'Arboussier was the child of a white French father and an African mother who died when he was quite young. He was raised lovingly by his father and a white stepmother. The story of a Black man being raised by white parents in the heart of Africa was utterly fascinating to Essie. They initially met over lunch, but there was not enough time for Essie to ask all of her questions, so she asked for more time. They developed a warm rapport, and apparently alternated between French and English in their conversations. Essie spent several more days with d'Arboussier.[28] He carved out a significant block of time to meet with her and sent a government car to transport her to their second meeting, at which she interviewed him at an inn in the countryside outside Brazzaville.[29]

One issue they discussed at length was the new colonial policies being proposed by the French, including a new set of citizenship laws that were due to go into effect on June 1, 1946. D'Arboussier supported these changes, which promised to abolish distinctions between colonial subjects and French citizens. All French colonies would become part of the French Union, and all colonial subjects would eventually become enfranchised citizens. Even though some of the details had not yet been worked out, d'Arboussier was hopeful. Essie was more skeptical about whether such a plan could work, given her knowledge of the U.S. Negro experience, but she kept silent. "One must not be too cynical, and one can always hope for the best, so I said nothing," she later wrote.[30]

At their third meeting, on June 13, d'Arboussier sat with Essie and helped her plan out the rest of her itinerary in French Equatorial Africa. By now they had become friends and Essie was quite comfortable with the young deputy, whom she found charming with a "great sense of humor." Even though they had some differing views, Essie and d'Arboussier clearly had a strong intellectual and personal rapport. But at least on Essie's part there were other attractions as well, and in her estimation, the feelings were mutual. Once she arrived at her first stop after traveling to the interior, she sent off a slew of pro forma letters to friends and family from her new outpost, then sat down to write a very intimate letter to her old friend Bess Rockmore (Bobby's first wife). In that letter, Essie confided: "I've met a man who is proving really companionable, besides being enormously attractive and right for me." She was excited about the prospect of a relationship and was thinking ahead to where that relationship might lead, but cautious at the same time. "He is tramping [flirting aggressively] heavily, and doesn't care about the implications, but I can't afford to, at the moment," she explained to Bess.[31]

It is unclear from Essie's letter whether the relationship was sexual or simply flirtatious (it seems to have been the latter), but it certainly indicates that at age fifty she was still open to and perhaps looking for romance and greater intimacy than Paul was prepared to provide. She goes on later in the letter to Bess, "The man I mentioned earlier in this letter has sent word ahead of me everywhere that I am to be slammed into hospital and kept there at the very first symptom of any illness or weariness and they have orders not to release me until he can arrive by plane and check!" She relished the doting attention she was receiving from her new friend, in contrast to Paul, who according to Essie had not checked on her since her departure. Ultimately the relationship with d'Arboussier, twelve years her junior, did not last, but Essie enjoyed imagining the possibility, albeit briefly.[32] For the most part, Essie and Paul's open marriage meant more romantic encounters for him than for her. But it seems that Essie was not shy to give opportunities serious consideration when they did present themselves.

The young and handsome Gabriel d'Arboussier was not the only man in Central Africa in whom Essie was interested. One of the goals of her trip to the Congo was to learn more about the curious and enigmatic colonial figure Félix Éboué, a French Guianan who was one of the first Black colonial officials to preside over a French territory.[33] Essie had not met Éboué before his death in 1944, but she knew of his reputation and had read accounts of his unusual career. The Council on African Affairs had written a favorable profile of him after his death. Essie had also heard some firsthand stories about Éboué from a young French archaeologist named Byron de Prorok, whom she had met in the summer of 1945 when they were both guest lecturers at Chautauqua, New York. De Prorok had known Éboué in Paris in the 1930s, and strongly encouraged Essie to pursue further research on him. De Prorok was quite a character himself, having traveled throughout Africa doing archaeological research, then allegedly fighting alongside the Ethiopian forces during the Italian invasion in 1935.[34]

Éboué was born in French Guiana in 1884 and educated in France. He rose up the ranks of the colonial bureaucracy and became an administrator in Chad during World War II. He led the colonial forces in Chad to break with the fascist Vichy government and side with the Free French forces of General Charles de Gaulle. In 1936 he had served as the first Black governor of a French colony (Guadalupe). He later was appointed to another post in French Equatorial Africa. During his tenure, Éboué promoted a number of policies to expand the rights of French colonial subjects. But he was also part of the colonial infrastructure, so overall his actions and his legacy were controversial among left-wing anti-colonial activists.

D'Arboussier was still a student in Dakar, Senegal, and quite the young militant, when Éboué issued his famous policy paper "Circulaire on Native Policy" in 1943. The paper called for African inclusion in French politics and culture, but stressed the importance of preserving indigenous African customs and cultures and making sure progress was consistent with those cultures and customs. When d'Arboussier first read the circulaire as a Marxist intellectual and organizer of the Rassemblement Démocratique Africain (African Democratic Group), he felt that Éboué was far too conservative, emphasizing culture over class.[35] "We recognized and saluted as very interesting and important, Éboué's idea of making the African conscious of his own civilization and culture; this is very necessary for his development, but it is insufficient," d'Arboussier told Essie.[36] This comment tempered her rosy view of Éboué, further complicated her assessment of d'Arboussier, and made her think long and hard about the challenges and dilemmas facing Africa. While Essie would later gravitate to the revolutionary language of independence-minded Africans, she realized, especially in the French territories, that there was a strong voice for reform and inclusion coming from Africans themselves, especially those who had been educated in France and enjoyed some degree of power and privilege under the French colonial regime. There were certainly parallels to this struggle between reformers and revolutionaries in the U.S. context as well. D'Arboussier would go on to play an important role in Francophone African politics and on the international stage.[37]

As she thought more deeply about Africa's history and its future,

Essie again took a special interest in the role of women, interviewing a number of women from different racial, ethnic, and class backgrounds during her time in the Congo. One of the most in-depth interviews she conducted was with a "métis" woman named Jeanne Vialle. A Marxist and ardent feminist, Vialle had married and divorced a wealthy French-man and had returned to the Congo to build an independent life for herself. Vialle had been "born in a Congo mud hut," but was sent to school in France. Her mother was from Gabon and her father was a French businessman.[38] During the German occupation of France in World War II, Vialle was a part of the underground French resistance. She was discovered and held by the Germans for a year as a prisoner of war. Once she returned to the Congo, she was elected to represent the Ubangi-Shari region of the French-dominated Congo in the colonial assembly.[39] Vialle worked as a journalist and later helped to form a Paris-based organization that advocated for women's rights in France and the French colonies.

The manifesto of Vialle's organization, the Association des Femmes de l'Union Française outre-mer et métropole, began, "We call upon all women of the French Union, the West Indies, North Africa, Black Africa, Madagascar, Indo-China, and all the overseas territories, who for six long years were separated from the metropolis and who suffered from the racist methods of the Vichy regime, to unite."[40] The group's objective was "to obtain for all women of the French Union the possibility to live in the dignity required by the human condition, upon the plane of complete equality, which is conferred by our rights of citizenship."[41] Essie and Vialle spent two days interviewing one another about their lives and talking about Africa and politics. Vialle was animated and passionate about the issue of women's rights, which was becoming a focus for Essie as well.[42] Still Vialle was talking about Africa's future within the context of a French structure. She was proposing that women demand French rights rather than African independence. Essie listened intently but skeptically. She enjoyed her intellectual conversations with the cosmopolitan Ms. Vialle, but she was eager to go deeper into the interior of the colony, especially because she hoped to write an article on labor conditions in Africa. Essie thus also spent some time in Elisabethville, where she visited with friends, and conducted informal interviews with the Congolese workers she met.

Before going further afield, Essie went back to Leopoldville to attend, as a journalist, a big conference of missionaries being held there. The Black American "race leader" Channing Tobias spoke, as did her professor at Hartford Seminary, Newell Booth. She liked Booth and enjoyed the chance to spend some time with him and his wife. The Booths were living in Congo when Essie arrived and she stayed with them in Elisabethville for several days. As for the missionary gathering itself, Essie was thoroughly disgusted by it. Despite good talks by Tobias and Booth, Essie essentially found the whole affair offensive and a waste of time, because she thought it reflected "the old paternalism" that had dominated missionary work in Africa for generations. "Almost all the time was taken up with what the white folks thought about this or that—very little about what the Africans thought," she complained.[43]

Fed up with the missionaries, Essie continued on her itinerary, determined in part to retrace the steps of Félix Éboué during his unique career in French Central Africa. Before continuing on her ambitious itinerary, Essie took time out to dispatch a few letters, including one to Paul requesting additional funds to carry her through the rest of the trip. She was trying to keep her expenses to a minimum but everything was expensive.[44] Her next stop was the League of Nations' mandated area of Ruanda-Urundi (later Rwanda and Burundi). She took a small bush plane to the administrative center of Usumbura and checked into the Paguidas Hotel on August 8, 1946—on crutches. The day before she left Elisabethville, she had twisted her ankle while walking on a cobblestone street.

An injured ankle was not enough to slow Essie down. She had been warned by her French colleagues that the area was rugged and off the beaten path, but she found it absolutely magical. "This place is divine," she wrote a friend, describing how from the balcony of her hotel room she could see bush fires igniting in the distance.[45] While in Usumbura, she conducted still more interviews, this time with white colonial officials as well as local Blacks. She also visited a military camp, a coffee farm, and a hospital along the way. "The trip [outside of Usumbura] was rugged but fascinating," Essie wrote in her journal. She traveled in a Studebaker car with a local colonial official escorting her. "There are not villages in Urundi," Essie observed: "people live in scattered groups all over the mountains and hills, in groupings too small to be considered villages." She and her escort moved onward to Astrida past fields of banana groves. She later reports that she "arrived at Kisnengo [Kinsenyi] at the Bugoyi Guest house with each room as a separate dwelling—round hut with thatched roof." Essie met with local chiefs, ordinary folks, and European officials and clerks.[46] Upon her arrival she found herself stricken with dysentery, a condition that plagued her repeatedly during her travels, along with other ailments. Ruggedly determined to persevere, she recovered enough within a few days to begin her research interviews as planned.[47]

One of her interviewees in the region was Mr. Kapenda Tshombe (she does not use his full name, Moïse Kapenda Tshombe), whom she described as "tall, dark, slim with a certain quiet elegance and dignity of manner and carriage, soft courteous voice, charming manner." Born in Musumba in Belgian Congo near the border of a colonial Portuguese area, he was one of eleven children from a poor family who started his own business under adverse conditions and managed to trudge his way up the economic ladder step by step. Essie seemed impressed with Tshombe's success but understood that he was the exception and not the rule.[48] Essie did not know at the time that Tshombe would become a pivotal, and much reviled, figure in the bloody drama that would surround the Congolese independence struggle a decade and a half later. More of a businessman than a freedom fighter, Tshombe, with the backing of Belgian mining interests and Belgian troops, in 1960 led a military campaign in Katanga province to secede from the newly independent Congo. He was later implicated in the torture and assassination of Congolese leader Patrice Lumumba, whom Essie admired and supported.[49] But in 1946 neither Essie nor Tshombe knew the political struggles and realignments that lay ahead. Her interview with him was personal and rather benign.

Another interviewee, one with whom Essie spent quite a bit of time, was Mr. E. Toussaint, a white colonial administrator based in Elisabethville who was the "native personnel chief." Essie walked a fine line in her dealings with white colonials. On the one hand, she had been given permission to do her research in areas under their control, and they were, for the most part, politely assisting her. On the other hand, she was a critic of the racist power they wielded and the structures they held in place. She was diplomatic and discreet when she had to be. But she often found ways to challenge and criticize local white authorities, even if she was their guest. After Essie's interview with Mr. Touissaint, she wrote him a long, subtly critical letter that read: "I found in my notes that one of the wonderful questions you asked your headmen was what is the difference between a boy and a workman? I don't think the answer to that one is included in the summary you gave me and I'd simply love to have it. And finally . . . I am still thinking very critically of the eight-hour stretch the workmen do without the usual hour off for lunch, as workmen in other countries always have. . . . You will all be faced with this question when the international labor board comes out, as I am very sure they will question this system."[50]

From Usumbura, Essie made her way to Tchad (Chad) where she planned to do still more research on Éboué. Each phase of her journey seemed more precarious. By this time she was traveling on very tiny planes and very bad roads. Several times along the way she had to leave luggage behind because there was no room or the cost was prohibitive on the once-a-week flight into, or out of, some small, remote location. During her one week in Tchad, she interviewed a few people, and visited the house where Éboué had lived when he was there. She returned to Leopoldville on July 14.

For most of the trip Essie traveled with her trusty little typewriter, a gift given to Paul Jr. by Freda Diamond that Essie had appropriated when Paul Jr. went off to college. But when she ventured into Tchad she was forced to leave it behind temporarily because of weight limits on her tiny aircraft. Between Tchad and Leopoldville, Essie stopped in a series of small towns, villages, and colonial outposts. Once she returned to Leopoldville, she typed up a batch of letters bulging with details of her experiences. One letter was addressed to Bobby Rockmore, who Essie thought would be efficient with group communications. She asked that he distribute it to her close circle of friends and family. The letter captures eloquently both the arduousness of the trip and the stimulation and excitement Essie felt about being there. She writes:

> I have just returned from a very strenuous trek up country, and Boy was it tough going. The French around here told me the trip would be "tres dure," and when these colonials say hard trip they really mean hard. But very hard. I went by car, de luxe Dodge 7 passenger fluid drive, from here on Tuesday, June 25th, in the morning, early. I went along with a young administrateur and his wife and baby, and our luggage, we have a schedule, but none of it worked out. Instead of sleeping at Grimari, and at Kembe, as our schedule indicated, we had a breakdown, carburetor trouble, and had to sleep at Ft. Sibut, the middle of tsetse fly area. . . . The country was beautiful and very fascinating, the weather was terrific, hot and very very heavy, and everything I ate disagreed with me. But Me Lemmerier [the administrator's wife] had a similar stomach, so I didn't feel too self-conscious. Everywhere we went people were marvelous, had everything ready to show me, and tell me, about Eboué, and I got so much material

that I was thrilled. But the rains had already begun and we never knew whether the roads would be washed out or not, and it was a bit nerve wracking. The night after we arrived at Bangassou there was a real tornado, which was something. Nearly every administrator's house where I found myself was a house which Éboué had built. It was quite exciting. . . . At Bangassou, which was one of his main posts, I stayed from Thursday to Monday, July 1st, gathering material and taking pictures. I set out Monday morning, early, alone in my magnificent but temperamental Dodge [presumably with her driver] . . . and made for Bambari. . . . I slept the night at Bambari, saw lots of folks, got lots of material, and took lots of pictures. Next day made for Bangui, and after lots of trouble, made it finally, on Wednesday night late, July 3rd. I took bed, mosquito netting, food, etc. and rum along with me, used the bed and net once, drank all the rum, and didn't use the food at all. They fed me everywhere. It was a wonderful experience, right into the bush, through forests, tsetse country, leper country, and savanna country, crossing rivers by pontoon ferry, crossing bridges that looked precarious to say the least, everyone flashing torches all around the rooms and under beds before letting me in, to check for serpents, and barring doors and windows heavily against leopards, which they call lee-o-pards, or panthers, and which are now roaming the countryside, coming to kitchens and stealing chickens, etc. I said I had fear and they said oh they won't touch you, they'll run if they see you, they will only attack if you threaten them. I said maybe we might come across one which didn't know the rules. They are very casual about it, and everyone proudly showed me the skins of the lee-o-pards they had just shot. Huge things. Whew. Well, I'm back in one piece, so that's OK. . . . leave tomorrow morning for Fort Lamy in Tchad.[51]

The conditions Essie encountered were not easy. She had to wash her hair with kerosene and suffered a swarm of flying mice that invaded her bedroom one night. Nevertheless she kept a positive attitude and was thrilled to be there. She had met "scads of interesting people," felt intellectually and physically challenged and emotionally buoyed by the whole experience, and was even beginning to map out a possible career path that would allow her to be based in Africa for an extended period of time.[52] She was unable to use a phone, obtain a newspaper, or even receive mail on a regular basis, however, and admitted that it felt "odd being isolated for so long." She was also disappointed that she had not received a single letter from Paul. Still, the trip had a powerful impact on her.[53]

It is possible to chart Essie's movements as she traveled around the world. It is more difficult to map her thinking as it evolved. Her public writings are a partial guide, her letters and diaries add even more insight, but sometimes it is difficult to determine precisely what her positions were on various issues, or to pinpoint exactly when a political or ideological shift occurred. Her public positions, for instance, are sometimes more cautious and discreet than her private thoughts expressed in personal letters and diary entries. It is clear, however, that her second trip to sub-Saharan Africa in 1946 had a very powerful influence on her thinking. For example, many of the French colonial officials and some of the anti-colonial activists she met with were advocating change far short of revolution, and were themselves relatively privileged as was she. When she returned to the States, however, her own spoken and written words on Africa were more militant than ever. As the Russian-born African scholar Lily Golden indicated years later, Essie was one of the first of those who were both writing about Africa and had spent time there who warned of the dangers of neo-colonialism.[54] Perhaps some of this awareness emerged out of her talks and experiences in the Congo, and it may not have been entirely the message those she interviewed sought to convey.

Although Essie's trip through the Congo was, in her words, "awe-inspiring," by early September she was feeling a little homesick.[55] She had been "roughing it" for nearly five months and by then she was ready for a hot shower, her own bed, and a good cup of coffee. She also jokingly wrote to a friend that she couldn't wait to see her hairdresser again, since her hair had turned back to "pure wool," adding proudly that "the Africans think it is beautiful."[56] When she finally returned home, she published small portions of her travel diaries in a series for the *Amsterdam News*. She had hoped to write an entire book, and even began that project while in Africa, but despite her best efforts, it never came to pass.

For the next two years Essie did work on a movie script, entitled "Congolaise," inspired, in large part, by her travels there. The plot of the film, which never made it from script to screen, is an interesting one. Essie focused her narrative on two young Belgian economists who fall in love and go off to Africa together, supremely naïve and unaware of the circumstances they will encounter. Initially they are uncritical of the colonial project, but eventually they come to see the situation through the eyes of their African colleagues and friends. They learn local languages and commit themselves to African development. Independence is hinted at but not clearly articulated by her young white protagonists. In the end, too, there is a tragic twist for the two main characters: the woman gives birth in the Congo to the couple's only child, and both mother and baby die. The husband stays on and continues to serve the local people's interests. His wife and child are buried there, he tells a friend, so he will never leave. The script is rough around the edges and clearly a draft, but one interpretation of Essie's narrative is that it was not enough for the idealistic young economists to come and help—rather, they had to suffer and sacrifice in order to truly be a part of the African struggle.[57] If they did suffer and sacrifice, and immerse themselves with the lives of the local people, such solidarity was, in fact, possible.

In November, a short time after her return from the Congo, Essie gave a provocative speech in New York City in which she declared "Africa is in revolution," a statement that the African Francophone leaders she had just met with would surely have distanced themselves from. Forces were in motion, she insisted, that would eventually bring an end to generations of colonial domination. Cognizant that fascism had only recently been defeated, she compared European colonial rule to Hitler's occupation of Europe. She insisted: "Liberation of the occupied countries was one of the dramatic, moving, gratifying achievements of our victory, [but] we have not finished with liberation. Africa has been occupied for more than 70 years; It is still occupied."[58] Essie had now positioned herself with a bold coterie of anti-colonial intellectuals and radical activists who argued for the full and immediate dismantling of white supremacist structures on the African continent and an end to colonial systems everywhere.

Much had transpired on the home front during Essie's five-month trip to Africa. After Hitler's defeat a new era of East-West tensions had begun, distancing the former war allies of the United States and the Soviet Union. As outspoken supporters of the Soviets, Paul and Essie would both soon become targets of U.S. Cold War animus. Paul, who had been traveling around the country speaking at "Win the Peace" rallies, had been summoned in October 1946 to testify before Senator Jack Tenney's California Senate Factfinding Subcommittee on Un-

American Activities. The Committee took advantage of the fact that Paul was touring in the state to haul him in for testimony. Around this time Paul also helped to convene a huge Madison Square Garden rally for African freedom; led a conference to launch an American crusade against lynching; and, with a small seven-person delegation, met with President Truman to register anger and concern about ongoing racist violence against Black Americans.[59] Truman's response was less than encouraging.

When Essie came home from Central Africa, even though she and Paul were in some ways more in sync politically than ever before, their family life was still not in harmony. Essie certainly knew about some of Paul's romantic partnerships; perhaps she did not want to know about others. She may have come home from Africa thinking about the charming man she had met in Congo. In any case, domestic life was not smooth for the Robesons in 1946. For one thing, Essie's aging mother was deteriorating rapidly and she needed more constant (and expensive) care. Paul Jr. had been inducted into the Air Force and was stationed on the West Coast, so Essie both missed his companionship and worried about him. All of these factors must have left Essie feeling emotionally strained as she spent time alone in her big rambling country house. Still, she had resolved to enjoy her life and pursue her own interests, in ways that she had not, or perhaps could not, have done in the past.[60] She returned from Africa thinking seriously about her next steps.

In December 1946, she and Paul had another run-in about money and respect. She felt once again, as she had fifteen years before, that her status as Mrs. Paul Robeson was in jeopardy. It was also the eve of her fiftieth birthday. Paul's prolonged absences and his continued relationships with other women, complicated by the sometimes heavy-handed financial management tactics of his lawyer, Bob Rockmore, had made Essie feel a bit vulnerable and insecure. So when she came back from her Congo trip, she wrote a long, cathartic letter to Paul letting him know exactly how she was feeling. As she put it bluntly, she sometimes felt like merely "a paid housekeeper," and a poorly paid one at that. "I feel I rate better than that," she added. Essie went on to complain about the inadequacy of the financial support she received for the house, the lack of a clear line of communication between them, the disrespectful treatment she felt she received from Bob Rockmore, and most importantly, the rumors she had heard that Paul might be considering divorce again. "Am I to continue to be Mrs. Paul Robeson? Yes or No?" she demanded to know.[61] The rumor appeared to have been just that, and the implicit answer to her question was yes. Paul was conciliatory in his response, more resources were promised, and the flare-up soon calmed.[62] Her Congo romance waned and life went on much as it had before.

On a more positive note, Essie's work on Africa was finally being noticed and recognized by an ever larger public audience. Earlier in 1946 the National Council on Negro Women (NCNW), a premier civic organization, honored Essie as one of their twelve outstanding women of the year (citing her work in the previous year), alongside civil rights activist Virginia Durr; poet and lawyer Pauli Murray; and labor leader and Africa activist Maida Springer.[63] NCNW founder Mary McLeod Bethune noted that Essie and the other recipients "have, each in her own individual way, made a distinguished and impressive contribution to the progress of America and the world."[64] While most of the media coverage referred to Essie as "author, anthropologist and wife of the famed Paul Robeson," it was Essie's public lectures, articles, and book, and her leadership role in the Council on African Affairs, that led the selection committee to include her among the distinguished group of recipients.[65] In a statement, members of the selection committee said they recognized Essie specifically for her "distinguished contribution to the concept of world brotherhood." Essie traveled alone to Washington, D.C., to receive the award at a ceremony and reception at the NCNW headquarters.[66] She felt very proud of the recognition, especially because it came from a respected Black women's organization. Women's issues and women's leadership were becoming central interests of her own.

ten

AMERICAN ARGUMENTS,
1946–1950

I have reluctantly come to the conclusion that everything now is
political: the price we pay for steak, if we can afford steak. . . . All is
political, make no mistake about that. So me, I'm political.

Eslanda Robeson

By the end of 1946, Essie's orientation and focus had shifted from arts and culture to politics, while still allowing for some overlap between the two. She had been moving in this direction for more than a decade. In 1949 Essie would produce her third book, *American Argument*, co-authored with the celebrated writer Pearl Buck. The book highlighted their differing philosophical views on life, race, and the state of the world. Politics was a theme throughout. A close look at the years leading up to the publication of *American Argument* illuminates the development of Essie's thinking and the deepening of her convictions.

Although Essie had some brushes with politics before 1946 — she campaigned briefly for Roosevelt in the 1944 U.S. presidential election, hoping to extend the progressive reforms of the New Deal, and her first experiences with the United Nations had taken place in 1945 — it wasn't until her return from Congo and the completion of *African Journey* that her own political analysis came into clearer focus.[1] Essie articulated her new politicized identity in a letter to her Delta sorority sisters in 1948, where she wrote, "I have reluctantly come to the conclusion that everything now is political: the price we pay for steak, if we can afford steak. . . . All is political, make no mistake about that. So me, I'm political."[2] It was around this time that she began lecturing and writing with a pragmatic purpose in mind, rather than solely for the sake of exploration or self-expression. Just as Paul had come to the conclusion that as an artist he was in service to the larger cause of freedom, Essie too had decided to use her words and her pen to agitate, advocate, and educate. She wanted to engage her audiences on the most pressing national and international questions of the day. She did so from a decidedly Left perspective, and although electoral politics were a part of the picture, they by no means were her entire political project.

In 1948, Essie agreed to collaborate with the writer Pearl Buck on *American Argument* because she hoped that the book would allow her to further disseminate some of her ideas and draw attention to the issues she was most passionate about. Essie had known Buck, a privileged white woman and prominent writer, for years, having met her in the 1930s at a dinner party at Carl Van Vechten's home. The daughter of white American missionaries, Buck grew up in China in the early 1900s. She won huge acclaim in the early 1930s for her novel *The Good Earth*, about life in rural China, and won the Nobel Prize in Literature in 1938.[3] Essie once told Van Vechten that she dreamed of writing a book that would "introduce readers to *my* people the way Pearl Buck introduced me to the Chinese people." So when Buck asked Essie to work with her on a book project in which the two of them would exchange views on a range of issues, Essie readily accepted. She didn't know Buck well, and she knew they had many differences, but she trusted Buck's intentions.

The resulting book, *American Argument*, was published in 1949. In it Essie, through interviews with her co-author, argued vociferously against many popularly held American beliefs. In a series of candid conversations, Essie and Buck squared off over race, patriotism, capitalism, world affairs, gender, and sex. They were both women of strong convictions who had traveled widely, lived abroad for significant periods of time, and defied easy labels. The free-flowing narrative in *American Argument* offers an interesting glimpse into what the fifty-three-year-old Essie wanted people to understand about her worldview, values, and politics at that moment in her life.

The co-authors argued four specific topics: the role of the intellectual, the nature of the political system in the Soviet Union, the politics of sexuality and families, and the meaning of patriotism. In terms of defining intellectual work, Essie embraced a populist position. She said mental labor should not be ranked more highly than manual labor and that scholars should not see themselves as above the rest of society. "I have never liked fancy intellectuals anywhere," Essie insisted. "I believe knowledge should be shared. And I believe that all knowledge can be reduced to clear words of one syllable, which can be understood by simple people."[4]

A topic on which the two women emphatically did disagree was the nature of politics and life in the Soviet Union. Contrary to the popular conception in the United States that Soviet citizens were simply mindless followers of the Kremlin, Essie argued that she had witnessed ordinary people engage in more frequent and informed debates about politics and ideas in Russia than she had in the United States. Having visited the country several times, and having traveled to various regions within it, Essie felt firmly that she was well informed and in the right. She praised the Soviet people at all levels of society and from all parts of that vast country as politically aware and perfectly able to "keep score for themselves" with regard to their leaders and policies, unlike most Americans, whom she deemed "politically illiterate."[5] Most important, Essie insisted that the Soviet Union was one of the few places on earth where racism was actually in decline, if not eradicated.

A fair-minded liberal, who never resorted to crude forms of red-baiting, Buck still disdained the Soviet Union and everything she felt it represented: rigid centralized bureaucracy, lack of individual freedom, and harsh political repression. She and Essie exchanged tough words about the Bolshevik revolution, the treatment of dissidents, and when a state has the right to use force in what its leaders believe is its own defense. Essie took a hard line. The Bolshevik Revolution had to be staunchly defended, she argued, and those who "deliberately worked against the government" had to be "'removed' if the government was going to survive." It is unclear whether at that point in the conversation the two women were talking only about the immediate aftermath of the 1917 revolution, or if they were at least implicitly also debating Stalin's purges in the 1930s and 1940s. The conversation occurred in the context of a larger discussion about the role of intellectuals in revolutionary societies, the overzealousness of revolutionary actors, and the importance of intellectual freedom. Buck tried to use the analogy of sheepdogs trying to contain a herd of sheep, and eventually killing those that would not stay with the herd. Speaking more directly, she then suggested that the Soviet leaders were guilty of "liquidating" dissenters and she could not condone it.[6] Essie responded in anger, and perhaps in haste. Still, she allowed her words to speak for themselves in print: "I'm not so afraid of liquidation as you are," she insisted. "I regret it, of course. I would avoid it if I possibly could. I like dogs, but I certainly wouldn't hesitate one moment to liquidate a mad dog. It's discouraging, but sometimes a few people behave like mad dogs—the people who lynch Negroes in the South, the people who exploited Africans to death, the people who foment wars, the people who cause millions of others to starve to death in famines, or to live their lives as serfs. These are mad dogs and must be treated as such."[7] Essie's words are chilling, especially the use of the word "liquidation," which was Buck's figure of speech, but Essie picked up on it. In the aftermath of the Holocaust, and given the ongoing repression inside the Soviet Union, it was a bad choice indeed.

Unable to reconcile her admiration for Essie Robeson, the gracious and intelligent friend, with Essie Robeson, supporter of the Soviet system, Buck insisted that Essie was not, and could not possibly be, a communist because she would not have been able to spend so much enjoyable time with her otherwise. Without apology, Essie seized on what she perceived as narrow-minded political prejudice. In a long but blunt footnote to this section of the book, Essie demanded to know how Buck could predetermine so absolutely that she could never be friends with a communist. When Buck responded that the issue was one of individual freedom, which citizens in communist countries did not have, Essie turned the tables. "I notice that the people who keep talking about individual freedom have quite a lot of it themselves. They are the haves." Essie pointed out that Blacks and poor whites sorely lacked individual freedom under U.S. capitalism. Buck asked Essie directly, did she see "any advantage in being an American?" Essie was equally direct. "When Americans treat me and my people like Americans, then I'll like it, and find advantage—and pride in being American—not before."[8]

On the issue of sex and marriage, Essie argued that sex and marriage could, and perhaps should, be viewed separately, and accused Americans overall of being immature about matters having to do with sex. While not directly addressing her own personal experience, she said that there was nothing at all sacred about sex, but that it was a basic human urge, pure and simple. At one point, most likely the late 1930s or early 1940s, Essie, curious about human sexuality and the realities of sex in America, had interviewed several prostitutes working the streets of New York City. This was the brazen ethnographer and anthropologist in her who felt she could apply her research skills to any subject including human sexuality. Moreover, she had confidence that sex workers had the capacity to analyze the nature of their work as much as any other woman could. She offered this bit of information to Buck as evidence of her matter-of-fact view of sexuality.[9]

The book ended with Essie issuing a challenge to Buck regarding the global balance of power and her relationship to it: would Buck, a rich, well-educated white woman, be willing to forfeit some of her privileges and comforts so that others with less could live better? Buck said yes, almost as a reflex it seems, but there was no further dialogue. "Eslanda and I have differed profoundly," Pearl concluded, "not just [on] our own country—we have differed on the whole world."[10] After the book was published, the women exchanged a few letters, remained in touch off and on, but both seemed to know the limits of the relationship.[11] In 1949, Buck would publicly condemn the political attacks made against the Robesons, but she could never really come to terms with many of Essie's political views.[12]

Even though Essie and Pearl Buck's disagreements were clear, there were many people who did share Essie's political views and with whom she found great common cause. In the wake of the war her primary political interests were twofold: the independence of Third World countries (especially those in Africa), and full citizenship rights for Negroes in the United States. She and many likeminded others thought it was an opportune moment to push for certain racial reforms. Even though most of her political career had been spent documenting, reporting, and speaking out on injustices of various sorts, she was rarely a hands-on organizer. In at least one instance, however, she embraced this role as well. In the fall of 1947 Essie took the lead to convene a broad-based group of Negro leaders that was poised to push for an array of postwar reforms, namely, legislation against lynching and poll taxes, as well as a permanent Fair Employment Practices Commission. All of these issues were already on the agenda of the NAACP and other groups.[13] But the goal of the new formation was to use the tactic of "mass pressure." The unnamed group first met on Monday, October 6, at the Harlem YMCA. Essie attributed the low attendance to the fact that the World Series game between the New York Yankees and the Brooklyn Dodgers was being played that very same day. Most importantly, Jackie Robinson was in the lineup. Although the meeting was officially called by Paul, it was organized and chaired by Essie. Before the meeting, she had personally telephoned Hubert Delaney, W. E. B. Du Bois, and Benjamin Mays, to try to secure their support for the idea of a new national coalition. A few people came to the gathering; most could not.

A second meeting was held on a rainy Saturday in November at the Harlem public library. This time the turnout was better. Eighteen people attended, including Dorothy Height, then president of the Delta

Sigma Theta Sorority; labor organizer Ewart Guinier; and Dr. Joe Johnson, dean of Howard University's medical school. Essie "occupied the chair unofficially" and gave opening remarks to the group gathered. She spoke "respectfully and warmly" about the NAACP efforts but suggested more action was needed. At the end of the meeting a working committee was formed. The group was scheduled to continue its work after the holiday season, but by early 1948 Essie and Paul were embattled with their onetime friend Max Yergan over the future of the Council on African Affairs, and the coalition Essie had envisioned was one of the casualties of that fight, because Essie and Paul were otherwise distracted and the increasing red-baiting made ideologically diverse coalitions less possible.[14]

One new political project did take hold after the war, however. In the late 1940s, both Essie and Paul lent their support for the newly formed Progressive Party, a left-leaning third-party alternative to the Democrats.[15] The Progressive Party was formed in 1948 with a platform emphasizing labor rights, peace, racial justice, self-determination, and dialogue with the Soviet Union. Henry Wallace, a former U.S. Secretary of Commerce and vice president under Roosevelt who had broken bitterly with the Truman administration over its Cold War policies, became the Progressive presidential nominee in 1948. Liberals and leftists, including Essie and Paul, rallied around him. They were both at the founding convention in Philadelphia in July 1948, and helped to get the party off the ground.

Essie was a vocal and active member of the party's platform committee and actually helped draft the 1948 platform, which reflected many of her political values. She also engaged in lively debates with committee members around key planks of the platform. One especially lively debate was on the U.S. colony of Puerto Rico. Essie invoked lessons from South Africa as the committee considered whether to call for a plebiscite or whether to change the platform position from support of independence to a more general call for self-determination.[16] The final platform was a very progressive document that consisted of a call for anti-lynching legislation, anti-discrimination laws, controls on the cost of rent and consumer prices, and pro-labor and anti-monopoly business legislation. There were also platform planks that called for federally subsidized childcare for working parents and "first class" citizenship rights for all women.[17]

Essie may have been drawn to the Progressive Party in part because it was especially appealing and hospitable to women, who made up half of the delegates to the Philadelphia convention and played key leadership roles throughout the organization. Historian Jacqueline Castledine points out that many members of the Progressive Party went on to be involved in leftist feminist politics in the 1960s and 1970s.[18] The party's platform of peace, civil rights, and social programs appealed to Essie, but Henry Wallace, the man, appealed to her too. He had rejected a safe career path to follow his conscience. Deeply religious but open to the views of others, Wallace was the kind of politician Essie and Paul could support. For embracing an anti-racist and racially inclusive platform and organization he was labeled a "nigger lover" and told to "go back to Russia" (despite the fact that he had come from a farming community in Iowa),[19] but the qualities and principles that made some right-wingers attack him with a vengeance were precisely those that attracted the Robesons to him.

Much of Essie's work for the Progressive Party was done through rallies, meetings, and forums in and around Connecticut. She spoke in union halls, cultural centers, schools, and private homes about the agenda of the party and its members. In June 1948 she was nominated to run for Connecticut secretary of state on the Progressive ticket.[20] She spoke at the Central YMCA in Waterbury, at the Labor Temple in New Haven, and at a private home in Greenwich, with secret FBI informants monitoring her every step of the way.[21] The campaign was historic in that it was "the largest slate of black candidates to run on a ticket since Reconstruction."[22]

Even though Essie got only 10,000 votes, while her Democratic and Republican opponents claimed roughly 400,000 each, she had made her voice heard.[23] In speech after speech around the state, she spoke to a broad array of issues that extended beyond Connecticut. "The major problem facing the American people today are high prices, housing and civil liberties and no amount of Communist red baiting is going to change that," Essie argued.[24]

She also participated on the national level, traveling the country to rally support for Wallace, even as many mainstream Black leaders campaigned for Truman. Essie accompanied Wallace on his eighteen-city 1948 Peace Tour, where she spoke out about the Progressive Party's opposition to the Cold War and U.S. militarism in Korea. "We know we can't stand for peace on one foot and war on the other," she wrote, which is why, she insisted, a third-party alternative was sorely needed.[25] Essie, echoing the platform of the Progressives, called for an end to the arms race, policies to support civil liberties, and an end to the poll taxes that excluded Blacks from the electoral arena. "Appropriating billions of dollars for arms, making military treaties with Canada and South American countries, actually fighting wars, with money, men and guns in Greece, China, Indonesia and Indo-China, and fighting what we call a Cold War in Russia . . . we of the Progressive Party don't think that program of the Republicans and Democrats adds up to peace."[26]

During the 1948 campaign Essie traveled in a private plane with Wallace and a small entourage to rallies around the country. In her speeches on behalf of the Progressive Party, she explicitly connected the nascent Black civil rights movement with the defense of civil liberties at home and peaceful coexistence worldwide. "The Progressive Party stands for freedom," she proclaimed, which meant, among other things, standing up to censorship and the intimidating tactics of the various un-American activities committees. While she was certainly not alone in making these arguments, Essie was an important advocate for internationalizing the Black Freedom struggle in the United States and for drawing parallels with socialist, communist, and anti-colonial movements abroad. She would expand greatly on this idea in her later writings, where she would emphasize the importance of being part of a global political family and developing a global Black identity.

Henry Wallace won only about 3 percent of the vote in the 1948 elections, and he split from the Progressive Party two years later, largely over the issue of communism.[27] Even after that break, and after Wallace's departure, the Progressive Party and its various affiliates continued to wage local and national campaigns and the party continued to enjoy Essie's support. In 1950, she ran unsuccessfully for U.S. Congress as a third-party candidate.[28] She must have known she had a slim chance of winning, and she pulled only 2,300 votes. But over the course of the campaign, she had the opportunity to make numerous speeches and media appearances. Her goal was simply to inject progressive ideas and policies into the conversation and perhaps influence voters and policymakers in the process.

On October 29, the Sunday before the election, Essie was a guest on a local radio program in Waterbury, Connecticut. She used the platform to oppose the war in Korea and the Cold War generally, insisting that security, civil rights, and economic justice could be realized only if a stable peace was achieved."[29] After a series of questions about communism, Essie fired back that she was tired of being asked questions about communism, and she didn't think that America could blame Moscow or Stalin for its own social problems like segregation, discrimination, and economic inequality.[30] Cold War fear mongering and accusations about communism were, she believed, simply tools of the political establishment intended to distract voters from issues of injustice within the United States. Essie's foray into electoral politics was relatively brief. Always a bit half-hearted in her campaigning, Essie, after failing to secure enough signatures on her nominating petitions to run for Congress again four years later, retired from third-party electoral politics.

Essie's agitation and advocacy in other areas, however, continued full throttle. Even as she worked with the Progressive Party and other organizations, Essie continued to support the Council on African Affairs, the group she had helped to get off the ground in its earlier incarnation a decade earlier. Friction and political divisions within the group were growing, however, and as with the Progressive Party those divisions centered around the accusation of communist affiliations. In other words, in the early 1950s red-baiting already was effectively undermining popular alliances between communists and non-communists who supported labor, peace, civil rights, and anti-colonialism.

Essie often had to defend her dual roles as an American citizen and an American dissident. She was an American by birth and by choice, but she reserved the right to criticize America for its intractable racism and persistent inequalities. While she announced publicly that she was not a communist, she was a supporter of the Soviet Union. And she backed friends like Ben Davis, Claudia Jones, and others who were in fact members of the Communist Party.[31] Essie saw her allegiance to the Soviets as devotion to the principles of anti-racism and anti-imperialism. "Until the rise of the Soviet Union, all the world powers were colonial countries whose economy, politics and military were built upon the cheap raw materials and labor of their colonies in Africa and Asia." As long as "we Negroes have a major world power on our side," she insisted, Blacks should be on its side as well.[32] These sentiments were considered "disloyal" by many in the late 1940s and 1950s.

Sadly for Essie, it was her old friend Max Yergan who in 1947 was stirring up the most trouble in the Council on African Affairs through red-baiting and strong-arm tactics. Yergan, once a liberal Christian social worker in Africa, had moved sharply to the Left, worked closely with the Robesons, and was now reversing his political views yet again. A complicated and curious figure, Yergan had come to the conclusion that in order for the work of the council to go forward, it had to purge itself of communists and communist sympathizers, mimicking the actions that other liberal reform groups were taking. He pushed for a statement of "non-partisanship" to distance the council from allegedly "communist-tainted" groups and individuals. Essie and Paul both adamantly opposed this kind of political litmus test, especially since they, along with council staff member Alphaeus Hunton, were among Yergan's prime targets. But Yergan pressed hard for a vote on the issue.

Essie was in the thick of the fray.[33] She wrote a blistering letter that condemned Yergan's power play to oust some of the council's founding members, indicted his duplicity, and even threatened to sue him over African artifacts and books she had loaned to the council office, which was at the time under his supervision.[34] Essie went on to point out that Yergan knew full well the political opinions of his fellow council members, and for a good many years had no problem associating with communists. In fact, she asserted, it was in Yergan's living room that she first met Earl Browder, former head of the Communist Party. Her open letter was reprinted by the Associated Negro Press in its entirety. In the end Yergen and several council members left the council. It was a bitter split in the organization and a nasty end to a long and treasured friendship between Essie and Max.

Another important but short-lived group that Essie worked with in the early 1950s was Sojourners for Truth and Justice, a group named after the legendary, a nineteenth-century crusader for Black equality and women's rights. Founded in 1951 and already in demise by 1952, the group was one of the first tangible demonstrations of what historian Erik McDuffie has called "a postwar black left feminism."[35]

Sojourners for Truth and Justice was made up of a dynamic mix of creative Black women, many of them leftists and communists. Essie, author Shirley Graham Du Bois, actress Beulah (Beah) Richards, author Alice Childress, Thelma Dale Perkins, and activist Louise Thompson Patterson were among the founding core. They were joined by California publisher Charlotta Bass, who served as the group's president. Many of these women were also supporters of the Council on African Affairs. They described the Sojourners as "a militant Negro women's movement . . . dedicated to the militant struggle for full freedom of the Negro people and an uncompromising fight against white supremacy."[36] Members of Sojourners picketed, rallied, lobbied politicians, and tried to form coalitions with other women activists internationally. The group petitioned the U.S. president to support meaningful domestic civil rights legislation. They focused on freeing Black women from the yoke of colonialism abroad. In a letter to South African women trade unionists who had launched a campaign against their government's pass law system, Bass and Patterson wrote, "We have been inspired by the example of militant action on the part of African women. We realize that our fight for freedom in the United States is inextricably linked to the struggle against the tyranny of the white supremacists not only in South Africa but throughout the entire continent. We further recognize that these struggles for full freedom on the part of colored women in Africa, Asia and in the United States must lead to the complete emancipation of women throughout the world."[37]

The Sojourners also confronted egregious instances of injustice close to home, such as the case of Rosa Lee Ingram and her family. Ingram was a tough Georgia sharecropper who had killed a white man in 1947. She and two of her teenage sons, who had come to her aid during the confrontation, had been sentenced to death for the killing, even though it was clearly an act of self-defense. She languished on death row for eleven long years while many groups and civil rights leaders spoke out demanding her release. Was a poor Black woman expected to endure assault without the right to defend herself? they argued. No one made Ingram's case more loudly or insistently than the Sojourners. A delegation of the organization's members, including Essie, went to the nation's capital to plead Ingram's case and to demand a hearing. It took more than a decade for the Ingrams to win their freedom, but the attention that the Sojourners and others brought to the case was critically important to their release.[38]

The Sojourners for Truth and Justice did not have a long lifespan, but the group made a definite impact. As McDuffie has explained, "the Sojourners formulated a black left feminist politics that incorporated a sophisticated understanding of the African American freedom as a struggle for human rights, one that had global dimensions, during the Cold War."[39] Even though Essie's time with the Sojourners was limited, it was precisely this kind of radical women's project that allowed her to exercise her multiple and overlapping passions. Such organizations' attention to the compound and linked variables of race, class, and gender resembles what late-twentieth-century feminists of color would call "intersectionality."[40]

The year 1949 was another difficult one for Essie, largely because of several politically motivated, personal attacks against her family. The first related to a speech that Paul delivered that year at the World Congress of Partisans of Peace in Paris. Tensions were high between the United States and Soviet Union; the onetime World War II allies were already engaged in the Cold War, and some observers worried that a hot war was on the horizon. In his speech, Paul was alleged to have stated that no Negro would fight against the Soviet Union if the Americans and the Soviets went to war. His actual words were more nuanced than that. But the international media seized on the sound bite and published a highly sensationalized account that caused a firestorm back home. Some African American leaders rushed to distance themselves from both Paul and his comments; others went even further and made overtly disparaging comments about him. Lester Granger, a leader in the Urban League and columnist for the *Amsterdam News*, criticized Paul as "Heaven's gift to his left wing sponsors," suggesting that his welcome home rally from his Paris trip would be a communist-orchestrated spectacle.[41] One especially nasty headline in *The Chicago Defender* read, "Paul Robeson: Is He a Man or a Soviet Mouse?"[42]

The criticism of Paul's comments sadly overshadowed the work of the conference itself and Paul's role in it. Nearly 1,800 delegates from around the world, including Africa, had gathered to express their commitment to world peace. Paul had delivered a rousing speech, and virtually all of the speakers had echoed some version of Paul's sentiments. Another war was in no one's interest, they said, least of all the poor and oppressed. Essie's friend Shirley Du Bois spoke at the conference and insisted that Black women in the United States were unwilling to have their sons "fed to another war." Bluntly put, she argued, Black people in the United States might not be willing to support their government's war plans. Gabriel d'Arboussier, now president of the French Union representing French West Africa, "made an impassioned plea for the deliverance of Africa from all forms of colonialism" and declared his own opposition to any impending war.[43]

The most painful attacks against Paul's Paris speech came from former friends, people he and Essie had once trusted and cared for deeply. One headline in the *Black Press* read, "Robeson Blasted for Paris Speech: White, Other Leaders Repudiate His Stand." Indeed, Walter White had written unforgivingly about Paul, a man he had once befriended and admired, and to whom he had given the NAACP's highest honor, the Spingarn Medal, only six years earlier. In an article in the February issue of *Ebony* called "The Strange Case of Paul Robeson," White referred to Paul as "a bewildered man who [deserves] more to be pitied than damned." White wrote that Robeson had done more for Russia than for democratic struggles in the United States and concluded that Paul had demonstrated "the atrophy of his critical faculty" by his persistent loyalty to the Soviet Union. The lengthy attack was illustrated with a photo of Paul at a reception at the Russian Embassy with a large portrait of Soviet leader Joseph Stalin looming in the background for dramatic effect.[44] In a few short years the political tides had turned. Because of his radical politics (and outspoken support of the Soviet Union), Robeson, once an unquestioned hero and cultural icon, was being shunned and disparaged by some even as he retained the respect and loyalty of others.

The harsh criticisms that Paul received were not respectful differences over ideology or strategy. These were personal attacks, and Essie was outraged. Regardless of any marital tensions that existed between them, Essie and Paul had always stood together in their political views and in their public positions. So when Paul was attacked for his 1949 comments, Essie immediately issued a strong statement defending her husband and lambasting his detractors. She did not actually know what Paul's remarks had been, but she felt she knew him well enough to guess his meaning, and without full consultation with Paul or anyone else, she leapt into action.[45]

Essie rhetorically turned the tables, casting Paul's critics, White included, as "professional" Black leaders, and underscoring the fact that they held well-paid positions in various organizations—and so implying that they were out of touch with the Black rank and file, and perhaps trying to curry favor with white political elites. "I know that every sensible Negro in this country, professional leaders notwithstanding, feels that if he must fight a future war for democracy, the proper place to begin such a fight is right here," she wrote, rewording and reinforcing what she assumed had been Paul's point.[46] A few Black American leaders agreed and stood by Paul. Writing in the *Atlanta Daily World*, the Baptist minister and columnist Reverend Taschereau Arnold said, "Paul Robeson represents a vast throng of young Negroes who have become embittered by the trend of affairs in America . . . and was speaking the unuttered thoughts of a great segment of our people."[47]

Essie had been defending Paul since 1944 against the allegation that he was a member of the Communist Party.[48] It's an "absurdly foolish" suggestion, she insisted—overstating her case—pointing out that nearly every intelligent Black person at the time was being labeled a "red." Her instinct was to defend Paul, and as the attacks against him increased in vehemence, so did her response.[49] In refuting the charge that Paul was a communist, Essie did not succumb to red-baiting herself. Rather, she pointed out how charges of communist membership were used to undermine all progressive struggles, including anti-racist struggles. In a lengthy essay published in her friend Charlotta Bass's newspaper, Essie posed the challenging question—were Paul's critics satisfied with the violence and discrimination that American Negroes experienced every day? If not, how could they criticize Paul for speaking the truth about the injustices of American racism, which she assumed were the focus of his remarks in Paris? Essie questioned whether Walter White or Adam Clayton Powell actually spoke for millions of Black Americans, as they so boldly claimed. Could they promise that Black people would indeed fight for "American interests" in a hypothetical war in a far distant land? The crux of her defense, however, rested not on Paul's words in Paris, but on his record as a champion of Black freedom. "There is no one who has done more on behalf of the Negro people than Paul Robeson," she insisted. At a dinner at the Commodore Hotel in New York hosted by the Progressive Party, Essie said, "Paul Robeson [is] the son of a slave who caught the ear of the world with his golden voice, and who has always used that voice to call the attention of the world to the plight of the Negro people."[50]

Why was Paul Robeson perceived as being such a threat to political elites in the United States that he had to be monitored, contained, and attacked so roundly when he spoke out? In 1949, the U.S. government under President Truman was eager to promote America's political and economic interests abroad, and an image of America as a multiracial haven for democracy and freedom was central to that effort.[51] In the competition with the Soviet Union for sympathizers and allies in the newly (or nearly) independent nations of Asia and Africa, one of America's great advantages was the fiction it had to peddle about a land of milk and honey for all.[52] America's long history of racism and discrimination against peoples of color within its borders tarnished that image to say the least. And Paul Robeson was not only speaking about the reality of race in America with eloquence and effectiveness to an enormous international fan base but, moreover, painting a positive portrait of America's main economic and ideological rival. Perhaps not surprisingly, the U.S. government considered this combined message to be dangerously subversive.

It is necessary here to write a few words about race and Cold War America in order to adequately understand the political and intellectual terrain on which Essie and Paul were navigating. Although both Essie and Paul had explicitly and repeatedly denied membership in the Communist Party as an organization, for nearly a decade they had, as a matter of principle, refused to sign affidavits to that effect. In the anti-communist hysteria of Cold War America, the line of demarcation between "being" a communist and "not being" a communist was important to many people. The answer to the now famous question "Are you or have you ever been a member of the Communist Party?" made or unmade careers, facilitated or impeded mobility, and sometimes determined who went to jail and who could stay free.

But the simple question of whether someone was officially a member of the Communist Party could be misleading. The fact is that Paul and Essie were very close to the U.S. communist movement, as well as the international communist movement. And while those alliances were not formal or official, they had been carefully considered. Both Paul and Essie explained their reasons time and time again. In a polarized world, smaller emerging nations had a better chance with Soviet support of resisting U.S. imperialist aims, or, with Soviets as a countervailing force, of forging a nonaligned third path. The Robesons viewed the struggle for Black freedom in the larger context of the fight against Western imperialism and capitalist exploitation. Obviously they were not alone. People of color the world over embraced and adapted various versions of Marxism as they mapped paths to liberation. In the aftermath of the Great Depression in the United States that ravaged so many lives and affected African Americans disproportionately, and given the brutality of decades of colonial exploitation in the Third World, many people of color in the world were skeptical of capitalism's promises, to say the least. The communist edict "from each according to his ability and to each according to his needs" was appealing to many who felt they had given (or had taken from them) more than they could afford and received less than they deserved.[53] To those who had been at the losing end of the capitalist and colonial enterprises, socialism and communism had a visceral and an intellectual appeal. Even though Essie and Paul enjoyed more material wealth than most, they increasingly identified with those at the bottom of the social and economic hierarchies as a matter of principle. The appeal of communism was also mediated by strong anti-racist and anti-colonialist sentiments, and a kind of left Pan-Africanism.

For many Blacks attracted to left-wing ideas, there was no contradiction between Pan-Africanism, radical nationalism, and their support for communism. As historians Robin Kelley and Sid Lemelle put it, by the time the Robesons first came into the orbit of the communist movement in the 1930s, "Black nationalism(s)—especially as it was expressed in culture—had much more in common with American communism than most scholars have admitted. Thus, for African-American Communists, like American Jewish and Finnish Communists, whose cultural and national identities constituted a central element of their radical politics, ethnic nationalism and internationalism were not mutually exclusive." This was certainly true for Essie. Her pride in her African ancestry and even her sometimes romantic views of Africa were intimately bound up with her radicalism. Her support and loyalty to the Soviet Union was linked to her view that the Soviets were loyal to the interests of African peoples.[54]

Essie was involved in many progressive, left-wing, and communist-affiliated groups in the 1940s. She also supported the American Labor Party (ALP), a left-leaning group that emerged during the Depression with a slightly different strategy than the Progressive Party. The ALP commonly co-endorsed candidates that were endorsed by one of the two major parties so they were rarely in competition with the Democrats or Republicans in federal elections; one notable exception was in 1948, when they opted to support the Progressive Party's candidate, Henry Wallace. Vito Marcantonio, the outspoken radical New York Congressman from East Harlem, and probably the best-known elected official associated with the ALP, was a friend of Essie and Paul's. He and Essie exchanged letters, shared speakers' platforms, and supported many of the same progressive causes and campaigns. In the fall of 1949 Essie made routine treks into New York City to volunteer her services and participate in meetings at the ALP offices.[55] Her work was a part of a larger Left-liberal effort in the postwar years. Demands for a more robust and inclusive electoral process, full voting rights, and an end to policies of racial subordination and practices of racial violence were on the agenda. As Martha Biondi documents persuasively, this was especially true in New York City.[56]

As their public political personas developed, Paul was certainly the more visible and influential of the two, but Essie was also a powerful messenger in her own way for this same set of ideas, and her audience was growing. The Robesons "saw the struggle of Black Americans as one with the struggle of oppressed people worldwide" and explicitly connected the dots among economic exploitation, class oppression, racism, and colonialism.[57] Indeed, the Robesons and their allies were among the earliest proponents of the view that the struggles for self-determination and independence in Africa and the efforts of working-class people worldwide to escape oppression were inextricably linked to the fight to abolish Jim Crow and white supremacy in the States. Their views represented a kind of radical Black internationalism that the U.S. government at the time definitely wanted to suppress. They both sought to expose the truth that American racism was alive and well, despite propaganda to the contrary. Essie, too, pointed out the role of ingrained sexism in keeping women subordinate. The Robesons' message stood in contrast to the more modest, national, and race-specific claims made by many of their Black American contemporaries in mainstream organizations.

The push to frame America's civil rights and economic justice movements as part of a broader struggle for international human rights and to link it to the larger anti-colonial and anti-imperialist movements abroad might actually have strengthened and accelerated, rather than derailed, the push for racial equality had the Black leadership at the time adopted that stance. A number of historians have noted that mainstream Black leaders' refusal to acknowledge the universality of their claims and their hesitation to align with a larger Black Diasporic and Third World project might have been short-sighted. There were some liberal Black leaders, as historian Carol Anderson's work suggests, who understood all along the international scope of Black oppression and the need to take an interest in foreign affairs. Many of them, however, felt compelled to prove their American loyalties above all else.

Only four months after the Paris Peace Conference fracas, Paul was under attack again. Racist and anti-communist mobs rioted to protest his appearance at a large outdoor concert in Peekskill, New York, in August 1949. In the hysteria of the Cold War and after his misconstrued comments in Paris, Paul was now seen as an open target by right-wingers of various stripes. Cars were overturned, Black passersby were attacked, and the concert had to be postponed and rescheduled for September 4, at which time his opponents protested violently once again. This time, however, thousands of Paul's supporters mobilized to defend the concert grounds. The second concert went on as planned, and the events at Peekskill made headlines across the country and beyond. Peekskill represented the second attack on Essie's family in 1949.

In the wake of the Peekskill violence, many spoke out against his attackers, even some who disagreed with Paul's politics, such as former first lady Eleanor Roosevelt, actor Henry Fonda, and Essie's co-author Pearl Buck. No defender was more strident or eloquent than Essie.[58] Just as she had done months before when the Peace Conference remarks stirred controversy, Essie quickly and fiercely lashed out at Paul's attackers. On September 1, 1949, only a week after the first clash at Peekskill, Essie stood before a crowd of five thousand in Mexico City to address the American Continental Congress for Peace.[59] After greeting her audience in Spanish with "Queridos Amigos," and delivering greetings from her husband who could not be there, Essie slammed those in the United States who would deny Paul Robeson the right to speak and perform because of his political views and associations.[60] As others had done, Essie smartly turned the very language of McCarthyism against its proponents by describing the vigilantes who had disrupted the Peekskill concert as un-American. She then turned her criticism toward the U.S. government itself for not pushing hard enough to make America's ideals a reality. "We in the United States . . . have been confused for generations by the large and elegant conversation about Democracy." That conversation, she argued, had often been vacuous, because the United States had systematically denied rights to so many of its own citizens and interfered with the affairs of other nations from Mexico to Greece to the small island nations and colonies of the Caribbean.[61]

During times of stress, with her adrenaline pumping to protect those she loved, Essie was unrestrained in her defense. Once she returned from Mexico, she had to go into battle mode once again when confronted by yet another family crisis: the controversy that erupted around her son's marriage in 1949 to a young white woman. Essie had a particularly emotional response to the attack on Paul Jr.

The young Paul Robeson had fallen in love with Marilyn Greenberg, a fellow student at Cornell University in Ithaca, New York, where he was studying engineering. Paul Jr. described Marilyn as "an attractive, five-foot-six, dark-haired, twenty-year-old with a flashing smile, beautiful eyes, and a witty sense of humor."[62] The young couple had met in progressive political circles at Cornell. He was highly visible on campus, given the Robeson name, and Marilyn was low-key by comparison. But the serious, smart, good-looking young woman who spoke her mind and exuded her own special charm caught Paul Jr.'s attention. Friendship evolved into romance, and they became engaged soon thereafter.[63] Marilyn's mother, Rae, did not initially approve of the interracial relationship for fear of the hardships it might represent for her daughter, but she eventually came around. Marilyn's father was not so amenable; during their courtship, he refused to let Paul Jr. into their home. Still, the determined young couple moved forward with their plans to marry. Paul Jr. took Marilyn home to Connecticut over Christmas break in

1948 to meet his parents and, rather inadvertently, announced their engagement. Actually Paul Sr. guessed their intentions and after a moment of surprise, Essie too embraced the news. Essie was impressed with Marilyn, and respected her son's level-headed judgment.

Paul Jr. and Marilyn's wedding was intended to be a small and quiet event at the New York City apartment of Freda Diamond, one of Paul's intimates who also maintained a close friendship with Essie. But as soon as news reached the mainstream media, reporters swarmed all around them. The media attention led to a flood of hate mail to Essie from white people angry at the idea of an interracial marriage. The day of the wedding, in particular, the mainstream media "sent squads of cameramen to the affair."[64] There were even a handful of hecklers in the street outside Freda's apartment.

The response probably should not have been too surprising, given that the wedding came on the heels of Paul's Paris Peace Conference speech, and followed by only a matter of hours his "Welcome Home" rally, which was held at the Rockland Palace on 155th Street in Harlem and attended by an overflow crowd of some five thousand people.[65] But when venomous attacks were hurled at Paul Jr. and Marilyn, Essie felt the critics had crossed the line. In response she sat down and wrote a biting essay entitled "Loyalty—Lost and Found." Essie began by satirically claiming to have misplaced her loyalty to a country that practiced racial inequality and tolerated vitriol and harassment. She protested that because her "beloved and only child married the girl he loves, I have taken a beating at the hands of my fellow countrymen: some of whom collected in the streets to boo my children, whom they did not even know." In conclusion she declared, "I do hereby declare war on my enemies and publicly notify them that I will fight them every step of the way."[66] And she meant it.

The year 1949 had been hectic and demanding, full of angst and conflict. So in December Essie was relieved to collect her passport, pack her bags, and go far, far away. That month she traveled without Paul to the Soviet Union, Eastern Europe, and the People's Republic of China. Little did she know it would be her last international trip for nearly a decade. The purpose of Essie's trip was to attend both the Women's International Democratic Federation (WIDF) Conference in Moscow, and the Asian Women's Federation meeting in Peking (later Beijing). She planned to stop for several days in Poland, Czechoslovakia, and Belgium on her return trip. Essie traveled with her New York acquaintance Ada Jackson, a Black Brooklyn-based American Labor Party (ALP) activist.[67] According to the *Amsterdam News*, Essie and Ada were the "first African American wom[e]n to visit China since the defeat of the Chiang Kai Shek government and the establishment of the new Chinese government, on October 1, 1949."[68] The FBI carefully monitored their trip, which Essie expressed to friends, in her usual upbeat manner, as an absolutely enlightening and "marvelous experience."[69]

Essie had an interesting and savvy travel companion in Jackson. There is no evidence that the two women ever became close friends, but a trip like this, of such historic significance, undoubtedly created some sort of bond between them. Jackson was a tough community organizer who was born in Georgia but cut her political teeth in the rough and tumble streets of Brooklyn's Bedford-Stuyvesant neighborhood. Described as a grassroots "powerhouse" by the Negro press, she pushed for safe and affordable housing as well as decent schools, and headed up the Interracial Assembly, a local coalition of community organizations in the city's southern borough.[70] She joined the progressive Congress of American Women, the U.S. affiliate of the WIDF; ran for office several times on the American Labor Party ticket; and the year before she traveled to the Soviet Union and China with Essie, she was a delegate to an international peace conference in Romania.[71]

After a brief stopover at the women's conference in Moscow, Essie and Ada took the Trans-Siberian Railroad into China, first to Peking and then to Shanghai. There were meetings in both cities. The trip to China was an eye-opener for Essie in many respects, and she took the ideas being discussed there seriously. It was a historic time for China, and in preparation for the conference Essie had read Mao Zedong's *The Chinese Revolution and the Chinese Communist Party*, and had taken meticulous notes on every section of it in her small, lined notebook.[72] The conference, which consisted of a series of lectures and panel presentations delivered in Chinese but simultaneously translated through earphones for international guests, gave participants an overview of the new Chinese government's vision and strategy for rebuilding the vast country, and of the political and economic changes under way. One lecture Essie attended in Shanghai on December 22 was delivered by Chen Yi, the mayor of that historic port city, and covered the complex process of reordering a major industrial center. The communists had been grounded in the rural areas, he explained, so it was a challenge for them to consider how to transform and redirect the resources of a city like Shanghai. The presentation suggested that the "take over" was as much a political battle as a technical one, given that there were many anti-

Mao Kuomintang supporters still embedded in the city bureaucracy.[73] It is unclear what kind of questions Essie asked or whether she was at all skeptical about any of the new developments she witnessed, but in her public statements after she returned, her accounts were glowing and supportive of the revolution's aims.

One person Essie met in China made a lasting impression on her: the Western-educated revolutionary heroine Soong Ching-ling, better known as Madame Sun Yat-sen. Soong Ching-ling had been born into privilege in China in 1893, married Sun (more than twenty-five years her senior) in 1915, and immersed herself first in the nationalist struggle to oust the monarchy and then, after Sun's death in 1925, allied herself with the communists. In 1949 she had just been appointed vice chair of the new People's Republic of China. She was also serving as honorary president of the All China Women's Federation. Soong Ching-ling was a much-revered figure who, at the time Essie met her, wielded considerable power. When Essie's train arrived in Shanghai after midnight on December 21, Soong was in the crowd that greeted the delegation. Essie would also spend two more days with her. On the evening of December 22, after the Chen Yi lecture, a small group of conferees met with Soong over dinner at the Golden Gate Hotel. And the following day, with an even smaller group, or perhaps alone, Essie and Soong met for lunch at her home, a converted mansion in the old International Settlement of Shanghai. They talked at length about world politics, the revolutionary changes taking place in China, and especially the condition of women. Essie recalled that Soong Ching-ling pointed out to her the importance of the new Common Law Article 6, which gave new rights to Chinese women. Essie was impressed by this "fragile" but tough woman who, in her view, stood as a "magnificent example of courage, warm humanity, and common sense."[74]

After the conference Essie traveled around the country, seeing centuries-old landmarks like the Great Wall and various palaces and temples. In addition to Peking and Shanghai, her itinerary included a short stay in Nanking, then a visit to the northern city of Tientsin (Tianjin).[75] The Chinese revolution was still very young, just two months old. So Essie was able to witness a socialist experiment in the making as local committees grappled with how to reconstruct their society after the ravages of civil war, and with political differences and social cleavages that were still very real.

Essie's decision to go to China was a bold and brazen political move in December of 1949. The communist forces of Mao Zedong had declared victory over the Nationalist forces of Chiang Kai-Shek just months earlier before declaring the formation of the People's Republic of China (PRC). The U.S. government, which had supported the Nationalists during the three-year civil war, immediately suspended diplomatic ties with the new communist regime. U.S. banks refused to give the PRC access to Bank of China funds, and the American embassy closed up shop and followed Kuomintang leader Chiang Kai-shek into exile in Formosa (later Taiwan). So while Essie wasn't breaking any laws by traveling to China, her actions were a dissident response to official U.S. foreign policy.

Essie returned to the United States in January 1950, eager to talk to audiences about what she had seen in "the new China." She held a press conference the Monday after her return, and called upon the U.S. government to formally recognize the PRC. One reporter observed admiringly that she "handled herself like an expert before a battery of cameramen and reporters." The *Afro-American* newspaper reported that Essie sharply "criticized Secretary [of State Dean] Acheson for 'talking in a vacuum on China,' and said he really knows nothing of what is going on there." In her typical irreverent manner, Essie bluntly advised Acheson to "get on his horse and go to China" so he could see firsthand what the Chinese people were doing and thereby establish the basis for a more fair and informed foreign policy. When she was challenged about the disrespectful tone of her comments, she quickly snapped back: "I have no respect for a Secretary of State unless he acts like one," adding that it was Acheson who should be accountable to her since she paid his salary as a taxpayer.[76]

Essie had harsh words for other U.S. government officials as well, and the State Department took all of those words seriously. The FBI kept an extensive file on Essie's pro-China remarks and her relationships with Chinese diplomats like her friend Kung Pu Shen. In December 1950 an FBI surveillance report noted: "The file on captioned individual [Essie] has been reviewed for the purpose of determining whether she is of such professed communist China sympathy that she would present a threat in the event of hostilities with Communist China."[77] Essie likely suspected she was under surveillance, but it did not deter her from speaking out loudly and with conviction.

In a 1951 article in the newspaper *Freedom*, Essie drew parallels between pre-revolutionary China and the Jim Crow South. She wrote: "Every Negro who has been called 'George' regardless of his right name, 'Uncle' regardless of his relationship, 'boy' regardless of his age

. . . who has not been allowed to enter the public libraries, parks, theatres, stores; every Negro who has been denied proper respect, human dignity and human rights—All these Negroes will be able to understand and fully appreciate what is happening in the Chinese People's Republic. In the new China, the old familiar signs, 'CHINESE AND DOGS NOT ALLOWED,' have been torn down," with other painful reminders of the era when British imperialists had their run of port cities like Shanghai, unimpeded by corrupt Chinese elites.[78] She suggested that the anti-Chinese racism that had dominated for years was a thing of the past, and that women's rights were being advanced as well.

Essie was inundated with invitations to speak about her China trip. She agreed to do a speaking tour in 1950 that was coordinated by her friend and colleague Louise Thompson Patterson, a key member of the Council on African Affairs and the second wife of Communist Party leader William Patterson.[79] The purpose of Essie's tour was to describe China's progress and promise. "Red Regime Lauded: New China Frees Masses, Mrs. Robeson Declares," was the headline in one newspaper. In the article itself, Essie was quoted as saying, "The new government has emancipated the nation's peasants from the feudal system that has chained them for centuries." She again compared the plight of the workers and peasants in China with that of the American Negro in the South, then added, "For generations now, everyone has owned China but the Chinese people, and now they own it." She concluded that the United States would eventually be forced to recognize the new regime in China. "You just can't ignore 450 million people and their government," she said.[80] Essie also spoke about her trip to the Soviet Union, highlighting the progress that women were making both there and in the PRC.

Essie talked to a wide range of groups about her travels in the East. The Centennial Christian Church hosted her in St. Louis. In Detroit, she spoke to an interdenominational alliance of clergy. But she especially enjoyed speaking to women's groups. The United Nationalities Committee in Youngstown, Ohio, hosted a women's dinner at which Essie spoke about the conferences in Peking and Moscow. On October 3, 1954, she flew out to Oakland, California, for an engagement with the California State Association of Colored Women. In speeches like these, she challenged other women to become more involved in world affairs and more educated about global issues.[81]

Essie also reached out specifically to the grassroots Black organizations that had nurtured and sponsored her in her youth—and challenged their members to think more globally. In March 1950, when Essie was passing through Detroit, her sorority sisters held a dinner there in her honor. She told them all about her China trip and even "broached the idea of their sponsoring a nursery for Chinese children." She reported that they were "crazy about the idea" and interested in sending books to the International Peace Hospital. Although there is no indication that these projects ever materialized, Essie was pleased that her Delta sisters were so open to her suggestion. She regretted only that similar proposals for projects in Africa "left them cold."[82]

Essie also made contact with the Chinese diplomatic community in New York when she returned from her trip, meeting in December 1950 with Kung Pu Shen of the PRC Ministry of Foreign Affairs and attending a function hosted by China's U.N. delegation at the Waldorf Astoria Hotel two years later. There was likely other undocumented contact as well. Essie was quite open in her praise for China's new communist government in the 1950s, and as a sympathetic journalist she was eager to monitor its progress. She particularly applauded the progress and leadership of women like Kung Pu Shen, who over the years became a valued personal friend.[83]

Essie was outspoken and never shy to express her views even when they were controversial, as hers were in the increasingly conservative climate of Cold War America. Wherever she went in the early 1950s, she was met with both praise and criticism, which did not seem to slow her down one bit. Opposition came with taking difficult stands. As long as controversy did not connote marginality or create isolation, she was fine. On this particular speaking tour, one of the first places she encountered stiff protest was Minneapolis, Minnesota. She was scheduled to speak at the city's interracial and liberal Phyllis Wheatley House, a local community center where public forums were routinely held, but at the last minute the board of directors determined that "the community house was [not] the proper place for so controversial a figure as Mrs. Robeson."[84] Undeterred, the local members of the Civil Rights Congress, the sponsoring organization, found a new venue at the union hall of the Congress of Industrial Organizations (CIO), where Essie spoke to an overflow crowd. She seized the opportunity to talk about the new freedoms she had witnessed in China and her concerns about curtailed freedom of speech and censorship at home. The following day, she spoke to students who gathered in the student union at the University of Minnesota. Opting not to stand behind a podium, Essie sat on a table, feet dangling over the side and wearing a dark suit and a stylish white hat, and engaged the students for hours in a relaxed interaction about world politics. Essie praised China's new land-reform policy and the fact that, in China, "equality extends to the women, who are recognized as citizens on the same basis as the men."[85]

The small town of Arden, Delaware, was the site of one of the most intense protests against Essie. In December 1952, she was asked by a liberal organization, the Arden Club's Scholars Guild, to come and speak about her research on Africa and her views on global affairs. Because of her recent visits to communist countries and her opposition to U.S. intervention in Korea, conservative groups responded to her appearance with protests that included death threats and harassing phone calls to her hosts. On the day of her speech, the organizers withstood a barrage of criticisms and harassment, but in the end the event was attended by an audience of more than a hundred people, most of them favorably inclined toward Essie's message. She fielded a few hostile questions, but overall she handled herself with confidence and aplomb.[86]

During the early 1950s, Asia was in conflict and flux, and China was only one site of contestation. War had broken out between communist North Korea and pro-Western South Korea in the summer of 1950, with China and the Soviet Union supporting the north and the United States and the United Nations supporting the south. Essie and Paul both spoke out against U.S. military involvement in Korea. One of Essie's largest audiences was on Randall's Island in New York City on August 20, 1952, when she spoke at the "Peace under the Stars" rally to a crowd of ten thousand that had gathered at the Triboro Stadium. This time the crowd was large and supportive. A veteran's group had threatened to protest the event but they did not. The rally represented a broad left-of-center coalition against U.S. militarism. It took place a little over a week after the U.S. Air Force dropped 650 tons of bombs on North Korean cities. Essie was one of a number of prominent New York peace activists, a group that included religious, civic, and labor leaders. Essie denounced U.S. involvement in Korea, condemned the arms race, and called for peace and peaceful coexistence.[87]

In the late 1940s and early 1950s, as the Cold War began and political intolerance took hold in the United States, Essie was indeed engaged in an "American argument" much bigger and fiercer than her book-bound exchanges with Pearl Buck. It was an argument about race and violence (Rosa Ingram and the attacks on Paul Jr.'s wedding); about China and self-determination; about peaceful co-existence (with the Soviet Union); about the right to dissent (Peekskill and her own disrupted speaking engagements); and about the narrowness and exclusivity of the two-party system (the Progressive Party initiative). And for Essie, it continued to be an argument about African and African American freedom movements, and about the United States' role in either furthering or obstructing that freedom.

(*top*): Eslanda at the American Continental Congress for Peace Conference in Mexico City, 1949. Paul and Eslanda Goode Robeson Collection, Howard University, Moorland-Spingarn Research Center, Manuscript Division.

Eslanda at a press conference at Hotel McAlpin in New York City, February 1952. Daily Worker/Daily World Photographs Collection, Tamiment Library, New York University.

(*top*): Eslanda (*center front*) with the Progressive Party's Peace Delegation, circa 1948. Daily Worker/Daily World Photographs Collection, Tamiment Library, New York University.

Eslanda with friends Alphaeus Hunton and Louise Thompson Patterson as she boards a plane for one of her many trips, circa 1958. Daily Worker/ Daily World Photographs Collection, Tamiment Library, New York University. Photo by Cecil Layne.

(*top*): Eslanda with co-author Pearl Buck, circa 1949. Paul and Eslanda Goode
Robeson Collection, Howard University, Moorland-Spingarn Research Center,
Manuscript Division.

Eslanda and Paul at the "Peace under the Stars" rally at Randalls Island, N.Y.,
August 20, 1952. Associated Press/Matty Zimmerman.

(*top*): Eslanda, on the campaign trail, with 1948 Progressive Party presidential candidate, Henry Wallace (*third from right*), H. Lester Hutchinson, British Labor MP (*second from left*), and Michele Giua, Italian socialist senator (*second from right*), Portland, Oregon, circa 1949. Paul and Eslanda Goode Robeson Collection, Howard University, Moorland-Spingarn Research Center, Manuscript Division.

Eslanda testifying before Senator Joseph McCarthy's U.S. Senate Permanent Subcommittee on Investigations of the Committee on Government Operations, Washington, D.C., July 7, 1953. Akademie der Künste, Berlin, Paul Robeson Archives/photo by UPI/Bettmann Newsphoto.

(*top*): Howard Fast receiving the 1953 Stalin Peace Prize with (*from left*)
Shirley Graham Du Bois, Paul and Eslanda, and W. E. B. Du Bois (*second from right*). Special Collections and University Archives, Rutgers University Libraries/
Julius Lazarus.

Eslanda speaking with U.N. Secretary-General Dag Hammarskjöld at the U.N.
headquarters in New York, 1958. Paul and Eslanda Goode Robeson Collection,
Howard University, Moorland-Spingarn Research Center, Manuscript Division.

(*top*): Eslanda in Australia with a Maori "challenge" staff that was given to her in New Zealand, 1960. © Newspix / News Ltd / 3rd Party Managed Reproduction & Supply Rights.

Eslanda with the Prime Minister of Burma, U Nu, 1950s. From the personal collection of Paul Robeson Jr.

(*top*): Eslanda with Nayantara and Chandralekha Pandit, daughters of her friend V. L. Pandit and nieces of India's future Prime Minister, Jawaharlal Nehru, at her home in Enfield, Conn., 1944. From the personal collection of Paul Robeson Jr.

Vijaya Lakshmi Pandit, Essie's lifelong friend, speaking at the United Nations in 1963, where she served as the first woman President of the General Assembly in 1953. UN Photo.

(*top*): Eslanda (*right*) with (*from left*) Alphaeus Hunton, Shirley Graham Du Bois, and President Kwame Nkrumah at the All-African Peoples' Conference in Accra, Ghana, December 1958. Paul and Eslanda Goode Robeson Collection, Howard University, Moorland-Spingarn Research Center, Manuscript Division.

Eslanda with friends and colleagues, Belgian Congo, 1946. Paul and Eslanda Goode Robeson Collection, Howard University, Moorland-Spingarn Research Center, Manuscript Division.

(*top*): Eslanda speaking at a public library lecture, Port of Spain, Trinidad, April 21, 1958. Future Prime Minister of Guyana, Cheddi Jagan sits in front of the podium in a white jacket. Paul and Eslanda Goode Robeson Collection, Howard University, Moorland-Spingarn Research Center, Manuscript Division/Photo by Shahadath Mohammed.

Eslanda greeted by Janet Jagan, future Prime Minister of Guyana, in Trinidad, April 21, 1958. Cheddi Jagan Research Centre, Guyana/Photo by Shahadath Mohammed. Photo courtesy of Nadira Jagan-Brancier.

(*top*): Eslanda with Senator Theophilus Albert Marryshow of Grenada at the
West Indies Federation in Trinidad, April 1958. Paul and Eslanda Goode Robeson
Collection, Howard University, Moorland-Spingarn Research Center,
Manuscript Division.

Eslanda and Paul in Tashkent, Uzbekistan, 1958. Akademie der Künste, Berlin,
Paul Robeson Archives.

(*top*): Eslanda and Paul seated with Soviet leader Nikita Khrushchev (*third from left*), at his vacation retreat near Yalta, Crimea, 1958. Library of Congress.

Eslanda speaks in Berlin at a mass rally for the International Commemoration Day for the Victims of Fascist Terror, September 13, 1959. Paul and Eslanda Goode Robeson Collection, Howard University, Moorland-Spingarn Research Center, Manuscript Division.

(*top*): Eslanda (*center*) at the trial of alleged Nazi collaborator Hans Globke, before the East German Supreme Court, July 8, 1963. Bundesarchiv, Bild 183-B0708-0014-004/Eva Brüggmann.

Eslanda (*right*) at the Women's International Democratic Federation Conference, Moscow, November 1949, with trade unionist Pearl Laws (*center*) and American Labor Party activist Ada Jackson (*left*). Paul and Eslanda Goode Robeson Collection, Howard University, Moorland-Spingarn Research Center, Manuscript Division.

(*top*): Eslanda speaking with Dr. Martin Luther King Jr. in London, October 1961. Claudia Jones Memorial Photograph Collection, Photographs and Prints Division, Schomburg Center for Research in Black Culture, The New York Public Library, Astor, Lenox and Tilden Foundations.

From left: Claudia Jones, Paul, Amy Ashwood Garvey, and Eslanda with friends in London, circa 1959. Claudia Jones Memorial Photograph Collection, Photographs and Prints Division, Schomburg Center for Research in Black Culture, The New York Public Library, Astor, Lenox and Tilden Foundations.

(*top*): Eslanda and Paul with Nigerian students, London, circa 1961.
Akademie der Künste, Berlin, Paul Robeson Archives.

Eslanda speaking at "Africa Women's Day" as part of the All-African Women's
Freedom Movement at the State Ballroom Hall in London, December 7, 1961.
On the left, Claudia Jones sits next to Kwesi Armah, Ghana's High Commissioner
to Britain and Nkrumah's Minister of Foreign Trade. Claudia Jones Memorial
Photograph Collection, Photographs and Prints Division, Schomburg Center
for Research in Black Culture, The New York Public Library, Astor,
Lenox and Tilden Foundations.

Eslanda (*back row, fourth from left*) with friends in London, including Claudia Jones (*on Eslanda's right*) and Peggy Middleton (*seated on floor, third from left*), circa 1963. Paul and Eslanda Goode Robeson Collection, Howard University, Moorland-Spingarn Research Center, Manuscript Division.

Paul, Eslanda, and Paul Jr. at their home in Enfield, Connecticut, 1941. Frank Bauman. From the personal collection of Paul Robeson Jr.

(*top*): Paul and Eslanda Robeson in 1965. From the personal collection
of Paul Robeson Jr.

Three generations of the Robesons (*left to right, top row*): Paul Jr.'s wife, Marilyn;
Eslanda; and Paul Jr.; (*left to right, bottom row*): Susan, Paul, and David, 1957.
From the personal collection of Paul Robeson Jr.

eleven

THE UNITED NATIONS
AND A WORLD POLITICAL
FAMILY, 1950–1956

The biggest, most widespread, most diverse, most cantankerous
and most potentially wonderful family, the World Family known
as the United Nations Organization, has been in labor.
Eslanda Robeson

By the early 1950s Essie's international interests were not just centered in Africa but spanned all of the colonized and post-colonial world, as well as socialist and communist countries around the globe. Her intellectual interests were broad as well. Although she was both a journalist and anthropologist, she sought to research, understand, and write about changing global realities not as a disinterested scholar or an ostensibly impartial reporter, but as a passionate and engaged historical actor, a scholar-activist, and a radical writer trying to both uncover the truth and influence the future. "The death moans of colonialism can be heard around the world mingled with the cries for self-government and independence and the shouts for peace and freedom," she wrote with excited anticipation.[1] Her own voice was among those shouting for peace and freedom, from the pages of newspapers and magazines and from the speaker's podium at venues throughout the United States and around the world. In her role as a journalist and U.N. correspondent, she also sometimes whispered her views discreetly into the ears of the policy-makers and power brokers to whom she had access.

With her speaking tour in 1950, and a series of articles that she published after her 1949–1950 trip to China and the Soviet Union, Essie felt she was truly coming into her own as a journalist, public speaker,

205

and writer on international affairs. In 1952 she became a regular correspondent for the *New World Review*, a Communist-allied leftist journal that reported on global issues and took a sympathetic view of both the USSR and China. "The purpose of our magazine is to bring the American people better understanding of the Soviet Union, Peoples China, and the people's liberation movements everywhere," the mission statement read. This affiliation gave Essie press credentials and a desk in the U.N. press room. A wide range of progressive writers and thinkers joined Essie in contributing to *New World Review*. Later in 1952 Essie also became the journal's editorial consultant on Negro and colonial issues. In addition, she wrote for various Black publications, including the *Afro-American*, the *Pittsburgh Courier*, the Associated Negro Press, *Challenge*, the *Sun Reporter*, the *California Eagle*, and the *Amsterdam News*. From 1950 to 1955, Essie also contributed writings to *Freedom*, the short-lived but influential newspaper that Paul had launched in November of 1950. The publication was ably edited by respected organizer Louis Burnham, but also buoyed by the efforts of three women whom Essie would later befriend and work more closely with on various projects in the years that followed: a young emerging playwright, Lorraine Hansberry; actress and writer Alice Childress; and actress and activist Beah Richards.

As for Essie, she was extremely prolific and outspoken, cranking out nearly two hundred articles and essays and delivering more than two hundred speeches during the late 1940s and 1950s.[2] Essie's initial focus in her political writing was the continent of Africa, but she widened her purview—and network—over the next decade and a half as she gained journalistic prominence and experience. Her perch at the United Nations provided her a special vantage point from which to observe global politics at work. She met and befriended a wide range of diplomats, writers, translators, and scholars from Latin America, Asia, the Caribbean, Africa, and Europe. Driven by her insatiable intellectual curiosity about the world, she ultimately created a niche for herself as a writer and observer of global affairs. No matter what part of the world she covered, Essie was a vociferous defender of the right of colonized people to self-rule, an unwavering critic of U.S. racism and chauvinism, and a strong advocate of peace and disarmament. "I am very happy to be able in some small way to participate in this work of searching out, accumulating, analyzing and then sharing constructive information about the countries and peoples of our New World," she reflected in a 1954 speech.[3]

In her coverage of international affairs, Essie always made clear the connections to domestic issues. For example, in an article for the *New World Review* called "What Is a Ghetto? Lessons from the Warsaw Ghetto Uprising for All People," Essie explicitly tied the treatment of Jews in Poland to that of Blacks in the United States. The article was based on a speech she gave at a rally in New York on April 20, 1954, to mark the eleventh anniversary of the uprising by Jewish residents of Warsaw against Nazi aggression and genocide in Poland. "Nearly every Negro knows what Ghettoes are," she began. "The Ghetto may be called by another name. But . . . most of us now understand the sinister meaning of the Ghetto. It is the place into which a section of the population is herded, and forced to live—alienated, segregated, separated from the rest of the population, and then subjected to exploitation, abuse and attack. The Ghetto is a pool for cheap labor. It is a source of high profits on rundown, outmoded housing. It is even a convenient place to run amok and kill people when the so-called advanced civilized, superior people feel the urge to some kind of destruction, a Pogrom, a Riot, a Lynching."[4] She then drew parallels between Jewish resistance to Nazi terror, the resistance to housing segregation in Detroit, and the fight against the brutality of Apartheid in South Africa.

Essie called on Black people to see their fate as tied to that specifically of other people of color worldwide. "We Negroes are becoming all the more impatient as we learn about what is going on among the colored peoples elsewhere in the great wide wonderful world. Our hearts beat faster when we learn that Africans in the Gold Coast are governing themselves, and that Africans in Nigeria will soon be doing likewise. We hold our breath with anxiety and sympathy for Africans in South Africa who have organized with Indians and colored people there to resist Malan's vicious policy of Apartheid. We worry about Africans in Kenya who are undergoing genocide," she wrote in 1955.[5]

Essie covered the United Nations at a turbulent time in her own life. As will be discussed in more detail in Chapter 12, she and Paul were under siege at home from the anti-communist crusades of Senator Joe McCarthy and his disciples. She could have become fearful and inward-focused but instead she looked outward to the rest of the world. Essie refused to be intimidated by her own government or back away from covering the most controversial international stories of the day. In the spring of 1953, for example, Essie reported on the Tenth Inter-American Conference in Caracas, Venezuela, that brought together delegates from North and South America. The U.S. delegation was led by U.S. Secretary of State John Foster Dulles, who "forced through" an anti-communist resolution and then left the conference, according to Essie's coverage. She criticized Dulles sharply. After Dulles left, the conference focused primarily on issues of "racism and colonialism."[6]

Essie was careful not to stereotype or idealize leaders in the Third World either, and she was willing to report on the internal problems and contradictions of their governments as well. People of color were not monolithic or immune to criticism. There was a right wing and a left wing in every national context, and Essie unapologetically located herself on the Left. After the conference in Venezuela, she wrote that a number of Latin American countries represented at the gathering were languishing under dictatorships. "It is freely admitted that President Jimenez of Venezuela has one of the most complete and ruthless right-wing military dictatorships in all Latin America, and that Trujillo of the Dominican Republic, Somoza of Nicaragua, and Batista of Cuba are all recognized as despots," she wrote, bluntly. "Costa Rica and Guatemala, two of the more democratic regimes in Latin America, publicly protested against some of these dictatorships at the Caracas gathering."[7] These internal struggles over politics and power within the Third World were as important as the big worldwide contestations, and they were related.

Essie applauded the Guatemalan delegation for taking a defiant stance against autocracy in Latin America and for "oppos[ing] emphatically the internationalization of McCarthyism" by the United States.[8] By this, she meant that the Guatemalans were opposing the push for smaller countries to choose sides in the Cold War. The Guatemalan government paid for that defiance less than a year later when the CIA orchestrated a coup that overthrew the government of the democratically elected president, Jacobo Árbenz Guzmán. When the coup occurred, Essie raised her pen in protest against the "barbarous attack" in an essay for *New World Review*. And she criticized the United Nations for its slow and tepid response to the pleas for help from the "defenseless and desperate" government of Guatemala.[9]

Around the same time, Essie weighed in on another heated debate: over whether the United Nations should seat leaders from the five-year-old government of the People's Republic of China (PRC) or exiled nationalist leaders in Formosa (Taiwan) who claimed to be the legitimate representatives of the Chinese people. A strong supporter of the PRC, especially after her 1949 visit, Essie predictably advocated for seating the communist-led government from the mainland. The fact that the United Nations had refused to seat a PRC representative, deferring instead to the relatively small anti-communist leadership in exile, infuriated Essie, and she made her views known through her writings and speeches.[10] In a January 1956 essay, she argued that the "Man from Formosa" had the "least claim of all to membership" in the United Nations and that his "presence deprives the 600,000,000 people of the Chinese People's Republic of their rightful seat at the family (United Nations) council table!" She went on to write, "No one in his right mind who is aware of the present day facts of life, would continue to insist that the representatives of Formosa truly represent anyone except Chiang Kai-Shek and his followers."[11] Essie then outlined the progress China had made in women's health and education, especially in rural areas, and concluded that much "might be gained from the presence of People's China in the United Nations."[12] Even though the United Nations was becoming more representative of the world, more "multi-colored," Essie argued it was still excluding millions of Chinese for being on the wrong side of the Cold War divide.

Throughout the 1950s, the United Nations was a critical forum for debate and political maneuvering as nations jostled to gain power. Membership in the United Nations was a major goal—and point of contention—because it conferred legitimacy, diplomatic relevance, and access to rights and resources. There were epic struggles within newly independent and post-revolutionary nations to set borders and establish new political structures. The victors of those battles were granted U.N. membership. Essie's disappointment about China's exclusion was somewhat tempered by the inclusion of sixteen new member states in the mid to late 1950s. "The biggest, most widespread, most diverse, most cantankerous and most potentially wonderful family, the World Family known as the United Nations Organization, has been in labor," she wrote—and was finally giving birth.[13]

Yet another critical issue facing the United Nations in the mid-1950s was France's battle to retain control over its North African colony of Algeria. Essie followed the debate about Algeria through various sources, including the foreign press, and wrote passionately on the subject. Responding specifically to the fierce struggle in Algeria, Essie wrote: "The death moans of colonialism can be heard around the world mingled with the cries for self-government and independence, and the shouts for peace and freedom," adding that "the formerly quiet, assured, occasionally arrogant voices of the Colonial Powers are not so confident these days."[14] In an article for the *New World Review*, Essie further outlined what she believed was at stake in the debate over Algeria: that Algeria posed a challenge to the United Nations as an institution that claimed to be an honest broker for international peace, and that the fragile and eclectic alliance of Third World nations coalescing to wage a fight on Algeria's behalf could represent a major shift in the balance of power in the world.

At first, France would not even acknowledge that the Algerian question was a legitimate issue for the United Nations to take up. France argued this was an internal matter, since Algeria was, France claimed, "part of Metro political France." The fact that Algeria lay across the Mediterranean on a different continent, Essie argued, was seemingly irrelevant to the French because France was still espousing the mind-bending illogic of colonial rule.[15] So the first order of business was to get Algeria on the agenda of the U.N. General Assembly. Initially, the fifteen-member general committee that set the agendas for the body refused. But a coalition of primarily Black and Brown nations ignored that decision and took the issue to the floor of the General Assembly anyway, requesting a special vote. "There was a bitter hard fought battle in the General Committee over the Algerian Question," Essie explained in one of her essays on the subject. "The Colonial Powers won the fight in the less representative body . . . [but] after another bitter battle [through a process of appeal, the progressive forces] defeated the Colonial Powers and won inscription of the item on the agenda."[16]

Citing the spirit of Bandung (referring to the 1955 'unity' conference of Third World non-aligned nations), Essie declared that no longer can the United Nations be labeled "a Colonial Club."[17] She quoted her friend Krishna Menon, a bold and outspoken Indian representative, who eloquently and defiantly proclaimed from the floor of the United Nations: "In this room . . . if an empire cannot be overthrown, if a conqueror cannot be displaced, if lost liberty cannot be re-won, then very few of us would have a place here."[18] In covering the role and scope of the United Nations, and the controversial issues like Algeria that came before the body, Essie often focused her stories on the voices of those who, like Menon, had taken great risks and made many sacrifices to defeat colonial rule in their own countries and had come to the United Nations to enlarge the contested meaning of postcolonial freedom. In a series of articles about Menon, Essie admiringly reminded her readers that he was often referred to as "India's trouble maker" and "Nehru's bad boy" for his militant anti-colonial stance and refusal to play Cold War politics. Essie respected the fact that Menon was not afraid, in the staid confines of the United Nations, to ask hard questions, to express anger at the lack of an adequate response, or to speak in defense of the oppressed and powerless from Asia to Africa.[19]

Another contested issue that came before the United Nations in the 1950s was the case of French-controlled Cameroon in Central Africa. Cameroon was supposed to be under the jurisdiction and oversight of the U.N. Trusteeship Council. But, Essie reported, U.N. officials and diplomats were looking the other way as France continued to dominate and overpower its former colonies. "Although hundreds of petitions from the Camerouns [claiming violent and illegal repression of independence forces] have flooded the UN," Essie wrote, "France so far has made no report, no comments, upon the apparently very alarming situation there, and has merely said in answer to pressing questions, that the petitions come from 'communist organizations.'" Whatever their political leanings, Essie argued, the U.N. member nations were still responsible for protecting the rights of the people of Cameroon and for monitoring France's actions—and they were falling far short of that obligation. Like so many of the parts of the world that she wrote about, Essie had a personal connection to Cameroon. She had met and corresponded with Ndeh Ntumazah, the militant leader of the Union of the Peoples of Cameroon (UPC), and the One Kamerun (OK) movement. Upon his return to Cameroon from a trip to the United States in 1958, Ntumazah wrote to Essie thanking her for her support and assuring her that "your name will remain ever fresh in our minds."[20]

In her writings, Essie took very seriously the fact that action—or inaction—by the United Nations meant life or death in colonized territories and for anti-colonial fighters like Ntumazah. Would the United Nations allow colonial powers to do what they wanted, as long as they claimed that "progress" was being made? Did the United Nations have the right and the ability to intervene? These were key questions in the years when colonialism was crumbling in some places and clinging to life in others.

As she watched the United Nations grow and mature, Essie was also hopeful about the growing role of women in that governing body and in diplomatic circles, although she lamented the relatively small numbers of women in key positions. In July 1954 she wrote the article "Women in the United Nations," in which she praised the "interesting and colorful" women who worked for the United Nations as national delegates and staff. She highlighted Agda Rossel of Sweden, "with a stunning white streak in her dark hair;" the "quiet wistful-looking" Mitra Mitrovic from Yugoslavia, and the "plump and irrepressible" Fortuna Augustin Guéry of Haiti. The physical descriptions reflect the personal connections and sense of familiarity and affection Essie felt toward these women, but her real source of pride was not in their appearances but in their work. All three were advocates for women in their respective countries, and added women's concerns to the larger U.N. debates. And in their strong, articulate, and confident presence in the predominately male assembly, they demonstrated to the world the power and potential of women's leadership. Rossel, for example, a Swedish Social Democrat trained as a social worker who went on to become a leading voice for women's issues and human rights in the international arena, served as the first woman "head of mission" to the United Nations when she was appointed Swedish ambassador in 1958. Mitrovic, a Communist Party leader from Serbia and wife of Yugoslav Minister Milovan Djilas, was an educator who wrote and lectured on the challenges and importance of mass education and educational access for women. And Augustin Guéry was not only a diplomat but also a fiction writer, historian, and memoirist who served on the U.N. Commission on the Status of Women after its formation, and was considered a respected cultural figure and intellectual in Haiti: she wrote about poverty, the Haitian revolution, and women's status in society.[21]

In July 1953, Essie covered the eighth annual gathering of the eighteen-member U.N. Commission on the Status of Women.[22] The commission was an advisory body, but its deliberations drew public attention to the plight and struggles of women all over the world. One resolution put forth by delegates from Haiti and Iran called for women to have "complete freedom in the choice of a spouse. . . . [and for] the rights of widows to custody of their children and their freedom as to remarriage."[23] Another resolution called for member nations to "take the necessary steps to ensure that women have equal access with men to all types of education, without distinction as to nationality, race or religion." Other proposals called for equal pay and full voting rights for women. Essie applauded all of these measures as steps in the right direction, even if there was still a long way to go.

She also turned her attention to equality within the United Nations itself. In a 1958 article, she noted that there were only twelve female full delegates to the General Assembly and two dozen female alternates. She expressed her hope "that some day in the near future the world organization, the United Nations, will properly represent the people of the world; not only the nations, but also the people of the world. This will mean that membership in the organization will be universal and that women will be adequately represented in the delegations."[24]

The constellation of U.N. diplomats, journalists, translators, and staff became a special community for Essie in the 1950s. She enjoyed friendly relations with her fellow U.N. reporters and observers, enjoying coffee and lunch discussions with them when she was there. She also had ties to the Chinese and Soviet representatives and made a special effort to reach out to and befriend the women delegates, alternate delegates, and aides of various ranks and ages and from a wide range of countries. Essie even enjoyed a rapport with the security guards, who noted her absence to her friends when they had not seen her for awhile.

In some ways the U.N. reporters and diplomats that Essie befriended became a kind of second family to her. Special among them was Ruth ("Rue") Gage-Colby, with whom she enjoyed an especially tender and loving friendship. Rue was a white middle-class Midwesterner, the wife of a respected physician and a prominent woman in the civic life of Minneapolis. Rue had been politicized by World War II, the threat of nuclear proliferation after the war, and the possibilities for change represented by the rise of newly independent nations of Asia and Africa. She became an anti-imperialist and a peace crusader—and she was unrelenting in her commitment. A prominent figure in the Women's International League for Peace and Freedom and Women Strike for Peace, Rue, like Essie, had traveled around the world many times over: always on a mission, a delegation, a journey of purpose and discovery. Both women were in San Francisco for the founding of the United Nations in 1945 and both observed and wrote about that international body for nearly twenty years. Rue befriended and sought to influence politicians and diplomats from Hubert Humphrey to U.N. Secretary-General Dag Hammarskjöld. She and Essie had much in common, and were in very close communication for many years.

By the early 1960s, Rue considered Essie Robeson to be her dearest friend. "I am lost without you. Never have I had such a precious friend," Rue wrote in 1960.[25] When Essie was sick and hospitalized, Rue longed to "sit by your bedside if only to watch you [sleep]."[26] There was a warm affection between these two dear friends that had grown from their common social and political projects. Ruth trusted Essie unequivocally. She sought her advice at critical moments as she moved around the world. She confided in her about the internal fights and tensions among political allies, and asked her to intervene in thorny international situations. There was an emotional and political understanding between these confidantes that animated the mutual affection and respect they had for one another.[27]

Essie's friendship with Rue came at a pivotal time in her life. In 1956, just when she was hitting her stride as a writer and U.N. correspondent, she was diagnosed with breast cancer. She relied on Rue and others for emotional support. In the fall of 1956 she had a mastectomy at Beth Israel Hospital in New York. Refusing to succumb to fear or pessimism, Essie wrote to her friend Cedric Belfrage in London in October, "I have been ill," she explained, but "oddly enough, I feel no self-consciousness whatsoever at the loss of a breast, and my recovery has been remarkable." Six weeks later she was back at the United Nations writing to colleagues about the conflict between Egypt and Israel over the Sinai Peninsula. She wrote to her friend George Murphy thanking him for his support during her hospitalization. She felt as though her successful treatment had given her "a second chance," and she was going to "reorganize" her life to be more effective in her work and healthier overall.[28]

By 1960, Essie's work was having a real impact. Through her travels, lectures, writing, and advocacy, she came in contact with thousands of people. She represented a Black American voice staunchly in support of socialist societies from the Soviet Union to China to Cuba, and was an unyielding advocate of self-determination and freedom not only for Africa, but for the entire Third World. She also stood up to Cold War repression and refused to pledge unconditional loyalty to any nation—including her own—that in her mind oppressed her people (defined broadly) and betrayed its own principles. She embraced a radical Black transnationalism and presaged the emergence of Black feminist notions of intersectionality in the late twentieth century. One measure of her influence and success in these arenas was the continued interest of the FBI, which monitored her work at the United Nations and instructed agents to report "any possible misuse of her accreditation." Clearly they were looking for an opportunity to silence her. She refused to be silenced.[29]

A progressive publication with which Essie had a unique and close association in the 1950s was the journal *Freedom*. Founded as an outlet for radical voices that were being increasingly censored in the Cold War climate, *Freedom*'s masthead read: "Where one is enslaved, all are in chains." The journal was named after the first independent Black newspaper published in the United States, in 1827.[30] It included articles, columns, and editorials by some of the leading Black Left thinkers and activists of the 1950s, including African National Congress leader Walter Sisulu, James Baldwin, and W. E. B. Du Bois. Its scope was thoroughly international, covering news and political movements from Vietnam to Kenya to Guiana (Guyana) to India. It was, for nearly five years beginning in 1950, a critical lens through which readers could view, learn about, and weigh in on the growing movement for Third World liberation. The changing tactics of the Puerto Rican independence movement; the sweeping arrest of tens of thousands of Kenyans, and their containment in "concentration camps" by the British in response to the Mau Mau uprisings; the detention of Cheddi Jagan and other Guyanese anti-colonial figures; the sustained protests against the notoriously repressive "pass laws" in South Africa—all were reported in the pages of *Freedom* in the early 1950s, along with reports from militants in the Southern civil rights movement like Robert Williams, whose article appeared in the June 1952 issue.[31] One particularly prescient article by Paul in March of 1954, entitled "Ho Chi Minh Is Toussaint L'Ouverture of Indo China," foreshadowed the growing global significance of the Vietnam War.[32] Essie was proud to be associated with such a cutting-edge publication.

The second important characteristic of *Freedom* was that it had a decidedly pro-feminist bent. Women were prominently featured both as contributors and as subjects of news articles. The roster of women writers, editors, and columnists was extensive, and included among many others Jane Gilbert, Charlotte Dorsey, Janet Wilson, Shirley Graham, and Linda Lewis. In addition, women's leadership and roles in world history were celebrated in feature stories and news. For example, there were articles on Harriet Tubman and Ida B. Wells Barnet; a feature on the organizing efforts of Nina Evans, a "leader of Domestic Workers"; an article on women quilters who were telling the story of the Black Freedom movement through their artistry; another article titled "1,000 Kikuyu Women March on the Prison Compounds"; another on South Africa titled "Women Lead Tenants Council Demonstrations"; and yet another, on efforts by low-income New York families to secure decent housing.[33] In addition, in one issue whose cover story was "the face of Africa," significantly, symbolically, that face was a woman's face. Further, the headline did not qualify or temper its assertion by labeling the image "the mother or daughter of Africa," but rather implied that hers was the face of *all* of Africa.

Freedom only lasted five years, but Essie appreciated its unique, groundbreaking role. After struggling for so many years to earn the attention of publishers and editors, Essie was rewarded at *Freedom* with a chance to write on her own terms.[34] Essie wrote several articles and reviews and supported and distributed the publication at her speaking engagements.[35]

As Essie moved around the globe, writing prolifically about international affairs, observing profound changes in the world, and intervening where she could, she felt increasingly connected to a varied, eclectic, and transnational group of friends and colleagues—a group that she would eventually describe as her "world political family." They spoke a myriad of languages and inhabited different cultures. Her political passions flowed from these relationships. Her interest in Africa, for example, was stimulated and deepened by the African students and other Black intellectuals she had met in London and Europe in the 1930s and later in Africa: Kenyatta, Kojo, Bokwe, Xuma, and others. And after meeting Gandhi in 1931 and developing a close friendship with Jawaharlal Nehru and his sister Vijaya Lakshmi (Nan) Pandit, she would develop a lifelong interest in the cause of Indian freedom. Finally, while her ties to the Caribbean were not as deep or longstanding as those to Africa, she did take a keen interest in the anti-colonial and revolutionary rumblings in that region as well, in part due to her personal friendship with Cheddi and Janet Jagan.[36]

There were three women whose decades-long friendships with Essie best reflect her transnational identity and both personal and political allegiances: Shirley Graham Du Bois, Vijaya Lakshmi (Nan) Pandit, and Janet Jagan—all three of whom appeared in the pages of *Freedom* on more than one occasion. Essie felt a kindred connection to these women in different ways and for slightly different reasons. And although she was never in daily contact with any of them and frequently found herself writing to them from different parts of the world, they were her political sisters and there was genuine affection and mutual respect among all four of these intellectuals, strategists, and outspoken leaders.

Essie met Shirley Graham Du Bois when she was still Shirley Graham and an aspiring playwright taking courses at Yale University. When they were first in contact, Essie was studying for her Ph.D. at the Kennedy School of Missions at the Hartford Seminary, and itching for greater intellectual companionship. So it was timely that the smart and similarly hungry young writer came her way when she did. Even though Shirley's initial contact was to explore the possibility of Paul accepting a role in one of her plays, it was her friendship with Essie that deepened and endured. The answer to the request of Paul, via Essie, was no. The response to the gesture of friendship, and the invitation that Essie read some of her work, was yes. The year was 1940. Their friendship lasted twenty-five years.

After Shirley married W. E. B. Du Bois in 1951, the two couples grew closer. Essie and Shirley combined their talents on several political projects: *Freedom*, which Shirley co-founded with Paul, and which Essie wrote for; Sojourners for Truth and Justice, which they both joined; and the Council on African Affairs, of which they were both active members. They also shared a commitment to African liberation struggles and a deep interest in communist movements throughout the world. Both women were targets of FBI surveillance and had their passports confiscated because of their politics. And they each lived, worked, and struggled in the shadows of famous husbands. Shirley's son David described his mother's friendship with Essie as "intense," complex, and sometimes a bit bumpy.[37] They were two very strong-willed women and it is not surprising that they did not always see eye to eye. The nature of the difference that David Du Bois refers to is unspecified, but the durability of their friendship is self-evident. A high point of Essie and Shirley's friendship was in 1958 when they walked arm in arm with the young Ghanaian president Kwame Nkrumah into a reception in Accra in celebration of the first year of the country's independence. They later sat next to one another during the historic proceedings of the All Africa Peoples' Conference.[38] Both women were beaming in photos taken that day. After years of anti-colonial agitation the Accra gathering was a high point. That same year Essie and Shirley celebrated New Year's Eve together with their husbands in Moscow at an elegant gala hosted by Soviet leaders.

Shirley was a prolific writer and historian. She was the author of more than a dozen books, including a short biography of Paul Robeson in 1946. She moved with W. E. B. Du Bois to Ghana in 1961 where they both became citizens, and where he died two years later. Shirley died in the People's Republic of China in 1977. Like Essie, she was a Black American woman whose sense of herself extended well beyond the boundaries of the United States and who developed a deep and abiding commitment to radical politics and anti-colonial ideals over the course of her life and career.

Vijaya Lakshmi (Nan) Pandit first entered Essie's life indirectly when she met Paul in London in 1932 during a turbulent time in his and Essie's relationship. Pandit was in London with her husband, Ranjit, and went backstage after one of Paul's *Showboat* performances, though Essie was not there. The two families connected again in 1938, after Paul and Essie had reconciled, and when Pandit was visiting London with her brother Jawaharlal Nehru, the future prime minister of India. Essie liked them both right away, as did Paul, and they invited them to their apartment for dinner, an evening that Pandit described as "memorable"—full of good food, meaningful conversation, and good humor. Paul and Nehru later shared a podium at a massive Indian independence rally at Kingsway Hall in Covent Gardens, where Paul offered high praise for the charismatic Indian leader and his Congress Party comrades. Nan sent a personal note to Essie after their first meeting. "I feel as though we were old friends," she wrote, thanking Essie for her "kindness and friendship."[39]

As for Nehru, he was quite the charmer and Essie confided to a mutual friend that she found him one of the most "fascinating men" she had ever met—which was meaningful given that Essie had met quite a few fascinating men in her time. In turn, Nehru was quite fond of Essie. When he had difficulty obtaining a visa to go to the Soviet Union, Essie contacted the Soviet consul in London on his behalf. They exchanged letters, ideas, and books: in the early 1940s while Nehru was in prison for his anti-colonial activities, Essie gave Nehru a book by Richard Wright as a special gift. Other books she sent him in prison were intercepted by colonial authorities and never reached him, and some letters were delayed by months. Essie also sent Nehru the proceedings of the National Negro Congress so that he would be kept abreast of the organizing efforts of Black activists in the United States. She, along with many others, wrote letters and signed petitions demanding his release. When his first book came out, he had an author's copy sent personally to Essie.[40]

Nehru and Essie enjoyed a personal friendship and each admired the other very much. Some of their letters were serious and formal, but others were rambling and contemplative exchanges about family, work, politics, and life. Essie wrote to Nehru about her upcoming trip to Central America in 1940. He, in turn, described to her his recent excursion to the Kashmir Valley, a beautiful northern region of the country that had great significance for the Nehru family, and invited her to come there one day and see it. Nehru once described Essie as "one of the most vital and energetic women I have ever met."[41] But it was Nan, more than Jawaharlal, whom Essie became even closer to over the years. Nan was a staunch anti-racist and a woman of strong and unwavering convictions, much like Essie. She came to the United States on a speaking tour in 1944, soon after her husband, Ranjit, had died tragically in an Indian prison where he had been incarcerated because of his anti-colonial views. During her speaking tour, Pandit adamantly refused to speak before segregated or all-white audiences.

Nan, one of India's first female cabinet ministers after independence, and according to one writer "one of the most remarkable women of the twentieth century," would also spend time in prison in India on three different occasions as a result of her political activism in the 1940s.[42] When she was in prison in 1943, Essie provided emotional support to her two daughters Nayantara (Tara) and Chandralekha (Lekha), who were attending Wellesley College at the time. The two young women were warmly welcomed into Essie's Connecticut home on weekends and during school holidays. They washed and aired their saris on the clothesline in the expansive yard of the Robeson home, and accompanied Essie to her classes at Hartford Seminary. In short, they were treated so much like a part of the family that Nan felt the Robesons were "like parents" to Tara and Lekha and Paul Jr. like a "brother" to them.[43]

The Pandits had told their children about their friends the Robesons before the girls left for college. Years earlier, too, Tara remembers her father reading aloud to her from Essie's book *Paul Robeson, Negro*. Tara and Lekha, then, were well acquainted with Paul and Essie's stories even before they met them. Paul was staying in New York the first summer they visited, so Paul Jr. took the two sisters to New York to a Broadway performance of *Othello* and then backstage to meet his famous father. They were so thrilled that Tara wrote fondly about the experience in her 1957 memoir, *Prison and Chocolate Cake*.[44] Nehru and Pandit were eventually released from prison and went on to help define and shape the politics of postwar India. Nehru became the country's first prime minister after independence. Pandit was appointed to several diplomatic posts abroad. She and Essie kept in touch.

Tara and Lekha were important threads of connection between the two families over the years.[45] They had grown quite close to Essie during their time in the United States. After college they continued to communicate with her and to refer fondly to their time spent at "The Beeches." They wrote to Essie from their travels in Switzerland, Russia, and France, confiding in her about their lives, and affectionately addressed their letters "Dear Mama" or "Dearest Mama," since they had regarded her as a surrogate mother during their years at Wellesley. "I hope you haven't forgotten your elder daughter," Lekha chided Essie in a 1947 letter from a trip to Moscow.[46] The Pandit sisters shared with Essie the news of their engagements, weddings, and pregnancies, and sent love and good wishes to "Mrs. Goode," Paul Jr., and "papa."[47]

Essie and Nan saw more of one another in the late 1940s and early 1950s when they were both absorbed in the business of the United Nations—Essie as a journalist, critic, and observer and Nan as a high-level official. They managed to see one another socially in those days, despite extremely busy schedules and complicated lives. On at least one occasion Nan shocked her U.N. colleagues, notably Secretary-General Dag Hammarskjöld, by soliciting an invitation to go to Essie's home for dinner. Essie, too, feared Nan might alarm her fellow U.N. officials if she trekked uptown for a home-cooked meal. Nan, however, insisted on coming, and likely earned an even greater margin of respect and affection from Essie in the process. She remained eternally grateful to Essie for the kindness she showed to her daughters while she was in prison. Nan and Essie also both enjoyed a friendship with Pearl Buck and both had found early political inspiration through their contact with Mohandas Gandhi. When she served as ambassador to the Soviet Union, Pandit had developed a coterie of socialist and communist friends and was, like Essie, decidedly left-leaning in her politics. Essie's relationship with the Nehrus and the Pandits represented the kind of cross-cultural Third World solidarity that Essie thought was essential to the realization of peace and justice in a postcolonial world.

In the climate of the Cold War, Essie and Nan's personal relationship, as well as the Robesons' relationship to Prime Minister Nehru, were often difficult to negotiate publicly. A letter marked "secret" that was written by Nan and dispatched to her brother in September 1949 on India Embassy letterhead read: "One thing that has troubled me greatly since I came here is my relationship with the Robesons. As you know, I am very fond of both Paul and Essie and they had treated me like a little sister. While the girls were here, the Robesons' home was open to them and they made full use of it. Since coming here, I have met Essie a couple of times in New York meetings and have always gone and spoken to her in spite of some criticism from the officials of my embassy. I know Essie would like to see you and I am wondering if it would be wise for me to arrange for her to come up to New York and meet with you for a few moments at your hotel. I feel that if I ignore her completely she will be greatly hurt . . . I should be glad if you could send me a telegram whether I should get in touch with Essie."[48] A week later

Nan wrote Essie an equally surreptitious note indicating that she was arranging her brother's itinerary and since he was being hosted by the U.S. president, the State Department wanted to be kept informed of all the details. Still Nan was able to get around official channels. "He has written that he wants to see you and Paul privately for a good talk. I have arranged for his official departure on the 5th of November, but actually he will be here until the 7th evening—incognito. Could you both arrange to be in New York on the 6th November?"[49] A brief meeting was arranged at the Sheraton Hotel on November 7, 1949, which Essie attended. Essie was quite glad to see her old friend after so many years and was not about to pass up an opportunity to do so. Paul, by contrast, was not pleased with some policy decisions Nehru had made, and refused to see him.[50] The two men reunited years later.

The third of Essie's political "sisters" was Janet Jagan. Born in Chicago to Jewish parents, Janet met and fell in love with the Indo-Guyanese socialist Cheddi Jagan, and moved to British Guiana (later Guyana) to join him in the anti-colonial struggle there. She shared many of the same political views as Nan, Shirley, and Essie. Together she and Cheddi formed the leftist People's Progressive Party (PPP), and Janet eventually served as prime minister and president of independent Guyana, but, like Nan Pandit, not before serving five months in jail followed by two years of house arrest. Cheddi Jagan had met and corresponded with Paul for several years, and at one point in the early 1950s, when Janet was in the United States visiting her family, she called Paul and asked if she could meet him. He and Essie welcomed her warmly and she developed a trusted friendship with Essie that lasted nearly fifteen years, until Essie's death (to Janet, it felt like she had known her for "decades").[51]

One of the last times Essie and Janet were together was in London in the winter of 1961. Paul was not well, and Essie's health was declining as well. It was hard for Janet to see the two people she remembered as so robust and vibrant grappling with ill health. Still, they were able to share a lot. Essie was eager to hear what her old friends from Guyana were up to politically. Janet's husband was premier in 1961 but Guyana was still in transition and the PPP was still pushing for full independence. Writing to Janet after her visit, Essie congratulated her on "the proud record of the PPP," but warned her she still had "lots of work ahead."[52] Essie's letter reflected the personal and political nature of their relationship. After asking about the family and updating Janet on her and Paul's health, Essie proceeded to offer a three-page commentary on the content of the most recent issues of *Thunder,* the paper of the PPP for which Janet, at one time, served as editor. She applauded Cheddi Jagan's reprinted speeches that called for an end to the arms race and an end to Cold War intimidation of smaller countries.[53] Essie had echoed the very same points in many of her own speeches and articles. Both Jagans were so fond of Paul and Essie—Cheddi was in the crowd that welcomed them back to England in 1958—that the FBI speculated that if the Robesons ever chose to relocate again outside of the United States, the Jagans would have eagerly welcomed them to Guiana.[54] In this assessment, at least, the FBI was quite right.

With their ties to the Caribbean, Asia, and Africa, Essie's friends Janet, Nan, and Shirley represented her connections to disparate parts of the Third World and the global anti-colonial movement. Each woman, like Essie, had a close relationship with a larger-than-life male persona, but nevertheless staked her own political and intellectual claims and made her own mark. The four women forged their own paths, took controversial positions, and refused to take the easy road of silence and conformity. Each woman paid a price. Still they persevered, sustained no doubt by their friendship and sisterhood.

twelve

STANDING TALL: THE COLD WAR AND POLITICS OF REPRESSION, 1950s

All I ever feared were cats.
Eslanda Robeson

On July 7, 1953, Eslanda Cardozo Goode Robeson walked confidently into Room 357 of the Senate Office Building in Washington, D.C., to provide testimony before the U.S. Senate Permanent Subcommittee on Investigations of the Committee on Government Operations, which was headed by Senator Joseph McCarthy of Wisconsin, the notorious and unrelenting anti-communist crusader. Essie wore a dark suit and black hat with a thin half-veil that was accented with velvet dots. She looked a bit like a stylish mourner, but her demeanor was more gutsy than grief-stricken. She was angry, annoyed, insulted, and wholly unapologetic. Even though people she knew were being threatened and jailed for their politics, Essie was undaunted. "All I ever feared were cats," she once declared. Still, the stakes were high. Julius and Ethel Rosenberg, a communist couple convicted of spying for the Soviet Union, had been executed just two weeks earlier, despite their insistence that they were innocent and a loud international outcry. Others were being jailed, blacklisted, and deported. In this climate of fear and persecution, it is impressive that Essie stood up to Joe McCarthy as forcefully as she did, refusing to be rattled or intimidated. I was "working very hard on an article about Mau Mau, when the McCarthy Senate Investigating Committee ordered me to appear before it in Washington, D.C.," she said in a statement reprinted by the Associated Negro Press.[1] Her bold and favorable reference to the militant anti-colonial resistance movement in Kenya underscored her refusal to be cowed.

McCarthy's committee, the Senate version of the more infamous House Un-American Activities Committee (HUAC), was conducting a witch hunt against anyone suspected of communist sympathies. In McCarthy's view, these sympathies were fundamentally un-American, and their adherents had to be rooted out. His definition of communist sympathizer grew to include basically anyone who disagreed with him politically, or dared to criticize the U.S. government: peace activists, civil rights leaders, dissident artists, and progressive labor organizers of all types. Both committees carried out an extensive intimidation campaign against dissidents in not only the film industry and academia, but also professional and civic organizations. Essie had ostensibly been summoned because her books, copies of which appeared on bookshelves in U.S. government libraries around the world (in embassies or U.S. government-funded programs), were alleged to be un-American. Her familial connection to Paul Robeson also was a source of concern.

As the Cold War heated up and domestic red-baiting became more ominous and widespread, those who were targeted generally either distanced themselves from any affiliations or individuals that might sully their reputations or damage their careers, or stood defiant and rightly accused the government of violating their basic civil liberties. Some "named names" to save themselves, accusing colleagues, friends, and neighbors of communist loyalties. Essie and Paul refused to cave in to such pressures, or to betray the trust of friends. By 1953, Essie had embraced a highly politicized public persona. She knew her role was not to lead organizations or run for office (she had given up on that after the Progressive Party experience), but she was determined to speak loudly and clearly about her idea of justice in the most public way possible, and to support others who did the same. To back down from this stance would undo all she had built and become. On some level, Essie relished the opportunity to confront McCarthy directly.

Essie sparred with the committee members from the start. "Did you write this book all by yourself?" asked McCarthy staffer G. David Schine, holding up her book *African Journey*. "All by myself," she replied, mocking the ridiculousness of the question. "Well I really think that is a very insulting question," she added. "I am quite capable of writing a book. I did write this book all by myself."[2] Schine backed off.

Essie refused to answer direct questions about whether or not she was a member of the Communist Party, claiming protection under both the Fifth and Fifteenth Amendments to the U.S. Constitution. While the Fifth Amendment protects citizens against compelled self-incrimination, Essie was making an additional statement about racism by asserting the Fifteenth Amendment, which guarantees voting rights regardless of race. When the committee told her she could not invoke the Fifteenth Amendment, Essie gave the committee a history lesson. "As a Negro and as a second-class citizen," Essie lectured, "I have been fighting racial discrimination all my life." She cited the longstanding practices of racism, racial violence, and Black disenfranchisement. "As a Negro, I know a lot about the force and violence used against my people in this country," she added.[3] When told her race had nothing to do with the hearings and that the Senate committee was all white as a result of voters' choices, not racism, Essie snapped, "Most Negroes are in the South, sir, and they don't have much right to elect senators."[4]

The committee grilled Essie: Why had she sent her son to a Soviet school? Did she know any communists? Had she been to a communist cell meeting and, if she had, were those in attendance plotting to overthrow the government by force? What did she think of the conflict in Korea? What did her husband think about communism and the Soviet Union? The questions went on and on, but Essie did not waiver. She insisted she knew very little about communism, "except what I read in the papers and hearsay." She answered questions with questions: "Why don't you ask [Paul]?" she quipped, in response to questions about his political views. "I don't know who, what or where," she said to questions about her meetings and friends. By the end of the exchange, the senators were stumped. They had gotten neither information nor deference and had been unable to intimidate her. McCarthy glared down at Essie as he brought the hearing to a close and said he had let her get away with too much. He said that she might have been cited for contempt if she were a man, rather than a woman, and warned future witnesses to be more compliant.[5]

The Black press applauded Essie's performance before the committee, and she was proud of herself. Veteran Black reporter Alice Dunnigan described Essie as "cool, intelligent and confident." Others praised her feisty courage and "clear-sighted" stance against the committee's intimidation tactics.[6] Months before Essie's testimony, her journalist friend P. L. Prattis lamented the onerous climate that existed throughout the country, where many people, paralyzed by fear, felt they could "no longer speak" their minds. "The future is terrible to contemplate. I wish you and Paul were not mixed up in it," he confessed in a letter to Essie, "but maybe that is a cowardly wish." Essie rejected fear and embraced a bolder and more optimistic stance, even in difficult times and situations.[7]

In addition to her lawyer, Milton Friedman, Essie's friend and political associate Thelma Dale Perkins had come down from New York to accompany her to the hearing. "I went to the hearing with much apprehension," Perkins recalled. Essie was a strongly independent woman who often spoke her mind regardless of the consequences. The consequences for being too blunt or candid with this committee could have meant, Perkins pointed out, "legal entrapment . . . [and] perhaps jail."[8] But Essie was pointed, candid, and careful. She did not take the bait when McCarthy sought to lead her down a particular path of inquiry, and the outcome of the testimony was as good as could have been expected: there were no charges, no indictments, and no incriminating comments. Perkins felt relieved. To congratulate Essie on her successful testimony, Perkins invited her to spend the evening at her parent's home in Anacostia, a predominately Black neighborhood in Washington. "On this day of triumph, I could not conceive of her going back home without some kind of celebration," Perkins recounted. "That afternoon, Essie relaxed and enjoyed the visit with my parents and their neighbors as if she had known them all her life." The two women then visited the Frederick Douglass historic home site nearby and stood on the front porch of the house, "looking across the river at the Capitol where Essie had begun this eventful day."[9] It was symbolically appropriate given that Douglass himself had been such an outspoken fighter against injustice and oppression roughly a hundred years earlier.

In newspaper articles, public speeches, and personal correspondence after her appearance, Essie spoke out vehemently against the tactics of McCarthy and his allies. She said that she was indeed a critic of the U.S. government, but that this did not make her a communist or any less of an American. As a self-aware Black woman, she argued, how could she not criticize the persistent racism she saw all around her? Radical activists and intellectuals from Frederick Douglass to Martin Luther King Jr. to Ella Baker have framed their criticism of America in precisely the same way: as a demand for America to realize its promise. Essie claimed she was a loyal citizen, a loyal Negro citizen, whose loyalty was "somewhat battered" but still intact.[10] Still, it's important to note that while Essie herself denied having a Communist Party affiliation, she did not condemn communism or those who were in fact party members. Her gripe with HUAC and McCarthy was not simply that they were making false accusations, but also that they were censoring political beliefs and punishing political dissidents.

In 1953, Essie accepted an invitation by the editors of the *Daily Worker* to write a response to President Eisenhower's State of the

Union address. Her lengthy essay, entitled "A Citizen's State of the Union," called for friendly relations with the Soviet Union based on a policy of "live and let live in this one world." She pointed out the duplicity of advocating democracy and freedom abroad while suppressing oppositional views and tolerating racial inequality at home. For Essie, racial injustice and the anticommunist crusades were intimately bound together because as long as people were afraid to speak out, injustice would continue. "Our citizens are no longer free nor brave," she wrote, warning that "fear is spreading like a plague among our citizens. Fear of losing one's job, home, education, fear of non-conforming, or of even being accused of non-conforming."[11] The real obstacles to racial progress, Essie argued, were not communists or so-called subversives; "the enemy are the powerful, lawless, ruthless, greedy, selfish, arrogant, un-Americans."[12]

Essie was also quick to praise other public figures who refused to be censored or intimidated. One of those people was the colorful Paris-based Black American performer Josephine Baker. When they first crossed paths in the 1920s, Essie had not been favorably impressed with Baker. But that changed when Baker became an outspoken critic of racism and repression and suffered government harassment as a result. "I feel Josephine Baker is a modern Negro heroine," Essie wrote to James Hicks, a reporter for the *Afro-American*. "All that talent, all that glamour, all those gorgeous clothes — and courage too. I'll bet her knees are beautiful, especially so because she does not live on them. . . . Since Jo has opened up her gorgeous mouth and spoken her piece, . . . [perhaps now] other heretofore timid and reluctant Negro artists will find their voices and also insist upon Negro rights."[13]

Even more significant and defiant than Essie's comments about Baker were her words of praise and support for jailed Communist Party leader Ben Davis, a personal friend of both Essie and Paul. In 1949 Davis, a Black Harvard-trained lawyer and onetime New York City councilman, was jailed for five years under the Smith Act, a 1940 federal law that prohibited participation in any group that advocated the overthrow of the government (with the implicit assumption that all communists advocated violent actions). Paul Robeson Jr. described Davis as his father's closest friend in the American Communist Party. He is also described as "a popular Harlem figure. Almost as big as Paul." A "jovial" and good-humored man, Davis loved tennis and the violin almost as much as he loved politics.[14] Paul was unwavering in his support and unsparing in his praise of Davis, and Essie shared his sentiments. They had both supported Davis in his 1943 bid for city council and enjoyed a warm personal relationship with him after that. Moreover, Essie's relationship with Ben Davis was not simply through Paul. She had independent conversations and correspondence with him in which they exchanged ideas about politics, international affairs, book writing, and other matters.[15]

In 1952 Essie wrote an article for *Freedom* entitled "I Know a Communist," in which she defended her friendship with Ben Davis.[16] In 1954 Essie agreed to write the foreword to a booklet by Claudia Jones, published as a tribute to Davis, entitled *Ben Davis, Fighter for Freedom*. In her opening passage, Essie wrote: "Ben Davis is in prison now because he has the courage of his convictions, I can't imagine a better reason to go to prison."[17] And Essie "admitted" in *Freedom* that she not only knew "a real live Communist" but he "was a wonderful guy," referring to Davis. This statement was in contrast to the thrust of her testimony before the Senate Committee in which she professed ignorance of communism. Of course she knew other communists as well, but she was especially fond of Davis.[18] "He is an old valued friend of ours. . . . We love the man."[19] In the 1940s when she and Paul were having some marital difficulties, Essie apparently confided in Ben, and he in turn praised her for being "such a strong and realistic mate" to such a great man.[20] The subtle veiled meanings here are not readily apparent. Perhaps it was Ben's way of thanking Essie for not making a big fuss about Paul's affairs, the publicizing of which would undoubtedly have tarnished Paul's image and made him less effective as a political figure. Or perhaps it was based on Ben's understanding of how demanding Paul's schedule was and how so many of those who claimed chunks of Paul's time and attention did not always recognize or appreciate Essie's contributions to their collective work.[21] It is clear that Ben understood Essie had made sacrifices for Paul, sacrifices that had in part enabled Paul to play an important role in national and global politics.

As American public officials focused on the Cold War, racial violence continued throughout the South and parts of the North. Essie accused politicians from Jim Crow states of hypocrisy for claiming to make the country safe from communism while leaving it quite unsafe for Negroes. In an essay for the *Afro-American* in the spring of 1955, Essie condemned the brutal murder of Reverend George Lee—a local grocer, printer, and NAACP activist in Belzoni, Mississippi. For his act of registering nearly one hundred Black voters in his small town, he was targeted and shot down in broad daylight as he drove home on May 7, 1955. The white local coroner ruled the death an accident, and Lee's killers went free. Essie argued that many "so-often blind, flag-waving patriots" were more concerned with rooting out alleged communists than tracking down the kind of thugs who had assassinated George Lee.[22]

Echoing concerns expressed by other Black radicals and some liberals at the time, Essie spoke and wrote about how red-baiting and anti-communism was dividing and weakening the Black Freedom struggle in the United States, and how it was convincing activists to turn away from the rest of the world and each other. "Our fight for civil rights is part of a worldwide civil rights fight," Essie reminded a crowd at a picnic and rally held by the American Committee for Protection of the Foreign Born in Wanaque, New Jersey. In her opinion, the government's indictment of the venerable African American intellectual and political spokesperson W. E. B. Du Bois, at the age of eighty-three, alleging that he was a "foreign agent" because he dared to speak out critically on U.S. foreign policy and colonialism, was a particularly low blow.[23]

The charges against Du Bois were eventually dropped, and after his acquittal in November 1951, Essie wrote an eloquent essay in defense of him and submitted it to the *Afro-American* newspaper for publication. In the essay, she argued that the government, "in its arrogance, made the mistake of picking on the wrong Negro." She applauded how Blacks and progressive whites had rallied to Du Bois's defense, but added that the very fact that the attack had occurred was evidence that "the bulk of the Negro people have been asleep at the switch too long." She also linked Du Bois's unjust treatment at the hands of the FBI to the treatment that many Black people had received for being "uppity." The nature of racism was to "cut down" those who tried to stand up, Essie insisted, recalling the words of the Congolese facilities manager she had met in 1946. "The Negro people have long experience with this kind of thing. We have seen Negro after Negro cut down, not because he had disobeyed any law, but because he had tried to vote, had moved into an illegally restricted neighborhood, was not meek enough, insisted upon his rights and his personal dignity, was too successful, was too militant, did not know 'his place.'"[24]

In the spring of 1954, a few short weeks before the historic *Brown v. Board of Education* Supreme Court decision declaring racial segregation in public schools unconstitutional, Essie wrote about the housing desegregation struggle in Chicago. A light-skinned Black family, the Howards, had moved into a previously all-white public housing complex in Chicago. Their neighbors, who had initially mistaken them for white, turned against them when the family's race was revealed—but the

Howards refused to leave. Surrounded by angry white mobs and chaotic protests, the family remained absolutely defiant.[25] Their stance paved the way for other Black families to move into the area, though they too came under attack. "A great deal is being said and written about the war in Indochina and our responsibility for the security of southeast Asia, but very little is being said and written about the war in South Chicago and responsibility for the security of these United States," Essie wrote. "The resistance of the French in the fortress of Dien Bien Phu has been dramatized for weeks by all the news media, but very little has been said about the really heroic resistance of the 10 Negro families in the fortress of Trumbull Park in South Chicago (where they, as citizens, have every right to be)," she added.[26]

Essie visited Chicago personally in April 1954 and attended meetings of local activists who were mobilizing around the Trumbull Park standoff. She went to a mass meeting at the Metropolitan Community Church one Sunday afternoon to listen to testimony from one of the Trumbull residents, a Black veteran named Frank London Brown. He stood up and pledged to defend his home. "Appeals to the Law have not protected us," he told the crowd in an emotional voice. "We have decided to protect ourselves. We have decided that from now, we will return fist for fist, brick for brick, pistol for pistol, period." Brown would go on to build a successful career as a writer. In 1959 he penned a widely acclaimed novel about his experiences with Chicago's fight for integrated housing called simply *Trumbull Park*.[27]

Essie herself did not rule out militant forms of resistance to achieve racial justice in the United States, or minimally to protect vulnerable populations against violence, and she at times deployed militaristic language and symbols quite powerfully to make her point. In fact, the perspective she advanced—that Blacks were very much under attack from their own countrymen and that they had the right of self-defense—presaged the radical civil rights and Black Power struggles of the late 1960s:

> All of us, every Negro man, woman and child, are soldiers at war; not an aggressive war against our Government and fellow-citizens, but fighting a defensive war for survival and progress. This war has been going on for a long time. Usually it is a cold war, waged against us by organized political, economic and social pressures; sometimes it waxes very hot indeed—in riots and street battles, bombings and dynamiting of our homes, lynchings, brutal and murderous attacks. In

STANDING TALL

this war that we Negroes fight, the enemy are not the North Koreans, Chinese, Russians, nor Communism; the enemies are the powerful, lawless, ruthless, greedy, selfish, arrogant Un-Americans who defy our laws, corrupt our local, state and federal officials, demoralize our young people, and over-throw our Constitution and Bill of Rights by force and violence, hatred, and prejudice, discrimination, segregation and terror.[28]

These are the kind of fiery words that drew the attention of the federal authorities. Essie and Paul had been under FBI surveillance off and on for years. The FBI, under its director J. Edgar Hoover, couldn't decide if Essie in particular was a "threat" or just an annoyance. (Sexism probably led them to underestimate the seriousness of her convictions.) As part of its campaign of intimidation and repression in 1950, the State Department confiscated Paul's passport. Soon thereafter, they denied Essie's passport as well because, like Paul, she refused to sign an affidavit stating she was not a communist. This development hampered both of their careers, but Paul's inability to perform abroad was a major financial blow for the family.

Almost immediately after Paul's passport was confiscated, his friends, allies, and supporters rallied to defend his right to travel.[29] In fact, the denial of Paul's passport resulted in an international protest campaign. Lloyd Brown, a Black leftist journalist, a co-author with Paul Robeson of *Here I Stand*, and a former editor of *New Masses*, wrote the pamphlet "Lift Every Voice for Paul Robeson" and the Committee to Restore Paul Robeson's Passport was born. Silent film star Charlie Chaplin and other celebrities spoke out in Paul's defense. "To deny a great artist like Paul Robeson his right to give his art to the world is to destroy the very foundation upon which our culture and civilization is built," Chaplin insisted. But others were not so forthcoming. The lines were drawn, with some friends and colleagues rushing to the side of Paul and Essie, and others turning away.[30]

Essie aided with the domestic and international campaigns around Paul's passport, even as she refused to let it interfere with her other work. She was fighting on multiple fronts. In addition to composing outreach letters and coordinating signatures for the amicus brief to be filed on Paul's behalf, Essie accompanied Paul to meetings with their lawyers and to hearings. She had a very active communication with leftist lawyer Leonard Boudin from 1956 to 1958 when the legal fight to regain Paul's passport shifted into high gear. She attended meetings about overall strategy and exchanged letters and phone calls with Boudin about how to pay the mounting legal fees.[31] Some of Boudin's services were provided gratis since he and his law partners felt politically supportive of Paul. There were, however, court fees to pay, researchers to compensate, and travel expenses to cover. Fundraisers paid some of the fees and the Robesons eventually covered the rest.

If government officials had hoped that the loss of their passports would silence Essie or Paul, they were sorely mistaken. The more that Cold War paranoia informed American foreign and domestic policy, the more Essie had to say. The more that the government tried to quiet her down, the more she turned up the volume. For example, Essie gave a number of speeches calling for peace and an end to U.S. militarism in Asia, most notably its involvement in Korea. On Mother's Day in 1952, in a church in Bridgeport, Connecticut, Essie appealed to the mothers in the audience to accept their obligation to stand and fight for peace and economic justice. She was articulating a kind of mainstream maternalism that belied her more progressive views on gender roles, but in this case she deployed the words she thought would work to get more women involved in the peace movement:

> On this Mother's Day, I think it would be well if we all give a thought to the Negro Mothers and the Poor-White mothers, especially in our Deep South, where no matter how hard they work, they cannot give their children the proper food, education and medical care in our rich and powerful country. This does not have to be. We mothers must get together and change this. On this Mother's Day it would be well for us to give a thought to the mothers in Africa and Asia— mothers who, with their children, have never had enough to eat in all their lives: in this rich world, this does not have to be . . . There is enough food for everybody. It is wicked for some to feed like hogs, while others starve. . . . I think Mother's Day is a proper time, not just to buy flowers and presents; it is a proper time for mothers, and all women, to think about these things, and to make a solemn vow to defend our children by putting a stop to war."[32]

Paul Robeson had been one of the most highly sought-after and highest paid Black artists in the world. Now, blacklisted at home and unable to travel abroad, he found it difficult to book his more lucrative performance engagements and the family income plummeted. In July of 1953

Essie finally had to sell the Beeches, the rambling white house in Connecticut that she so loved, because they simply could not afford it any longer.[33]

In one sense Essie felt more grounded than ever. She knew what she believed, who her friends were, and she had settled on a career that suited her. But in other ways, financially and physically, much of the security she had relied on for years was starting to diminish. After the house in Connecticut was gone, Essie moved in temporarily with Paul Jr. and Marilyn until she could get her bearings. Paul was living here and there: sometimes at the parsonage of his brother Ben's church in Harlem, sometimes with friends in Manhattan. Essie was unsure of where Paul was going to ultimately settle down, so she next moved herself to another temporary residence: the historic Hotel Dauphin on Broadway and 67th, which offered closer proximity to her desk at the United Nations as well as a bit more privacy. Within a year she had found a more permanent residence and persuaded Paul that they should purchase a modest townhouse on Jumel Terrace in Washington Heights on the edge of Harlem. After that, in the fall of 1955, they settled back into a domestic life together.

Even though Paul and Essie's lives had been in flux during this time, they were still a family. It was an unconventional family, to be sure, and not without tensions, but their connectedness to one another was clear to those who knew them well. As their mutual friend Freda Diamond insisted long after Paul and Essie had passed on, there was never a question about their marriage being threatened, despite Paul's affairs with other women, including Freda herself. There were only a few years in their four-decades-long marriage that Paul and Essie did not share a home together—not always a bed, but always a home.[34] And Freda, herself married, was a devoted friend to both of them.

Still the early 1950s had been difficult years for Essie. In the spring of 1953, her elderly mother had died after a prolonged illness. Even though it was not wholly unexpected, Ma Goode's death was yet another blow for Essie. Ma Goode, a single mother, had lived with Essie, her only daughter, a good part of her adult life, and had stood by her through many of life's ups and downs. Moreover, Ma Goode had not aged gracefully. Sharp-witted until well into her seventies, she had become slightly demented in her final years. Out of concern for her safety and the realization that Ma Goode needed fulltime care, Essie had placed her mother in a nursing home in Connecticut. Mrs. Goode was not at all happy there, and she wrote numerous letters to Essie begging to be allowed to come home, but Essie could not change the difficult situation. It did not help that her mother's death came at a time when she and Paul were having more difficulties in their relationship. Ma Goode was quietly cremated and there was no service to mark her passing.

Throughout the 1950s, despite personal, emotional, and financial losses, the Robesons continued to speak their minds and to fight political persecution, albeit sometimes on different stages. In many respects the difficulties of the 1950s brought the couple closer. After nearly two years of living mostly apart, their new townhouse on Jumel Terrace provided a fresh common ground. At a banquet in their honor hosted by Essie's colleagues at the *New World Review*, Paul stood up and publicly praised Essie extensively for her many accomplishments, for her "contributions to his own development as a man and an artist," and for her political efforts in the interest of "Negro people" and the larger cause of peace and justice in the world.[35] His affection and admiration were sincere.

As the decade wore on, Essie became increasingly active in the campaign to restore Paul's passport, and by extension her own. She worked mostly on the international front, keeping in close communication with friends in England who were trying to bring pressure to bear from the other side of the Atlantic. Sometime in the mid-1950s the London Paul Robeson Committee was formed. At the helm were activist councilor (local representative) Peggy Middleton and *National Guardian* editor Cedric Belfrage, who had been deported from the United States to his native England for refusing to cooperate with the House Un-American Activities Committee. Essie wrote, cabled, and phoned them both regularly, urging them to keep up the outside pressure and brainstorming with them about tactics and strategy. Progress was indeed made on that front. The committee was able to garner considerable visibility in the British press. In April 1958, as a result of the committee's agitation, the British Actors' Equity passed a statement of support for Paul. It also organized a "virtual" concert where Paul sang "live" over the radio to a sizeable British audience in symbolic defiance of his enforced confinement to the United States. For Paul's sixtieth birthday on April 8, 1958, an illustrious crowd of diplomats, artists and writers, and leftist labor leaders were on hand for various celebrations.[36] Peggy Middleton, in consultation with Essie, encouraged and kept track of tributes to Paul that occurred in more than twenty cities from Tokyo to Mexico City to Delhi.

Essie was especially touched that her Indian friends, notably Nehru,

India's head of state, refused to succumb to U.S. State Department pressures to shun Paul. Under the direction of Nehru's daughter, Indira Gandhi, the country's future prime minister, India organized several Robeson celebrations in multiple cities, topped off by an eloquent statement from Nehru himself, who praised Paul as "one of the greatest artists of our generation."[37] Essie followed up with a personal thank-you note indicating her gratitude that the friendship between the Robeson and Nehru families had endured.[38] Months later she met with Indira at the airport in London to thank her personally for her and her father's support.

The support that Paul and Essie felt from their Indian friends was not always matched at home. The couple had retained close ties to the Black American community throughout the Cold War, but fear and suspicion were rampant, and some leaders of the mainstream civil rights organizations bought into red-baiting as a way to protect themselves from harassment and mark their image as patriotic and respectable. Some bought into Cold War ideas because they genuinely believed them. Whatever the motivation, the NAACP, major labor unions, and even some newer civil rights groups went out of their way to exclude those they believed to be communists or so-called "fellow travelers" who were associated and sympathetic to communism. For instance, when the NAACP and other civil rights leaders sponsored the Prayer Pilgrimage—a massive civil rights rally held in Washington, D.C., on the anniversary of the *Brown v. Board of Education* decision—Paul was not invited to be a speaker. The Robesons attended the 1957 rally anyway, situating themselves among the thousands of people in the crowd. Surprised that he was in the audience and not on the stage, many fans approached Paul for autographs, which did not assuage Essie's annoyance at the snubs Paul received from those she had deemed "professional Negro leaders."

It is important to note that while Essie and Paul stood on the sidelines at the 1957 Pilgrimage, they by no means stood on the sidelines in general. Essie in particular remained very much engaged. Not only did she write about Black American and global events for the foreign and domestic press; she reached out directly to grassroots civil rights leaders, and urged friends to support the growing mass-based struggles (even as she criticized some of the top leadership). After a rare Robeson family visit to Paul's brother Ben's church in 1957, for example, Essie railed that churchgoers were not being urged to attend the Pilgrimage. This was not a personal criticism of Ben but a comment on the Black religious establishment in general.[39] In 1958 Essie also got in touch directly with Daisy Bates, NAACP leader of the Central High School desegregation struggle in Little Rock, Arkansas, to express her support and offer herself as an ally if she could help. Bates responded graciously to Essie's letter.[40] Despite the Robesons' history and persistent efforts, there were those who sought to push them to the margins of mainstream Cold War Black politics, but they in turn pushed back, carving out a new political, cultural, and intellectual space from which to continue to do the work they had done for years. Fortunately, they had friends who stood by them during their ordeal, and they in turn, stood by others who were facing even greater persecution and harassment. For instance, both Essie and Paul were so galled at the treatment that had been meted out to the aging and venerable W. E. B. Du Bois that when his ninetieth birthday rolled around in 1958, Essie agreed to head up a committee to organize an elaborate celebratory event.

The gala was attended by a thousand guests and held at the Roosevelt Hotel in Manhattan on March 2, 1958. Tributes and good wishes poured in from around the world: Russia, Guyana, Nigeria, London, and India. The event was a rousing success and an important statement of support for Du Bois, who like the Robesons was being denied his right to travel because of alleged communist affiliations.[41] In a letter to her friend George Murphy, Essie remarked somewhat jokingly that she had been asked to co-chair the committee because it was a lot of work and no one else wanted to shoulder the burden. Still, she was pleased to do it, and even more "thrilled" with the outcome.

In the spring of 1958, after Du Bois's birthday bash and Paul's own sixtieth birthday celebration, Essie looked to test the waters and travel outside of the country for the first time in seven years. In August of 1957 the government had partially lifted some of its travel restrictions on the Robesons, indicating that they could travel to places in the Western Hemisphere that at the time did not require a passport.[42] Essie was invited to participate in the celebration surrounding the formation of the West Indies Federation, a precursor to the regional Caribbean Community (CARICOM). Many at the time, including the radical thinker C. L. R. James, viewed the new group as both a step toward independence as well as a Pan-Africanist effort to unify the disparate islands of the region and give them a stronger voice in world politics. The federation lasted only five years but in 1958 there was much excitement about its potential and promise. In April people from dozens of islands across the region, and many from the United States and Latin America, converged on the small city of Port-of-Spain, Trinidad, for the first meeting of the federal parliament of the West Indies Federation. With her journalist's credentials in hand, Essie went too.

For more than a week, Essie talked, lectured, and socialized with friends old and new. She first spoke to a packed house at the main public library in Port-of-Spain, with heavy tropical heat and a rapt audience. The program began late and Essie was introduced by Speaker of the Federal House of Representatives E. R. L. Ward, who had begun his career as a labor organizer in the sugar cane fields of Barbados. Her topic was "The Negro in World Focus." Next she had the pleasure of addressing the Communication Services and General Workers Union, again speaking about global affairs and international solidarity. She remarked with delight, "This is the first time I have addressed a Trade Union consisting only of women." Finally, she was a speaker at a forum hosted by the Women's League of the newly constituted People's National Movement of Trinidad, which would soon become the ruling party of the island.[43]

Her appointment book was full, but not too full to do a bit of socializing.[44] During her stay in Trinidad, Essie spent time with the Grenadian journalist and Pan-Africanist Theophilus Albert Marryshow, a delightfully eccentric West Indian man who had been the catalyst behind the federation idea. Dubbed the "father of the federation," Marryshow, with his silver hair, stylish glasses, and dapper bowtie, was at age seventy-one an attractive, charming man with a fierce passion for Black politics and a sharp tongue to match. A journalist and trade unionist, he was a self-taught intellectual who had attended W. E. B. Du Bois's Pan-African Congress in 1919 and had written a book condemning South Africa's white supremacist policies.[45] He and Essie enjoyed weighty conversations and equally robust laughter during her short stay. Sadly, although Marryshow was touted at the first parliament and enjoyed a brief term as a federation senator, he died several months after the Trinidad gathering.[46]

Essie also spent time with her friends the Jagans while in Trinidad in the spring of 1958. They were immersed in the ongoing and complex freedom struggle in Guiana at the time and must have been both happy and relieved to be able to travel to Trinidad for the first parliament of the new federation. Like Paul and Essie, Cheddi Jagan's travel had been restricted from 1953 to 1957, so he was just emerging from political captivity, so to speak. He had won the seat of prime minister of the country only to be ousted by the British and banned from travel. He would return to hold government office in the 1960s and then again in the 1990s. A resilient man, Cheddi, who was of Indian descent, was the son of sugar plantation workers. After attending college in the United States, he had returned to British Guiana with his U.S.-born wife, Janet, to work with labor and left forces.

Another important landmark for Essie and Paul, and another example of their refusal to be silenced or intimidated, was the publication in 1958 of Paul's book *Here I Stand*, in which he countered the negative and narrow depictions of him in mainstream media, outlined his political views in his own words, and indicted the U.S. government for harassment, repression, and racism. Paul worked with his friend Lloyd Brown to complete and edit the book. In a move that underscored the Robeson family's determination to speak freely, unfettered by either the government or timid publishers, it was published by the Robesons' own Othello Associates, a company run by Paul Jr. to facilitate Paul's career and indirectly to advance the views and causes the family believed in. *Here I Stand* was part memoir and part manifesto for Black America. In it Paul described the "warm feeling of friendship" he felt toward the Soviet people, and reiterated his belief in "scientific socialism" as a more egalitarian and just way to organize society. He went on to outline his analysis and aspirations for the growing civil rights movement, eschewing "gradualism," and like Essie had done on numerous occasions and in multiple publications, linking the fate and aspirations of Black Americans to "the world beyond our borders."[47]

Essie had offered her input while the book was in development and she was pleased with the results. In spite of her fragile and fluctuating health, she leapt into action to help with publicity, sending out a plethora of letters urging friends, colleagues, and strangers to buy the book and encouraging media allies to review it. Her efforts helped ensure that the book reached a wide audience. It was befitting then, that after all they had been through together—the muck and the mire on all levels—that Paul, in all sincerity, and with characteristic eloquence and grace, dedicated *Here I Stand* as follows: "To Eslanda Goode Robeson, Distinguished writer and anthropologist. Thanks for many things—For your untiring labors in the interest of the African peoples. For your devotion to the struggle of our folk here in America for full freedom. For your constructive analyses of the momentous events at the United Nations, which affect all manner of human societies. For the deeply shared belief in and labors for the attainment of a lasting peace for all peoples of the earth. And deepest gratitude for your help and guidance over many years of struggle, aspirations, achievements, and the constant awareness of a better future for our children and grandchildren."[48]

thirteen

A FAILING BODY AND A
HOPEFUL HEART, 1958-1961

I'm not going to sit quietly . . . They'll have to put me
in jail or kill me before I'll permit it.
Eslanda Robeson

In June of 1958, after a long, hard, eight-year fight, Essie and Paul finally won the return of their passports. In two historic decisions, *Kent v. Dulles* and *Briehl v. Dulles*, the U.S. Supreme Court determined that the State Department could not revoke or withhold the passport of a U.S. citizen because of his or her political views, recognizing the right to travel as a basic liberty. When Shirley Graham Du Bois heard the good news, she wrote to Essie from Paris to congratulate her, exclaiming that this proved "the people" can win when their cause is righteous.[1] Paul performed before a full house at Carnegie Hall in New York City in that same month, and just a month later, in July 1958, he and Essie had packed their belongings and set sail for London. The Robesons left the United States both to protest the treatment they had received by their own government and also with the hope that Paul's career would flourish again in Europe. A rented flat on Connaught Square in London would be their home base for the next five years, but they kept their apartment on Jumel Terrace in Harlem and continued to travel widely. They had other tempting options during this period. For example, their old friend, President Nkrumah, offered to make Paul, and presumably Essie as well, citizens of Ghana. There they could have had a permanent solution to their troubles with the U.S. government, he reasoned.[2] They graciously declined. The Du Boises would accept a similar offer a few years later.

Neither Essie nor Paul ever considered themselves true expatriates. To fully embrace that identity would have been to allow the U.S. government to succeed in making them foreigners to their own country. They were very much a part of the United States in many ways—family, friends, culture, and history had created strong bonds—even as they continued to be critical of the United States' many flaws. They felt fully rooted in America, specifically Black America. Yet through their extensive travels and wide social networks, Essie and Paul had on some level also become citizens of the world. They both felt strong connections to the larger African Diaspora and to the many countries and cultures with which they had come to identify.

Immediately upon their arrival in London in 1958, Essie began reestablishing contacts with friends and colleagues there while Paul went to work. He appeared on British television, signed a contract to perform *Othello* at the Royal Shakespeare Theatre at Stratford-upon-Avon, and joined his old friend Larry Brown for a sold-out concert at the renowned Royal Albert Hall. Peggy Middleton, who had helped to coordinate the London Paul Robeson Committee and who had become a dear and trusted friend, threw a big welcome back party for Essie and Paul right before his Royal Albert Hall concert with food, drink, old friends, and a Ghanaian drummer who led the Robesons into the gathering with a loud and lively processional. Essie loved it and spent the rest of the evening talking to the young drummer about Africa and anthropology.[3] The Robesons were welcomed warmly to London by their Indian friends as well. They attended a cocktail party hosted by Krishna Menon, the U.N. diplomat Essie so admired, and Nan Pandit had them to tea at the Indian embassy in London.[4]

Essie would also see quite a bit of exiled Black communist leader Claudia Jones over the next few years. Jones, a native of Trinidad, had been jailed and deported from the United States under the McCarran-Walter Act for her communist beliefs, and had resettled in London. Essie liked and admired Jones, describing her once as an absolutely "brilliant" woman.[5] Jones greeted Paul and Essie upon their arrival, and Essie would work with her in an African women's organization in the early 1960s. Essie would also enthusiastically support Jones's cultural projects that involved London's large and diverse West Indian community.[6]

In August 1958 the Robesons went to the Soviet Union for a month of work and relaxation. Paul gave a major public concert in Moscow, attended by eighteen thousand cheering Russian fans. The couple also traveled to a resort in Yalta where they dined and socialized with Soviet premier Nikita Khrushchev. A personal highlight of the trip for Essie was a reunion with her brother Frank, whom she had not seen in nearly a decade. Frank had had a hard time during the war; he had worked as a stevedore and freight handler in Siberia when not performing with his wrestling team. "I worked like John Henry" during the war years, he later recalled, referring to the fictional Black character who worked himself to death—a character Paul would play on stage. But Frank's drama was real. Every Russian citizen, including Frank, had been called on to make sacrifices for the war effort. So after leaving or having been fired from his job as a weight lifter in the circus, Frank did some very grueling manual labor during the war years. He then returned to Moscow, where he tried to make a new life for himself.[7]

The Robesons were welcomed warmly everywhere they went in the Soviet Union in 1958. Paul was a popular and much beloved figure. The legal case concerning his passport and his consistent statements in solidarity with the Russian people had garnered wide publicity in the Soviet Union, adding to his celebrity. The most eventful and physically challenging part of their Russian visit in 1958 was their trek into the remote region of Uzbekistan for the Asian and African Film Festival in Tashkent. It was hot and dusty in the Central Asian republic, and Paul and Essie were on a tough and tight schedule, being toasted and honored at one place and then another. During their time in Tashkent, while attending the historic film festival and concurrent Asian-African writers' conference along with Du Bois and others, they managed to meet with Lily Golden, the daughter of the Black Russian Oliver Golden, whom the Robesons had met twenty years earlier. The twenty-four-year-old Lily was honored to meet Essie and Paul as an adult (she had encountered them as a child in the 1930s) and she had a specific purpose in mind for their meeting. She had been asked by senior Soviet scholar Ivan Potekhin to broach the subject with the Robesons of starting an Institute for African Studies in the Soviet Union that would be a national center for research and teaching.[8]

Essie was thrilled at the prospect of such an institute, and participated actively in the conversations with Lily and subsequent discussions with Potekhin, whom Essie would cross paths with a few months later in Ghana. Those discussions led to the formation of the Institute for African Studies of the Soviet (now Russian) Academy of Sciences, which Lily would later direct.[9] Essie would not be able to see the project to fruition, but she had made her small contribution at an early, critical stage. In fact, according to writer and activist Esther Cooper Jackson, by the 1970s key Soviet scholars at the institute were crediting Essie with having had an important role in its creation. During a visit to the institute around that time, Jackson recalls a talk by historian Anatolii Gromyko in which he praised Essie by name, and suggested that the institute may never have come into existence if not for her quiet efforts. Another example of Essie's close collegial relationship with Potekhin is that he wrote the introduction to the Russian edition of her book *African Journey*, which was published in 1957, twelve years after its original English version and twenty years after the trip that had inspired it.[10]

In his introduction, Potekhin had praised *African Journey* as "the first-hand impressions of a witness who relates to the African people with deep sympathy." He went on to mark it as an important historical text that took a snapshot of colonial Africa through the eyes of an anti-racist observer, at a time when such sensitive observations were rare. Potekhin's introduction also chronicles the two intervening decades between Essie's 1936 visit to south and east Africa and publication of the Russian edition. Much struggle and change had occurred, and the early mobilizations and discussions that Essie had witnessed in 1936 were coming to fruition in the anti-colonial campaigns that had peaked in 1957 and the years that immediately followed. In summing up the value of Essie's contribution to African anti-colonial literature, the respected Russian historian wrote: "Eslanda Robeson went to Africa to gather material herself in order to refute the racist claims of the colonizers. She accomplished this task with flying colors. Her book will, without a doubt, play a positive role. And now, in their active struggle against colonialism, the African people themselves are confirming Eslanda's conclusions."[11]

In December of 1958 Essie would make her third and last trip to the African continent—this time to West Africa. Paul had been invited to attend the All-African Peoples' Conference (AAPC) in Ghana, but he was heading off on a concert tour and could not accept. Essie had no intention of missing this historic event, so she went in his place. More than three hundred delegates and observers gathered from across Africa as well as from India, Canada, Australia, Indonesia, and various European countries. Representatives from twenty-eight African colonies still in the throes of their independence struggles would be present. By 1960, eighteen of those colonies would be independent. At the Accra meeting Essie would meet some of the most influential African leaders on the continent: Tom Mboya from Kenya, Patrice Lumumba of Congo, and Hastings Banda of Nyasaland (Malawi).[12]

Essie arrived at the tiny airstrip just outside Ghana's capital, Accra, on the morning of December 8, 1958. She immediately felt the excitement all around her. The airport was "buzzing with activity," and there were welcome signs along the roads leading to the conference site.[13] The Ghanaian government hosted Essie at what she described as a lovely African villa. Having missed the 1955 Bandung Conference of African and Asian nations in Indonesia and the five Pan-African conferences held in Europe over the years, Essie was ecstatic to be a part of this historic event in Ghana. "Africa is on her way," she exclaimed.[14] Ghana and President Nkrumah held a special place in the history of African independence, and in Essie's mind and heart. The former British Gold Coast colony was the first sub-Saharan nation to achieve full independence after World War II. Ghana and its eloquent and politically savvy new leader, Nkrumah, had a great appeal to African Americans. A year earlier, "Martin Luther King Jr. [had] stood on Accra's polo grounds, along with half a million other weeping and cheering people, when Nkrumah declared Ghana's independence."[15] For her part, Essie knew Nkrumah from her London years and had corresponded with him during the years leading up to Ghana's independence in 1957. For her, visiting the independent nation of Ghana, after all the anti-colonial resistance she had witnessed, documented, and supported for nearly twenty years, was a truly spectacular experience. Even though the continent as a whole had a long way to go, Essie was thrilled that Ghana was leading the way, not only by achieving independence for itself, but also by convening the AAPC to lend support to others.

Essie attended the official sessions of the conference, notebook in hand, and dined at the newly built Ambassador Hotel. The Accra conference provided Essie an opportunity to reconnect with many members of her international political "family" as well as make new acquaintances. She especially enjoyed spending time with the powerful group of women who had gathered at the AAPC that year. She was disappointed by the small number of women in the group—only eight women out of hundreds of official delegates—but they were an impressive lot. Shirley Graham Du Bois was one of only two women invited to address the plenary session of the conference, and she was there as a representative of her esteemed but ailing husband. Mallama Gambo, the other woman who spoke, discussed the suffering that she and her compatriots had endured during Nigeria's struggle for independence. Even before she entered the fight for national liberation, Gambo had waged a personal war for her own emancipation. A child bride of a polygamist aristocrat in northern Nigeria, Gambo, pregnant at the time, had defied custom by leaving her husband and returning to her parents' home. Soon after, she became involved in the struggle against colonialism. Gambo told of being jailed and beaten for her political activity. She refused to be deterred, and she insisted that other Africans also stay the course toward freedom. Essie was inspired both by Gambo's personal story and her political message.

Two other women impressed Essie at the Accra meeting: Saiza Nabarawi, a leading Egyptian feminist, and Geeta Mukherjee, a radical Indian activist. Geeta would later be written about as a formidable figure in the political evolution of India. Nabarawi, with whom Essie enjoyed a great personal rapport, had already made a name for herself in the Arab world by staging defiant symbolic protests in the 1920s against the requirement that Muslim women wear the veil. She was a part of the Egyptian Feminist Union and a member of the international advisory council to the U.S.-based Woman's Party founded by suffragist Alice Paul.[16] Saiza was outspoken and edgy, just the kind of dinner companion Essie loved, and they shared many meals together during the conference. Geeta, more than twenty years younger than Essie and Saiza, was a sharp political voice in India's powerful Communist Party. After the 1958 conference, she returned to India and became one of its leading left-wing voices and one of the few women in India's parliament.[17]

Essie also met and spoke with "Miss Hirtu Imru of Addis Ababa" about the situation in Ethiopia.[18] She was clearly drawn to the other women, perhaps in part because, as another conference participant observed, there was both palpable sexism and a powerful women's presence at the AAPC. "The women, particularly the French-speaking women, were on fire!" wrote Black labor leader Maida Springer, who was at odds with Essie politically but shared her sentiments on women's leadership. Springer described overhearing men complain and even mock some of the female delegates, an experience that for her underscored that the African liberation struggle still had a long way to go before achieving gender equity.[19] Essie openly expressed her own disappointment that more women were not at the gathering, since "100 million women in Africa have undertaken their responsibility in the fight" and so in her view should be fully represented at international gatherings.[20] "A whole population cannot be properly mobilized if half of it is officially ignored," Essie added.[21] Even so, Essie beamed with a hopeful pride as she sat next to her old friend Shirley Du Bois in an independent Ghana, surrounded by leaders of the anti-colonial movement and under posters and banners proclaiming "Africa Will Be Free," "Africa for the Africans," and "Self-Determination for All People." At this historic event, Essie was reminded of the emotions she had experienced at the United Nations' founding a little over a decade before.[22]

The Ghana conference was significant on many levels. In Essie's view it achieved three critical political objectives: greater unity between leaders in northern and southern Africa; a vow of support for the armed liberation movements that were under way; and a powerful show of "Afro-Asian solidarity." In particular, Essie reported positively on Ghanaian president Kwame Nkrumah's notion of "Pan-African socialism." She observed that new African leaders were building on African traditions of communalism but rejecting the divisiveness and often corrupt traditions of "chieftainships" and tribalism. And she was hopeful about a greater Pan-African unity that would include north and sub-Saharan Africa. The depth and skill she demonstrated in her reporting showed just how much she had developed as a writer and thinker since her visit to the African continent in 1936, when she had simply offered admiring praise for the African royalty she had met.

In her review of the events at Accra, Essie also insisted that rumors of a split between Nkrumah and Egypt's Gamal Abdel Nasser were overblown if not fabricated altogether, and supported the use of militant tactics in the campaigns for African independence. She admiringly paraphrased delegates to the Accra conference—many of whom were embroiled in, or had recently emerged from, armed struggles for liberation—as having "declared that 'Africans will not turn the other cheek,' and 'if you hit us we will hit you back.'"[24] In support of this position, she asked rhetorically, "How effective will non-violence be against the brutality of the French in Algeria or Cameroons, against white settlers in Kenya and South Africa?"[25] Significantly, in Essie's view, this was a critical way in which the struggles in the United States and Africa differed: that is, while nonviolent protest seemed to be making modest headway against racism in the United States, many colonial elites were unmoved by such protests, so other tactics had to be employed. At the same time she recognized the right of housing activists in Trumbull Park in Chicago to defend their homes against violent racist mobs.

Essie was pleased, too, that a delegation of Indian representatives like Geeta Mukherjee was on hand to show solidarity for the event. More than anything, Essie was optimistic that this landmark gathering represented a new point of departure for Africa. As she saw it, "Africans plan to assert, as from now, a new African personality in world affairs and at world forums, and above all, this African personality will express an independent sovereign African people." By contrast she condemned "African Uncle Toms, these would-be Frenchmen, Britons etc., the especially-trained Black 'elite,'" who had been allowed to speak for Africa and would be displaced by "the authentic voice of the African people."[26]

What did she mean by African authenticity? Essie made a clear distinction between leaders who demonstrated a commitment to ending colonial rule in all of its forms and empowering the African masses, and those who saw themselves as extensions of or in alliance with white colonial elites. Authentic leaders were defiant; they refused to acquiesce to the desires of the West and were relatively unconcerned with how they were perceived by American and European leaders. She and others were rightly concerned about the specter of neo-colonialism. Essie applauded the rise of the "new type of leader" who was "saying a healthy resounding NO! to their former masters (not even a respectful, no sir), and are starting out on their own road to freedom." Accordingly, she praised Kenyan Tom Mboya's militant support for "all fighters for freedom in Africa," even those "who are compelled to retaliate against violence," and touted Hastings Banda's brazen remarks about rejecting "stooges" who collaborated with colonialism. "This is a new era," Essie exclaimed, perhaps remembering the more modest proposals she had heard in the Congo in 1946—"and a new African leadership is emerging . . . . the end of colonialism is at hand."[27] Sadly, all of the young African leaders who spoke with such idealism in 1958 would not live up to their promises to serve the African masses, but that future was not evident at the Accra gathering.

Essie left Ghana on a turbulent flight through stormy skies, stopping in Kano, Nigeria, and Barcelona, Spain, before heading back to London. She was anxious to monitor the political rumblings back home in the United States.[28] A new Black leadership was emerging there and changing the social, cultural, and political landscape. Before Essie and Paul left the States, she had watched and read with great interest as the Montgomery Bus Boycott unfolded over the course of 1956, and she had listened on the radio to—and read quotes in the newspaper by—the young charismatic minister Martin Luther King Jr. She and Paul had attended the 1957 civil rights march and waited with hopeful anticipation to see what would come next. Essie praised the new direct-action tactics that were being deployed and recognized the great potential in the new Southern-based Black freedom struggle.

During the early 1950s, years before Rosa Parks's defiant stance that triggered the Montgomery Bus Boycott, Essie had covered political stories about Southern Black resistance efforts and the violence they sparked in others seeking to undermine those efforts. She wrote a powerful essay in 1951 condemning the Christmas Day bombing of the home of NAACP activist Harry T. Moore and his wife, Harriette, in Mims, Florida. The couple was killed in the blast. Moore had led the fight for pay equity for Black and white teachers, spoken out against lynching and police brutality, and advocated for Black voter registration. The local Ku Klux Klan was implicated in the case, but no arrests were ever made.

The Moores' case and other instances of unpunished racist violence drew Essie's ire. For months before the Moore murders she had been advocating a more militant stance against racisim. In "A Call to the Negro People: Begging Should End Now," penned in April 1951 and published in *The California Eagle*, she issued her own call to action.[29] "I believe the time has come for us, the Negro People, to stop thinking of ourselves in terms of inferiority—asking, pleading, begging for a crust or two of the bread of citizenship. The time has come for us to demand the whole loaf." She then posed a provocative rhetorical question: In light of the anti-colonial struggles the world over, "shall we, the Negro people, be quiet?" Her answer was no. "We must revolutionize our thinking," Essie insisted, pointing to the former colonial subjects around the world who had risen up to claim independence.[30] "The majority of the Colored people of Asia have fought their way up and out from under white Colonial domination," she wrote. "The rest of Asia, Africa and the West Indies are fighting now to come up and out from under. 'There are rumblings in every village from the Mediterranean to the Pacific'—yet here we are, the Negro people of the United States, still thinking and talking and behaving as though the Colored Peoples of the world, including ourselves, were still in slavery, still servants of the 'Free Nations.'"[31] Her words were brazen, even more so since she and Paul were at that very moment being hounded, harassed, and spied on. Rather than succumb to the intimidation, Essie went out of her way to voice her dissent as loudly as she could. "I'm not going to sit quiet," she insisted. "They'll have to put me in jail, or kill me, before I'll permit it."[32]

In a speech to the National Association of Colored Women (NACW) in 1954, Essie had injected a gender analysis into her Black internationalist perspective. "It isn't a man's world any longer. It never was—men just said it was, and took over," she told her "sisters" at the NACW meeting in Oakland. As always she framed the Black experience in a global context. To make these issues relevant to her audience, she created analogies among colonialism, slavery, and domestic service. "Negro people know and understand," she intoned, "what happens when you are forced to build a house for somebody else, and to take care of somebody else's children, when the Master or Mistress has no interest in you, consideration for you, and doesn't even pay you well for your work, but treats you with, not respect nor dignity, [but] as a slave or animal. . . . You definitely will have no love or respect for the tyrant who forces you to work." She described socialist countries and former colonies where people, particularly women, no longer felt the yoke of oppression, having been freed from their colonial "masters." Citing India, Indonesia, China, Burma, and Eastern Europe as examples, she argued that there had been stark improvements in the lives and opportunities for women, not because of benevolence of men or "because of advanced thinking, but because of necessity."[33] Women, she said, are essential to the struggle and critical for building a new society. As a starting point for her American "sisters" to demand and expect greater inclusion, she suggested that they see themselves as people first and women second.[34] Contemporary feminists might bristle at this formulation, but Essie did not mean to say that gender should be put on the back burner; only that traditional notions of womanhood should be.

Essie even used her eulogy at the funeral of Black Communist Party leader James Ford to underscore the importance of women's leadership. After apologizing for Paul's absence, expressing her condolences to the family, and commenting on Ford's integrity and good humor, she chose to highlight his progressive attitude on women's leadership in Left politics. "I especially appreciated his awareness of the status of women in our world. He understood—as not enough men do—the contribution that women have made, and continue to make, in the struggle for freedom, equality and democracy in our country."[35]

Ford's death in 1957 at age sixty-three may also have prompted Essie to think long and hard about her own life and mortality. Essie had already survived a bout with breast cancer. Treatments at Beth Israel Hospital had been successful: in 1956 Essie had confided to a friend that she felt hopeful about her prognosis.[36] In 1958, however, she was diagnosed with cervical cancer and then uterine cancer. It was unclear if the breast cancer had recurred and metastasized after her mastectomy or whether these were new cancers, but either way, the treatments she received beginning in 1958 were painful and prolonged. Throughout it all, Essie was as tough in her fight against the disease that had colonized her body as she was in the political struggles she waged so tirelessly. True to form,

Essie worked a lot and complained only a little. She adopted the attitude that she had already overcome a lot of hurdles in her life and could conquer this one as well.

In January 1959, Essie traveled to the Soviet Union to undergo radiotherapy for her cancer. Paul also received treatment at the same hospital for a matrix of ill-defined ailments, which were later diagnosed as a form of depression. Essie was in the hospital five long and difficult weeks. She tried to be upbeat in her letters to Paul Jr. and Marilyn as well as other friends back home. She wrote about the lovely accommodations, the kind and competent staff, and the flowers, cards, and fruit baskets from well-wishers around the world. She boasted of her improved Russian language skills and that she had a lovely typewriter in her room so that she could continue her writing projects. She told friends that her doctor, a young Russian woman, was "very skillful and very very expert. . . . I have every confidence in her."[37] As much as possible Essie tried to convince others, and perhaps herself, that she and Paul would be okay at the end of this ordeal.[38] She wanted desperately to recover and resume her life.

Essie had to admit at one point that the medical procedures she was having were absolutely "rugged." Since Essie was generally tough as nails and not prone to complain, it must have been pretty bad. Her primary treatment consisted of having radium injected into her uterus over a twenty-four-hour period, during which she had to lie perfectly still. The procedure was repeated five times over the course of her stay, each time followed by twenty-five gamma ray treatments, which left her in "continuous pain" and feeling absolutely "wicked." Paul was discharged from the hospital before Essie's therapy regimen was complete. He returned to their London apartment, leaving Essie to endure the rest of her medical treatments alone. Health problems notwithstanding, Paul still had to earn a living and he had contracted to appear in another production of *Othello*, this time at the famed Royal Shakespeare Theatre at Stratford-upon-Avon, outside London. He felt he had to return to prepare for the part. Essie persevered.[39] In fact, she worried aloud to friends not about herself, but about how Paul would manage in London without her.[40]

Essie was discharged soon after Paul's departure. Her British friend Peggy Middleton, who had become so devoted to her, met Essie during her flight's layover in Paris to help her the rest of the way back to London. Essie accepted the help because, as she put it, she was feeling "just a bit wobbly."[41]

The very difficult year of 1959 was punctuated in the summer by an extended visit from Paul Jr. and his family. In these years, family—including her extended family of friends—was more important to Essie than ever. After losing her mother, she had become doubly devoted to Paul Jr.; his wife, Marilyn; and their two children, David and Susan, who were eight and six, respectively. Essie absolutely adored her grandchildren, and gushed when describing them to friends. So she was thrilled when "Pauli" (which is how she continued to address her grown son) and his family came to London for several weeks in July of 1959. Paul was so immersed in the *Othello* production, which co-starred Laurence Olivier, that he rarely made it back to the Connaught Square flat—instead, for the duration of the production, he stayed in a rented room just outside Stratford-upon-Avon in order to devote all of his energies to the play. When the younger Robesons came to visit Essie, then, she had them all to herself for several days, which gave her a "new lease on life."[42] After Essie arranged for the whole crew to go up to Stratford for one of Paul's performances, Paul Jr. and Marilyn left for the World Youth Festival in Vienna (where Paul Sr. flew in briefly to deliver the closing remarks and to sing for a crowd of 25,000), leaving David and Susan behind with their thrilled grandmother. Paul Jr. reflected years later that Essie "delighted in being a grandmother, and [the children] adored their 'Nana.'"[43]

Despite these happy interludes, Paul and Essie's family life overall was far from blissful. Essie was tired and frustrated. They were still being spied on by United States and British intelligence, and at times Essie did not feel safe, let alone secure. Paul's sometimes erratic behavior continued to grind on her, especially when she was ill. When Paul, Marilyn, and Paul Jr. returned from Vienna, Paul began to discuss the possibility of returning to the States on a permanent basis. Essie, however, was nervous about the prospect of going home. They had been persecuted and hounded by the U.S. government, and some friends had suffered even worse fates. The situation came to a head one evening when she overheard Paul expressing to Paul Jr. his desire to go back to the States. Angry and afraid, she accused Paul of selfish pursuits, of philandering and recklessness, and then, nearly in tears, confessed her real fear: that he was "going to get himself killed." It was obvious to Paul Jr. that his mother was under enormous emotional strain and that the relationship between his parents was tense, to say the least.[44] But this storm cloud, too, would pass. As she had done many times over the years, Essie pulled herself together and carried on.

At the end of 1959 Paul ended *Othello* in what Essie described as "a blaze of glory." She, however, was not doing well at all. In November she woke up in the middle of the night "with screaming pain." Paul took her to the hospital where she was admitted right away. The diagnosis was an ulcer caused by the radiation she had received as a part of her cancer treatment. She was given codeine to relieve the pain, but her mobility was compromised. She was grateful that Larry Brown was nearby and helped with errands. Her friend, Peggy Middleton, whom she increasingly treated as extended family, also came by regularly to help with the correspondence and other business that filled Essie's desk. It was a grueling winter.[45] In addition to her physical suffering, Essie was horribly frustrated by these periods of incapacitation; it made her furious that illness was getting in the way of her plans. She lived on the move; she lived to make things happen. In an apology to the head of the Associated Negro Press, Claude Barnett, for missing an interview with Guinea's president when the president was in London, she fumed: "I am disgusted with myself as a reporter. . . . Sekou Toure and his wife were in London, searching for me, and I was in hospital, very very sick."[46] Essie also had intended to travel as a journalist with Soviet Premier Nikita Khrushchev on his first visit to Africa, but that too had to be put on hold. (In the end, Khrushchev canceled the trip for other reasons.)[47]

Although Essie was wrestling with an array of health problems, both hers and Paul's, from across the Atlantic she was still carefully observing and weighing in on U.S. politics. George Murphy wrote to Essie about the desegregation student sit-in movement that had begun in February in Greensboro, North Carolina, and spread quickly throughout the South. Other friends sent her newspaper clippings indicating that the Black Freedom movement was gaining momentum.

In October and November of 1960, during a brief window of simultaneous good health, Paul and Essie traveled to Australia and New Zealand for a ten-week concert tour. Essie was pleased to receive her own press coverage this time. While Paul and Larry performed in concerts, she helped with the tour and set up meetings with local activists, artists, and scholars. The press there loved her. One article with the headline "Mrs. Robeson Is Notable Too" described Essie as "a woman of great charm and intelligence who has had a fascinating career of her own." Another article in a Melbourne paper noted with praise that she "devotes much of her time and many-sided talents to supporting the advancement of the Negro people in the United States and Africa." Positive media coverage aside, Essie and Paul both recognized immediately the racism suffered by the indigenous people in Australia and New Zealand, and spoke out against it.[48]

On November 10, Essie gave a keynote address at a luncheon hosted by the Union of Australian Women (UAW) in Sydney. The UAW had been formed in 1950 by women involved in leftist, labor, and peace organizations, and it embraced a "militant policy and action-oriented programme."[49] While the group focused primarily on women's economic issues, they also allied themselves with indigenous struggles: "We have always supported the aboriginal people in their struggle for land rights and self determination."[50] In her remarks before the UAW, Essie took the opportunity to address not only U.S. race relations and African decolonization, the two topics she spoke about most frequently, but also the importance of women's leadership "in all spheres" of society. "I am not a feminist," she said (although her remarks suggest otherwise), "but I believe very strongly that since women are half the population on earth that they should exert at least half the power."[51]

While they were in New Zealand, Paul and Essie encountered representatives of the indigenous Maori people. Essie was pleased to meet, talk, and exchange gifts with the Maori, because she was eager to show her solidarity with their struggle. In one of their meetings she was given a traditional "challenge staff," also referred to as a "rakau," which the Maori lay down before distinguished guests as part of an honorific welcoming ritual. This rakau became one of Essie's treasured possessions, one that she proudly displayed in a photograph taken for a local paper during her visit.[52]

Essie and Paul both seemed to find the trip to Australia and New Zealand deeply meaningful and affirming, albeit "exhausting."[53] And while politically they were on the same page, personally they were again experiencing some friction. Paul was depressed and tired and seemed to take it out on Essie. She wrote a frustrated letter to Freda Diamond complaining, "He is angrier than ever, and it makes me shudder, because he is so often angry at all the wrong people, and so often unnecessarily angry."[54] Even though Essie confessed that she was literally "fed up" with Paul's behavior, she persevered, and they returned to England together. Paul required more medical care soon after their return.[55]

More than simply angry and frustrated, Essie was becoming increasingly worried about Paul. A particularly alarming incident occurred in March 1961. Paul was in Moscow without Essie and there was a party in his hotel room in which there was a lot of drinking and several uninvited guests. The next morning, Paul found himself in a Moscow hospital bed, having slashed his own wrists with razor blades in an apparent suicide attempt. Essie was called and immediately booked a flight from London to Moscow to help. Few people know exactly what happened that night; Paul had been discovered in the bathroom of his hotel room by his translator, Irina. Years later, Paul Jr., through his own investigations and review of declassified U.S. government documents, obtained compelling evidence that the CIA and the British intelligence agency may have conspired to administer LSD to Paul in an effort to undo him completely. The Russian hotel incident may have somehow been a part of that scheme. Although there is no ironclad proof, the theory is not farfetched, given the threat that Robeson still represented to the Cold War agenda, the powerful political influence he could have had on the growing Black struggle in the United States, and what recent scholarship has revealed about what the FBI and CIA were capable of doing in those days to undermine leftist and radical leaders. It is also significant that right before his alleged suicide attempt, Paul had been preparing to travel to Cuba. Had this incident not occurred, he would have likely been with Fidel Castro when the failed U.S.-led Bay of Pigs invasion took place in April 1961.[56]

As disturbing as this incident was, Paul survived and was back on his feet, even if not fully recovered, within a few short weeks.[57] He was still vulnerable, though, and lacked much of the vigor and vitality of his former self. His Soviet doctors diagnosed him with "depressive paranoiac psychosis" and began treating him with mild tranquilizers, which seemed to help for a time.[58] He was then referred to Barveekha (or Barvikha) Sanitorium, a highly regarded Russian facility where W. E. B. Du Bois had gone to rest and rehabilitate. By early May, Paul Sr., Essie, and Paul Jr. were all recuperating in a "luxurious cottage" on the sanatorium's grounds. Having come to Moscow to investigate what had happened to his father in March, Paul Jr. also suffered an inexplicable mental breakdown that included "severe hallucinations and extreme paranoia," symptoms remarkably similar to those his father had experienced before the suicide attempt. Since he never suffered from a similar episode before or after that incident, Paul Jr. later concluded that his breakdown was also drug induced.[59] Whatever the cause of this strange series of events, Essie found herself in a familiar but foreign country tending to the two men she loved most in the world, unsure what the future held for any of them. With her physical energies depleted and nerves frayed, Essie welcomed the opportunity to stay at Barveekha with her two Pauls for several weeks to rest and get her strength back.

Paul Jr. returned to the States first, and Essie and Paul left for London in June. Essie was glad to get back to her own flat, her own things, her own life. But she enjoyed the comforts of home only briefly—they were both back in the hospital in Moscow by the month's end. They trusted their Russian doctors and so they were willing to make the trek to get the very fine health care that was provided to them for free. Still, Essie was beginning to become "seriously discouraged" about Paul's condition. And moreover she had to navigate a minefield of queries from worried family and friends. In a letter to Paul Jr. and Marilyn in July 1961, Essie insisted that she was telling those who inquired exactly "what Paul asked me to tell them" about his condition. She said he did not want all of the details spread about, and she was abiding by his wishes. A week later, she curtly turned the problem over to Paul Jr. and Marilyn. "As to explanations, we will leave that entirely to you and Marilyn from here on in," she wrote, "I have too much on my hands on this end to even care." She confessed that she was simply "trying to survive and cope."[60] But inquiries and complaints about how she was handling Paul's condition persisted. A letter from Paul's lawyer and friend Bob Rockmore, whom Essie had never liked and considered Paul's friend and not hers, must have been especially exasperating. "I have been and still am extremely disturbed over the whole situation — the more so because of the vague and ambiguous statements you make to me," Rockmore declared.[61] At that point, his concerns were simply not a priority for Essie.

Despite all the difficulties and strains, Essie did keep up her personal correspondence with individuals whom she respected and cared about from Harlem to Accra to Delhi. Even though the letters were sporadic and there were periods when Essie was simply too worn out to write, her spirited passion for Africa, social justice, and her colorful coterie of friends was unwavering. For example, she continued exchanging candid letters with Shirley Graham Du Bois throughout the early 1960s on issues ranging from personal health to world politics.[62] When Shirley and W. E. B. Du Bois relocated to Ghana in 1961, Shirley wrote to Essie with all the details of the move, their accommodations, and her hopes for their new life in Africa. Essie in turn confided in Shirley about the ups and downs in her own life, and indulged in hopeful speculation about new political changes on the horizon.[63] So close were the two couples that the Du Boises stayed at the Robesons' London flat when Essie and Paul were in Moscow.[64]

By October 1961, Paul was in residence at an exclusive nursing and psychiatric facility on the outskirts of London called The Priory, where he remained off and on for nearly two years. His symptoms of depression and disorientation had persisted and Essie placed him there, in her mind, as a last resort. She had made the difficult decision on the advice of his London doctors. She felt she was doing what was best for Paul under the circumstances. His Russian doctors did not agree with the treatment plan mapped out at The Priory, and Essie did not consult with Paul Jr. in making the decision, a fact that caused considerable tension between them. The decision to place Paul in The Priory proved to be a fateful one, since he received debilitating electroconvulsive therapy at the facility, after which, according to Paul Jr., his father was never the same.[65]

Essie surely made decisions about Paul's health with the best of intentions. She loved Paul dearly, even after all they had been through, or perhaps because of it. She visited him dutifully when he was at The Priory, even though doing so required taking a complicated route, and she brought him home-cooked meals to try to lift his spirits. For his birthday in 1962, she sent a letter to all their friends urging them to send "an avalanche" of cards to cheer him up.[66] She also took a regular stream of visitors to see him, and on weekends she would shuttle him to their London flat in the hope that the familiar and comfortable surroundings would aid in his recovery. Above all, she wanted "her Paul" back. One Sunday afternoon in October the two of them sat around and watched rugby matches on television, "had tea," talked, and napped. Essie was being her most nurturing self.[67] And once again she was putting her own needs on the back burner. Although the future was uncertain, Essie's devotion to Paul was not.

Essie Robeson was a willful woman. If she could have willed Paul back to good health, she certainly would have. But this was a problem that sheer willpower could not entirely resolve, and Essie was no longer a healthy young woman. Caring for Paul and overseeing his care and treatments was a sacrifice for Essie: it took her away from the writing and public speaking projects she so enjoyed, and much of her effort was at the expense of her own deteriorating health, which unbeknownst to her was to be again severely challenged by cancer. Nonetheless she did all that she did willingly and lovingly. Essie navigated the straightest path she could through dark and uncertain waters.[68]

fourteen

ALWAYS THE FIGHTER:
A PEN AS HER WEAPON,
1961–1965

In fighting a just cause, in resisting oppression, there is dignity.
Eslanda Robeson

Throughout her protracted bouts with cancer and other illnesses, Essie wrote. For her, writing was cathartic and clarifying. Long before her words were published, writing was her way of coping with and understanding her life and the world around her. In the 1920s and 1930s, she kept a diary to chronicle life's twists and turns, to vent her frustrations and clear her head. In the late 1950s and early 1960s, in addition to her political journalism, and as she wrestled with her own mortality, writing took on even greater therapeutic importance, and she wrote with great ferocity and urgency, this time for a public readership. There were always writing projects on her desk. One especially consuming enterprise was her effort to sort, revise, and edit her notes from her 1946 trip to Congo—a project that she hoped would become another book. She also drafted a proposal for a collection of her articles and essays that she intended to pitch to a publisher. Finally, and most ambitiously, she dreamed of crafting a comprehensive "survey" text on sub-Saharan Africa, but ultimately life was too short for that too. More modest writing assignments were manageable, and would have to do.

Essie did publish numerous articles in the 1960s on topics including the United Nations, civil rights protests, and the fast-changing political world. In fact, she turned out an amazing volume of essays and articles in this period. It was as if she was racing against time to have her say. And she had something to say about a wide range of international issues, from the Caribbean to North Africa to Asia to sub-Saharan Africa, to the changing racial landscape in the United States. With strong opinions and heartfelt loyalties, Essie wielded her pen as a political weapon, and she was unafraid of controversy.

One hotspot Essie wrote about in the early 1960s was Cuba. Although she had never visited the island (she and Paul had planned to do so but their plans were thwarted by illness), she came to know it through books, articles, and films. The Caribbean nation had undergone a revolution in 1959 to oust the U.S.-backed dictator Fulgencio Batista. By 1961, the new Cuban leaders had embraced communism and allied themselves with the Soviet Union. In April of that year, President John F. Kennedy authorized an ill-conceived invasion of the island at the now famed Bay of Pigs, an effort spearheaded by U.S.-trained anticommunist Cuban exiles living in Miami. The plan was to topple Fidel Castro's two-year-old government and strike a blow against Soviet encroachment into the Western Hemisphere. Essie actually wrote one piece about Cuba right before the invasion; she then added a postscript about the failed foray. In the essay Essie used the film *Island in Flames*, which she had just seen in Moscow, to introduce readers to Cuban history and politics. She described a country in transition, moving from an oppressive dictatorship to something more hopeful. "The Cuban people, led by Fidel Castro, fought their way out from under Batista and the American Dollar, and are now happily building Cuba for themselves," she wrote.[1] The unpublished postscript was harshly critical of the U.S.-led invasion: "The island WAS in flames for several days recently when the United States sponsored and supported an émigré invasion of Cuba. But the people of Cuba rallied immediately to their Leader and successfully defended their revolution."[2]

In 1961, Essie wrote a series of articles for the Chicago-based Associated Negro Press about the annual meeting of the Family Council of the British Commonwealth of Nations (BCN) in London, where prime ministers from former and current British colonies and territories had gathered to discuss issues of common concern. Essie analyzed their discussions and debates about South Africa, a place and a struggle dear to her.[3] Indeed, of all the issues addressed by the gathering, South Africa was the most contentious and prolonged. South Africa was scheduled to officially become an independent republic in May, and the white leadership had requested that it continue to enjoy the rights and privileges of membership in the commonwealth. As Essie noted, although the question had been buried in the agenda, perhaps to disguise its significance, the leaders of formerly colonial African and Asian nations rose up in protest. They demanded that South Africa's system of apartheid be on the table for examination if it was going to be a part of the commonwealth. And they questioned whether Black- and Brown-led nations would be afforded the courtesy of having embassies in Pretoria and whether their diplomats would be able to live and travel freely in the country. South African prime minister Hendrik Verwoerd balked at that idea, and his government's effort to gain commonwealth acceptance collapsed under the pressure.

Essie applauded the roles played by Ghana's president, Kwame Nkrumah, and her old friend Jawaharlal Nehru, India's prime minister, in thwarting South Africa's plans.[4] Still invigorated from their recent independence movements, these leaders successfully pushed back against the longstanding hegemony of the West. South Africa was still a racist country with a system of whites-only rule, but at least it had been denied the veneer of respectability that membership in the BCN would have afforded. This small victory was all the more meaningful because it occurred almost exactly one year after the Sharpeville massacre in South Africa, when sixty-nine Black South Africans in the Transvaal region had been killed by authorities for protesting the country's repressive laws.

On March 19, 1961, the one-year anniversary of the Sharpeville massacre, just after the BCN meeting ended, Essie was one of the speakers at a massive outdoor rally in London's Trafalgar Square. She spoke to a crowd of two thousand alongside other anti-apartheid activists, including members of Parliament, but the rally was not without opposition. A tiny group from the "Keep England White" movement heckled the speakers from the periphery and scuffled with police. Thirty people were arrested, though none of the hecklers had much of an effect on the group's message.[5] The Trafalgar rally was a rousing success and, along with similar protests around the world, signaled the beginnings of the international anti-apartheid movement.

The Congo was also on Essie's mind in 1961. The newly independent nation's charismatic young prime minister, Patrice Lumumba, whom Essie had met in Ghana in 1958, had been overthrown in a violent coup and later assassinated. The CIA was implicated. Essie had a special attachment to the Congo because of the time she had spent there, and she was deeply troubled by Lumumba's tragic death. She wrote to a friend that she derived some hope from the people's response to the crisis in the Congo; instead of silence, there had been "riots all over the world in protest."[6] There was so much upheaval that U.N. Secretary-General Dag Hammarskjöld, with whom Essie was acquainted, responded to the crisis by arranging to travel there to see for himself what was going on. He died in a suspicious plane crash en route.[7]

Kenya was yet another important anti-colonial battleground in the early 1960s. Essie's old friend and former classmate at the London School of Economics, Jomo Kenyatta, who would in a few short years become the first prime minister and later president of Kenya, was at the center of that fight. Kenyatta had been jailed in 1952, after the famous "Kapenguria Six" trial, for allegedly attempting to overthrow the colonial regime during the Mau Mau Uprising. He remained in prison for seven years. In 1961, Kenyatta was under house arrest in a remote area of the colony, and there was growing pressure on the colonial authorities to free him. In January of that year, Essie wrote an open letter defending Kenyatta and demanding his immediate release.[8] Petitioners throughout Africa and around the world did the same. Essie's letter referred in part to her personal relationship with Kenyatta, which began in the 1930s when they both attended one of Bronislaw Malinowski's anthropology seminars at LSE.[9] Kenyatta had even played an extra in the film that Paul and Essie so came to regret, *Sanders of the River.* Essie and Kenyatta had an intellectual bond, and he had had a great influence on her thinking. "Before I met Kenyatta," Essie wrote, "I was studying anthropology (and Africa) in theory. Kenyatta brought it to life for me, and took me out of the textbooks into African life itself. I was fascinated by his stories, and he, recognizing this, gave me much interesting and useful information about his tribe, the Kikuyu, and about their lives in his country, Kenya." She described Kenyatta as "a brilliant, informed, gentle, tolerant, courageous human being." Essie knew his character and actions were being distorted by the British press, which described him as "violent" and "dangerous." She recalled the patient and methodical activist who compiled petitions and legal arguments to put before the British authorities. In her letter, Essie argued that the "trial of Kenyatta was a world scandal. His conviction and imprisonment [were] a disgraceful injustice."[10]

Essie lent her support to African independence struggles directly (through expressions of solidarity and her advocacy) and indirectly (by lobbying non-African friends also to lend their support). One such friend was Indian prime minister Jawaharlal Nehru. Essie sent him many articles on Africa and African anti-colonial struggles. In 1955, in the wake of the historic Bandung conference, he expressed how their exchanges had influenced him and reaffirmed his own commitment to African freedom. He wrote to Essie: "The more I think of it, the more deeply I feel how important this question of Africa is. I am overwhelmed at the thought of the long agony of the African people."[11]

By the early 1960s, Africa was on fire. The year 1960 had marked the culmination of independence struggles in some seventeen countries, and for the next several years the peoples of the continent were experiencing the volatility and danger that came with transitions of political power. Essie was an astute observer and student of the social and political developments on the African continent. When she first went to Africa in 1936 she had been a bit naïve in her expectations and observations, but by the early 1960s she had become a savvy analyst and largely self-taught scholar and expert. She was clear in general about what side she was on in the fight against colonialism, but she also wanted to ground her articles, pamphlets, speeches, and editorials in solid evidence and accurate information. Excerpts from her weekly notebooks illustrate how seriously she took the task of researching and writing about Africa. In a converted address book, Essie took fastidious and copious notes on the daily developments in Africa and beyond. Citing several U.S. and British newspapers as well as meetings, lectures, and press conferences that she had attended, Essie essentially made her own up-to-date encyclopedia of Africa. The "A" section, for example, begins with detailed notes from her study of Angola. She doesn't cite specific sources in this entry, but her comments are extensive. The forces in Angola are "split into the union of Peoples of Angola (UPA) . . . led by Roberto Holden [Holden Roberto]," she writes. "MPLA is the strongest liberation movement in Angola, is completely multiracial and has branches in both towns and cities, [and] has a program not only for political independence," she observes significantly, "but also for economic and political changes after liberation. Both groups have guerilla armies."[12]

Essie monitored all the various gatherings on the African continent as they pertained to the terms of the rapidly evolving political situation. In reading her political journal we are reminded of the extensive activity and multiple deliberations that marked this period when new African nations came onto the world stage. Significant conferences included a gathering in Monrovia in May of 1961; a "conference at Addis Ababa of the Pan African Freedom Movement in East, Central and Southern Africa" in March of 1962; a meeting of the "French African Malagasy Union" in "March of 1961 at Yaounde (Cameroon)";

"the third annual African Peoples Conference, also in March of 1961," where Congo hosted delegates from thirty-two African countries and liberation struggles who declared that "neo-colonialism is [the] greatest menace in Africa"; and a convention in Casablanca in January of 1961 that brought together leaders from West Africa and North Africa.

In addition to recording the cold, hard facts about Africa, Essie kept extensive notes on the people she met and the events and meetings she attended. In her notes about individuals, Essie reminded herself of their family backgrounds, views, affiliations, and even physical characteristics so she would not forget them. One entry read: "Elizabeth Renner (or Penner), tall dark lawyer I met at British Commonwealth League luncheon when I spoke. (Sierra Leone)." She also reminded herself of a "little man with beard," Ngumbu Njururi, whom she had met in London, and another diplomat she had met on her flight to Accra in 1958. Listed under "W" for West Indies, she mentions "Daniel N. N. George, J. S. Donaldson, parliamentary ministry, communications, Port of Spain, Trinidad (I met at federation celebrations)." Finally she cites "Eric Williams, brilliant economist," referring to Trinidad's first prime minister. No more details about Williams are given, but clearly Essie wanted to remind herself of who he was.[13]

A resurgence of Black-led protests was occurring in the United States at this time as well, and writers like Essie stepped up to document and support the U.S.-based movement. Essie initially chronicled the U.S. Black Freedom movement from afar. For example, she praised the "young Martin L. King Jr., the Negro Minister who so effectively advocates continuing, active, non-violent resistance to segregation." In a lengthy article that was published in the *Sun-Reporter*, Essie highlighted King's more militant rhetoric, quoting him admiringly as saying, "We will turn America upside-down, in order that it turn right side up." She read that comment through a distinctly international lens and concluded, "The Negro is saying to his Government: never mind all this advertising and trying to sell this false image around the world; never mind spending all that money broadcasting Voice of America, and sending all those salesmen, missionaries, Peace Corps, diplomats and soldiers to impose the false American image over there. Do something over here and now to make that image a true one by practicing what you preach."[14]

When King visited London in the fall of 1961 to speak out in support of nuclear disarmament for a British peace group, Essie was in the audience to hear him. She thought King's remarks were good and he handled himself with great "dignity" despite a handful of hecklers who shouted from the floor. The evening lecture was in a large auditorium and included a South African speaker who had been one of the defendants in the 1956 Treason Trial. The previous afternoon, October 29, Essie had attended a smaller reception for King organized by Claudia Jones at Africa Unity House, where she had a chance to chat with him about the Black Freedom movement in the United States, and to convey Paul's regards and his regrets.[15] He would have been there with Essie, had he been well, but at the time he was still an inpatient at The Priory.

The next time Essie saw Dr. King she and Paul were watching him deliver his famous "I Have a Dream" speech on television. It was August 1963, and the March on Washington had drawn 250,000 people to the nation's capital to protest racism. In a letter to Shirley Du Bois Essie marveled at how much things had changed in recent times. It had only been six years since the Prayer Pilgrimage in 1957, when Black leaders shunned militants as unpatriotic, and now there were signs of real progress—not only the March on Washington, but also the increasingly confrontational direct-action tactics of the Student Nonviolent Coordinating Committee. Essie viewed these developments with great optimism.[16]

There was a lot of political activity in London in the fall and winter of 1962. Two weeks after King's departure, Essie's old friend Jomo Kenyatta was in town, his student days far behind him and his prison days finally over. As leader of the Kenya African National Union (KANU) delegation, Kenyatta had arrived to participate in historic negotiations, the Lancaster House talks that would lead to Kenya's independence the following year. On November 12, Essie went over to the Cumberland Hotel near Hyde Park where Kenyatta was staying to see her old friend, tell him how things were going with her and Paul, and of course, talk politics. "Kenyatta was in good form," Essie reported to Paul Jr. in a later phone call. The two friends reminisced about old times and their days at LSE. "They didn't think we would use our knowledge against them, did they?" Kenyatta joked with Essie. They talked about the United Nations, the nonviolent movement in the United States, and the negotiations he was involved in. Essie also asked several questions about the status and involvement of women in Kenyan politics. She was pleased to have had that time with Kenyatta, and they both must have regretted Paul's absence from the reunion.[17]

Since issues of women's leadership and women's rights had become a passion of Essie's almost as much as the issue of African freedom, it is not surprising that one of the organizations she became involved in when she moved back to England was a new left-leaning Pan-African women's organization that included her friend Claudia Jones. The All-African Women's Freedom Movement (AAWFM) was founded in part by the sixty-five-year-old Essie, who also participated in their inaugural "Africa Women's Day" event held on December 7, 1961, at London's new State Ballroom Hall. Essie shared the podium with Jones and several others. The diverse array of Africa-descended people who attended reflected the broad Pan-African unity that Essie and Jones were trying to build through this organization. In addition to Essie the program included an Afro-Cuban dancer, a Jamaican singer, and Kwesi Armah, a Ghanaian high commissioner.[18] The AAWFM recruited twenty-eight new members at the event and Essie thought it was a "very great success" overall.[19]

In Essie's remarks that day she proclaimed that she was "happy [to be] recognized and accepted as a Sister. I am [an] American Negro of African descent, and therefore DO belong to the African family. My son, very young once, said to me isn't it too bad you haven't got more brown? I said I feel brown, and I think brown, and I am brown, so that makes it enough. As a member of our great African family, indeed as a member of the greater non white family in our world, I am of course very much interested and concerned with our family joys and sorrows and our many problems. That's why you see me at meetings. I am especially happy to belong to this new organization, the All Africa Women's Movement, because I do believe that women have an important and urgent role to play in our new World."[20] The following year, the group's annual program, which was held at Africa Unity House in London, had an even more diverse representation of African women and women from the Diaspora, and at least one male speaker. Essie was on the roster once again. This time she spoke under a banner that read "Long Live Lumumba" alongside Princess Lalla Fatima Zohra of Morocco; Mahmoud Abdi Arraleh, the Somalian ambassador to Britain; and Rose Chibambo, founder of the League of Malawi Women from what was then Nyasaland (later, Malawi). Chibambo had spent a year in jail for her political activism back home and had even delivered one of her five children while serving her prison sentence.[21]

As a result of her work with AAWFM, Essie was invited to speak to the Committee of African Organizations' special forum on "The Role of Women in the Emancipation of Africa," held on April 14, 1962. The committee was a coalition of forces that included the West African Students' Union, the Uganda People's Congress, the Zanzibar nationalist party, the Basutoland African Congress, the Somali Student Association, and the Society of African Culture, all of which were based in London.[22]

While Essie championed the rights of women around the world, and took great interest in promoting women's leadership, she did not consider herself a "feminist" per se. It is only now, looking back from the vantage point of the twenty-first century, and with the nuance and textured meaning given today to "feminism" by women of color, Third World women, and indigenous and postcolonial women, that Essie's words and deeds look very much like those of a radical feminist of color, like the "Black Left feminists" that scholars Mary Helen Washington and Erik McDuffie describe in their work.

Between 1960 and 1963, and despite many personal challenges, Essie was primarily a writer and her advocacy was expressed in that medium. But she also did not hesitate to use her extensive personal contacts and the respect she had earned to try, in her own limited way, to influence policymakers and world leaders on behalf of Africa. Three examples in the early 1960s illustrate this kind of personal intervention. In the spring of 1960, while Essie was recuperating from her cancer treatment in Moscow, the high-ranking Soviet official Nuriddin Mukhitdinov visited Essie and Paul in the hospital to pay his respects. While he was there, Essie engaged him in a lengthy discussion about what was going on in the various African liberation struggles. Mukhitdinov was an Uzbek Communist Party leader who had risen in the ranks to become a close adviser to Khrushchev. He became, as one historian later described him, "the major Soviet Asian spokesman for Khrushchev's new campaign to woo the so-called Third World."[23] In 1960, he was well positioned in the Soviet leadership, so his visit presented Essie with a unique opportunity. The Soviet Union was an important countervailing force against European colonial powers and the neo-colonial policies of the United States, so Essie wanted the Soviet leadership to be informed of the complex and rapidly changing situation on the continent of Africa, as she understood it.

Toward that end, she gave Mukhitdinov her analysis of what was going on in the African countries and colonies, from Ghana and Guinea to Uganda. In a conversation and later in lengthy follow-up letter, she carefully outlined her assessment of the forces involved in the various liberation struggles. She further explained the "idea of federation" in Central Africa, which she defined as "Nyasaland, Northern and Southern Rhodesia," while pointing out that this notion was initially proposed by Europeans for the "security" of white settlers and "all Africans vigorously oppose the Federation, and continue to resist and denounce it." Essie was also concerned with the looming threat of neo-colonialism in those areas where the African leaders most closely allied with the metropole would be positioned to "lead" the new African nations.[24]

In her letter to Mukhitdinov, Essie demonstrates a sophisticated understanding of the intricate architecture of colonialism as well as of the internal politics of the various liberation struggles then under way in sub-Saharan and North Africa. She is interested not simply in the vague principle of "freedom," but in how it will happen on the ground, how it will affect people living on the continent. And she made it her business to know the viability and implications of all the policies being proposed and to share that analysis widely, especially with those who had some influence.

In June 1962, Essie made a second effort to use her connections to intervene in policy matters on the occasion of the "World without Bombs" assembly in Accra, Ghana—an event that showcased Nkrumah's anti-imperialist and egalitarian stance. At the time, the Ghanaian president was playing a pivotal role in international affairs, and was being wooed by both the Soviets and the Americans. In 1962 Nkrumah decided to appeal to all nonaligned nations to come together, during a frightening nuclear arms race between the two reigning superpowers, in order to "propose new and bold solutions to disarmament questions," and to "fire the imaginations of the peoples of the world with the possibilities for development in a world without the bomb." Nkrumah gave an eloquent and rousing opening speech, which went on for a full eighty minutes and received a robust standing ovation from the more than two hundred invited guests and observers. In his remarks, he contradicted the notion that new African leaders would be silent pawns and proxies in the Cold War–era arms race. "In regard to Africa," he concluded, "I should like the continent to become not only a non-nuclear zone, but also a zone where no foreign military bases are allowed. I should like this to be paralleled with an ideological truce and an agreement not to try to convert Africa into an economic appendage of any other continent."[25]

Essie could not attend the conference, due to health reasons, both hers and Paul's. But many of her associates were there and in the end, she made her presence felt indirectly. On the eve of the opening session,

Essie was contacted at her flat in London by her friend, the peace activist Ruth Gage-Colby, who wanted Essie's help in order to minimize the influence of several anti-communist American delegates. Essie agreed and hurriedly sent Nkrumah a letter to alert him about what she and Gage-Colby felt were efforts to subvert the goals of the historic conference. "I am hastening to enclose extracts from a very urgent letter regarding the Accra meeting now in session," she wrote. She enclosed excerpts from a letter from a "trusted colleague" (whom she does not otherwise name but is Gage-Colby) that sharply criticizes Homer Jack, a U.S. Unitarian clergyman and peace activist, as one of the "coldest, bitterest cold war fighters" who has "infiltrated the African scene." The fear was that Jack was there to undermine the Soviet Union more than to support Nkrumah's leadership or to build a truly nonaligned antiwar alliance. It is unclear whether this assessment was valid, but Gage-Colby was convinced that it was. Essie then added, "Sorry to bother you with this, but I think it is important for you to know, and I hope you get it in time."[26] The conference, although it did not achieve Nkrumah's goal of ending nuclear proliferation, was a short-term success, and no major East–West flare-ups occurred. It is unclear whether Essie's letter made much of a difference, but from past exchanges it appears that Nkrumah did respect her contributions a great deal, so it is likely that he duly noted her concern.

A third example of one of Essie's behind-the-scenes policy interventions occurred in 1963 when her friend Carlton Goodlett, a Black newspaper publisher from California, asked her to contact Kremlin officials to help reverse a decision that threatened to deny Black American jazz performers an opportunity to tour in Russia. In March of 1963 Goodlett wrote to Essie to tell her that the USSR had declined entry to Duke Ellington and Count Basie, who wanted to travel as a part of an established cultural exchange program. "Our State Department has twisted the Russian position, which is not to accept any form of jazz," wrote Goodlett. In other words, he thought that the U.S. State Department might use the omission of jazz performers on a Russian tour as an opportunity to suggest that the Soviets were not such good friends to Blacks as they professed to be. He continued, "After Benny Goodman's tour, Khrushchev decided that no jazz . . . from USA should be included in cultural exchange program." It was all a big misunderstanding, according to Goodlett, who added, "how damaging it would be to the reservoir of good will which exists in Negro America for the Soviet's appreciation of art, if they are permitted to believe that only

Negro jazz musicians are being rejected" from the cultural program. He pointed out that Ellington would be more "decorous" than Basie, who would have the Russians "dancing in the aisles," something that "would of course be distasteful to Khrushchev [smiles]." Khrushchev was not a dancer and had only a tepid appreciation for the genre of jazz. Goodlett and Essie had an inside joke about Khrushchev's rigid personality. But Goodlett's appeal was a serious one and reflected an appreciation of Essie's influence and contacts. "I want you to use your influence through the Cultural Attaché in the Soviet Embassy in London," he asked, "and also through connection with the minister of culture, to get this problem adjusted."[27] There is no paper trail indicating how or whether Essie intervened, but her past practice suggests that she probably at least made a few phone calls.

Even though Essie kept up her writing and her activism in the early 1960s, she and Paul were both still facing profound medical problems. Paul's precise diagnosis was still vague. He was tired, intermittently depressed, and eventually, despondent—and the shock treatments in London made his symptoms worse. Throughout the ordeal, Essie continued to be loyal, supportive, and highly protective. Writing to an old friend, the journalist P. L. Prattis, Essie explained that Paul had "been going at the same tough pace for thirty years, or more, and felt that he was indestructible. But wear is wear, and exhaustion is quite a thing." She assured him that Paul would soon be "fully recovered." Two years later, when Paul was still not back to normal, she wrote to "Pratt" again, thanking him for a column that mentioned Paul favorably. "We are just not ready to take on the Press barrage yet. The western, reactionary Press, that is. . . . Forty years of work and fight have taken their toll," she wrote. Her assessment surely glossed over what was a painful time for both of them.[28]

Even though both Paul and Essie were still receiving treatments, recovering and cautiously looking to the future, Essie was not one to sit still. In July of 1963, for example, she agreed to be a spectator in the trial in absentia of the alleged Nazi collaborator Hans Globke, which was being heard by the East German Supreme Court. Historian Jeffrey Herf describes it as one of the "show trials" put on largely for public relations purposes by the East German government (in fact Globke would receive a life sentence that he never served), but Essie had strong anti-fascist politics and had spent time in Germany under vastly different circumstances over the years. She was an observer at the trial for all those reasons, and likely because her German friends asked her to be there.[29] There is a photo of Essie at the proceedings wearing head-phones for translation and sitting next to a frail, gaunt-looking woman who looked like a vivid embodiment of the ravages of war, and perhaps a concentration camp survivor. The woman was, in fact, Greta Kuck-hoff, vice president of the German Peace Council and a very interesting character indeed. A native of Frankfurt who studied literature for two years at the University of Wisconsin, Madison, Kuckhoff had returned to Germany to lead an underground anti-Nazi resistance group called Rote Kapelle, or Red Orchestra. In 1942, Kuckhoff and her husband, Adam, were arrested and jailed. Adam was executed on Hitler's orders and Greta spent three years in prison until she was freed at the end of the war by the Soviet army.[30]

Essie may have continued to be involved with many causes, and on many fronts, but her 1963 diary entries are filled with the two issues that truly consumed her thoughts and her energies: the state of world poli-tics and the state of Paul's health. The diary does not include many of Essie's personal feelings about either subject—rather, it contains copi-ous painstakingly detailed notes written in tiny cursive script, page after page, on material she was reading about both topics. She seemed to read at least five national and international newspapers every week and chronicled the articles and events that caught her eye. In some cases, she nearly transcribed entire articles about issues ranging from de-velopments in India and Indonesia, to civil rights marches in the U.S. South, to pending U.N. resolutions and debates. No doubt these notes provided the raw material for some of the essays she wrote for various publications in the 1960s. In her diary she also summarizes the scien-tific and medical journals that she read in order to try to dissect and better understand Paul's symptoms, adding citations and punctuating her summaries with her own questions. She was worried about Paul and in some ways she did not feel strong enough to take care of him in the way that she always had. Still, she tried.[31]

Essie was especially protective of Paul when it came to the main-stream media, which had been so blatantly biased and ruthless in its coverage of him during the 1950s. One evening in August 1963, as she and Paul were flying from London to Berlin, Essie lost her patience, and her temper, when a nosy British reporter from the *London Daily Telegraph* refused to leave them alone. Essie was furious when he left his seat to come over and ask Paul questions about his views on commu-nism. First she attempted to summon the flight attendant. When she was unsuccessful, she confronted him herself. "I know judo," she told the stunned reporter. And she did. She informed him that she would "happily" kick him in the groin or break his glasses if he did not leave them alone at once. She issued a few more choice comments, which convinced the reporter to return to his seat and to conclude astutely that Paul had a "formidable protector" in Essie. After hustling the reporter back to his seat, Essie lingered to talk with him on her terms. She discovered that he was not such a terrible fellow, but that he had a terribly skewed view of things. Because the great March on Washington had just occurred, and here Paul and Essie were on the other side of the planet, the reporter had concluded that Paul was being "spirited away" to keep him from politics. There was also rampant gossip that Paul had repudiated his left-wing views, rejected the Soviet Union, and was being kept out of the public eye to hide that fact.[32] After agreeing not to beat him up after all, Essie allowed the stunned reporter to ask Paul a few questions to set the record straight. She was eager to combat the wild rumors that Paul had been "kidnapped" to keep his new allegedly anti-Soviet views a secret.[33]

When the airplane incident occurred, Essie and Paul were on their way to the famous Buch Clinic in East Germany for medical treatment. A family friend had recommended the clinic, and Paul Jr. had checked it out, after which he strongly encouraged Essie to take Paul there. After Paul's disappointing treatments at London's Priory hospital, the family was eager to see what German doctors could do for the constellation of symptoms that still plagued him. While they were there, Essie decided to get herself checked out as well. It turned out to be a prolonged stay for them both. Her cancer had reappeared yet again, and the German doctors offered very little hope for a successful remission; in fact, there were no treatment options left for her. True to form, Essie kept this terrible news to herself.[34] She didn't want anyone to feel sorry for her, and ever the optimist, she wanted to believe that she might just beat the odds.

The staff at the Buch Clinic was very kind to Essie during her stay, especially when her birthday rolled around in December. "My birthday this year has been something special," she wrote on a sheet of paper, as if it were a diary entry, "I am a patient, along with Paul, at Buch clinic, just outside Berlin." Birthdays were not a big event in the Robeson family, so Essie had learned not to expect a big hoopla. But when her nurse brought her a small present and later a cake with candles, Essie was touched. She was comforted when among these strangers, so far from home, and with Paul not at all himself, her birthday was acknowledged so sweetly.

While in Berlin in 1963 Essie was invited to give a presentation at

Humboldt University as a part of a panel on "The Negro in the United States." Other panel members included the Chicago lawyer Earl Dickerson, who had been a college classmate of Essie's in Illinois nearly fifty years earlier, and other Americans visiting Germany at the time. It was a lively discussion and, according to Essie, the African students she met there were very curious about Black politics in the United States. She also met with African students at Herder Institute at Leipzig University, where she talked about "the racial upheaval" in the United States and "the young leadership" in that struggle. In addition, she attended a film festival in Leipzig and had a friendly debate with two white filmmakers whose film, Essie argued, presented a skewed picture of Black American youth. "We exchanged very different opinions on the subject," Essie wrote. "Mine was impatient and militant; theirs was liberal, with good intentions."[35]

By the winter of 1963, Paul and Essie were making their way back to the United States. It was time to go home again. Essie was excited that she would be closer to the Black struggle going on there and was eager to see the action for herself. Her vibrant, active, and inquisitive approach to life in 1964 was amazing, given her increasingly precarious physical condition and Paul's steep decline. But as her body grew weaker, her convictions grew stronger. She may have been more physically fragile, but she was politically and intellectually fiercer than ever.

In many of the articles that Essie wrote in 1963 and 1964—articles like "The New Negro Movement," "Long Hot Summer," "Black Revolution and White Backlash," and "The Time Is Now"—Essie sided with the increased militancy of the Black freedom movement. She was thrilled by the upsurge in protest. "We Negroes have now passed the Point of No Return. We are determined, determined to claim our full citizenship and human rights, now, period," Essie wrote. "The situation in our country is frightening and dangerous," she went on. Negroes were burning with "the fire of deep anger, fed by disillusionment [and] frustration."[36] When she returned to London for a short visit in July of 1964, she agreed to take part in a panel hosted by the Committee of Afro-Asian-Caribbean Organizations, again at Africa Unity House, to discuss "The American Negro Rights Struggle." The flyer for the event condemned the assassination of civil rights leader Medgar Evers, and praised "our Negro brothers and sisters who are engaged in sharp liberation struggles to rid their land of the scourge of [the] colour bar and Jim Crow [and] . . . U.S. imperialism."[37]

Essie respected Dr. King's nonviolent approach, and she respected

King, the man, whom she had met on at least one occasion in London.[38] Still she reserved the right to self-defense against violent attacks. In response to those who counseled patience and passivity, she replied, "There is no need for all this talk about non-violence unless it means non-violence for everybody," referring indirectly to the lynchings and vigilante violence of the Jim Crow South. She advocated "building up the idea of Resistance and Self-Defense," and she supported a range of tactics, from taking Negro grievances to the U.N. Human Rights Committee, to taking to the streets in a massive general strike.[39] In her 1965 written eulogy for Malcolm X, Essie noted her disagreements with Malcolm, but praised his "fearlessness and militant challenge" to American racism.[40] Another fearless and militant young Black artist whom Essie admired in the 1960s was Lorraine Hansberry, author of the acclaimed Broadway play *Raisin in the Sun*. Essie had met Hansberry in New York when she had worked on the journal *Freedom* in the early 1950s. Essie was deeply saddened by Lorraine's premature death at age thirty-four of pancreatic cancer. She had spent time with Lorraine and her mother, Mamie, as Lorraine's illness progressed, sitting at her bedside to provide comfort. And she had sat in the pew of a crowded Harlem church in January 1965, undoubtedly overwhelmed with sadness as Paul eloquently eulogized their talented young friend.[41] Ossie Davis and Ruby Dee were there as well, along with actress Shelley Winters and a myriad of other celebrated artists, actors, and playwrights.

While Essie's status as Mrs. Paul Robeson was still the first thing people said about her, by the early 1960s she had achieved a level of recognition for her own work as a writer, lecturer, anti-colonial and anti-racist activist, and anthropologist that was incredibly gratifying for her. Sadly, most of her public recognition came at a time when Paul's health and prominence were in decline. Still she enjoyed the accolades she received as affirmation that her life's work had some larger meaning.

Essie was especially proud to receive in 1963 Germany's Clara Zetkin medal for her "services in the struggle for peace and human equality."[42] Zetkin had been a communist, feminist, and anti-fascist heroine in the 1930s, and the medal was awarded by the German Democratic Republic's Council of Ministers. Essie had traveled to Germany many times between 1934 and 1963, both before and after it was divided into East and West. On one trip after the war, she had visited the site of the Ravensbrück concentration camp and helped dedicate a memorial to its 92,000 victims.[43] During her 1963 trip to accept her award, Essie addressed a large crowd of more than ten thousand East Germans who had assembled to mark the "Memorial Day for the Victims of Fascism." In her speech, Essie delivered a message to the German people that she had articulated in multiple articles and speeches over the years. She urged her listeners to see a connection between the struggle against fascism in Europe, which was so compelling in their own lives, and Black Americans' ongoing fight against racial tyranny and terror in the United States. As Essie so eloquently urged, "Ever since I can remember, from my childhood as an American Negro, I have worked and fought against and resisted fascism in all its forms . . . including the fight against exploitation and lynching. My husband, Paul Robeson, and I will continue to fight fascism in all its forms."[44]

Personally and physically, life was difficult for Essie during her final years. She tried as best she could to look after Paul and take care of herself at the same time, but she did a better job of caring for Paul than attending to her own needs. Essie was eternally grateful to Paul Jr. and Marilyn for their nurturing support. She confided to a friend that she was so pleased and lucky to have them close by. "Paul Jr. and Family have risen to the occasion," she wrote, "and are really out of this world, so helpful, so RIGHT, so tactful, and so reliable and sustaining. It was worth coming home [from London] just for that."[45]

Essie returned to Harlem in December of 1963 knowing better than anyone the gravity of her illness. Still, she was determined to keep up her pace of activity as much as she could, to speak out as loudly as she could, to embrace and engage friends and family, and not "go quietly." Essie continued to go to the United Nations to observe proceedings, for instance, although not as frequently as she had done in the past.[46] She enjoyed the liveliness of the place. She had earned the respect of colleagues there. As her friend the writer Alice Childriss later reflected, Essie used "the fullness of each day with little, if any, time for retreat or despair."[47] At the same time she kept up the struggle, with the help of Paul Jr. and Marilyn, to take care of Paul: to make the right medical decisions, to keep his spirits up, to protect him from intrusions and unnecessary pressures, and to guard his public image.

As she grappled with her terminal illness, Essie treasured her loyal friends, including her colleague and fellow leftist George Murphy Jr., the Washington, D.C., editor of the *Afro-American* and member of that newspaper's founding family. For the last decade of her life Essie kept up a lively and personal correspondence with George, and they shared meals and visits when they could. She told him the details of her medical condition, confided her frustrations about Paul's health, and carefully outlined her political views on key world events. In turn he shared his ups and downs with her, including his own health challenges, concerns about his marriage, and his efforts to manage a slightly rebellious teenager. George had visited her and brought her flowers when she was in the hospital in 1956 during her first bout with cancer. They had sat together and had a long talk, which Essie enjoyed very much. After that he had allowed her to use his New York apartment when she was covering the United Nations, because it was much closer than her uptown apartment on Jumel Place. He had made a typewriter and desk available to her as well. Essie had deemed George an absolute "angel" for his kindness. And the friendship was reciprocal. When George was called before the House Un-American Activities Committee (HUAC) three years after Essie's appearance before the Senate Committee, she was one of his vocal supporters despite battling cancer at the time: she wrote a letter to his editors at the *Afro-American* newspaper praising George's testimony as "dignified and fearless" and sent a note to George signed with "a big Robeson hug and kiss."[48]

The year 1965 was both rewarding and arduous, with a series of public tributes and testimonials for both Paul and Essie. The couple's American friends were glad to have them back on their side of the Atlantic, and everyone knew what trials they had endured. Perhaps some knew too that Essie's days were numbered and it was best to honor her sooner rather than later. In February the W. E. B. Du Bois clubs honored Paul with a lively reception. On March 26, Essie was the mistress of ceremonies at a festive gala honoring Uvee Mdodana Arbouin, the National Baptist Women's leader, at the Waldorf Astoria hotel, where Essie's friend Ruth Gage-Colby sang Essie's praises in her introduction—extolling her as an amazing and brilliant woman who was a staunch fighter for freedom and peace in the world.

In April there was a gala tribute for Paul where, appropriately, Essie was acknowledged too. It was a star-studded event with Ossie Davis as master of ceremonies; other celebrity participants included the actress Ruby Dee, writer James Baldwin, jazz legend Dizzy Gillespie, folksinger Pete Seeger, and movie stars Lena Horne and Diana Sands. It was the occasion of Paul's sixty-seventh birthday, as well as a belated welcome home celebration. The staff of the radical *Freedomways* magazine hosted the event at the Americana Hotel in Times Square. Editors Esther Cooper Jackson and Jack O'Dell had visited Essie and Paul at their home several months beforehand to plan what they hoped would be a high-profile event to signal Paul's importance to the Black community and the Black Freedom struggle in general. It was a beautiful celebration. Essie and Paul decided to stay overnight in the hotel, and a small group of friends including Esther Cooper Jackson, her husband, Communist Party leader James Jackson, and James Baldwin joined them in their suite after the event to talk and share a more intimate conversation about life, art, and politics. They laughed and talked until the sun came up. It had been a memorable evening. Even though Essie was sick, she was happy that night, proud of Paul, and content with their devoted circle of friends.[49] It had been a rough few years and she was pleased to see Paul looking well and happy.

In May 1965, Essie and Paul went to California for what was to be a three-week visit. Paul Jr. was worried that his father, having suffered lapses of depression and other ailments, was not well enough for the trip, but Essie plowed ahead. Paul made several public appearances at churches and community centers in Los Angeles, gave an interview to the *Los Angeles Times*, and then the couple traveled together to San Francisco. But Essie's pain grew worse and Paul "began to sink into a withdrawn and uncommunicative state." They had to cut the trip short and return home earlier than planned.[50]

Upon their return to New York, two friends from California agreed to move in with Paul and Essie to help look after them. Essie was not used to being cared for, but in her depleted state, she could not afford to turn down the help. Paul's condition was very shaky. One evening he left the house on Jumel Terrace, wandered into a nearby park, and was found bruised and injured the next morning after an apparent fall. After he was released from the hospital, the family decided it was best for Paul to go to Philadelphia for an extended visit with his sister, Marian, since he seemed to feel more settled and at ease there. He had never been the same after the unexplained suicide attempt in Moscow, and the subsequent shock therapy in London.

By August 1965 Essie was back in Beth Israel Hospital suffering severe pain related to her cancer. Even before she was admitted to the hospital Essie knew that her disease was terminal, but she had tried to stay optimistic, or at least to put a positive face on things to the outside world. In October of that year she wrote about her various illnesses to her friend Florence Luscomb, a civil rights, labor, and feminist activist. She and Florence had gotten to know one another during the Progressive Party campaign of 1948 and had kept in touch intermittently over the years. After thanking Florence for a recent letter, Essie explained frankly: "I had a hesterectomy [*sic*] recently when the surgeons found I had cancer there [in her uterus]. It seems that they got it out intact, but now I am undergoing cobalt treatment daily, five times a week, and they are very enervating. But they do say they stall off any recurring growth, so I have to put up with it. This is my third cancer, first breast, then cervix, now this. So, I'm lucky to have come this far. I will be 70 in December."[51]

Essie Cardozo Goode Robeson died in a hospital room at Beth Israel Hospital in New York City on December 13, 1965, two days before her seventieth birthday. During her last few weeks, she received many visitors and messages from friends, all of whom wanted to pay their respects and express their affection for a woman who had lived such a large, generous, and unconventional life; a principled, complicated life, but one that was rich and full and rewarding. The list of those who paid their respects to Essie at the end of her life is a reflection of and tribute to the eclectic and far-reaching network of relationships she enjoyed and the many people she touched around the globe. Paul's poor health meant that he could not be with Essie in her final days, but her son and daughter-in-law attended to her dutifully. They visited daily and made sure she was as comfortable as possible.

There was no public service to mark Essie's passing, which saddened some of her friends and colleagues.[52] There was instead a very private service held before Essie was cremated, attended only by Paul Jr., Marilyn, and their two children. Paul remained in Philadelphia. The family had decided that given Paul's precarious health condition, any sort of memorial or funeral for Essie would be too difficult for him. And so, their forty-four-year partnership came to a quiet end.

Since Essie had found her calling as a writer and a journalist, it was fitting that her friends, admirers, and fellow activists would celebrate her legacy in print. In 1966 *Freedomways* magazine, where Essie had served as contributor and correspondent, devoted a special issue as a tribute to her life. Her multilingual and multinational colleagues at the United Nations celebrated her contributions. Her editors and fellow journalists in the Black and left-wing press mourned their loss. And her anti-colonial and anti-imperialist allies from India to South Africa asserted that her fierce and unrelenting voice would be dearly missed. "A Great Lady Passes," proclaimed the *Sun Reporter*, describing her as an "institution" and "a highly cultured woman of photogenic beauty and great personal charm. . . . Her personality variously expressed a combination of human warmth and compassion, the carbon hardness of determination, and the explosive power of righteous indignation. She had no penchant for pedantry but wore her academic titles with dignity, placing her immense knowledge at the service of mankind, especially the darker races. She was steadfast in her friendships and dependable in her response."[53]

Published eulogies and private expressions of sympathy heralded Essie's unique personal qualities. The Afro-Russian author Lily Golden, whom Essie had met in Uzbekistan in 1958, commented admiringly that Essie's life "was an example of devotion to the progressive ideals of our epoch." And her friend Peggy Middleton, who saw or spoke to Essie almost every day when she was in London between 1958 and 1963, recalled that "there was not a single day in her life of which some part was not given to 'our struggle.'" Others praised her dual devotion to the world and to her family, with the special caveat that it was not always easy to be Mrs. Paul Robeson.[54] Activist Vicky Garvin sent a long handwritten letter from Ghana to express how "distressed" she was to hear of Essie's death. Langston Hughes sent a telegram of condolence to Paul describing Essie as "a gracious and lovely human being."[55]

Janet Jagan wrote from Guyana: "For me personally, it was the loss [of] a very dear friend and one whose friendship and guidance meant so much."[56] The day before Essie died, her good friend Ruth ("Rue") Gage-Colby came to the hospital with an arm full of holly "thinking it wise to begin celebrating the Holidays a bit early." Essie was too weak to speak, but Rue sat at her bedside, feeling both sadness and admiration. Rue later reflected respectfully: "Eslanda Robeson's last action, almost with her last breath, was dictating a letter which was delivered to U Thant [then secretary-general of the United Nations] before she died, with new proposals for the UN that she hoped might be of use toward bringing to an end the war in Vietnam."[57] Over the years, Rue had become a dear friend and colleague. After Essie passed, she wrote a eulogy to Essie in the form of a letter to her beloved friend: "How invincible is your faith in the human spirit! It is the source of my joy in working with you at the United Nations these many years. Despite the burden of complicated personal responsibilities you have never lost sight of the world." Concluding with words for the audience, she proclaimed that Essie "loved life and she loved humanity. And to all whom her life touched, she lent pleasure, luster and honor. In utter truth it can be said there is no one to take her place."[58]

EPILOGUE

A life story is not a theory or an ideology, nor even a precisely crafted work of fiction. Despite a writer's best efforts to whip the facts into line, an individual life is not a neat chronicle of events and themes. It is therefore the biographer's task to give a kind of artificial coherence to a human journey that is by definition messy, circuitous, at odds with itself, and at times utterly inexplicable. A biographer is at once a guide, an interpreter, a skeptical reporter, a framer, and an advocate. As an advocate for Essie, I have not told you to love or to hate her, to agree with her or to champion her causes. Instead I have tried to persuade you that out of all the billions of people who have lived and died on this planet, this one life is worth knowing more about. And I have tried to make sense of that life as best I can.

So, why is Essie Robeson's story worth knowing and remembering? Simply put, she lived an extraordinary life — a rich and robust life sometimes brimming with contradictions, even painful ones, but a life that was never small. She inhabited many roles, was at home in many places, and embraced many cultures.

By the late 1930s Essie had found her political voice. She was not afraid to take sides. She was a passionate anti-colonialist, siding with the Africans and Indians over the British, French, and Belgian colonizers. She placed her faith in the promise of socialism and communism, rather than capitalism. And she sought out, supported, and affirmed the leadership of radical women of color. Once she had staked her political claims, she made no apologies.

Essie Robeson was a part of the Black Atlantic world. She traversed the rough waters of the Atlantic more than a dozen times by boat and many more times by air: from New York to Ghana to London to Cairo to Cape Town and back again. And in the process of talking, working, arguing, making friends, writing, and listening to other people's stories, she ultimately synthesized that amalgam of experiences, and local histories, into her own hybrid Black identity, which was at the same time a political identity. She became one of Robin Kelley's "race rebels," fighting simultaneously for "the race" and the working class across many national borders.[1]

She situated herself with the Third World project, as Vijay Prashad describes it—a bold strategy to link the Asian and African peasants, Black and Brown intellectuals, and the multilingual global tribe of have-nots in protest against the rigid binary of the Cold War world.[2] The Third World project, its limitations notwithstanding, was an attempt to reconfigure the global political playing field, and at a minimum, to leverage greater power, resources, and autonomy for those on the bottom of various intractable hierarchies. Essie, initially with wild optimism, and later with sober realism, believed in and fought for the Third World project as a matter of principle and as a gesture of solidarity. She studied, internalized, and made her own the struggles of Indians, South Africans, Chinese, Guyanese, and Congolese.

While Essie's story is indisputably a part of Black radical and international Left histories, it is also a part of a Black women's intellectual and political tradition. Even though Essie eschewed the term "feminist," her actions belie her words. By always questioning the absence of women in leadership, comparing class exploitation and racial subjugation to gender oppression, and refusing to dissect the entangled issues and variables from one another, Essie anticipated contemporary Black feminist theories of intersectionality. In speech after speech, and article after article, she insisted that the relationships among capitalism, sexism, colonialism, racism, and empire were symbiotic. Women were half the population and should wield half the power, she insisted. Conventional marriage was outdated and overrated, she argued. Throughout her life she was outspoken and self-assured. For this she was labeled "aggressive," "controlling," "manipulative," and "pushy" by people who were enamored of Paul but resented the central role that Mrs. Robeson occupied in his life, and the confidence with which she did so.[3]

As much as she was Mrs. Paul Robeson, Essie remained her own woman. Recognizably her mother's daughter, she was tough, strong-willed, and unshakable. Essie pursued an independent career as a writer, activist, and scholar, traveling on her own to Asia, Africa, Central America, and the Caribbean. She used her title as Mrs. Paul Robeson to open doors, but once those doors opened, a smart, pragmatic, and fiercely independent woman walked through them.

Early in their marriage Essie supported Paul as an artist and was indispensable to his early career, but at that time, both of their ambitions were rather conventional. Later in life, however, after Bloemfontein and Kabarole, Madrid and Berlin, Moscow and Brazzaville, Essie supported him with equal intensity, but for different reasons, political reasons. Their views of the world coincided, and in fact had evolved out of many years of conversations, arguments, and intellectual exchanges with one another. By the 1940s Essie backed Paul not only because of their personal and familial ties, but also because of the ideals they shared. And so she stood by him, she stood up for him, and she loved him deeply. There were other loyal friends and relatives, of course, who supported him throughout his life, and he had a devoted son and daughter-in-law. But no one stayed the course as long as Essie did. No one believed in him more, fought for him harder, or loved him with greater ferocity. Her love was not always "sweet" love or even romantic. Instead her love was bound up with who he was and what he represented on the world political stage and within the Black Freedom struggle to which they were both devoted.

Eslanda Robeson's life is worth knowing about because it offers us a prism through which to see, feel, and assess what was going on in the world that she inhabited. Rather than view her as a marginal subject, what does the world, in the four and a half decades that followed the end of World War I, look like if we situate her at the center? After all, she was a kind of alternative Zeitgeist. She engaged the literary and artistic luminaries of New York, London, and Paris in the 1920s and 1930s, assessing their flaws as well as their talents with her caustic wit, and tapping their influence to further Paul's career. Her social calendar read like a cultural who's who of the postwar decade. And then came Africa, the African Diaspora, and radical ideas. Essie traveled extensively in Africa at a time when few Americans had passports and even fewer knew or were interested in the geography of the African continent. She developed friendships with independence leaders and became deeply committed to the struggle for African liberation. She was on a first-name basis with at least four heads of state, traveled on both sides of the so-called Iron Curtain during the Cold War, stood side by side with anti-fascist fighters from Madrid to postwar Berlin, and defended communists who were under attack. She was at the founding of the United Nations and covered its proceedings as a journalist for nearly two decades. She interviewed Mahatma Gandhi and maintained close and enduring friendships with the powerful Nehru and Pandit families of India. She and Paul suffered the McCarthy witch hunts, and years of government surveillance and harassment, but remained steadfast in their beliefs. She witnessed and supported the growing Black Freedom movement of the 1960s. In other words, Essie had an intimate relationship with history and with the historic figures and movements of her time—from war zones to the advent of new nations, from the treacherous waters of the Congo to the grand ballroom of the Waldorf Astoria and the opulent dining room in the Kremlin.

To look at a sweep of twentieth-century world history through the eyes of a radical African American female subject is to turn many common assumptions upside down. And because Essie Robeson weighed in on the large ideological struggles of the century, we are invited, by reading her life, and taking her seriously, to entertain a different set of truths and sensibilities about power and patriotism; about freedom and repression; about capitalism and communism; about democracy and self-determination; about gender and leadership; about race and identity; and about the twentieth-century world and how it was transformed.

CHRONOLOGY: ESLANDA
CARDOZO GOODE ROBESON

1895
December 15   Eslanda Cardozo Goode (ER) is born in Washington, D.C.

1901
January 25   ER's father, John J. A. Goode, dies and ER's mother (Eslanda Goode) moves ER and her two brothers to New York City (Harlem)

1907   ER witnesses a riot to protest police brutality in Harlem

1912   ER and her mother relocate temporarily to Chicago
ER attends the Lucy Flower High School for girls
ER enrolls at the University of Illinois, Urbana

1916   ER transfers to Columbia University's Teachers College in New York City

1917   ER's mother supports Harlem socialist Hubert Harrison

1919   World War I ends and the Harlem Renaissance gets underway
Paul Robeson (PR) and ER meet in Harlem

1920   ER graduates from Columbia University and ER and PR begin dating seriously

1921
August 17   ER and PR elope and marry in Port Chester, N.Y.
December   In Philadelphia, ER and PR announce their marriage at their joint sorority/fraternity national meeting

1922
April   PR accepts his first professional acting job in the musical *Taboo* (later renamed *Voodoo*)

June	PR sails to England for European tour of *Voodoo*
	ER has surgery and is hospitalized for weeks
	PR returns to New York to care for ER during her prolonged recovery
1923	PR graduates from Columbia Law School
1924	
March	PR performs in *Roseanne*
May 6	PR performs in *Emperor Jones*
May 15	PR performs in *All God's Chillun Got Wings*
	ER begins working as PR's manager
August	ER meets Prince Kojo Touvalou Houénou of Dahomey and her interest in Africa is piqued
Fall	ER negotiates for PR to appear in Oscar Micheaux's landmark silent film *Body and Soul*
1925	In New York, PR reconnects with Lawrence Brown and begins musical collaboration that lasts for decades
April 19	ER arranges for PR and Larry Brown's first public concert at the Greenwich Village Theatre
August 5	ER and PR travel to England for London production of *Emperor Jones*, which closes after a few weeks. They remain in Europe for four months
Summer/Fall	The Robesons meet and spend time with feminist/anarchist Emma Goldman in London
	ER and PR go on a six-week vacation in village of Villefranche-sur-Mer on the French Riviera where they meet and spend time with socialist Max Eastman, his wife, Elena Krylenko, and poet Claude McKay
	ER finishes her first play, "Aunt Hagar's Children"
December 16	ER celebrates her thirtieth birthday with PR and friends in Paris, and the Robesons sail for the United States
1926	
January–March	ER accompanies PR on concert tour through the U.S. Midwest and Northeast
1927	
October 15	PR and Larry board a ship to Europe for concerts in France and England

October 29	PR is in Europe for his debut concert in Paris
November 2	ER gives birth to Paul Jr. (PRJ) and suffers complications
	Paul returns home in December
1928	PR travels back to Europe to perform in the musical *Show Boat*
1929	Stock Market crash and Great Depression begins
May	ER sails for London and leaves her six-month-old baby in her mother's care
	ER learns about Russian anti-Semitic pogroms from friend Naomi Bercovici
1930	ER's first book, *Paul Robeson, Negro*, is published
January	ER accompanies PR and Larry on a concert tour through Central and Eastern Europe. They visit Prague, Bucharest, Dresden, Düsseldorf, Cologne, Brno, Czernowitz, and Vienna
March	ER and PR go to Territet, Switzerland, where ER co-stars, with PR and Hilda Dolittle, in the experimental silent film *Borderline*
	In a concert tour through Scotland, ER and PR meet with Nigerian and West Indian students
	PR has an affair with a British woman named Yolande Jackson, which threatens his marriage. ER and PR separate and contemplate divorce
April	PR stars in *Othello* in London
	ER travels to South Carolina to write a novel on the women in her family called "The Three Eslandas"
1931	
January	ER finishes writing her second play, "Black Progress"
Spring	ER makes a brief return to the States, where she spends time with her old boyfriend, Dr. Grant Lucas
March	ER has an illegal abortion in New York
October	ER lands an interview with the legendary Indian spiritual and political leader Mohandas Gandhi
1932	
Spring	ER and PR make plans to divorce (but never actually do). PR announces he will marry Yolande Jackson
June	ER spends several weeks in Paris escorted by Kojo Touvalou Houénou. She meets with the French

Guyanese writer and intellectual René Maran, Paulette Nardal, Habib Benglia, and others

ER meets and befriends Ada Beatrice Queen Victoria Louise Virginia (Bricktop) Smith, owner of a legendary club in the Montmartre neighborhood of Paris

July 31	ER spends an eventful day with Leonard and Beatrice Barnes. Her interest in Africa is heightened
August 17	ER writes the essay "I Believe in Divorce"
September	PR and Yolande call off their wedding plans
December	ER and PR reunite and settle into an open marital arrangement
1933	ER enrolls at London School of Economics to study anthropology with Bronislaw Malinowski. There, she meets Jomo Kenyatta
	Hitler comes to power in Germany
1934	ER is encouraged by novelist and anthropologist Zora Neale Hurston in her study of African cultures
December	ER and PR travel to the Soviet Union because PR has agreed to make a film with Sergei Eisenstein. En route to Moscow, they pass through Nazi Germany and see signs of fascism
1935	PR and ER fly to Hollywood to film the movie version of *Show Boat*
	ER visits and exchanges letters with anthropologist Melville Herskovits
January	PR and ER see her two brothers, who have recently relocated to the USSR, during their first visit there
April	PR stars in the film *Sanders of the River*, which debuts in London and is a source of embarrassment to ER and PR because of its pro-colonial message
	Paul Robeson Jr. (PRJ) and ER's mother live together in the United States and Canada for more than a year
1936	Italy invades Ethiopia and begins a five-year occupation
May 29	ER and PRJ sail from England for a four-month journey through southern and eastern Africa
June 15	ER and PRJ arrive in Capetown, South Africa, and stay for several days

June 19	ER and PRJ arrive in Port Elisabeth and meet with an old friend from London, Rosebery Bokwe, and a new friend, Max Yergan, who host them in South Africa
	ER visits the African reserve of Ntselemantzi, as well as Basutoland
July 2	ER and PRJ stay with Dr. Alfred Bitini Xuma in Sofiatown, South Africa
	ER attends the historic All-African National Convention, held in the town of Bloemfontein in the Orange Free State region of South Africa
July 15	ER and PRJ arrive in Mombassa, Kenya
	ER and PRJ travel to Kikuyu countryside, then leave Kenya and enter the British Protectorate of Uganda
	ER and PRJ arrive in Kampala where they are guests of Akiki Nyabongo, cousin to the King of Toro
	ER and PRJ spend four weeks in the village of Kabarole in Uganda, where ER does anthropological field work
August 5	ER and PRJ take a safari into the Congo
October	ER and PR travel to Soviet Union with PRJ and enroll him in a Soviet school in Moscow for what they believe will be a racist-free education
	ER and PR leave Moscow, stop in London, and continue on to Egypt for one month, for production of PR's new movie *Jericho*
1937	PR gives concerts and speeches in England in support of the Spanish Loyalist cause
	PR and ER help to establish the International Committee on African Affairs (ICAA)—later Council on African Affairs—in London. ER becomes the first "contributing member" when she writes a check for $300 to Max Yergan
1938	
January 21	ER and PR leave for wartorn Spain with British leftist feminist Charlotte Haldane, in order to support the Loyalist cause against Franco. After their return, ER travels to Soviet Union alone to check on her brother Frank
	ER and PR are silent about Stalin's purge trials and executions

ER and PR meet Indian anti-colonial leaders
Jawaharlal Nehru and his sister V. L. Pandit who
become lifelong friends

1939
September   World War II reaches England
               PR finishes the final scene of his film *Proud Valley* in
               London and the family sails for the United States after
               eleven years in England
October   PR, ER, and PRJ stay with their old friend Hattie
               Bolling for a few weeks while they resettle in New York
               City
               ER rents apartment for the family at 555 Edgecomb
               Avenue in Harlem

1940   ER writes her third novel, "Your Color Is Showing"
               (later renamed "Color")
Summer   ER travels to Central America and Mexico alone on a
               cargo ship
               ER travels to Mexico City to visit her old friend
               Fernando Castillo, whom she had met in Spain in 1938,
               and his family

1941   Robesons move into a large estate home known as
               "The Beeches" in Enfield, Connecticut
               ER visits the Southern United States, staying with
               old friend Ira Reid and his wife, Gladys. They travel
               together to Mississippi, Louisiana, and Alabama
               Japan attacks Pearl Harbor and the U.S. enters World
               War II

1943   ER is under FBI surveillance for her outspoken
               political views
               PRJ is accepted at Cornell University to study
               engineering
September   ER accepts an invitation from anti-racist Southern
               writer Lillian Smith to meet with an interracial group
               of influential women at Smith's home in Georgia
               ER enrolls in the Hartford Seminary Foundation to
               pursue her Ph.D. in anthropology. She is a candidate
               for the degree but never completes it

1945	
April	ER decides to go to Chicago for PR's forty-seventh birthday and the opening of *Othello*. Tensions surface again between ER and PR
May 13	ER attends founding conference of United Nations in San Francisco
August	ER's second book, *African Journey*, is published
October	ER is with PR when he receives the Spingarn Medal for outstanding achievement from the NAACP
1945–1948	ER begins to speak and lecture widely on Africa and race policies in the U.S.
1946	
March	ER travels to Washington, D.C., where she is honored at the National Council on Negro Women as one of their twelve outstanding women of the year
May 22	ER leaves for a month-long research trip to French Equatorial Africa and Belgian Congo
	The British intelligence agency MI5 follows ER in Congo, describing her anti-colonial views as "dangerous."
	ER travels to Brazzaville in French Congo, then takes a six-day trip along the mighty Congo River
	ER meets, befriends, and shares a spark of romance with French-Sudanese anticolonial leader, Gabriel d'Arboussier
June 25–July 14	ER travels to Ft. Sibut and Bangassou, as well as Bambari and Bangui in Central Africa
August 8	ER visits League of Nation's mandated area of Ruanda-Urundi (later Rwanda and Burundi), then travels to Tchad (Chad)
October	PR is summoned to testify before the anti-communist California State Tenney Committee while ER is still in Africa
November	After returning from the Congo, ER declares that "Africa is in revolution" in a speech in New York City
1948	ER attends a founding convention of the newly formed Progressive Party in Philadelphia, joins the platform committee, and travels to the country with Henry Wallace, as he campaigns for President

	ER begins a third play called "Uncle Tom's Cabin"
June 26	ER attends People's Party State Convention (the CT branch of the Progressive Party) and is nominated as a candidate for Connecticut secretary of state
1949	PJR marries Marilyn Greenberg and the Robesons get hate mail
	PR's Paris Peace speech stirs controversy
	PR's concert at Peekskill, N.Y., attacked by mobs
November 9	ER leaves the United States to attend the Women's International Democratic Federation meeting in Moscow as a delegate of the Congress of American Women. She then travels to China for the Asian Women's Federation meeting in Peking (Beijing)
1950	U.S. State Department revokes PR and ER's passports
	ER and PR's first grandchild, David, is born
1953	
Spring	Essie's mother dies after long illness and her second grandchild, Susan, is born
July 7	ER testifies before Joseph McCarthy's infamous Senate Permanent sub-committee on investigations of the Committee on Government Operations
1954	
December	ER and PR on Executive Committee of the American Labor Party
1955	
April 4	ER gives speech at American-Soviet Friendship Annual Meeting
1956	ER diagnosed with breast cancer and has a mastectomy
1957	Ghana obtains independence
May 1	ER, PR, and PRJ go to Prayer Pilgrimage, major civil rights rally in Washington, D.C.
1958	ER's and PR's passports returned
April	ER goes to Trinidad to cover the West Indies Federation's first parliament. Sees Cheddi and Janet Jagan and delivers a series of lectures
July 22	ER meets Indira Gandhi on July 22, 1958, in London

	ER visits Tashkent with PR and meets with Lily Golden about forming an African institute in Moscow
December	ER attends historic All-African Peoples' Conference (AAPC) in Accra, Ghana, attended by Patrice Lumumba and other key African independence leaders
December 31	ER and PR celebrate New Year's Eve in Moscow along with W. E. B. and Shirley Graham Du Bois

1959

June–August	ER and PR in Czechoslovakia, Austria, and Romania

1961

March 26	PR attempts suicide under mysterious circumstances in a Moscow hotel room. ER flies to Moscow to look afer PR, followed by PRJ
	PR and ER go to Barveekha Sanitorium in Russia for rest after their medical treatments
	ER speaks at "Africa Women's Day" in London on behalf of All African Women's Freedom Movement

1963

July	ER attends the Berlin show trial of alleged Nazi supporter Hans Globke (tried in absentia)
August	ER and PR become inpatients at the BUCH clinic in Berlin for nearly four months; ER receives treatment for cancer
	ER is diagnosed with cervical and uterine cancer
	ER receives Clara Zetkin medal from German Democratic Republic Council of Ministers
December	ER and PR return to the United States after five years abroad

1964

	ER authors a dozen articles on Black Freedom Movement including "Long Hot Summer" and "The Time Is Now"
July	ER speaks at Africa Unity House in London hosted by Afro-Asian-Caribbean Organization

1965

April 22	ER attends *Freedomways* gala reception in honor of PR at the Americana Hotel. The program includes James Baldwin, Lena Horne, Ossie Davis and Ruby Dee

| December 13 | A few days before her seventieth birthday, ER dies of cancer in Beth Israel Hospital, New York City |

1976

| January 23 | Paul Robeson dies at age 77 |

ABBREVIATIONS TO THE NOTES

ABX A. B. Xuma Papers, Manuscript and Historical Papers Library, University of the Witwatersrand, Johannesburg

AMGP Anna Melissa Graves Papers, Swarthmore College, Swarthmore, Pa.

ASP Abbott Simon Papers, Tamiment Library and Robert F. Wagner Labor Archives, New York University

BMP Bronislaw Malinowski Papers, London School of Economics Library

CBP Papers of Claude Barnett, Director of the Associated Negro Press, Chicago History Museum

CJMC Claudia Jones Memorial Collection, Schomburg Center for Research in Black Culture, New York Public Library

CVVP Carl Van Vechten Papers, Beinecke Rare Book and Manuscript Library, Yale University, New Haven

DWP Dorothy West Papers, Schlesinger Library, Harvard University, Cambridge, Mass.

EFFP E. Franklin Frazier Papers, Moorland-Spingarn Research Center, Howard University, Washington, D.C.

EGA Emma Goldman Papers, Emma Goldman Archives, International Institute of Social History, Amsterdam

EGP Emma Goldman Papers, University of California, Berkeley

ETL Evanston Township Library Special Collections, Evanston, Ill.

FBIR FBI (Federal Bureau of Investigation) Records: The Vault. Available online: http://vault.fbi.gov/PaulRobeson

FLP Florence Luscomb Papers, Schlesinger Library, Harvard University, Cambridge, Mass.

GMP George Murphy Papers, Moorland-Spingarn Research Center, Howard University, Washington, D.C.

JWJP James Weldon Johnson Papers, Beinecke Rare Book and Manuscript Library, Yale University, New Haven

LBP Lawrence Brown Papers, Schomburg Center for Research in Black Culture, New York Public Library

LSE London School of Economics Archives, London

LTPP Louise Thompson Patterson Papers, Emory University Library, Atlanta

MYP Max Yergan Papers, Kautz Family Papers, YMCA Collection, University of Minnesota, Minneapolis

NAACP NAACP Papers, Library of Congress, Washington, D.C.

NMML Nehru Memorial Museum Library, Delhi, India

PERC Paul and Eslanda Robeson Collection, Moorland-Spingarn Research Center, Howard University, Washington, D.C.

PLPP	P. L. Prattis Papers, Moorland-Spingarn Research Center, Howard University, Washington, D.C.
PRAB	Paul Robeson Archives, Musikarchiv, Akademie der Künste, Berlin
PRC	Paul Robeson Collection, microfilm, Schomburg Center for Research in Black Culture, New York Public Library
PPP	Progressive Party Papers, University of Iowa Special Collections, Iowa City
RBC	Rabinowitz and Boudin Collection, Tamiment Library and Robert F. Wagner Labor Archives, New York University
RBP	Ralph Bunche Papers, University of California, Los Angeles
RFP	Ray Firth Papers, London School of Economics
SHP	Stella Hanau Papers, University of Wyoming, American Heritage Center, Laramie
RGCP	Ruth Gage-Colby Papers, Minnesota Historical Society, St. Paul
UIC	University Archives, University of Illinois, Chicago

NOTES

The Paul and Eslanda Robeson Collection (PERC), located at the Moorland-Spingarn Research Center, Howard University, is an extensive collection of thousands of items related to the lives and careers of Eslanda and Paul Robeson from 1922 until Paul's death in 1976. The collection has been carefully organized, but many items have been pulled from the files for various exhibitions related to the Paul Robeson centennial and some have landed in special boxes upon their return. The collection was also organized in stages and so there is some asymmetry to the collection. Unless otherwise specified, letters cited here can be found in the "Correspondence" files, where they have been arranged in alphabetical order in either the Paul Robeson or Eslanda Robeson section, according to who wrote or received that letter. Essays, novels, plays, and other writings by Eslanda Robeson, published and unpublished, can be found in the Eslanda Robeson section of the collection, in series E, boxes 8–15. These boxes are labeled "Writings" and have been arranged in chronological order with undated items at the back of the files. If a document has been placed in a specific topical file, box and folder numbers have been provided here. In addition, all of the Robeson declassified FBI files can be located online at http://vault.fbi.gov/Paul%20Robeson%2C%20Sr.

INTRODUCTION

1. Eslanda Robeson, "My Mind Is Wandering," n.d., in "Writings by Eslanda Robeson," folder 1, box 9, PERC.
2. Eslanda Robeson, "Airborne," May 25, 1946, in "Writings," PERC.
3. A number of secondary sources, including her *New York Times* obituary, report her birth year as 1896. Census data report her year of birth both as 1895 on one census and 1896 on another. Her passports indicate 1896, as do her speaker's bios, which she crafted. Her official birth certificate obtained from the Washington, D.C., Office of Vital Records indicates that 1895 was her year of birth. It is unclear why Eslanda would misrepresent her age or when the misrepresentation began. It is possible that she was uncomfortable with the three-year age difference between herself and Paul and wanted to make herself seem a bit younger. This is only speculation. See "Eslanda Goode Is Dead: Writer and Wife of Singer, 68," *New York Times* obituary, Dec. 14, 1965, 43. Eslanda Robeson was widely referred to as "Essie" by friends, family, and acquaintances. She almost always referred to herself this way. Therefore she will be referred to by that name in the text and notes of this book.
4. Although the branches of the Cardozo family tree are a bit tangled, the following seems to be true: David Cardozo was the uncle of Justice Benjamin Cardozo. David had at least two sons, Isaac and Jacob, one of whom "married" (or had a long-term common-law relationship with) a free Black woman in Charleston, South Carolina, named Lydia Williams, who was Francis

Lewis Cardozo's mother. And Cardozo was Essie's maternal grandfather. See Andrew L. Kaufman, *Cardozo* (Cambridge, Mass.: Harvard University Press, 1998), 6–7; Joe M. Richardson, "Francis L. Cardozo: Black Educator during Reconstruction," *Journal of Negro Education* 48, no. 1 (Winter 1979): 73–83; and Euline Brock, "Thomas W. Cardozo: Fallible Black Reconstruction Leader," *Journal of Southern History* 47, no. 2 (May 1981): 183–206.

5. Office of Vital Records, Washington, D.C., Deaths and Burial Records, film no. 2115107. Date of death listed for John J. Goode, as Jan. 23, 1901, and date of burial listed as two days later, Jan. 25, 1901.

6. Essie moved to New York City in 1916, after completing the second semester of the 1915–1916 academic year. See her University of Illinois transcript in "Transcripts," PERC; Eslanda Robeson, "Changes in Manuscript," in "Writings," 22, PERC; and the letter from Teachers College indicating she received her bachelor's degree in June 1920 but had to withdraw for illness at some point. University documented dated Sept. 12, 1923, in "Transcripts," PERC.

7. Eslanda Robeson, "Africa—No Longer the 'Dark Continent,'" *New World Review* (Aug. 1952): 3–6; "Is US-USSR Co-Existence Possible?" *New World Review* (Mar. 1952): 14–15; "Felix Eboué: The End of an Era," *New World Review* (Oct. 1952): 44–48; "The Rising Tide," *New World Review* (Nov. 1952): 10; "Which Way for Africa?" *New World Review* (Dec. 1952): 24–29.

8. By "radical," I mean a set of left political ideas that critique fundamental injustices and inequities in the capitalist political and economic system and that seek to transform the system in some way. Essie was affiliated with communist movements but her own ideological positions were never precisely defined by her.

9. Essie stated repeatedly that she was not a communist or a member of the Communist Party. There is no evidence that she was either. Even the FBI concluded at one point that she was not a communist. But she maintained ties to pro-communist organizations, visited and applauded communist countries that she felt were making strides on the issues of race and equality, and maintained relationships with many longtime members and leaders of the U.S. Communist Party.

10. Eslanda Robeson did write about her views on the Soviet Union in the book *American Argument*, co-authored with Pearl Buck, and in several articles, including Eslanda Robeson, "Why I Am A Friend of the USSR," *New World Review* (Aug. 1953) and her eulogy for Soviet leader Joseph Stalin, "On Stalin's Death," Mar. 31, 1953, in "Writings," PERC. Paul Robeson Jr. notes that she knew of at least some of the violence and repression that was going on in the Soviet Union in the 1930s and 1940s. She did not focus on those issues for either personal reasons (her brother was living there) or pragmatic reasons (she thought it would hurt rather than help the larger cause). She may have convinced herself that the problems were exaggerated.

11. Eslanda Robeson, "Open Letter to Fisk University Students," Sept. 1943, in "Writings," PERC.

12. Essie identified with Pan-Africanism in the same way that W. E. B. Du Bois did. She was an internationalist above all, and her calls for African unity did not preclude Afro-Asian unity or international political solidarity.

13. Robeson, "Changes," 38.

1. Eslanda Robeson to P. L. Prattis, Oct. 27, 1961, PLPP.
2. Pearl S. Buck and Eslanda Robeson, *American Argument* (New York: John Day, 1949), 9.
3. Ibid., 7.
4. William Grant, ed., "The Graduates," (features alumni bios) in *Evanston Village High School* (N.p.: S. D. Childs and Company, 1907), ETL, 60.
5. John Cardozo Goode, U.S. Army Registration Card; Francis Cardozo Goode, U.S. Army Registration Card, both in Office of Vital Records, Washington, D.C. All noted Office of Vital Records documents are available online at www.ancestry.com (last accessed May 12, 2012).
6. Office of Vital Records, Washington, D.C., Deaths and Burial Records, indicates that John J. Goode died in 1901. Essie Robeson was born on December 15, 1895, so she was five not four, having turned five in December 1900. He died Jan. 1901. In several written accounts Eslanda Robeson states she was four when her father died, and Paul Robeson's biographies echo this slight miscalculation.
7. Paul Robeson Jr., telephone interview with the author, Aug. 16, 2010.
8. Eslanda Robeson, "Changes in Manuscript," in "Writings by Eslanda Robeson," 39, PERC.
9. Buck and Robeson, *American Argument*, 8; Robeson, "Changes," 23.
10. Ibid., 40.
11. There is some dispute about whether it was Jacob or Isaac who married Lydia Williams. In Essie Robeson's account it is the brother, Jacob. Benjamin Cardozo's biographer A. L. Kaufman suggests it was actually Isaac, a "weigher" and vice president of the Reformed Society of Israelites, who lived with Lydia. See Andrew L. Kaufman, *Cardozo* (Cambridge, Mass.: Harvard University Press, 1998), 7; Robeson, "Changes," 14. Kaufman's documentation is more persuasive.
12. Robeson, "Changes," 14. I note that much of this family history is Essie's second- or third-hand account, and much of it is not wholly verifiable. But I am as interested in how the stories are told and remembered in the family as I am in their precise accuracy, since all of them played out well before my subject was born. Note that "Changes" was originally intended to be a part of Essie's book on Paul—*Paul Robeson, Negro*—but either she or the editor decided to cut it, and it was never published in its entirety.
13. Robeson, "We Go to Spain," 1937, in "Writings," PERC.
14. U.S. Bureau of the Census, *United States Federal Population Census Schedule* (Washington, D.C.: Government Printing Office, 1880), available online at www.archives.gov (last accessed May 12, 2012).
15. Joe M. Richardson, "Francis L. Cardozo: Black Educator during Reconstruction," *Journal of Negro Education* 48, no. 1 (Winter 1979): 83.
16. Euline W. Brock, "Thomas W. Cardozo: Fallible Black Reconstruction Leader," *Journal of Southern History* 47 (May 1981): 183. Brock contrasts Francis with his less accomplished and more controversial brother, Thomas.
17. Robeson in "Writings," folder 1, box 9, 14, PERC.
18. Erwin Knoll, "The Truth about Desegregation in the Washington, D.C., Public Schools," *Journal of Negro Education* 28, no. 2 (Spring 1959): 92–113; Richardson, "Francis L. Cardozo," 83; and Robeson, "Changes," 16.

19. Robeson, "Changes," 19.
20. Ibid.
21. Buck and Robeson, *American Argument*, 40.
22. Eslanda Goode (Essie's mother) to Eslanda Robeson, June 30, 1949, in "Correspondence," PERC.
23. The Bureau of the Census, Washington D.C., 1880, microfilm, roll 121, page 157B, ED 19, image 0801, census record group 29, available online at www .archives.gov (last accessed May 12, 2012). In her manuscript "Changes," Essie names her maternal grandmother as Romena Howell. It appears her full legal name was Catharine Romena Howell. Also, see William J. Simmons, *Men of Mark: Eminent, Progressive and Rising* (Cleveland: Rewell, 1887), 430.
24. Robeson, "Changes," 15.
25. Ibid., 14. For more Cardozo family history, see William C. Hine, "Black Politicians in Reconstruction Charleston, South Carolina: A Collective Study," *Journal of Southern History* 49, no. 4 (Nov. 1983): 555–584; Richardson, "Francis L. Cardozo," 73–78; and Knoll, "The Truth about Desegregation," 92–113.
26. Richardson, "Francis L. Cardozo," 78, 80.
27. Office of Vital Records, Washington, D.C., Marriages, 1820–1921, vol. 28, 83.
28. The Bureau of the Census, U.S. Federal Census Population Schedule, 1900, Washington, D.C., roll T623_160, enumeration district 52, 4B, available online at www.archives.gov (last accessed May 12, 2012).
29. Paul Robeson Jr., *The Undiscovered Paul Robeson: An Artist's Journey, 1898–1939* (New York: John Wiley & Sons, 2001), 48, 50, regarding Eslanda Goode's color bias. According to Essie, however, her mother did not harbor any bias based on color; see Robeson, "Changes," 19.
30. Eslanda Robeson, "I Am an American," in "Writings," series E, box 9, folder 3, 2, PERC.
31. Some records indicate that John Goode was born in Ohio ("The Graduates") while others indicate he was born in Cook County, Illinois. It is such a common name and the spelling alternates between Good and Goode, so it is difficult to say for certain which record is accurate. We do know that John Goode grew up in Chicago and its northern suburb, Evanston, which had a small but significant Negro population in the late 1800s and early 1900s. In 1870 John Goode is listed as age eight and living in Chicago with his mother, Susan. According to the 1880 census, John Goode is eighteen years old and living as a student boarder in Evanston, Illinois. This record lists his place of birth as Chicago and his birth year as 1862. See U.S. 1880 Census, Evanston, Ill., district 1, enumeration no. 218, sheet 40. The 1900 census, by contrast, lists John J. A. Goode's year of birth as 1868 (six years off from the 1880 census), and his place of birth as Chicago. See U.S. 1900 Census, District 1, Chicago, Ill., enumeration no. 52, sheet 4, available online at www.archives.gov (last accessed May 12, 2012).
32. Records of the Office of the Secretary of War, RG 107: "Register of Civilian Employees of the War Department in Washington, D.C.," entry 281, National Archives, available online at www.archives.gov (last accessed May 12, 2012).
33. Barbara P. Josiah, "Providing for the Future: The World of the African American Depositors of Washington, D.C.'s Freedmen's Savings Bank, 1865–1874," *Journal of African American History* 89, no. 1 (Winter 2004): 1–16; James Bor-

chert, *Alley Life in Washington: Family, Community, Religion, and Folk Life in the City, 1850–1870* (Urbana: University of Illinois Press, 1980), 91–94, 165–95; Allan Johnston, *Surviving Freedom: The Black Community of Washington, D.C., 1860–1880* (New York: Garland, 1993), 75–186; U.S. Department of the Interior, U.S. Census of Population, "District of Columbia—Race and Hispanic Origin: 1800 to 1990." Sept. 13, 2002, www.census.gov/population/www/documentation/twps0056/tab23.pdf (last accessed May 14, 2012).

34. Eslanda Robeson diary, Aug. 2, 1925, PERC.

35. Robeson, "Changes," 39.

36. Ibid., 20.

37. Ibid.

38. Buck and Robeson, *American Argument*, 14.

39. Robeson, "Changes," 20.

40. Ibid., 21.

41. Buck and Robeson, *American Argument*, 39.

42. Ibid., 11. Essie's protest probably occurred at the Liggett's Store on Broadway and 34th Street. See "The Man behind the Idea That Brought Liggett's to New York," *New York Times*, Oct. 6, 1912, 5.

43. Buck and Robeson, *American Argument*, 10. Although in 1949 Essie recalled that she was fourteen years old when the Harlem riot took place, the events she so vividly described more accurately resemble the 1907 uprising in response to police harassment than the 1910 racial violence in New York that followed the prize fight between Black boxer Jack Johnson and a white opponent, James Jeffries. Therefore, Essie was more likely eleven years old, not fourteen. She was remembering the events thirty-eight years after the fact. See "Arrest Leads to Great Race Riot," *Chicago Daily Tribune*, July 8, 1907, 1.

44. Robeson, "Changes," 23, 39; and "Relative of Robeson Back Here in School," *Amsterdam News*, Mar. 6, 1937.

45. Robeson, "Changes," 45.

46. Ibid., 20–21.

47. Ibid., 21.

48. "Relative of Robeson Back Here in School."

49. "Eslanda Goode," under heading "Persons Nominated for Scholarships in the Household Science Department," University of Illinois, *Annual Report of the Illinois Farmer's Institute, 1912–1913* (Springfield: Illinois State Printers, 1913), 18:416.

50. Philip T. K. Daniel, "A History of Discrimination against Black Students in Chicago Secondary Schools," *History of Education Quarterly* 20, no. 2 (Summer 1980): 151.

51. FBI files indicate that Essie attended both Lucy Flower High School in Chicago and Urbana High School in Urbana, Illinois; FBI Files, Robeson, 100-56680, p. 2, available online at http://vault.fbi.gov/Paul Robeson, Sr. (last accessed May 14, 2012); Robeson, "Changes," 21–22.

52. Teresa Armitage, *Our Songs* (Sacramento: California State Department of Education, 1942); Teresa Armitage, *Let Music Ring!* (Boston: C.C. Birchard, 1949); Teresa Armitage, Peter W. Dykema, and Gladys Pitcher, *Music Everywhere: Teacher's Manual, Book of Accompaniments* (Boston: C.C. Birchard, 1945).

53. Robeson, "Changes," 21–22, 52–53.

54. Yet another publication lists Lucy Flower High School as her alma mater, but Chicago Public Schools records for that school do not list Essie as a graduate. We can infer that Essie transferred to Urbana High School and graduated from there as indicated on her University of Illinois transcript.

55. The precise details of Essie Robeson's early academic career remain a bit fuzzy. Her London School of Economics student records also indicate that she attended both Lucy Flower and Urbana High School. FBI files, which are notoriously unreliable for empirical data, indicated the same. The newspaper announcement of the test that Essie took for the Illinois scholarship gives her address as 406 E. Clark Street, Champaign, Illinois. See "Fourteen Try for Scholarships," *Urbana Daily Courier,* June 1, 1912, 1.

56. Eslanda Robeson, draft of *Paul Robeson, Negro,* 22; and "Fourteen Try," 1. Essie's name is misspelled in the newspaper article, but all other information fits the account she provides in her manuscript draft, "Changes."

57. University of Illinois yearbook, 1912, vol. 18, Library of Health Sciences-Chicago, Special Collections, UIC.

58. Eslanda C. Goode, University of Illinois transcript, Sept. 24, 1923, in Eslanda Robeson personal papers, box 2, MSRC.

59. Eslanda C. Goode, Face Pack, U.S. Patent No. 649, 734, filed July 5, 1923.

60. "Mrs. Goode Resigns," *Chicago Defender,* Oct. 26, 1918, 4.

61. Jeffrey Babcock Perry, *Hubert Harrison: The Voice of Harlem Radicalism, 1883–1918* (New York, Columbia University Press, 2009), 305, 315, 350–351, 13.

62. Ibid., 305, 315, 350.

63. Robeson, "Changes," 22.

64. Eslanda C. Goode, official transcript, issued Sept. 15, 1923, Columbia University Teacher's College, in "Awards, Tributes, and Memorabilia," box 2, folder "Transcripts," PERC.

CHAPTER 2. A HARLEM LOVE STORY, 1919–1927

1. Eslanda Robeson, "Changes in Manuscript," in "Writings by Eslanda Robeson," PERC, 28.

2. Ibid., 40.

3. Ibid.

4. Ibid.

5. There are differing versions of how Essie and Paul actually "met," as distinct from when they "became better acquainted." Although in Pearl S. Buck and Eslanda Robeson, *American Argument* (New York: John Day, 1949) Essie places the year at 1920, other evidence suggests they "met" in 1919 and became closer friends and lovers in 1920. Martin Duberman marks their meeting as the time Paul was a patient at Columbia Presbyterian Hospital, where Essie worked, and they were introduced by Dr. Henry Murray, a young surgeon. This scenario was described to Duberman by Murray some seventy years later. There may certainly have been some contact during Paul's hospital stay, but I find Essie's version of the first actual meeting more persuasive, even though her recollections also varied. Duberman, *Paul Robeson,* 37; Buck and Robeson, *American Argument,* 25.

6. Lloyd L. Brown's quotation can be found in Deborah Willis, "The Image and

Paul Robeson," in *Paul Robeson: Artist and Citizen* (New Brunswick, N.J.: Rutgers University Press, 1998), 61. See also Lloyd L. Brown, *The Young Paul Robeson: "On My Journey Now"* (New York: Westview, 1997), 3.

7. Martin Duberman, in *Paul Robeson: A Biography* (New York: Knopf, 1988), 60, quoting Millia Davenport, a costume designer in New York City in 1922.

8. Ibid., 70. The statement was based on his interviews in the 1920s with Robeson's acquaintances.

9. Robeson, "Changes," 23–25, 38, 40.

10. The description of Paul and Essie's early relationship is drawn from Essie's autobiographical manuscript, "Changes."

11. Ibid., 24–25.

12. Buck and Robeson, *American Argument*, 59.

13. Paul Robeson Jr., *The Undiscovered Paul Robeson: An Artist's Journey, 1898–1939* (New York: John Wiley & Sons, 2001), 50. Also see Kuwana Haulsey, *Angel of Harlem* (New York: One World/Ballantine, 2006). Haulsey's book is a carefully researched novel based on May Chinn's life. For biographical information on Chinn, see George Davis, "A Healing Hand in Harlem," *The New York Times*, Apr. 22, 1979; Wini Warren, *Black Women Scientists in the United States* (Bloomington: Indiana University Press, 1999); and the May Chinn interview by Ellen Craft Dammon in the Black Women's Oral History Collection, Radcliffe College, Schlesinger Library, Cambridge, Mass. In *Undiscovered, 1898–1939*, Paul Robeson Jr. gives an account of Essie's abortion and the advice of her physician "that she should never have a child." He also adds that Paul was angry Essie had kept the news from him and that Essie had done so, in part, because she was "determined to not make Paul feel obligated to her," 50–51.

14. Robeson, "Changes," 25.

15. Robeson, "Changes," 26. There are competing interpretations of Paul and Essie's early relationship and their decision to marry. Precisely when and how they met seems less relevant than the terms of their early relationship. But I differ with Martin Duberman's suggestion that a "shrewd" and manipulative Essie "noisily connive[d]" to "snare" Paul into matrimony (Duberman, *Paul Robeson*, 38–40). Essie was certainly an assertive woman unafraid to claim her feelings and desires and determined to pursue her goals, including her amorous ones. She admitted to taking the initiative in the relationship with Paul (see Buck and Robeson, *American Argument*, 23). She was not, however, a woman desperate to find a husband. She had been raised to be independent, and she had other suitors, and therefore other romantic options. She loved Paul and despite some ambivalence and hesitation, he apparently loved her too. The gushing love letters that Paul wrote to Essie in 1922, less than a year after their marriage, are evidence that her feelings toward him were reciprocated. These letters, which I believe reflect Paul's true emotions at the time, belie the notion of a man tricked, trapped, or railroaded into wedlock. At age twenty-three Paul might have been ambivalent about marriage, but by the time he proposed, he seemed quite certain about Essie.

16. Robeson Jr., *Undiscovered, 1898–1939*, 51.

17. Ibid., 50.

18. Ibid.

19. Robeson, "Changes," 26.

20. Ibid., 27.

21. Buck and Robeson, *American Argument*, 62.

22. Robeson, "Changes," 29.

23. Ibid., 31.

24. Ibid.

25. Ibid., 32.

26. Ibid., 35–37, 44–45.

27. Robeson Jr., *Undiscovered, 1898–1939*, 60. Robeson, "Changes," 33.

28. Robeson, "Changes," 39.

29. Paul Robeson to Eslanda Robeson, Portsmouth, July 21, 1922; Paul Robeson to Eslanda Robeson, Plymouth, Aug. 23, 1922, in "Correspondence," PERC.

30. Paul Robeson to Eslanda Robeson, Glasgow, Aug. 2, 1922, in "Correspondence," PERC.

31. Robeson Jr., *Undiscovered, 1898–1939*, 60, 66–68. Extant documentation of Essie and Paul's exchanges during his trip abroad in 1922 is limited. Only his letters to her were kept. Her letters to him are not in the PERC. See Paul to Eslanda, Portsmouth, July 21, 1922; and Paul to Eslanda, Plymouth, Aug. 23, 1922.

32. Robeson Jr., *Undiscovered, 1898–1939*, 71.

33. Ibid., 73–78.

34. *Opportunity*, Dec. 1924, 368.

35. Duberman, *Paul Robeson*, 76, 118.

36. Eslanda Robeson diary, Jan. 3, 1926, in "Writings by Eslanda Robeson," PERC. The description of Essie is a composite of primary and secondary sources.

37. Paul already knew Otto Khan, a trustee of Rutgers, whom he had approached unsuccessfully for help with his career a few years earlier. See Robeson Jr., *Undiscovered, 1898–1939*, 73.

38. Nathan Irvin Huggins, *Harlem Renaissance* (New York: Oxford University Press, 1971), 99.

39. David Levering Lewis, *W. E. B. Du Bois: The Fight for Equality and the American Century, 1919–1963* (New York: Henry Holt, 2000), 180. Eslanda Robeson to Carl Van Vechten and Fania Marinoff, n.d. (March 1928).

40. Nancy Kuhl, *Extravagant Crowd: Carl Van Vechten's Portraits of Women* (New Haven: Yale University Press, 2007).

41. Robeson diary, Jan. 3, 1925.

42. Eslanda Robeson to Carl Van Vechten and Fania, July 10, 1949, "Correspondence," CVVP. By the 1940s Essie had serious political differences with Carlo, but she remained in touch and on relatively good terms with him.

43. Robeson diary, Feb. 12, 1924; Aug. 17, 1924; Apr. 10, 1925; Apr. 21, 1925; and May 1, 1925. See also Walter White, *A Man Called White: The Autobiography of Walter White* (Bloomington: Indiana University Press, 1948); and Kenneth R. Janken, *Walter White: Mr. NAACP* (Chapel Hill: University of North Carolina Press, 2006) for more details on Walter White's influential career.

44. According to the scholar Iheanachor Egonu, "The great merit of *Les Continents* was perhaps not so much in its indictment of colonialism as in the fact that it provided Afro-French intellectuals an organ of uninhibited political expression at a critical moment in the Pan-Negro movement in France." See Egonu,

"*Les Continents* and the Francophone Pan-Negro Movement," *Phylon* 42, no. 3 (1981): 246.

45. Robeson diary, Aug. 17, 1924; and Sept. 7, 9, 12, 16, 17, 1924.

46. Even though Paul and Essie did not criticize their fellow Harlem Renaissance artists or dubious white "supporters" like Carl Van Vechten, their future friend and close associate W. E. B. Du Bois did not hesitate to do so. He viewed Van Vechten's novel *Nigger Heaven* as an "affront" and described some of the so-called primitivist writings of the Renaissance—that is, novels and stories that celebrated a wild Harlem nightlife and an uninhibited Black sexuality—as "the literary tradition of denigration." See Lewis, *W. E. B. Du Bois*, 177, 180; and Robert E. Washington, *The Ideologies of African American Literature: From the Harlem Renaissance to the Black Nationalist Revolt* (Lanham, Md.: Rowman and Littlefield, 2001).

47. Robeson diary, Oct. 17, 1924.

48. Charles Musser, "Troubled Relations: Paul Robeson, Eugene O'Neill and Oscar Micheaux," in Jeffrey C. Stewart, ed., *Paul Robeson, Artist and Citizen* (New Brunswick, N.J.: Rutgers University Press, 1998), 82, 88–89.

49. Robeson diary, Nov. 3, 1924; Duberman, *Paul Robeson*, 593.

50. Robeson diary, Oct. 17, 1924, and Nov. 3, 1924.

51. Robeson, "Changes," 58. Even though Essie and Paul both worked hard to ensure his success in *Emperor*, and the concurrent O'Neill play that Paul was starring in, *All Gods Chillun Got Wings*, both roles met with political criticism from Black leaders. By Essie's own admission the lead role of Brutus Jones was a negative one—Paul played "a murdering crap-shooting swaggering pirate"—and *Chillun* can be read as a cautionary tale about miscegenation. Still she reassured Paul that his success would pave the way for other actors and be a source of pride for the race. In 1924, in a seemingly unself-critical stance that she held as late as 1930, she urged Paul to ignore Mr. Negro-with-a-Chip-on-His-Shoulder and his criticisms of the plays. Later in the decade Essie would develop a sharper and more critical view of the nexus between art and racial politics.

52. Paul's letters reflect a strong physical attraction and close emotional bond with Essie in 1922 as they bagan their life together. Paul Robeson to Eslanda Robeson, July 1922 and Aug. 1922, in "Correspondence," PERC.

53. Paul Robeson to Eslanda Robeson, 1925 (n.d.), in "Family Correspondence," PERC.

54. "'I Owe My Success to My Wife' Says PR, Star in O'Neill's Drama," *Pittsburgh Courier*, June 14, 1924, 13.

55. "Biography of Stella Hanau," collection guide, SHP; and Robeson diary, May 15, 1924; June 28, 1924; Aug. 30, 1924; Nov. 27, 1924; Feb. 27, 1925; June 28, 1925; and May 20, 1926.

CHAPTER 3. ONTO THE WORLD STAGE, 1920s

1. Eslanda Robeson diary, Mar. 23, 1925, in "Writings by Eslanda Robeson," PERC.

2. Marie Seton, *Paul Robeson* (London: Dodson Books, 1958), 59.

3. Robeson diary, Mar. 29, 1925.

4. Ibid., Mar. 3, 1925; Feb. 29, 1925; and Apr. 11, 1925.

5. Ibid., Apr. 19, 1925.

6. Ibid., May 11, 1925.

7. Ibid., Mar. 21, May 14, Jun. 1, 1925.

8. There are dozens of letters between Essie and Lawrence Brown between 1927 and 1945 that demonstrate their friendship, familiarity, and trust. Essie signs her letters "affectionately," and refers to Larry as "Larry, dear," "Toots," or "Hi Ya, Honey!!!" See Essie to "Larry [Brown] dear," Correspondence file, LBP.

9. Eslanda Robeson to Lawrence Brown, Aug. 14, 1945, Correspondence file, LBP.

10. Eslanda Robeson to Lawrence Brown, Oct. 23, 1949, Correspondence file, LBP.

11. Robeson diary, May 23, 1925, and May 26, 1925.

12. The 50/50 split with her 10 percent cut as manager is spelled out in Eslanda Robeson's diary, Mar. 24, 1925. In Paul Robeson Jr., *The Undiscovered Paul Robeson: An Artist's Journey, 1898–1939* (New York: John Wiley & Sons, 2001), we learn that Essie "rehearsed with him day and night" (75), that she "developed a strategy and presented it to Paul" about how to launch and advance his career in 1922 (56), that "his dependence on her was real" (60), and that he "need[ed] her criticism and advice" in England while she is back home, writing, "I want you and only you to help me" (64).

13. Pearl S. Buck and Eslanda Robeson, *American Argument* (New York: John Day, 1949), 12–13.

14. Robeson diary, Oct. 15, 1925.

15. Essie telephoned Kahn's office to make an appointment to request the loan. See Theresa M. Collins, *Otto Kahn: Art, Money and Modern Time* (Chapel Hill: University of North Carolina Press, 2002), 162, 168. For the interactions that led to Kahn's loan, see Martin Duberman, *Paul Robeson: A Biography* (New York: Knopf, 1988), 84. According to Duberman she asked for $5,000.

16. Robeson diary, Aug. 13, 1925.

17. Ibid., Aug. 15, 1925.

18. Eslanda Robeson, "Changes in Manuscript," in "Writings," 45, PERC.

19. Eslanda Robeson to Carl Van Vechten, Sept. 28, 1925, CVVP.

20. William Roger Louis et al., *The Oxford History of the British Empire* (Oxford, Eng.: Oxford University Press, 2001), 282–283; and Deborah Hughes, "Kenya, India and the British Empire Exhibition of 1924," *Race and Class* (Apr. 2006): 47, 66–85.

21. David Simonelli, "'Laughing Nations of Happy Children Who Have Never Grown Up': Race, the Concept of Commonwealth, and the 1924–25 British Empire Exhibition," *Journal of Colonialism and Colonial History* 10, no. 1 (Spring 2009); and Sarah Britton, "'Come and See the Empire by the All Red Route!' Anti-Imperialism and Exhibitions in Interwar Britain," *History Workshop Journal* 69, no. 1 (Spring 2010): 68–89; H. J. Braunholt, "Ethnographical Exhibition in the South African Pavilion, British Empire Exhibition," *MAN* 98 (Sept. 1924): 129–132.

22. Robeson diary, Aug. 28–29, 1925; Eslanda Robeson to Carl Van Vechten, Sept. 7–8, 1925, CVVP. For an example of a 1925 news article on Eslanda Robe-

son in Paris see *Paris Tribune*, Dec. 11, 1925. See also Eslanda Robeson, *Paul Robeson, Negro* (New York: Harper & Brothers, 1930), 102–103.

23. Carl Van Vechten gave Eslanda a letter of introduction to present to Gertrude Stein when she and Paul arrived in Paris, telling Gertrude how wonderful Essie and Paul were. About Paul, Van Vechten wrote, "I like him more than almost anyone I have ever met," and he is "a lamb of God." Carl Van Vechten to Gertrude Stein, Aug. 1, 1925, in Edward Burns, ed., *The Letters of Gertrude Stein and Carl Van Vechten, 1913–1946* (New York: Columbia University Press, 1986), 120. Other letters between Eslanda Robeson and Stein, and between Stein and Van Vechten, mention Essie and Paul and chronicle their continued association with Stein and her friends and associates in Paris. Stein to Van Vechten, Nov. 28, 1928, mentions one of Paul and Essie's parties in London after they moved there in 1928; see Burns, *Letters of Gertrude Stein*, 184.

24. Robeson diary, Aug. 22, 1925 (meeting Goldman); Sept. 5, 1925; and Sept. 25, 1925 (dinner) all cite Emma Goldman, as do other entries.

25. Emma Goldman, *My Disillusionment with Russia* (New York: Doubleday, 1923).

26. Ibid., chapters 28 and 32.

27. Robeson diary, Sept. 10, 1925. Goldman attended the performance of *Emperor Jones* again on Oct. 5, 1925; see Robeson diary entry for the same date.

28. Ibid., Sept. 23, 1925.

29. Emma Goldman to Eslanda Robeson, October 4, 1925, in "Correspondence," PERC. For mentions of the Robesons in Goldman's other correspondence, as well as her copies of letters from Essie, see reels 36, 39, and 41, EGP.

30. Richard Drinnon, *Rebel in Paradise: A Biography of Emma Goldman* (Chicago: University of Chicago Press, 1961); Candace Serena Falk, *Love, Anarchy, and Emma Goldman* (Piscataway, N.J.: Rutgers University Press, 1990); for Essie and Emma's correspondence, see "Correspondence," PERC; and Goldman correspondence files, 1925, 1927, 1930, EGP.

31. Robeson, *Paul*, 106.

32. Robeson diary, Oct. 15, 1925; Goldman to Eslanda Robeson, Nov. 18, 1925; Sept. 5, 1926; June 7, 1926; Nov. 21, 1927; Dec. 1, 1927; and Sept. 16, 1930, all in "Correspondence," PERC. Emma was enormously fond of Paul too, and was exuberant in her praise of his talents as an artist. See, for example, Goldman to Robeson, Mar. 7, 1930, in "Correspondence," PERC.

33. Robeson diary, Aug. 28, 1925, and Aug. 27, 1925.

34. Ibid., Aug. 24–28, 1925.

35. Robeson, *Paul*, 112.

36. Ibid., 113; Robeson diary, Nov. 10, 11, 12, 1925.

37. Robeson, *Paul*, 121.

38. Claude McKay to Paul Robeson, "Monday," n.d., 1925, in "Correspondence," PERC. In the letter McKay wrote, "I am a friend of Walter White's and I understand he is also a great friend of yours," and asked if they could meet while Paul was in France.

39. Robeson diary, Nov. 28, 1925.

40. Kate A. Baldwin, *Beyond the Color Line and the Iron Curtain: Reading Encounters in Black and Red, 1922–1963* (Durham, N.C.: Duke University Press, 2002), 37–39, 51.

41. Robeson, *Paul*, 116.

42. Robeson diary, Nov. 21, 1925.

43. Claude McKay to Eslanda Robeson, n.d. (Dec. 1925), in "Correspondence," PERC.

44. Robeson diary, Feb. 18, 1926; Dec. 1 and 3, 1925. Regarding Essie's use in her private diary of the word "nigger," which had clear and negative meanings about race, class, and color embedded in it, that word choice by no means gives a full or accurate picture of Essie's attitudes on these subjects.

45. Claude McKay (and Gene Andrew Jarrett), *A Long Way Home* (New Brunswick, N.J.: Rutgers University Press, 2007), 204.

46. Robeson diary, Feb. 18, 1926; Dec. 30, 1930. For mention of Ulric in blackface, see David Lewis, *W. E. B. Du Bois: The Fight for Equality and the American Century, 1919–1963* (New York: Henry Holt, 2001), 173.

47. Duberman, *Paul Robeson*, 238, which details the Duberman interview with Bayard Rustin on Mar. 25 and Apr. 20, 1983.

48. Robeson diary, Dec. 25, Dec. 26, Dec. 28, and Dec. 30, 1925 (socializing separately); Robeson, *Paul*, 126 (where we learn that apparently they slept in separate rooms when on tour; Essie says she could hear Paul's cough "through the bedroom wall").

49. Robeson diary, Jan. 18, Feb. 13, 1926.

50. Ibid., Feb. 14, 1926.

51. Ibid., Mar. 8, 1926; The African American Registry, "A'Lelia Walker, Harlem Businesswoman," available online at www.aaregistry.org/historic_events/view/alelia-walker-harlem-businesswoman (last accessed May 14, 2012); and Cary D. Wintz et al., *Encyclopedia of the Harlem Renaissance*, vol. 2 (New York: Routledge, 2004), 1222.

52. Robeson diary, Dec. 26, Dec. 28, 1925; and June 3, June 4, June 5, June 13, 1926.

53. Ibid., June 14, 1926.

54. Frances E. Rivers to Mrs. Eslanda Robeson, May 1, 1926, in "Correspondence," PERC; Eslanda Robeson, "Aunt Hagar's Children: The Outline of a Negro Play," n.d., in "Writings," PERC.

55. Robeson diary, Mar. 20 and Apr. 8, 1926.

56. "Raid on Rooming House 'Love Nest' Reveals Double Life of Married Pair," *Amsterdam News*, Jan. 20, 1926.

57. Paul's letters to her from England in 1922 mentioned her concern that she might not be able to have children and her desire to do so. See Robeson Jr., *Undiscovered, 1898–1939*, 68, 142.

58. See Paul Allen Anderson, *Deep River: Music and Memory in Harlem Renaissance Thought* (Durham, N.C.: Duke University Press, 2001) for the importance of Paul's musical contributions to 1920s Black culture.

59. Paul Robeson to Eslanda Robeson, Dec. 10 and 12, 1927, in "Correspondence," PERC.

CHAPTER 4. REMAPPING A MARRIAGE, CAREER, AND WORLDVIEW, 1927–1933

1. "Across the Pond," *Amsterdam News*, Nov. 8, 1927.
2. Paul Robeson Jr., *The Undiscovered Paul Robeson: An Artist's Journey, 1898–1939* (New York: John Wiley & Sons, 2001), 143–144.
3. See Eslanda Robeson to Carl Van Vechten, Nov. 11, 1927, CVVP; also see *Amsterdam News*, Nov. 17, 1927; and Eslanda Robeson to Lawrence Brown, Jan. 8, 1928 (explaining her illness), LBP.
4. Eslanda Robeson to Lawrence Brown, n.d. (1928), LBP.
5. Eslanda Robeson to Carl Van Vechten and Fania Marinoff, Long Island College Hospital, Brooklyn, Nov. 11, 1927, CVVP.
6. Eslanda Robeson to Carl Van Vechten, Nov. 18, 1927, CVVP.
7. Essie's diaries from the 1920s mention numerous evenings, afternoons, and special occasions shared with Clare Scott Delaney: see, for example, Eslanda Robeson diary, Sept. 22, 1924; Dec. 28, 1924; Dec. 30, 1924; Apr. 30, 1925; and Apr. 7, 1926, PERC. She was obviously a valued friend, and Essie and Ma Goode knew Clare's family as well.
8. See Robeson diary entries for Aug. 30 and Aug. 31, 1925, as well as May 1928 (day not known; Essie's lengthy reflections on Clare Delaney upon her return to London); "Death Takes Daughter of Emmet Scott," *Chicago Defender*, national edition, Oct. 15, 1927; and Ruth Randolph, "Another Day Will Find Me Brave: Clarissa Scott Delaney, 1901–1927," *SAGE: Scholarly Journal of Black Women* (1988): supplement, 14–18.
9. Robeson diary, n.d. (May 1928). On Bercovici, see Kathy E. Ferguson, *Emma Goldman: Political Thinking in the Streets* (Lanham, Md.: Rowman and Littlefield, 2011), 269.
10. Robeson diary, n.d. (May 1928; mentions "cheering and tremendous applause for a packed house"); Robeson to Carl Van Vechten, June 14, 1928, and July 8, 1929, CVVP.
11. Eslanda Robeson, *Paul Robeson, Negro* (New York: Harper & Brothers, 1930), 139, quoting James Douglas, "A Negro Genius in London," *Daily Express*, July 5, 1928.
12. Others noted Essie's instrumental role in Paul's career advancement as well. See, for example, Marvel Cook, "Mrs. Paul Robeson, Manager and Mate," *Amsterdam News*, Oct. 5, 1935.
13. Robeson, *Paul*, 156.
14. Robeson diary, n.d. (May 1928); Robeson to Carl Van Vechten, June 14 and July 8, 1928; Aug. 5, 1929, CVVP.
15. While Essie's brother, Frank, did have a daughter, he also became a Soviet citizen, married a Soviet woman, and settled down there. Consequently, the grandchild with whom Ma Goode had the most contact was Paul Jr.
16. Paul Robeson Jr., interview with author, Nov. 4, 2005.
17. Robeson diary, Jan. 17, 1930.
18. Robeson diary, Jan. 2–27, 1930. Essie suffered an infection in her foot or leg during the trip, which slowed her down a bit toward the end of it, but she rebounded quickly.

19. Jez Connolly, "Close-up Look at Kenneth MacPherson's *Borderline*," *AllVoices* (UK), June 16, 2010. *Borderline*. Directed by Kenneth MacPherson. 1930; Territet, Switzerland. Zodiac, 2007.

20. James Donald, "*Borderline* and *Paul Robeson: Portraits of the Artist* (review)," *Modernism/modernity* 15, no. 3 (Sept. 2008): 594–598.

21. Robeson to Van Vechten and Marinoff, Aug. 3, 1930, CVVP.

22. Robeson diary, Mar. 20–29, 1930.

23. Hilda Doolittle (H. D.), who was openly bisexual and had many lovers, was rumored to have a crush on Paul (which was not acted on). See Susan Stanford Friedman, ed., *Analyzing Freud: Letters of H.D. and Bryher and Their Circle* (New York: New Directions Press, 2002), 131.

24. Ibid., 131 n.18.

25. Robeson diary, Mar. 9, 1930.

26. Ibid.

27. In January of 1925 Essie confided to her diary that Paul had flirted openly with a woman at a party. In July of that year he met a woman who would become a longtime friend of the family, Freda Diamond, who also, Paul Robeson Jr. and Martin Duberman both assert, was a long-term intimate partner of Paul's. It should be noted that later in life Freda Diamond disputed how biographer Martin Duberman characterized her relationship with Paul Robeson, but not the fact that they were intimately involved. Freda insisted that she and Essie were friends independently of her relationship with Paul. Details can be found in "Corrections to Revised Galleys (Chapter 21 1955–1956)," and "Corrections," 2, Abbott Simon Papers, TAM 346, box 3, folder 2, The Tamiment Library and Robert F. Wagner Labor Archives, New York University.

28. Pearl S. Buck and Eslanda Robeson, *American Argument* (New York: John Day, 1949), 113.

29. Robeson diary, Sept. 1, 1930.

30. Paul Robeson to Eslanda Robeson, Aug. 2, 1932 (where he writes, referring to Yolande, "guess I'm really in love this time"), in "Correspondence," PERC; "Robeson's Decision Leaves Harlem Amazed," *Atlanta Daily World*, June 30, 1932, 1; and "Romance of Robeson with English Society Girl O.K.'d by Harlem; Score U.S. Bias," *The Pittsburgh Courier*, July 2, 1932, A8. "Attractive" is from Robeson Jr., *Undiscovered, 1898–1939*, 163.

31. Robeson diary, n.d. (Oct. 1930).

32. Ibid.; (no byline), "Brother-in-Law of Paul Robeson Visits Moscow," *The Chicago Defender*, June 16, 1934.

33. Robeson to Van Vechten and Marinoff, Dec. 19, 1930, CVVP.

34. Robeson diary, Dec. 5, 8, 10, 1931; Jan.–Dec. 1931).

35. Ibid., Aug. 19 and Sept. 1, 1931.

36. Here I refer to the women characters in her unpublished novels, her writings on women in Africa and China and at the United Nations, and her interviews with women in Paris and French Equatorial Africa.

37. Robeson diary, Mar. 30 and Apr. 3, 1931.

38. Ibid., Mar. 4, 1931, in which Essie refers to her abortion as her "job" that she was going to have performed by Dr. West, who had performed the same procedure ten years earlier. The indication that it was a covert medical procedure

is her reference in her diary to the fact that West would do the procedure near Columbia Presbyterian hospital in case anything went awry. The abortions are also discussed in Robeson Jr., *Undiscovered, 1898–1939*, 184, and mentioned by Duberman, *Paul Robeson*, 150. This was likely a difficult and fraught decision considering the risk of abortions at that time.

39. Robeson diary, Apr. 6, 1931.

40. Ibid., Apr. 14, 1931.

41. It is unclear whether the terminated pregnancy in the spring of 1931 was a result of amorous liaisons with Coward or Harrison, though Coward was gay later in life and may have been gay at the time. It is unlikely that her relationship with Lucas resulted in a pregnancy because she came to the States intent on the procedure and seems to have reconnected with Grant Lucas only once she had arrived. It is also unclear whether the relationship with Lucas was sexual or simply flirtatious.

42. Robeson diary, Dec. 30, 1930, 3.

43. Ibid., June 15, 1932. The friend was Kojo Touvalou Houénou.

44. Eslanda Robeson to Grace Nail Johnson, Sept. 6, 1931, from Kitzbuhel, Tirol, Austria, JWJP.

45. Robeson to Brown, Mar. 7, 1932, LBP.

46. Ibid.

47. Robeson to Van Vechten, July 13, 1932, CVVP.

48. She was hoping to "break into the journalism game"; see Robeson diary, June 25, 1932.

49. Robeson diary, Jan. 30, 1931.

50. I make this assumption because her diary is replete with mentions of various "attractive" men she is seeing. She comments on who she thinks "likes her," and whom she finds delightful and a romantic prospect. Kojo Touvalou is mentioned often but never in this way. Kojo married the Black American soprano Roberta Dodd Crawford in 1932 and moved back to Dahomey with her soon thereafter.

51. Robeson diary, June 3, 1932.

52. Dorothy West, "Black Paris," *Challenge* (Jan. 1936): 18.

53. There are multiple spellings of Kojo Touvalou Houénou's middle and last names. I have chosen the most common version.

54. Eslanda Robeson, interview with Kojo Touvalou, n.d., box 3, 29, DWP.

55. Babacar M'Baye, "Marcus Garvey and African Francophone Political Leaders of the Early Twentieth Century: Prince Kojo Tovalou Houénou Reconsidered," *Journal of Pan-African Studies* 1, no. 5 (Oct. 2006): 2–19; Melvyn Stokes, "Kojo Touvalou Houenou: An Assessment," *Transatlantica* 1 (2009): 2–7.

56. Michel Fabre, *From Harlem to Paris: Black American Writers in France, 1840–1980* (Urbana: University of Illinois Press, 1993), 146–147.

57. See ibid., 146–147; William Shack, *Harlem in Montmartre: A Paris Jazz Story Between the Great Wars* (Berkeley: University of California Press, 2001), 59, 68–69, 151n14.

58. For more details and nuanced discussion of La Défense de la Race Noire (LUDRN), see Robert A. Hill, ed., *The Marcus Garvey and Universal Negro Improvement Association Papers, 1923–1945* (Berkeley: University of California Press, 2006), vol. 10, 172–173.

59. Claude McKay, *Banjo: A Story without a Plot* (New York: Harcourt Brace Jovanovich, 1957), 194.

60. Stokes, "Kojo Touvalou Houenou," 3; M'Baye, "Marcus Garvey and African Francophone Political Leaders," 2–19; Christopher L. Miller, *Nationals and Nomads: Essays on Francophone African Literature and Culture* (Chicago: University of Chicago Press, 1998), 2, 10, 50.

61. Robeson diary, June 6 and June 8, 1932.

62. Cultural critic Brent Hayes Edwards points out that while some charged that *Batouala* by René Maran (London: Heinemann, 1973) incited Africans to rebel, a closer read of the novel and Maran reveals him to be "a reformer, not a revolutionary." See Brent Hayes Edwards, *The Practice of Diaspora: Literature, Translation, and the Rise of Black Internationalism* (Cambridge, Mass.: Harvard University Press, 2003), 83–84.

63. Robeson diary, June 16, 1932; and Robeson, "Black Paris" (June entry in the series), *Challenge: A Literary Quarterly* (June 1936): 13.

64. Robert Hill, *The Marcus Garvey and Universal Negro Improvement Association Papers*, vol. 3, 181; vol. 7, 176, 185; Robeson diary, June 13, 1932.

65. Robeson, "Black Paris"; Robeson, "1936 January, Black Paris" (January entry in the series), *Challenge: A Literary Quarterly*, 1, no. 4 (Jan. 1936); Robeson diary, June 4–18, 1932. In 1934, Dorothy West created *Challenge* magazine as a vehicle to showcase Harlem Renaissance authors. West was the founder and editor of the magazine until it closed in 1937 due to lack of funding. See Laurie Champion and Emmanuel Sampath Nelson, *American Women Writers, 1900–1945: A Bio-Bibliographical Critical Sourcebook* (Santa Barbara, Calif.: Greenwood, 2000). After *Challenge* folded, West and Langston Hughes founded *New Challenge*. *Challenge* is archived in DWP. The issues edited by Dorothy West are Mar. and Sept. 1934, May 1935, Jan. and June 1936, and Spring 1937.

66. Robeson diary, Aug. 27 and Nov. 3, 1925; Robeson, "Black Paris," 14.

67. Robeson, "Black Paris," 14.

68. Brenda Dixson Gottschild, *Waltzing in the Dark: African American Vaudeville and Race Politics in the Swing Era* (New York: Palgrave, 2000), 158; Roi Ottley, *No Green Pastures* (New York: Charles Scribner's Sons, 1951), 73. Benglia is sometimes referred to as a Sudanese and sometimes as a Senegalese. This is partly explained by the shifting borders and varied names attached to the French-controlled regions of Central and West Africa. As Patrick Manning writes in *Francophone Sub-Saharan Africa, 1880–1995* (Cambridge: Cambridge University Press, 1998), 4: "The nation known today as Mali was known as French Sudan from 1922 to 1959, as Upper Senegal–Niger from 1900–1922, and by other names in earlier periods." Benglia, then, was from the region of French Soudan (Sudan) and Senegal. But it is important not to confuse "French Sudan" in West Africa with modern-day Sudan in East Africa.

69. See the "filmography" online as well as Bennetta Jules Rosette, *Black Paris: The African Writer's Landscape* (Urbana: University of Illinois Press, 2000), xi.

70. Robeson diary, June 8, 1932. For more on Benglia see Richard Brender, "Reinventing Africa in Their Own Image: The Ballets Suedois' 'Ballet Negre': La Création du Monde," *Dance Chronicle* 9, no. 1 (1986): 119–147; and Rosey E. Pool, "The Negro Actor in Europe," *Phylon* 14, no. 3 (1953): 258–267.

71. Robeson, "Black Paris," 9–15.

72. Brent Hayes Edwards, *The Practice of Diaspora: Literature, Translation, and the Rise of Black Internationalism* (Cambridge, Mass.: Harvard University Press, 2003), 119.

73. Shireen K. Lewis, *Race, Culture and Identity: Francophone West African and Caribbean Literature and Theory from Negritude to Creolite* (Oxford, Eng.: Lexington Books, 2006), 55–70. For more on the Nardal sisters and their role in the complex and multifaceted Black transnational intellectual community in Paris, see Emily Kirkland McTighe Musil, *La Marianne Noire: How Gender and Race in the Twentieth-Century Atlantic World Reshaped the Debate about Human Rights* (Berkeley: University of California Press, 2007).

74. For more biographical and background information, see James Haskins, *Bricktop* (New York: Atheneum Press, 1983).

75. Robeson diary, June 10 and June 13, 1932.

76. Ibid., June 13, 1932.

77. Ibid.

78. Ibid., June 16, 1932.

79. Ibid., June 17, 1932.

80. Ibid., June 18, 1932. Jim Newell is possibly James Michael Newell, the American muralist who was studying in Paris at that time and later returned to the United States to work with the Works Progress Administration's artists program.

81. Ibid., June 3, 1932; Shack, *Harlem in Montmartre*, 157 n.19. A sad epitaph to Essie's Paris trip is that in 1936, the same year that she finally made her first, long-awaited trip to Africa, her old friend, Kojo, having been forced to leave France, died of typhoid fever in a prison in Dakar. Some accounts cite Kojo's year of death as 1938 but the details and circumstances of his death are essentially the same. In *Francophone Sub-Saharan Africa*, Patrick Manning suggests that Kojo's demise was a result, in part, of French government harassment. He was disbarred in 1925, and in 1936 he was jailed for contempt of court in Dahomey, where he eventually "succumbed to typhoid" and died (102). Also see Iheanachor Egonu, "Les Continents and the Francophone Pan-Negro Movement," *Phylon* 42, no. 3 (1981): 245–254.

82. Robeson diary, July 31, 1932. For more on Barnes, see Julius Lewin, "Leonard Barnes: The Man and His Books," *African Affairs* 74, no. 297 (1975): 483–484.

83. Ibid.

84. Robeson diary, July 31, 1932.

85. Eslanda Robeson, *African Journey* (New York: John Day, 1945), 88; as well as "Press Release," Council on African Affairs (CAA), Aug. 31, 1945; and CAA, "Press Release: Robeson" (announcing that Essie has joined the CAA staff), Dec. 27, 1945, both in PERC.

86. Introduction, *Guide to Anna Melissa Graves' Papers*, AMGP. Graves edited or authored numerous essays and pamphlets on anti-racism, anti-imperialism, and various other international issues. In 1942 she wrote *Africa: The Wonder and the Glory*. In addition to her exchanges with Barnes, Graves, and others, Essie seemed eager to talk to anyone about Africa in 1932. She enjoyed a lively conversation on the subject with Virginia Woolf's husband, Leonard, at a London dinner party that same summer. See Robeson diary, Mar. 17, 1932.

87. Robeson diary, May 23 and May 25, 1932.

88. Eslanda Robeson to Paul Robeson, n.d. (Nov. 1931), PERC. Eslanda's application for a Guggenheim Fellowship to travel to Africa is also referenced in this letter.

89. Robeson Jr., *Undiscovered, 1898–1939*, 183.

90. Robeson diary, Aug. 17, 1932.

91. J. A. Rogers, "White Woman Shielded in Robeson Divorce Suit," *Amsterdam News*, Oct. 26, 1932, 1; "English Noblewoman Resents Interracial Scandal Rumors," *Pittsburgh Courier*, July 16, 1932, 1.

92. T. E. B. Clarke, "The Feminist Viewpoint: The Robeson Rift," *Amsterdam News*, Nov. 2, 1932, 4.

93. The reason I question Essie here is that she was profoundly ambivalent about her relationship with Paul. Her "I Believe in Divorce" essay is much more resolute and unambiguous than were her diaries and private correspondence; see "Writings" and "Correspondence," PERC. She also writes to Carl Van Vechten in July of 1932 describing her impending divorce as "evil." See Robeson to Van Vechten, July 13, 1932, CVVP.

94. Robeson, "Divorce." The reason I question whether Essie fully believed what she wrote in the article is because her diary entries belie the essay's main argument. Essie was often angry and hurt by her husband's infidelities in the 1930s, but she eventually made her peace with a reality that she could not totally control.

95. Rogers, "White Woman Shielded," 1.

96. Robeson, "Divorce," 4.

97. Paul Robeson to Eslanda Robeson, Aug. 2, 1932, "Correspondence," PERC.

98. Robeson, "Divorce," 3.

99. Buck and Robeson, *American Argument*, 82.

100. There are two reasons to question the resoluteness of Essie's opposition to monogamy: first, in a 1949 interview she admitted her desire to essentially "snag" a husband in 1921, and second, once her own divorce was averted she wrote much more sympathetically about the institution as a whole.

101. There is a discrepancy between what Essie wrote in her diary that she was receiving in support and what the couple's financial records indicate. A number of bills and expenses were routinely covered by Robert Rockmore on Paul's behalf, in addition to cash that was made available to Essie.

102. Robeson diary, Sept. 16, 1932.

103. Ibid., Dec. 31, 1932; also see Paul Robeson Jr., "The Counterfeit 'Paul Robeson': A Legacy Demeaned," unpublished version in author's possession, courtesy of Paul Robeson Jr., 5; and Duberman, *Paul Robeson*, 163.

104. Robeson biographer Martin Duberman tried to track down Yolande Jackson's whereabouts years later but there was thin evidence of what ultimately became of her. Also see "The Other Woman," by Linda Grant, *The Guardian*, Oct. 6, 2006, which tries to locate Yolande Jackson decades after her relationship with Paul but with little significant results. Grant's short article and radio play about Paul and Yolande's affair give the relationship a kind of Romeo and Juliet quality and offer a one-dimensional portrait of Essie as a "nag" ill-suited for Paul who refused to let him go. This is by no means a fair or accurate representation of Essie or the Robeson marriage.

105. Robeson diary, Sept. 29, 1932, and Oct. 1, 2, and 4, 1932. As a part of a small group Essie had dinner with Duchamp on Sept. 28 and 29. She then spent the afternoon with him on Oct. 1, and they had lunch at La Source café on Oct. 2.

106. Ibid., Dec. 16, 1932, 11. Also see Ted Poston, "Interview with Eslanda Robeson," *Amsterdam News*, Feb. 8, 1933.

107. Essie and Paul Robeson's marital arrangement was not unique in the entertainment industry, including other African American couples like Ossie Davis and Ruby Dee, who had an open marriage for some years in the 1950s, or their white friends, Carl Van Vechten and Fania Marinoff.

108. "Singing in Harmony Again," *Chicago Defender*, national edition, Feb. 11, 1933, 1 (photo headline, no byline).

109. Buck and Robeson, *American Argument*, 96–97.

CHAPTER 5. BECOMING A WRITER AND ANTHROPOLOGIST, 1930s

Epigraph: Eslanda Robeson, *African Journey* (New York: John Day, 1945), 14.

1. Ruth Dudley Edwards, *Victor Gollancz: A Biography* (London: Victor Gollancz, 1987). Gollancz started his publishing company in 1927, and published works by Leonard Woolf and H. G. Wells. *Paul Robeson, Negro* was later reprinted by Harper's.

2. Eslanda Robeson diary, Sept. 1, 1930, PERC.

3. Paul Robeson Jr., *The Undiscovered Paul Robeson: An Artist's Journey, 1898–1939* (New York: John Wiley & Sons, 2001), 173.

4. Eslanda Robeson, *Paul Robeson, Negro* (New York: Harper & Brothers, 1930), 154, 87, 157, 160–162.

5. See Robeson Jr., *Undiscovered, 1898–1939*, 173.

6. Robeson, *Paul*, 47–55, 61, 64–67.

7. Ibid., 171, 52.

8. Langston Hughes, "Ambassador to the World," review of *Paul Robeson, Negro* by Eslanda Robeson, *New York Herald Tribune*, June 29, 1930, 1.

9. Eslanda Robeson to Mr. Crane, Apr. 3, 1932, PERC (in folder "Uncle Tom's Cabin," a play by Eslanda Robeson, Mar. 1932).

10. Eslanda Robeson, "Leave Them Alone," thirty-page script, 1930s, in "Writings by Eslanda Robeson," PERC.

11. A cover letter addressed to Mr. Crane on Apr. 3, 1932, mentions that the publisher cannot have two "Negro" books published at the same time (in folder "Uncle Tom's Cabin," a play by Eslanda Robeson, Mar. 1932, and cover letters Mar.–Apr. 1932).

12. Eslanda Robeson, "1932 Oliver Golden," in "Writings."

13. Robeson diary, Oct. 22, 1931, in "Writings."

14. Ibid., 2.

15. Gerald Horne, *The End of Empires: African Americans and India* (Philadelphia: Temple University Press, 2008), 132, 133, 136, 168.

16. Robeson Jr., *Undiscovered, 1898–1939*, 178. Paul Robeson, "How I Discovered Africa," *Freedom* (June 1953), reprinted in Philip S. Foner, ed., *Paul Robeson Speaks* (New York: Citadel, 1978), 351.

17. See photo and caption (circa 1940) in Susan Robeson, *The Whole World in His Hands: Paul Robeson, a Family Memoir in Words and Pictures* (New York: Citadel Press, 1981), 57.

18. Marc Matera, "Black Internationalism and African and Caribbean Intellectuals in London, 1919–1950," Ph.D. diss., Rutgers University, 2008, 12.

19. In addition to Eslanda Robeson's correspondence and mentions of African friends from London in *African Journey* (New York: John Day, 1945), other scholarship indicates that a coterie of such folks met and mingled in London at this time. See Paul Rich, "The Black Diaspora in Britain," *Immigrants and Minorities* 6, no. 2 (July 1987): 151–173. See Duberman, 171, 198.

20. University of London transcript, Feb. 16, 1943, PERC. The dates of her attendance were 1933 to 1935.

21. Winston James, "The Black Experience in Twentieth-Century Britain," in Philip D. Morgan and Sean Hawkins, eds., *Black Experience and the Empire* (Oxford, Eng.: Oxford University Press, 2004); and Matera, "Black Internationalism."

22. Robeson, *African Journey*, 14–15. On Malinowski, see Dan Stone, "Nazism as Modern Magic: Bronislaw Malinowski's Political Anthropology," *History and Anthropology* (Sept. 2003); and Michael Young, *Malinowski: Odyssey of an Anthropologist, 1884–1920* (New Haven: Yale University Press, 2004).

23. For biographical information on Malinowski and excerpts of the debate about his allegedly racist views, see the following texts and essays: Bronislaw Malinowski, *A Diary in the Strict Sense of the Term*, with introduction by Ray Firth (1967; Stanford, Calif.: Stanford University Press, 1989), xxiv; Young, *Malinowski, Odyssey of an Anthropologist*, xxii; R. F. Ellen et al., eds., *Malinowski between Two Worlds: The Polish Roots of an Anthropological Tradition* (Cambridge: Cambridge University Press, 1988), 151; and review of *A Diary* by Clifford Geertz, *New York Review of Books*, Sept. 14, 1967.

24. Eslanda Goode Robeson to Professor Malinowski, Mar. 8 (no year, but likely 1935 based on the document's content), BMP.

25. "Intercultural and Interracial Relations," speech given Apr. 7, 1944, at Springfield College, PERC. In speech Essie recounts Malinowski's advice.

26. Eslanda Robeson, "The Book I Should Have Written," 1955, 1, PERC. Essie writes that once she had reviewed the diaries and other materials she had collected during her 1936 research trip to Africa, she decided she "could not bury it in a scientific thesis for a few other anthropologists"—so she published the material in her book *African Journey*.

27. Robeson diary, Oct. 26, 1932.

28. Eslanda Robeson to Harold Moody, Mar. 3, 1934, "Correspondence," PERC; also see Anne Spry Rush, "Imperial Identity in Colonial Minds: Harold Moody and the League of Coloured Peoples, 1931–50," *Twentieth Century British History* 13, no. 4 (2002): 356–383.

29. Robin D. G. Kelley, in "Afric's Sons with Banner Red," in Kelley, *Race Rebels: Culture, Politics and the Black Working Class* (New York: Free Press, 1996), articulates the kind of internationalist Pan-Africanism that very much resembled Essie's views.

30. Eslanda Robeson to D. G. Tendulkar, June 17, 1938, and July 15, 1938, in "Correspondence," PERC; and Nico Slate, *Colored Cosmopolitanism: The Shared Struggle for Freedom in the United States and India* (Cambridge, Mass.: Harvard University Press, 2012).

31. Carla Kaplan, *Zora Neale Hurston: A Life in Letters* (New York: Anchor Books, 2003), 5.

32. Zora Neale Hurston to Eslanda Robeson, Apr. 18, 1934, in ibid., 299.

33. Throughout her life and in all other contexts Eslanda was referred to as "Essie." For some reason, either in response to someone else giving her a new nickname, or perhaps her own choice to self-identify differently as a mark of her new intellectual and academic identity, she was called Landa by several friends and professors. African friends like Kenyatta who would later know her in other contexts referred to her as "Essie."

34. See Robeson to Ray Firth, (n.d.), "the more I see you, the more I like you"; Firth to Anna Grimshaw, Sept. 22, 1984 (about her Robeson research); Firth to Richard Ruda, Jan. 20, 1975, all in RFP. Essie's intellectual curiosities were fertile in this period, because she was moving about and seeing the world and talking to all kinds of people about all kinds of things. She noted in one letter to Firth that while in Moscow she had met and had a series of intriguing conversations with the Russian neuropsychologist Alexander Luria about how the mind works. Eslanda to Firth, Jan. 1, 193(5), (a postcard that mentions Luria), RFP.

35. Robeson to Ray Firth, n.d. (circa fall 1935), postcard, RFP.

36. Marie Seton, *Paul Robeson* (London: D. Dobson, 1958), 79–80.

37. Erik S. McDuffie, "A 'New Freedom Movement of Negro Women': Sojourning for Truth, Justice, and Human Rights during the Early Cold War," *Radical History Review* 101 (2008): 2–63.

38. Seton, *Paul Robeson*, 81.

39. Robeson diary, Dec. 21, 1934. Both Paul and Essie had the same reaction; see Robeson Jr., *Undiscovered, 1898–1939*, 218. Also see ibid., 83–84. Seton gives a very similar account and attributes a strikingly similar set of observations to Paul. Seton, *Paul Robeson*, 81–82.

40. In fact, Jews and ethnic minorities in Russia were still suffering under very real persecution and discrimination despite public pronouncements and even certain policy changes to the contrary.

41. David Levering Lewis, *W. E. B. Du Bois: The Fight for Equality and the American Century, 1919–1963* (New York: Henry Holt, 2000), 200–203.

42. Eslanda Robeson to "Carlo Darling and Dearest Fania" (Carl Van Vechten and Fania Marinoff), Jan. 6, 1935, CVVP.

43. See Chatwood Hall, "Paul Robeson's Kin Is Famous Wrestler," *Chicago Defender*, July 20, 1935, 13, xi; Francis Cardozo Goode's U.S. Military Registration Card, dated June 5, 1917, U.S. National Archives and Records, College Park, Md., available online at www.archives.gov/research/alic/reference/military/ww1.html (last accessed May 22, 2012); and the dates of Essie's brother's arrival noted in Eslanda Robeson to "Carlo" (Van Vechten), Jan. 6, 1935, CVVP.

44. There is additional information about Goode in Homer Smith, *Black Man in Red Russia* (Chicago: Johnson Publishers, 1964), 197–210.

45. Frank Goode to Eslanda Robeson, n.d. (Oct. 1957), in "Correspondence, Goode, John and Frank," box 6, PERC.

46. Allan Keiler, *Marian Anderson: A Singer's Journey* (Urbana: University of Illinois Press, 2002), 72, 80, 144; and Raymond Arsenault, *The Sound of Freedom:*

Marian Anderson, the Lincoln Memorial and the Concert That Awakened America (London: Bloomsbury, 2010), 41, 107. The ongoing friendship between the two women is documented in numerous primary sources, including "Mass Meeting for Famine Relief in South Africa," n.d., CAA Emergency Appeal for South Africa Press Release, CAA, Max Yergan Papers. Kautz family YMCA Archives. University of Minnesota.

47. Robeson Jr., *Undiscovered, 1898–1939*, 219.

48. Ibid., 220.

49. Robeson to Van Vechten, Jan. 6, 1935.

50. Eslanda Robeson to "Mama dear" (Eslanda Goode), Jan. 20, 1935, PERC.

51. Robeson to Walter White, Nov. 24, 1935, box C-107, NAACP.

52. Robeson to Van Vechten, Nov. 21, 1935, CVVP; Robeson postcard to Ray Firth, n.d. (circa fall 1935), RFP.

53. Jerry Gershenhorn, *Melville J. Herskovits and the Racial Politics of Knowledge* (Lincoln: University of Nebraska, 2004), 31-32.

54. Ibid., 129.

55. Ibid., 161–167.

56. Charlene B. Regester, *African American Actresses: The Struggle for Visibility, 1900–1960* (Bloomington: University of Indiana Press, 2010), 40-43.

57. Robeson (signed "Chile") to Goode, Jan. 20, 1935, in "Correspondence," PERC.

58. Marcus Garvey, "Paul Robeson and His Mission," reprinted in Robert A. Hill, ed., *The Marcus Garvey and Universal Negro Improvement Association Papers*, vol. 7 (Berkeley: University of California Press, 1983), 730; Robeson Jr., *Undiscovered*, 224–225.

59. Robeson, *African Journey*, 48.

60. Mary G. Mason, "Travel as Metaphor and Reality in Afro-American Women's Autobiography, 1850–1972," *Black American Literature Forum* 24, no. 2 (Summer 1990): 337-356.

61. Robeson, *African Journey*, 20.

62. Robeson Jr., *Undiscovered, 1898–1939*, 233.

63. Robeson to Goode, Jan. 20, 1935; Mar. 29, 1935; and May 6, 1935, all in "Correspondence," PERC.

64. Robeson Jr., *Undiscovered, 1898–1939*, 232.

65. In ibid., Paul Robeson Jr. suggests that his father "proposed that Essie should go" to South Africa and East Africa in 1936 once he realized that he could not easily accept an invitation to do the same, and despite his desire to go. Essie's trip may have been a convergence of an opportunity offered by Paul and her own longstanding desire. Independently of Paul, for nearly four years she had plotted and strategized on how to go to sub-Saharan Africa.

66. Robeson, *African Journey*, 17.

67. Ibid., 18.

68. Ibid., 19.

69. J. D. Rheinallt Jones to Eslanda Robeson, June 12, 1936, PERC.

70. See Harold G. Marcus, *A History of Ethiopia* (Berkeley: University of California Press, 1994).

CHAPTER 6. AFRICA AT LAST, 1936

1. Robeson, *African Journey* (New York: John Day, 1945), 18–20.
2. Eslanda Robeson to Carl Van Vechten and Fania Marinoff, June 6, 1936 (postcard), CVVP.
3. Robeson, *African Journey*, 28.
4. Ibid., 24.
5. Ibid., 25.
6. Ibid., 30.
7. Ibid., 28.
8. Ibid., 31.
9. Ibid., 32–33.
10. "Colour Bar Abroad: Question Discussed by Mrs. Robeson, Research Visit to Africa—'Mistake to Ape Europeans,'" *The Cape Times*, PERC.
11. Jean Le Fontaine, "Professor Isaac Schapera: Anthropologist and Champion of the Tswana," *Independent* (Eng.), July 7, 2003, obituary. Malinowski may have provided Essie with Schapera's contact information before her departure, since this is the one person she and Schapera seemingly had in common.
12. Phone conversation by the author with Gow's niece, Charlene W. Coleman, Apr. 11, 2010. Also, see *Songs of Zion* by James T. Campbell (Oxford University Press, 1998), 255.
13. Robeson, *African Journey*, 35.
14. Ibid., 41.
15. Ibid., 39.
16. Ibid., 38.
17. Ibid., 37.
18. Ibid.
19. Ibid., 38.
20. Ibid.
21. Ibid., 39.
22. Ibid., 72.
23. "Colour Bar Abroad."
24. Robeson, *African Journey*, 41.
25. Ibid., 42.
26. Ibid., 41–42. Essie does not specify, but we can assume by the detailed description of the conversation with the "nursemaid" that they spoke directly to one another in English, although English was not likely this person's first language.
27. Ibid., 17.
28. See Sept. 1954 interview with Z. K. Matthews by George Houser available online at the African Activist Archive Project, http://africanactivist.msu.edu (last accessed May 14, 2012); Tim J. Juckes, *Opposition in South Africa: The Leadership of Z. K. Matthews, Nelson Mandela, and Stephen Biko* (Westport, Conn.: Praeger, 1995).
29. Eslanda Robeson to Paul Robeson, June 21, 1936, PERC.
30. For more on Yergan, see David H. Anthony III, *Max Yergan: Race Man, Internationalist, Cold Warrior* (New York: New York University Press, 2006); also see MYP. Essie's quote about liking Yergan "on sight" is in Robeson, *African Journey*, 42.

31. Anthony, *Max Yergan*, 1, 50, 160, 161–163, 228–232.

32. Robeson, *African Journey*, 43.

33. Ibid., 47.

34. Ibid., 42, 44–45.

35. Ibid., 49. Most common spelling is "Ntselamanzi."

36. Ibid., 50.

37. For a short biography of Moroka, see L. R. Olivier and J. R. Kriel, "A Job Well Done: A Short History of Dr. James Moroka," *South Africa Medical Journal* 54 (Aug. 19, 1978): 331.

38. Robeson to Van Vechten and Marinoff, July 19, 1936, CVVP.

39. Robeson, *African Journey*, 51–52.

40. Ibid., 54.

41. Ibid., 56–58.

42. Ibid., 65.

43. Ibid.

44. Ibid.

45. Steven Gish, *Alfred B. Xuma: African American, South African* (New York: New York University Press, 2002), 82.

46. Robeson, *African Journey*, 77. Also see V. L. Allen. *The History of Black Mineworkers in South Africa* (London: Merlin Press, 2005); and Jonathan Crush, "Power and Surveillance on the South African Gold Mines," *Journal of Southern African Studies* 18, no. 4 (Dec. 1992).

47. Robeson, *African Journey*.

48. Eslanda Robeson to Paul Robeson Sr., June 21, 1936, in "Correspondence," PERC.

49. Robeson, *African Journey*, 61.

50. Ibid., 81.

51. Ibid., 82.

52. Ibid., 84–85.

53. Ibid., 84.

54. Eslanda to Paul, June 21, 1936 in "Correspondence," PERC.

55. Eslanda met Akiki Nyabongo in England "when he was studying anthropology at Oxford" (Robeson, *African Journey*, 89). Nyabongo would publish his own book on Africa in 1936 entitled *Africa Answers Back* (London: Routledge, 1936). He went on to study at Yale University and to teach in the United States. For more, see Tobias Doring, "The Fissures of Fusion: Akiki Nyabongo's 'Africa Answers Back' (1936) and What It May Teach Us," in Peter O. Stummer and Christopher Balme, eds., *Fusion of Cultures?* (Amsterdam: Rodopi Press, 1996), 140–154. Nyabongo's *Africa Answers Back* is one of the important early works on Uganda written by someone from the region.

56. Robeson, *African Journey*, 88.

57. Ibid., 89–90.

58. Ibid., 91.

59. Ibid.

60. Ibid.

61. Ibid., 89.

62. Nyabongo, *Africa Answers Back*; and Doring, "The Fissures of Fusion," 141n.

63. In this movement, Nyabongo was a "spirit" that guided followers of a woman named Muhumusa into anti-colonial resistance. After Muhumusa led a series of military skirmishes, she was jailed by the British for decades.

64. Terisa E. Turner and Bryan J. Ferguson, *Arise Ye Mighty People! Gender, Class and Race in Popular Struggles* (Trenton, N.J.: Africa World Press, 1994), 22–24; A. D. Roberts, "The Sub-Imperialism of the Baganda," *International Journal of African Historical Studies* 3 (1962): 435–458; and Murindwa Rutanga, "Nyabingi Movement: People's Anti-Colonial Struggles in Kigezi, 1910-1930," working paper no. 18 (Dakar, Senegal: Council for the Development of Social Science Research in Africa, 1991); T. O. Ranger, "The Connexions between 'Primary Resistance' Movements and Modern Mass Nationalism in East and Central Asia," *Journal of African History* 9, no. 4 (1968): 631-641.

65. Robeson, *African Journey*, 89, 93–94.

66. Ibid., 95–96.

67. Ibid., 103, 105, 106.

68. Kenneth Ingham, *The Kingdom of Toro in Uganda* (Suffolk, Eng.: Methuen, 1975), 1. The Kingdom of Toro had a tumultuous history. It was set up, dissolved, reestablished in the 1800s, abolished again by the independent Ugandan government in the 1960s and then reestablished in 1993.

69. Ibid., 1, 59, 137.

70. These Ugandan and Toro historical facts were derived from multiple overlapping sources, including Jan J. Jorgensen, *Uganda: A Modern History* (London: Croom Helm, 1981); Aili Mari Tripp et al., *The Women's Movement in Uganda: History, Challenges, and Prospects* (Kampala, Uganda: Fountain Publishers, 2002); Arthur Syahuku-Muhindo, "The Rwenzururu Movement and the Democratic Struggle," in M. Mamdani and J. Oloka-Onyango, eds., *Uganda: Studies in Living Conditions, Popular Movements and Constitutionalism* (Vienna: JEP Book Series, 1994), 273-317; and ibid.

71. Robeson, *African Journey*, 101; and Ingham, *Kingdom of Toro*.

72. Melvin L. Perlman, "The Changing Status and Role of Women in Toro (Western Uganda)," *Cahiers d'études Africaines* 6, no. 24 (1966): 564-591 (translated into English in the Persee Scientific Journals database).

73. Robeson, *African Journey*, 108–109.

74. Ibid., 109.

75. Ibid., 103.

76. Ibid., 110–111.

77. Ibid., 107–108.

78. Ibid., 92, 95.

79. Robeson to Carl Van Vechten and Fania Marinoff, July 19, 1936, CVVP.

80. Robeson, *African Journey*, 113, 117.

81. Ibid., 120.

82. Ibid., 121-122. "Pygmy" is a pejorative term. The echnic group Essie encountered were most likely the BaAka or Mbuti people. See, Michelle Robin Kisliuk, *Seize the Dance!: BaAka Musical Life and the Ethnography of Performance* (New York: Oxford University Press, 1998), 6.

83. Ibid., 136.

84. Ibid., 130.

85. Ibid., 128–129.

86. Ibid., 138.

87. Ibid., 139.

88. Robeson to Carl Van Vechten and Fania Marinoff, July 4, 1936, from Johannesburg, South Africa, in "Correspondence," PERC.

89. Eslanda Robeson, "Proud to Be a Negro" (an article describing her departure from Uganda), *Asia and the Americas*, n.d., 108, PERC. (Note: there are several versions of this article with the same general information but slightly differing details.)

90. Robeson, *African Journey*, 147.

91. Ibid., 145–146.

92. Ibid., 150–151.

93. Ibid., 151–152.

94. Eslanda Goode Robeson, "Is Black a Handicap?" *Negro Digest*, Feb. 1945.

95. *Woman's Day* magazine article, n.d. (around Aug.–Sept. 1936), in "Writings," PERC.

CHAPTER 7. MADRID TO MOSCOW, POLITICAL COMMITMENTS DEEPEN, 1936–1939

1. See Kate A. Baldwin, *Beyond the Color Line and the Iron Curtain: Reading Encounters in Black and Red, 1922–1963* (Durham, N.C.: Duke University Press, 2002); David C. Engerman, *Modernization from the Other Shore: American Intellectuals and the Romance of Russian Development* (Cambridge, Mass.: Harvard University Press, 2003); and Homer Smith, *Black Man in Red Russia* (Chicago: Johnson Publishing, 1964). From the 1920s on, there was an ideological divide on the left (in the world and in the United States) between communists and socialists. Simply put, communists sought the ultimate goal of a "classless" and "stateless" egalitarian society, which would be brought about through social revolution—although the terms, means, and conditions under which such revolution(s) would come about was hotly debated. Socialists, by contrast, saw the necessity of a state and worked within apparatuses of the state in various contexts to create better conditions for poor and working-class people and to oppose capitalist practices. Another layer of complication is this. While communists had the long-term goal of a society without class exploitation, most saw a socialist society with a strong pro-worker state as a necessary phase in the move toward communism. This simplified definition is offered to minimize confusion about the reference to communist-led societies as socialist given that many socialist parties were at odds with communists. The Robesons leaned toward the communists in their ideological disposition.

2. Eslanda Robeson to Carl Van Vechten and Fania Marinoff, Jan. 6, 1935, CVVP; also see Sidney and Beatrice Webb, *Soviet Communism: A New Civilization?* (New York: Scribner, 1936; reprinted and digitized, University of California Press, 2009).

3. Paul Robeson, "How I Discovered Africa," *Freedom* (June 1953), reprinted in Philip S. Foner, ed., *Paul Robeson Speaks* (New York: Citadel, 1978), 351.

4. John Cardozo Goode, Military Registration Card dated June 5, 1917, available

online at www.ancestry.com, *World War 1 Draft Registration Cards, 1917–1918* (Provo, Utah: Ancestry.com Operations Inc., 2005).

5. John Goode to Eslanda Robeson, Sept. 3 and Sept. 15, 1935, Cardozo Family Correspondence, PERC.

6. Paul Robeson Jr., *The Undiscovered Paul Robeson: An Artist's Journey, 1898–1939* (New York: John Wiley & Sons, 2001), 218–222. Soon after John Goode's departure in 1937 the Soviet police issued a warrant for his arrest. The charges were unclear but his name was apparently given to the authorities by an acquaintance who was eager to save himself yet was later executed. Joseph Stalin's purges from 1936 to 1938 were widespread and ruthless. For whatever reason, after his return to the United States, John Goode chose not to criticize the Soviet Union publicly, underscoring in a newspaper article that he encountered "no hint or sign of racial or color prejudice against any race or nationality" while living there and that he had returned home mainly to pursue his education.

7. Ibid., 280.

8. Esther Cooper Jackson, telephone interview with the author, Nov. 30, 2011.

9. Robeson Jr., *Undiscovered, 1898–1939*, 280.

10. Eslanda Robeson to Carl Van Vechten, Feb. 9, 1937, postcard, PRC and CVVP; Robeson Jr., *Undiscovered, 1898–1939*, 281–283.

11. Eslanda Robeson, postcards to and from Carl Van Vechten, Feb. 9, 1937, CVVP.

12. Stephen Bourne, *Black in the British Frame: The Black Experience in British Film and Television* (London: Continuum International, 2005), 23. *Big Fella*. DVD. Directed by J. Elder Wills (1939; Beaconsfield, Buckinghamshire, England: Kino Video, 2000).

13. George Orwell, *Farewell to Catalonia*, with introduction by Lionel Trilling (1938; New York: Harcourt Brace Jovanovich, 1952), v.

14. Robin D. G. Kelley, "'This Ain't Ethiopia, But It'll Do': African-Americans and the Spanish Civil War," in *Race Rebels: Culture, Politics and the Black Working Class* (New York: Free Press, 1996), 132–133.

15. Ibid., 157.

16. "Robeson Relative in Aid Spain Drive," *The Chicago Defender*, Oct. 8, 1938.

17. Robeson Jr., *Undiscovered, 1898–1939*, 243.

18. Ibid., 283.

19. For more on the Spanish Civil War, see: Alvah Bessie and Alberto Prago, *Our Fight: Writings by Veterans of the Abraham Lincoln Brigade, Spain 1936–1939* (New York: Monthly Review Press, 1985); Robert Rosenstone, *Crusade of the Left: The Lincoln Battalion in the Spanish Civil War* (New York: Pegasus, 1969); and Burnett Bolloten, *The Spanish Civil War: Revolution and Counter-Revolution* (Chapel Hill: University of North Carolina Press, 1990).

20. Eslanda Robeson, "We Go to Spain," 1937, 1, in "Writings by Eslanda Robeson," PERC. For more on Blacks and the Spanish Civil War see Danny Duncan Callum, ed., *African Americans in the Spanish Civil War: This Ain't Ethiopia But It'll Do* (New York: Macmillan, 1992); Kelley, "'This Ain't Ethiopia,'" and Robert Rosenstone, *Crusade of the Left: The Lincoln Battalion in the Spanish Civil War* (New Brunswick, N.J.: Transaction Press, 2009).

21. Robeson, "We Go to Spain," 1.

22. See Judith Adamson, *Charlotte Haldane: Woman Writer in a Man's World* (Basingstoke, Eng.: Macmillan, 1998), 119; Charlotte Haldane, *Truth Will Out* (New York: Vanguard, 1950).

23. Ronald Clark, *J. B. S.: The Life and Work of J. B. S. Haldane* (Oxford, Eng.: Oxford University Press, 1968).

24. Regarding Charlotte Haldane's divorce and affair, and J. B. S. Haldane's troubles at Cambridge, see Adamson, *Charlotte Haldane*, 47–49.

25. Ibid., 135.

26. Under Haldane's editorship, the left-wing feminist journal *Woman Today* did a profile on Essie in 1939 that briefly highlighted her trip to Spain. See "Intimate Interviews," *Woman Today* (London), 1939, a copy of which is in Robeson, "Writings."

27. Robeson Jr., *Undiscovered, 1898–1939*, 321. Eslanda Robeson, untitled speech on Spanish Civil War, Jan. 1947, folder 416, 5, PRAB.

28. Robeson, "We Go to Spain," 6.

29. Ibid., 37.

30. Ibid., 29.

31. Eslanda Robeson diary, "Trip to Spain," Jan. 27, 1938, TAM.

32. Ibid., 37, 40–41.

33. Ibid., 43.

34. Ibid., 49.

35. Ibid., 55.

36. Kelley, "'This Ain't Ethiopia, But It'll Do,'" 150.

37. Robeson, "We Go to Spain," 16, 18, 46, 68; Robeson, *Here I Stand*, 61.

38. Eslanda Robeson diary, Feb. 1939 (n.d.), PERC.

39. Eslanda Robeson to Emma Goldman, Nov. 24, 1935, in EGA.

40. Emma Goldman to Eslanda Robeson, Dec. 16, 1935, EGA.

41. Emma Goldman to Paul Robeson, Jan. 17, 1938, EGA.

42. Marie Seton, *Paul Robeson* (London: D. Dobson, 1958), 85.

43. Based on conversations with his father years later (his parents would not discuss Kazakov's execution or the purge trials with the adolescent when they occurred), Paul Robeson Jr. describes a lunch meeting between his father and his old friend Kazakov at a Moscow hotel in August 1937. Paul was worried about Kazakov, according to Paul Jr., after having been told by a mutual friend that Kazakov had been arrested. Paul reached out to his friend, perhaps in the hopes of finding out what was going on or to offer his support in some way. It was unusual that when he came to lunch with Paul, Kazakov was accompanied by "translators," who, as Paul told Paul Jr., Paul suspected were actually undercover police. Paul never saw Kazakov again.

44. Eslanda Robeson to "My dear Pat" (William Patterson), Apr. 4, 1938, reel 1, PRC. Details about Kazakov are available in Hans Schoots, *Living Dangerously: A Biography of Joris Ivens* (Amsterdam: Amsterdam University Press, 2000), 98; and Yakov Rapoport, *The Doctor's Plot of 1953* (Cambridge, Mass.: Harvard University Press, 1991), 28–29.

45. Robeson Jr., *Undiscovered, 1898–1939*, 306.

46. We can only speculate about how much Paul and Essie knew about what was going on in the Soviet Union at the time, and how they gauged their response

based on that knowledge. It is likely that their reaction was a complex combination of fear and faith. They were surprised by Kazakov's execution. They were undoubtedly fearful of what would come next. But we don't fully know the tangled web of relationships, conversations, confidences, and political debates that may have played out behind the scenes. Even if there were sharp disagreements in pro-Soviet circles, the mistrust of Western media, the rising threat of fascism, and the fear that any public criticisms of the Soviet Union or certain Soviet leaders would be used to indict the whole enterprise of socialism and communism may have inhibited the Robesons from speaking out publicly against the Soviet Union in the 1930s or later. We should not conclude from this that there were not serious private conversations and debates. Still, although they did not sever ties with the Kremlin during the purges, they also continued to ally themselves with the Soviet Union after Khrushchev denounced Stalin's practices in 1956. As a ten-year-old, Paul Jr. remembers his own frustration with his parent's public silence, and at one point screamed at his father that he had known Kazakov was innocent and had said nothing (ibid., 293–306). Adding another layer to the mystery is the third-hand account of the granddaughter of the Black American expatriate Oliver Golden, who recalls her mother, Lily Golden, telling her that she overheard her grandfather and Paul Robeson in an animated discussion in the summer of 1937 in Kislovodsk and she (Lily) learned later that it was about mutual friends who had vanished, presumably victims of the purges. See Yelena Khanga with Susan Jacoby, *Soul to Soul: The Story of a Black Russian American Family, 1865–1992* (New York: Norton, 1992), 89.

47. Eslanda Robeson diary, n.d. (Sept. 1939), PERC.
48. Robeson Jr., *Undiscovered, 1898–1939*, 331.
49. There were various camps or tendencies among the opponents of capitalism in the 1930s. Some located themselves in the socialist camp and others defined themselves as communists, and even both of those camps were divided, with vehemently different ideas and theories about how to reform or overthrow capitalism. While Essie Robeson used the term socialism at times to describe the economic policies to which she subscribed, in the partisan world of left politics, she moved more in communist circles than in socialist ones. Also, the term feminist is not one that Essie Robeson used. In fact in one speech, she specifically says she is not a feminist but then goes on to spell out her own characteristics and beliefs, which one would likely ascribe to a feminist. So here I take the liberty to describe her conditionally as part of a feminist tradition based on her consistent actions as a woman's rights advocate for many years.

CHAPTER 8. RETURNING HOME AND
FINDING A NEW VOICE, 1939–1945

1. Eslanda Robeson to "Carlo, Dear" (Carl Van Vechten), Nov. 7, 1940, CVVP. For a short time after the Robesons moved to Edgecomb Ave. Paul Jr. stayed in a separate apartment with his grandmother.
2. T. E. B. Clarke, "Chatter and Chimes," *New York Amsterdam News*, Oct. 21, 1939, 16.
3. Paul Robeson Jr., *The Undiscovered Paul Robeson: Quest for Freedom, 1939–1976*

(Hoboken, N.J.: Wiley, 2010), 9, 13, 20, 27; also Eslanda's correspondence in PERC.

4. T. E. B. Clarke, "Chatter and Chimes," *New York Amsterdam News*, June 19, 1941, and Sept. 27, 1941.

5. Marie Seton discusses this in her book *Paul Robeson* (London: D. Dodson, 1958).

6. *Chicago Defender*, Aug. 3, 1940, n.p. (regarding Grant Park rally in Chicago).

7. Paul Robeson Jr., *Undiscovered, 1939–1976*, 29.

8. Eslanda Robeson to Jawarhalal Nehru, Apr. 10, 1940, in folder 436, "Nehru letters," 1938 to 1940, PRAB.

9. FBI files, Robeson, 100-14994, p. 79 (robes 1a), available online at http://vault .fbi.gov/Paul Robeson, Sr. (last accessed May 14, 2012).

10. Eslanda Robeson to "Dearest Carlo" (Carl Van Vechten) and "Fania" (Fania Marinoff), Aug. 30, 1940, postcard, CVVP.

11. Eslanda Robeson, "Central America Diary 1940," Eslanda Robeson Papers, "Writings by Eslanda Robeson," box 17, PERC.

12. Eslanda Robeson to Carl Van Vechten and Fania Marinoff, Nov. 17, 1941, CVVP. Biographical information on Ira Reid taken from Henry Louis Gates and Evelyn Brooks Higginbotham, *African American Lives* (Oxford, Eng.: Oxford University Press, 2004), 705.

13. FBI Files, Robeson, New Haven Files, 100-8032, Dec. 18, 1943, p. 69, copied to FBI HQ under file 100-12304, section 1, available online at http://vault.fbi .gov/Paul Robeson, Sr (last accessed May 14, 2012).

14. See Robeson Jr., *Undiscovered, 1939–1976*, regarding Enfield high school (120) and for a photo of him in his Springfield school uniform (325).

15. Paul Robeson Jr., interview by author, April 3, 2009.

16. Lillian Smith to "Dear Vandi" (Haygood), Sept. 6, 1943, in Margaret Rose Gladley, ed., *How Am I to Be Heard? Letters of Lillian Smith* (Chapel Hill: University of North Carolina Press, 1996), 75–76; and Lynne Olson, *Freedom's Daughters: The Unsung Heroines of the Civil Rights Movement from 1830 to 1970* (Chapel Hill: University of North Carolina Press, 2001), 66.

17. Penny M. Von Eschen, *Race against Empire: Black Americans and Anti-Colonialism, 1937–1957* (Ithaca, N.Y.: Cornell University Press, 1997), 70.

18. Gerald Horne, *The End of Empires: African Americans and India* (Philadelphia: Temple University Press, 2008), 169.

19. Hollis R. Lynch, *Black American Radicals and the Liberation of Africa: The Council on African Affairs, 1937–1955* (Ithaca, N.Y.: Africana Studies and Research Center, Cornell University, 1978), 25; and Minutes of Council on African Affairs (CAA) meetings, 1943, EFFP.

20. Lynch, *Black American Radicals*. Essie's relationship with Bunche is marked by their exchange of letters, her loan of a camera for his trip to Africa, and her time with him and his family when all were visiting Paris in 1932.

21. Mary Church Terrell to Paul Robeson, Feb. 16, 1947; and "CAA Conference Proceedings," 1944, Paul Robeson Collection, Organizations and Itineraries, box 39, series J, both in PERC.

22. Von Eschen, *Race against Empire*, 18–19, 60–61.

23. FBI Records, FOIA files, Paul and Eslanda Robeson, 1942–1950, copy in author's possession.

24. Von Eschen, *Race against Empire.*

25. Eslanda Robeson, "What Do the People of Africa Want?" (New York: Council on African Affairs, 1945); *Amsterdam News,* May 5, 1945.

26. See Vijay Prashad, *Darker Nations: A People's History of the Third World* (New York: New Press, 2008); Robeson, "Editorial," *New Africa,* n.d. (Aug. 1946), 30.

27. Photo of Eslanda Robeson being greeted by Charlotta Bass and other women after her arrival, Charlotta Bass Collection, Southern California Library for Social Studies and Research, Los Angeles.

28. Robeson, "UN Founding in San Francisco," in "Writings," PERC.

29. Robeson, "Unofficial America Goes to the Conference," in "Writings," PERC.

30. Robeson, "UN Founding."

31. Eslanda Robeson, "Women at the Conference," n.d., box 9, 5 (she is writing about the 1945 UN founding conference), PERC.

32. Pearl S. Buck and Eslanda Robeson, *American Argument* (New York: John Wiley & Sons, 2001), 99–101.

33. Robeson, "Women at the Conference," 14. See also Hilkka Pietila, *The Unfinished Story of Women and the United Nations* (New York: United Nations Press, 2007).

34. "Mrs. Paul Robeson Talks on Charter," *Amsterdam News,* July 4, 1945, A8.

35. Robeson, "What Do the People of Africa Want?" 8–9. Note Eslanda published this pamphlet under the name "Mrs. Paul Robeson." It is unclear if she opted for this title or if Max Yergan, then executive director of the Council on African Affairs (the publisher), advised it in order to garner more public attention for the publication (since Paul's name carried more cachet than hers).

36. Ibid., 11.

37. Ibid., 19.

38. Ibid., 23.

39. "News Release," Aug. 31, 1945, Council on African Affairs files, PERC. She joined the staff in 1945.

40. Tarika Powell, "Conference Honors Mozambique Liberator," *Oberlin Review* 127, no. 6 (Oct. 9, 1998).

41. Darrell Randall and Mildred Randall, "Africa Letter" to "Dear Friends," Nov. 1948, in "Correspondence," PERC. This is one of a series of letters titled "Africa Letter."

42. Randall and Randall, "Africa Letter," Aug. 1949, in "Correspondence," PERC.

43. Randall and Randall, "Africa Letter," Nov. 1948, in "Correspondence," PERC.

44. Randall and Randall, "Africa Letter," Aug. 1949, after having arrived in the United States and becoming based in New York.

45. "Dear Friends" letter from Ruth Longstaff, Ganta, Liberia, Apr. 28, 1947, which included a June 24, 1946, newsletter from Ganta, Liberia; also letter dated Oct. 11, 1946, to "Dear Mrs. Robeson" from "Richard and Edith Scotti" Gombari, Congo; "Dear Friends" letter from Bishop Newell Snow Booth, Elisabethville Area, Congo Belge, Nov. 25, 1946; Letter Sept. 4, 1946 to "Dear Mrs. Robeson" from "Omar and Eva"; "Dear Friends" letter from "Hattie and Gertrude" from Mondombe, Congo Belge, Feb. 27, 1947; "Dear Friends" letter dated Nov. 1948 from Johannesburg, and from the Randalls; May 10, 1946 personal, handwritten letter from Eva Hartzler, wife of Rev. Omar Lee Hartzler (his name on letterhead) from the evangelical mission in Malange, Angola;

another letter from the Hartzlers (typed) dated May 12, 1948; "Dear Friends" letter dated May 10, 1948 from Lavinia Scott at Inanda Seminary, Phoenix, Natal, South Africa. All in "Congo notes," located in "Writings," PERC.

46. *New York Times*, June 7, 1946; *New Africa*, Dec. 1946; and Lynch, *Black American Radicals*, 33.

47. Steven Gish, *Alfred B. Xuma: African, American, South African* (New York: New York University Press, 2000); and Richard D. Ralston, "American Episodes in the Making of an African Leader: A Case Study of Alfred B. Xuma (1893–1962)," *International Journal of African Historical Studies* 6, no. 1 (1973).

48. Eslanda Robeson, *African Journey* (New York: John Day, 1945), but also see Iris Berger, "An African American 'Mother of the Nation': Madie Hall Xuma in South Africa, 1940-1963," *Journal of Southern African Affairs* (Sept. 2001).

49. Gish, *Alfred B. Xuma*, 82, mentions Essie's speech and how it must have impressed Xuma. See also Arnold Benjamin, "Africa's Eccentric Loner," *(Banda) Star*, Nov. 10, 1993.

50. A. B. Xuma to Eslanda and Paul Robeson, May 21, 1937, Correspondence files, ABX. The letter proposed a visit to the Robesons in London as part of a trip that Xuma planned to make to the United States in June 1937.

51. Eslanda Robeson, "Town Hall" speech, n.d. (1946), folder 40, PERC.

52. "1000 Hear Mrs. Paul Robeson Speak In Akron on Negro in World Affairs," *Call and Post*, Feb. 14, 1946, 13.

53. Eslanda Robeson, "Missionary Personnel in Africa," in "Writings," folder 42, box 10, PERC.

54. Dr. Charles G. Chakerian to Eslanda Robeson, in box 2: Eslanda Robeson Personal Papers, "Awards and Tributes, Memorabilia," folder "Examination on subjects, Hartford Seminary foundation, 1944," PERC.

55. Hartford Seminary did not have an official record of Essie's Ph.D. completion, but a draft of her thesis is in "Writings," PERC.

56. I have refrained from further describing the book, since it so closely corresponds to her 1936 diaries and has been cited extensively in an earlier chapter that recounts the trip itself.

57. Herman Shumlin to Essie Robeson, Oct. 5, 1944; Essie to Shumlin, Oct. 16, 1944, both in "Correspondence," PERC.

58. See box 2: Eslanda Robeson Personal Papers, "Awards and Tributes, Memorabilia," folder "Program, 1946," PERC.

59. Maureen Mahon, "Eslanda Goode Robeson's African Journey: The Politics of Identification and Representation in the African Diaspora," in M. Marable and V. Agard-Jones, eds., *Transnational Blackness: Navigating the Global Color Line* (New York: Palgrave Macmillan, 2008), 120. K. Gough, "Anthropology Is the Child of Imperialism," *Monthly Review* 19, no. 11 (1968); Wendy James, "The Anthropologist as Reluctant Imperialist," in Talal Asad, ed., *Anthropology and the Colonial Encounter* (New York: Humanities Press, 1973); and James R. Hooker, "The Anthropologists' Frontier: The Last Phase of African Exploitation," *Journal of Modern African Studies* 1, no. 4 (1963); J. Stauder, "The Relevance of Anthropology to Colonialism and Imperialism," *Race* 16 (July 1974).

60. See George P. Potamianos, "Visions of a Dying Africa: Ralph Bunche and His Second African Journey, 1936-1938," *Journal of Black Studies* 26, no. 4

(Mar. 1996): 447–466; Correspondence file, RBP; Gerald Horne, *Mau Mau in Harlem: The U.S. and the Liberation of Kenya* (New York: Palgrave Macmillan, 2009); Brian Urquhart, *Ralph Bunche: An American Life* (New York: W.W. Norton, 1993), 67, 74. In the mid-1930s Bunche felt a rapport with the Robesons, was curious about the Soviet Union because of them, and was eager to see the African vistas that Essie had told him about. During his time in London in 1937, Bunche and his family spent time with Essie and Paul and with the cadre of young African students whom they all knew, including Kenyatta. By 1949 he had deemed Paul (and by extension Essie) "radically wrong" in their political views (100).

61. E. Franklin Frazier to Eslanda Robeson, Oct. 15, 1946, in "Correspondence," PERC.

62. Prince A. A. Nwafor Orizu, "Africa Speaks," Aug. 25, 1945, published in 1990 as a book by the same name by Horizontal Publishers, Anambra State, Nigeria.

63. Robeson, *African Journey*, dedication page.

64. Hartford Seminary Foundation was able to verify that Eslanda Robeson (she is listed as Mrs. Paul Robeson on some class lists) was a Ph.D. candidate there but it could not verify that she obtained her degree. Transcript records indicate she was a candidate in 1943, 1944, and 1945.

65. Council on African Affairs, "News Release," Aug. 31, 1945, CAA files, PERC.

66. Eslanda Robeson to Marian Forsythe, Apr. 4, 1945, in "Correspondence," PERC.

67. Robeson Jr., *Undiscovered, 1939–1976*, 214–215; Paul Robeson to Eslanda Robeson, n.d. (Aug. 1943), in "Correspondence," PERC.

68. Robeson Jr., *Undiscovered, 1939–1976*, 218–219; Eslanda Robeson to Paul Robeson, Sept. 20, 1943, in "Correspondence," PERC.

69. Eslanda Robeson to Paul Robeson, Dec. 1, 1946, in "Correspondence," PERC. Also see Robeson's letters to Carl Van Vechten, July 15, Aug. 12, Sept. 9, and Nov. 14, 1943, CVVP. Also, see Duberman, 291–292.

70. Eslanda Robeson to Lawrence Brown, Aug. 14, 1945, LBP. In this letter, Essie tells Larry of the letter sent to Paul.

CHAPTER 9. INTO THE CONGO, 1946

1. Beatrice E. Penman, Grand President of Deltas (Kansas City), to Eslanda Robeson, May 13, 1946, in "Correspondence," PERC.

2. Eslanda Robeson, "Airborne," May 25, 1946, in "Writings of Eslanda Robeson," PERC.

3. Ibid., 60.

4. Ibid., 8.

5. Ibid., 9.

6. Adam Hochschild, *King Leopold's Ghosts: A Story of Greed, Terror and Heroism in Colonial Africa* (Boston: Houghton Mifflin, 1998).

7. Georges Nzongola-Ntalaja, *The Congo from Leopold to Kabila: A People's History* (London: Zed Books, 2002), 52.

8. Eslanda Robeson diary, Dec. 1, 1932 (describing her visit to the Congo Museum), in "Writings," PERC; and Eslanda Robeson, *African Journey* (New York: John Day, 1945).

9. Robeson, "Congo Diary," May 28, 1946, in "Writings," PERC.

10. See Robeson, "Airborne," 8.

11. Robeson, "Congo Diary," May 28, 1946, 3.

12. Ibid., May 26, 1946, 7.

13. Ibid., May 26, May 27, and May 28, 1946.

14. Eslanda Robeson, "Angola," July 1946, Congo folder, PERC. But she met him in May and the interviews were in July (or perhaps that is just when she logged the experience in her journal).

15. "African Opinion on Colonialism," folder 390, n.d. (but surely 1946), PRAB.

16. Untitled Notes, "Congo Essays, 1946" folder, PERC.

17. British Consul General in Leopoldville to the Director of Passport Control, Surveillance Files, KV/2/1829 June 2, 1946, MI5 files, available online at www.nationalarchives.gov.uk/documentsonline (last accessed May 14, 2012).

18. Eslanda Robeson, "Picturesque Journey in the Congo by Boat," Feb. 25, 1951, 1, in "Writings," PERC.

19. Ibid., 1.

20. Ibid., 4. *Amsterdam News* announced the series but no extant copies have been located.

21. Ibid., 3.

22. Eslanda Robeson to "Dearest Carlo and Fania" (Carl Van Vechten and Fania Marinoff), Sept. 12, 1946, CVVP.

23. Robeson, "Picturesque Journey," 4.

24. Robeson to "Dearest Carlo and Fania," Sept. 12, 1946.

25. Eslanda Robeson to Bess Rockmore, Aug. 9, 1946, folder 431, PRAB.

26. For biographical information on d'Arboussier, see Elizabeth Schmidt, *Cold War and Decolonization in Guinea, 1946–1958* (Athens: Ohio University Press, 2007), 25, 36, 48, 200 n.9; Victor T. LeVine, *Politics in Francophone Africa* (Boulder, Colo.: Lynne Rienner, 2004), 75–77. D'Arboussier was on the cusp of some important changes in his own politics and career just as Essie left the region in 1946. Details of that shift are outlined in Schmidt's book.

27. Eslanda Robeson, "Days with a Deputy," June 1946, 5, in "Writings," PERC.

28. Robeson, "Congo Diary," June 5, 11, and 13, 1946.

29. Robeson, "Days with a Deputy," 1.

30. Ibid.

31. Eslanda Robeson to Bess Rockmore, Aug. 9, 1946.

32. Ibid. Essie does not identify her mysterious love interest by name but indicates enough details that, when combined with other descriptions and references to d'Arboussier, lead me to conclude that he is the man she is referring to in her letter to Bess. One clue to his identity is Essie's description of him as holding a high-level position there, and he was the highest-ranking non-white person with whom she met. She met with him at length and wrote in her journal how attractive she found him. After looking at the profiles of all the other men she mentioned by name during her trip, too, there are no other likely candidates. It is interesting to note that Essie also mentions to Bess she is considering doing more work in Africa, having "decided to reorganize my life entirely." She adds that her new "man" makes annual visits to the United States.

33. Brian Weinstein, *Eboué* (Oxford, Eng.: Oxford University Press, 1972); Morris

Siegel, "Felix Eboué and Colonial Policy," *Journal of Negro Education* 16, no. 4 (Autumn 1947): 534–544.

34. Eslanda Robeson, "Felix Eboué, First Negro Governor-General in Africa," ca. 1946, in "Writings," PERC.

35. Robeson, "Days with a Deputy," 2. Note that d'Arboussier had become more moderate in his own thinking between 1943 (when he criticized Éboué) and 1946 (when he was interviewed by Essie Robeson).

36. Ibid., 2. Éboué was advocating acceptance of French rule, albeit with constraints and protections and greater inclusion and rights for the African population.

37. "Gabriel d'Arboussier was Secretary-General of the Rassemblement Démocratique Africain (African Democratic group) from its inception. He tried to reconcile leanings towards autonomy from the metropolitan government in the dependant territories with a search for an African unity based on federalist principles. In 1958, Gabriel d'Arboussier became, first, Vice-President and, later on, President of the Grand Council of the French Western Africa where he continued to promote African solidarity. In 1960, he was appointed Minister of Justice of a newly independent Senegal and, two years later, he became Ambassador of Senegal to France. In 1965, Gabriel d'Arboussier was appointed Executive Director of a newly created UNITAR (a United Nations unit) and occupied this position until 1967." See www.unitar.org/fr/anciens-directeursgeneraux-unitar#arboussier (last accessed May 14, 2012).

38. Eslanda Robeson, "African Women," 1946, unpublished, in "Writings," PERC. The document includes a set of interviews with Jeanne Vialle held June 23, 1946, and July 4, 1946, in Oubangui-Chari, French Equatorial Africa.

39. "Hunter College Students Hear Senator Jane [*sic*] Vialle of Africa," *Amsterdam News*, May 5, 1951, 18, 21.

40. Robeson, "African Women," 2.

41. Ibid., 3.

42. Robeson, Jeanne Vialle interview, 1946, PERC.

43. Eslanda Robeson to Malcolm Pitt, Sept. 4, 1946, folder 433; and Eslanda Robeson to Bess (Rockmore), Aug. 9, 1946, folder 431, both in PRAB.

44. Robeson to "Paul, Dear," June 14, 1946, folder 337, PRAB.

45. Robeson to Bess Rockmore, Aug. 9, 1946.

46. Eslanda Robeson, box 17: Eslanda Robeson Personal Papers, Diaries, folder "African Diary no. 4," 205, 206, 241, PERC.

47. Robeson to Bess Rockmore, Aug. 9, 1946.

48. Robeson, "1946 Congo Diary," in "Diaries," box 17 of "Writings," PERC.

49. For more on Tshombe's role in Lumumba's murder in 1961, see Ludo De Witte, *The Assassination of Lumumba* (London: Verso, 2001).

50. Eslanda Robeson to Mr. E. Toussaint, Aug. 12, 1946, in box 17: Eslanda Robeson Personal Papers, Diaries, PERC; Robeson, "1946 Congo Diary," PERC.

51. Robeson to Bobby Rockmore, July 5, 1946, in folder 434, PRAB.

52. Robeson to Bess Rockmore, Aug. 9, 1946, where Essie outlines her thoughts about getting a job in Congo.

53. Robeson to Bobby Rockmore, July 5, 1946; Robeson to Bess Rockmore, Aug. 9, 1946.

54. "Remembrances," *Freedomways*, no. 4 (1966): n.p. (comments by Lily Golden).
55. Robeson, "Picturesque Journey," 2.
56. Eslanda Robeson to "Elmer" (no last name given), Aug. 9, 1946, folder 432, PRAB; Robeson to Bess Rockmore, Aug. 9, 1946.
57. Eslanda Robeson, "Congolaise," outline of a film script attached to a letter to Laurence Olivier, Apr. 20, 1949, in "Correspondence folder," PERC.
58. Eslanda Robeson, "Africa," speech, New York Town Hall International Programs, Nov. 11, 1946, in "Writings," PERC.
59. Martin Duberman, *Paul Robeson: A Biography* (New York: Knopf, 1988), 307, 318.
60. Robeson to Bess Rockmore, Aug. 9, 1946. In the letter Essie notes that her mother "is proving to be a problem" but she won't let her "interfere with my future." In the long, cathartic letter, Essie, who had been the center and anchor for her family for decades, was considering moving to another country on her own, entertaining the possibility of a serious romantic relationship, and mapping her career trajectory with precision and focus.
61. Eslanda Robeson to Paul Robeson, Dec. 1, 1946, in "Correspondence," PERC.
62. Freda Diamond did not deny that she had an intimate relationship with Paul. But she simultaneously insisted that his marriage to Essie was never in jeopardy and that she and Paul never had plans to marry. She objected strenuously to any suggestions otherwise. Her sentiments are expressed in letters and editorial essays given to Robeson biographer Martin Duberman around 1988, which were copied to her friend Abbott Simon. See "Corrections to Revised Galleys (Chapter 21 1955-1956)," and "Corrections," TAM 346, box 3, folder 2, ASP.
63. The award was for accomplishments in 1945 and hence was "women of the year for 1945," but the award was given in March of 1946.
64. "Bethune Group Announces Vote for Twelve Women of the Year," *Chicago Defender*, national edition, Mar. 9, 1946, 19.
65. The quotation can be found in an undated news clip on microfilm reel 9, no. 00270, Mary McLeod Bethune Papers, PRC.
66. "Outstanding Women of 1945 Honored by Nat'l Council," National Newspaper Publishers Association (NNPA), paper not listed, microfilm reel 9, number 00270, Mary McLeod Bethune Papers, PRC.

CHAPTER 10. AMERICAN ARGUMENTS, 1946–1950

1. Eslanda Robeson, "Election Speech," New Haven, Conn., Oct. 30, 1944, in "Writings of Eslanda Robeson," PERC.
2. Eslanda Robeson to Delta Sorors, 1948–, and Eslanda to Sorors in Delta Sigma Theta, Aug. 4, 1949, both in "Correspondence," PRC.
3. Pearl S. Buck, *My Several Worlds* (New York: John Day, 1954).
4. Eslanda Robeson, *African Journey* (New York: John Day, 1945), 131–132.
5. Pearl S. Buck and Eslanda Robeson, *American Argument* (New York: John Wiley & Sons, 2001), 136–137.
6. Ibid., 129.
7. Ibid., 130.
8. Ibid., 130–137.
9. Ibid., 196.

10. Ibid., 201.

11. See FBI Files, Eslanda Robeson, 13–22 (1958–1965), available online at http://vault.fbi.gov/Paul Robeson Sr. (last accessed May 14, 2012).

12. Buck and Robeson, *American Argument*, 214.

13. Martha Biondi, *To Stand and Fight: The Struggle for Civil Rights in Postwar New York City* (Cambridge, Mass.: Harvard University Press, 2003), for further discussion of postwar New York City Black politics.

14. "Robeson Report," in box 39, series J, folder "Organizations: CAA, Minutes and Reports," 6, PERC.

15. For more details about the party, including the Connecticut Party, see PPP. For more on Wallace and the Progressive Party, see John C. Culver and John Hyde, *American Dreamer: A Life of Henry A. Wallace* (New York: W.W. Norton, 2001); and Graham White and John Maze, *Henry A. Wallace: His Search for a New World Order* (Chapel Hill: University of North Carolina Press, 1995).

16. Curtis MacDougall, *Gideon's Army* (New York: Marzani & Munsell, 1965), 545–546.

17. Progressive Party Platform Committee, "Proposed Platform: Peace, Freedom and Abundance," July 24, 1948, 1–21, PPP.

18. Jacqueline Castledine, "In a Solid Bond of Unity: Anticolonial Feminism in the Cold War Era," in *Journal of Women's History* 20, no. 4 (Winter 2008): 2.

19. Culver and Hyde, *American Dreamer*, 496.

20. No title, *Hartford Courant*, June 27, 1948.

21. FBI files, Robeson, clipping without date, available online at http://vault.fbi.gov/Paul Robeson, Sr (last accessed May 14, 2012).

22. MacDougall, *Gideon's Army*, 664.

23. "Statements of Vote," 1948, State of Connecticut Archives, Hartford.

24. *Stamford Advocate*, July 30, 1948; FBI files, Robeson, 4b, 3–10, available online at http://vault.fbi.gov/Paul Robeson Sr. (last accessed May 14, 2012).

25. Eslanda Robeson to Sorors in Delta Sigma Theta, Aug. 4, 1948, in "Correspondence," PERC; Eslanda Robeson, box 9, folder 17: "Notes for Progressive Party" speech, n.d., in "Writings," PERC; and series E of "Writings," PERC.

26. Eslanda Robeson, "Peace" speech, n.d., in "Writings," PERC.

27. For more details of the split from Wallace's perspective, see Henry Wallace, "Where I Was Wrong," *New York Herald Tribune*, Sept. 1952 (n.d.). Wallace increasingly resisted association with the Communist Party or related groups.

28. "Statements of Vote."

29. "Waterbury Peoples Party," radio script, Sunday, Oct. 29, 1950, 3, in "Writings," PERC.

30. Ibid.

31. Conrad Clark, "'I Am Not A Communist' Declares Mrs. Paul Robeson," Associated Negro Press, in author's possession.

32. Eslanda Robeson to Sorors in Delta Sigma Theta, Aug. 4, 1948.

33. W. A. Hunton to Eslanda Robeson, Mar 7, 1948, in "Correspondence," PERC; "Robeson's Wife Explains Husband's Political Issue: Clarifies Alleged Role of Doctor Max Yergan in The Red Tag," June [ca. 1948], by special correspondent, CBP.

34. Eslanda Robeson to "My dear Fellow Council Members," Apr. 17, 1948; Es-

landa Robeson to Max Yergan, Apr. 18, 1948; Thomas Russell Jones, attorney, to Eslanda Robeson, Apr. 27, 1948; and Eslanda Robeson to Council Members, Apr. 8 and Apr. 17, 1948, all in "Correspondence," PERC.

35. Erik S. McDuffie, "A 'New Freedom Movement of Negro Women': Sojourning for Truth, Justice, and Human Rights during the Early Cold War," *Radical History Review* 101 (2008): 81. McDuffie credits historian Mary Helen Washington with introducing the term "black left feminism."

36. Charlotta Bass and Louise T. Patterson to Miss Ray Alexander, Food and Canning Workers Union, South Africa, Apr. 5, 1952, in folder "Sojourners for Truth and Justice," LTPP.

37. Ibid.

38. Charles H. Martin, "Race, Gender and Southern Justice," *American Journal of Legal History* 29, no. 3 (July 1985): 251–268.

39. McDuffie, "New Freedom Movement," 98.

40. Kimberle Crenshaw, "Mapping the Margins: Intersectionality, Identity Politics, and Violence against Women of Color," *Stanford Law Review* 43, no. 6 (July 1991): 1241–1299.

41. Lester B. Granger, "Manhattan and Beyond," *Amsterdam News*, June 25, 1949, 18.

42. "Paul Robeson: Is He a Man or a Soviet Mouse?" *The Chicago Defender* (in author's possession).

43. P. L. Prattis, "Robeson, Du Bois Cause Uproar at Paris Meet," *Pittsburgh Courier*, Apr. 30, 1949, 3.

44. Essie penned a sharply worded reply to White in defense of Paul entitled, "The Not So Strange Case of Paul Robeson," *California Eagle*, Apr. 5, 1951, 5. Essie deemed White's essay "a very serious mischaracterization of Robeson." Walter White, "The Strange Case of Paul Robeson," *Ebony* (Feb. 1951): 78–84.

45. Robeson, "The Not So Strange Case of Paul Robeson," 5.

46. "Wife Backs Paul's' 'Won't Fight' Quote," *New York Amsterdam News*, May 7, 1949, 1.

47. "On the Reel," *Atlanta Daily World*, June 4, 1949, 2.

48. In 1944 Paul was called to testify before the Tenney Committee, an investigatory committee set up by the California State Legislature to investigate alleged communist activity.

49. FBI files, Robeson, 100–8030, p. 70 (robes2A), available online at http://vault.fbi.gov/Paul Robeson Sr. (last accessed May 14, 2012); news clip, *Hartford Times*, Oct. 6, 1944.

50. "Wife Backs Paul's' 'Won't Fight' Quote," 1.

51. See Penny M. Von Eschen, *Race against Empire: Black Americans and Anti-Colonialism, 1937–1957* (Ithaca, N.Y.: Cornell University Press, 1997); Mary L. Dudziak, *Cold War, Civil Rights: Race and the Image of American Democracy* (Princeton, N.J.: Princeton University Press, 2000); Brenda Gayle Plummer, *Rising Wind: Black Americans and U.S. Foreign Affairs, 1935–1960* (Chapel Hill: University of North Carolina Press, 1996).

52. In 1947, India became independent and the sub-Saharan African nations were on the road to independence, with Ghana achieving it first, in 1957.

53. Karl Marx, *Critique of the Gotha Program* (1938; Rockville, Md.: Wildside Press, 2008), 27.

54. Robin D. G. Kelley, "'Afric's Sons with Banner Red': African American Communists and the Politics of Culture, 1919–1934," in Sidney Lemelle and Robin Kelley, eds., *Imagining Home: Class, Culture and Nationalism in the African Diaspora* (New York: Verson, 1994), 37.

55. Gerald Meyer, *Vito Marcantonio: Radical Politician, 1902–1954* (Albany: State University of New York Press, 1989); Eslanda Robeson to George Murphy, Oct. 10, 1949, PERC.

56. Biondi, *To Stand and Fight.*

57. Paul Robeson Jr., "The Counterfeit 'Paul Robeson': A Legacy Demeaned," unpublished version in author's possession, courtesy of Paul Robeson Jr., 5, 15.

58. *New York Daily News*, Aug. 27, Sept. 4, and Sept. 5, 1949; and Susan Robeson, *The Whole World in His Hands: Paul Robeson, a Family Memoir in Words and Pictures* (New York: Citadel Press, 1985), 178–193.

59. Joseph Starobin, "Mexico City Peace Parley Hail Wallace, Robeson," *Daily Worker* 26, no. 182, Sept. 13, 1949, 2.

60. Eslanda Goode Robeson, Mass Meeting, Mexico City, Sept. 11, 1949, "Report on Peekskill," microfilm document, reel 2, 6, PRC.

61. Ibid. See also postcard to Larry Brown from Essie, Sept. 11, 1949, LBP.

62. Paul Robeson Jr., *The Undiscovered Paul Robeson: Quest for Freedom, 1939–1976* (Hoboken, N.J.: Wiley, 2010), 495.

63. Marilyn Robeson, interview with the author, 2006.

64. "Press Rabid as Robeson Son Weds," *Daily Worker*, June 21, 1949.

65. "5,000 Jam Harlem Rally to Welcome Paul Robeson Home," *Daily Worker*, June 20, 1949, 1.

66. Eslanda Goode Robeson, "Loyalty—Lost and Found," June 1949, PRC.

67. James Allan, "Mrs. Robeson Tells of Trip to China," *D.C. Compass*, Jan. 24, 1950. The WIDF was formed after an international meeting in 1945 convened by a communist women's group in France, which included a small delegation of American women. The Congress of American Women was formed as a U.S. affiliate of WIDF but it was attacked by HUAC and was in demise by 1948. See WIDF Records, 1945–1979 (MS594) at the Sophia Smith Collection at Smith College, Northampton, Mass.

68. "Ada Jackson to 'Reveal' All at Boro ALP Rally," *New York Amsterdam News*, Jan. 28, 1950, 21.

69. Essie to "Larry Dear" Lawrence Brown, Dec. 26, 1949, postcard, LBP; also see FBI files, Robeson, 100–12304–316–318, Feb. 4, 1955, New York Bureau file memo mentioning her China trip, available online at http://vault.fbi.gov/Paul Robeson, Sr (last accessed May 14, 2012).

70. "Norman Robinson Is Named Year's 'Top Brooklynite' In Annual Poll: Norman Robinson Selected Year's Leading Boroughite, Major Myles Paige Runs a Close Second In Race for Brooklyn's Annual Honors," *Amsterdam News*, Jan. 1, 1944, 13.

71. "Ask Leader To Resign Post on Home Board: Board Feels Ada Jackson Hurts Drive, Denies Any Connection with Communists at Any Time," *Amsterdam News*, Feb. 14, 19, 21, 1949; "Leave for Georgia to Help Free Ingram Family," photo caption, *Daily Worker*, Apr. 1, 1949, 1; and Biondi, *To Stand and Fight*, 51.

72. Robeson, China 1950 diary, no. 3, in box 17: Eslanda Robeson Personal Papers, Diaries, PERC.

73. Ibid.

74. Jung Chang and Jon Halliday, *Madame Sun Yat-Sen: Soong Ching-Ling* (London: Penguin, 1986); and Eslanda Robeson, "World Woman Number One," *New World Review* (July 1951): 7.

75. Eslanda to E. F. Frazier, Dec. 21, 1949, postcard, EFFP; and Essie Robeson's China diaries, 1949, PERC.

76. Jimmy Hicks, "Mrs. Robeson Regrets Having Defended Nehru," *Afro-American*, Jan. 28, 1950.

77. FBI files, Paul and Eslanda Robeson, available online at http://vault.fbi.gov/ Paul Robeson Sr. (last accessed May 14, 2012); "New York Banks Refuse to Reds Access to Funds of Bank of China," *New York Times*, Nov 2, 1949, 41.

78. Eslanda Robeson, (no title), in *Freedom* 1, no. 6 (June 1951): 6.

79. "Announcing a Lecture Tour by Eslanda Goode Robeson upon Her Return from China and the Soviet Union," microfilm reel 1–71, PRC.

80. "Red Regime Lauded: New China Frees Masses, Mrs. Robeson Declares," *Minneapolis Morning Tribune*, Apr. 12, 1950. Robert Freidman, "'They're Ours,' Say Chinese of Land and Buildings," *Daily Worker*, Jan. 29, 1950.

81. Eslanda Robeson, Speech to NACW in Oakland, CA, Oct. 3, 1954, PERC.

82. Eslanda Robeson's speech to Delta sorors; Eslanda Robeson's Notes on Detroit for Progressive Party, Mar. 6, 1950, both in PERC.

83. Robeson FBI files, no. 100–12304, New York Bureau file, Feb. 4, 1955.

84. "Open Forum, How the Phyllis Wheatley Board Decided," *Minneapolis Morning Tribune*, Apr. 12, 1950.

85. "Red Regime Lauded," 3. There is no byline (the photo provides the basis for this physical description).

86. "Win Speech Fight for Mrs. Robeson," *Daily Worker*, Dec. 22, 1952.

87. "10,000 Attend Rally Opposed by V.F.W.," *New York Times*, Aug. 21, 1952, 13; "The Korean Bombings," *New York Times*, Aug. 16, 1952, 14; "Peace under the Stars," *Amsterdam News*, Aug. 16, 1952, 12. As historian Michael E. Robinson writes: "Beginning in the winter of 1951 . . . [in] two years, the U.S. Air Force destroyed every North Korean city, its industrial capacity, and its railroad infrastructure. . . . and napalmed villages suspected of harboring troops." See Robinson, *Korea's Twentieth-Century Odyssey* (Honolulu: University of Hawai'i Press, 2007), 119.

CHAPTER 11. THE UNITED NATIONS AND
A WORLD POLITICAL FAMILY, 1950–1956

1. Eslanda Robeson, "The Last Stand of Colonialism in the UN," *New World Review* (Oct. 1955): 1.

2. The texts or even logistical details of all of her many public talks are not extant, but this estimate is based on a calculation of speeches, lectures, readings, and greetings cited or mentioned in primary and secondary documents.

3. Eslanda Robeson, "Peace, Friendship and Progress," *New World Review* (Nov. 1954): 32.

4. Eslanda Robeson, "What Is a Ghetto?" *New World Review* (Aug. 1954): 25–26.

5. Eslanda Robeson, "Some Thoughts on Negro History Week," *New World Review* (Mar. 1955): 20.

6. Eslanda Robeson, "U.S. Smokescreen at Caracas," *New World Review* (Apr. 1953): 28.
7. Ibid., 29.
8. Ibid., 30.
9. Eslanda Robeson, "Guatemala," draft article, n.d., in "Writings by Eslanda Robeson," 13, 2, PERC.
10. Several articles on China cited here include Eslanda Robeson, "The World Family Grows," *New World Review* (Jan. 1956); and Eslanda Robeson, "China and the UN," *New World Review* (June 1957).
11. Eslanda Robeson, "If the UN Seated China," *New World Review* (Aug. 1954): 21.
12. Ibid., 23.
13. Robeson, "China and the UN." Robeson, "The World Family Grows."
14. Eslanda Robeson, "War in Algeria," n.d., in "Writings," PERC.
15. Robeson, "Last Stand of Colonialism."
16. Ibid., 3.
17. Ibid., 1.
18. Ibid., 7.
19. Eslanda Robeson, "Krishna Menon: A New Type of Diplomat," *New World Review* (June 1956).
20. Ndeh Ntumazah to Eslanda Robeson, Feb. 20, 1958, in "Correspondence," PERC; also see Linus Asong and Simon Ndeh Chi, eds., *Ndeh Ntumazah: A Controversial Autobiography* (Bamenda, Cameroon: Langaa Research Publishing Common Initiative Group, 2010); and Horace Campbell, "Remembering Ndeh Ntumazah: An African Freedom Fighter," Oct. 22, 2010, available online at www.horacecampbell.net (last accessed May 14, 2012).
21. Eslanda Robeson, "Women in the United Nations," *New World Review* (July 1954). Also see Agda Rossell, "Human Rights and the Rights of Women: Retrospects and Perspectives on Work in the United Nations," in Mary Ann Tetrault and Robin L. Teske, *Partial Truths and the Politics of Community* (Columbia: University of South Carolina Press, 2003), 265–274; and a review of Fortuna A. Guery, *Témoignages* (Port-au-Prince: Henri Deschamps, 1950); Mercer Cook, "*Témoignages*" (review of Guery's book), *Journal of Negro History* 35, no. 3 (July 1950): 329; Josef Korbel, *Tito's Communism* (Denver: University of Denver Press, 1951), 79; Marcel David, *Adult Education in Yugoslavia* (New York: UNESCO, 1962), 17, 43; Sabrina P. Ramet, *Gender and Politics in the Western Balkans* (State College: Penn State Press, 1999), 76; and Nick Miller, *The Nonconformists: Culture, Politics and Nationalism in a Serbian Intellectual Circle, 1944–1991* (Budapest: Central European Press, 2007), 44, 73, 77.
22. Robeson, "Women in the United Nations," 7.
23. Ibid., 9.
24. Eslanda Robeson, "Women in the United Nations," *New World Review* (Mar. 1958): 33. This later article has the same title as that published in July 1954.
25. Ruth Gage-Colby to Eslanda Robeson, Jan. 15, 1960, PRAB.
26. Ruth Gage-Colby to Eslanda Robeson, Dec. 13, 1962, PRAB.
27. Ruth Gage-Colby Papers in the Peace Collection at Swarthmore College, Swarthmore, Pa.; and "Introduction" to the Ruth Gage-Colby Papers, both in RGCP.

28. Robeson to Cedric Belfrage, Oct. 12, 1956, folder 333, PRAB; and Robeson to George Murphy, Oct. 14 and Nov. 23, 1956, GMP.

29. Robeson FBI files, 100-12304-338, Nov. 18, 1955, memo from R. R. Roach to H. O. Bartlett, available online at http://vault.fbi.gov/Paul Robeson, Sr (last accessed May 14, 2012). It was recommended in the memo that, although her file was officially closed, reconnaissance on her be "reported to espionage and subversive controls sections."

30. See George Murphy to Essie, Dec. 3, 1951, GMP; Martin Duberman, *Paul Robeson: A Biography* (New York: Knopf, 1988), 392–393, nn.29 and 30; Paul Robeson Jr., *The Undiscovered Paul Robeson: An Artist's Journey, 1939–1976* (Hoboken, N.J.: Wiley, 2010).

31. Robert Williams, "North Carolina Militant Youth," *Freedom* (June 1952): 5.

32. Paul Robeson, "Ho Chi Minh Is Toussaint L'Ouverture of Indo China," *Freedom* (Mar. 1954): 1.

33. "1,000 Kikuyu Women March on the Prison Compounds Where 500 Men Had Been Imprisoned by British Colonial Office," *Freedom* (Dec. 1952): 3; Lorraine Hansberry, "Mrs. Mabel McLin Who Led the Militant Mothers with Their Children in the 20 Hour Vigil," *Freedom* (May 1951): 5; "Women Voice Demands in Capital Sojourn," *Freedom* (Oct. 1951); 6; "Freedom Salutes Nina Evans, Leader of Domestic Workers," *Freedom* (Sept. 1952): 2.

34. In the *Freedomways* tribute to Essie, Alice Childress remarks that Essie often gave guided tours of the publication's offices to visitors, a sign of her strong identification with the paper and her pride in it. *Freedomways*, no. 4 (1966).

35. Select examples of Eslanda Robeson's contributions to *Freedom* include Robeson, "I Know a Communist," *Freedom* (Mar. 1952): 4; and Robeson, "Mrs Edith Sampson Tells Europeans Negroes Are Happy," *Freedom* (June 1952): 2.

36. Her encounters with Francophone intellectuals Paulette Nardal and René Maran in Paris triggered her initial interest in Caribbean culture and politics in the 1930s.

37. Gerald Horne, *Race Woman: The Lives of Shirley Graham Du Bois* (New York: New York University Press, 2000), 143.

38. See a photo of Shirley Graham Du Bois, Kwame Nkrumah, and Eslanda Robeson in Ghana in 1958 (with Alphaeus Hunton also in the photograph), in Photos, PERC.

39. Vijaya Lakshmi Pandit to Eslanda Robeson, Sept. 15, 1938, in "Correspondence," PERC.

40. For the "fascinating" quotation, see Marie Seton, *Panditji: Portrait of Nehru* (New York: Dobson, 1967), 95–96; see also Nehru to Eslanda Robeson, June 26, 1947, and Dec. 27, 1950, in Nehru folder, "Correspondence," PERC.

41. Jawaharlal Nehru to Betty (sister), Oct. 12, 1943, in *Selected Works of Jawaharlal Nehru*, vol. 13 (New Delhi: Jawaharlal Nehru Memorial Fund, 1984), 255.

42. Clive Bush, *The Century's Midnight: Dissenting European and American Writers of the Second World War* (New York: Peter Lang, 2009), 245.

43. Vijaya Lakshmi Pandit, *The Scope of Happiness* (New York: Crown, 1979), 216–217.

44. Nayantara Sahgal, *Prison and Chocolate Cake* (New York: Knopf, 1954), 137.

45. The FBI took note of the Pandit sisters' visits to the Beeches. See FBI HQ 100-12304, section 1; and 100-8032, New Haven File, Robes 1a, 69.

46. Lekha Pandit to Eslanda Robeson, n.d. (1947), in "Correspondence," Pandit folder, PERC.

47. Lekha Pandit to Robeson, Oct. 1, 1949, and Mar 25 (no year) from Vienna, Austria; Tara Pandit to Robeson, July 12, 1949; Lekha's wedding invitation, Apr. 14, 1949; and Nan announcing May 27, 1950, that both daughters are pregnant, all in "Correspondence," PERC.

48. Vijaya Lakshmi Pandit to Jawaharlal Nehru, Sept. 16, 1949, Pandit catalog 482, subject file 59, NMML.

49. Nan Pandit to "Essie darling," Sept. 26, 1949, in "Correspondence," PERC.

50. See an untitled itinerary that gives the dates and time of Nehru meeting, in "Awards, Tributes and Memorabilia," box 2, folder "Itineraries," PERC; also see Robeson Jr., *Undiscovered, 1939–1976*, 183. Paul Robeson Jr. indicates the meeting occurred on Nov. 6, but Essie suggests it was Nov. 7. See, Duberman, *Paul Robeson*, 378–379, 698–699n38.

51. Janet Jagan, "Reminiscences: Che and Robeson," 2003, courtesy of Nadira Jagan-Brancier, Cheddi Jagan Research Centre, copy in author's possession.

52. Eslanda Robeson to Janet Jagan, Feb. 3, 1962, courtesy of Nadira Jagan-Brancier, copy in author's possession.

53. Ibid.

54. FBI files, Robeson, 100–12304, available online at http://vault.fbi.gov/Paul Robeson, Sr (last accessed May 14, 2012).

CHAPTER 12. STANDING TALL: THE COLD WAR AND POLITICS OF REPRESSION, 1950S

1. News release entitled "Mrs. Robeson Denounces McCarthy Quiz," partial document in "primary sources" folder, 15 extracted from Associated Negro Press (ANP) files with ANP byline, in author's possession; for what Eslanda was wearing, see the photograph in Susan Robeson, *The Whole World in His Hands: A Pictorial Biography of Paul Robeson* (New York: Citadel Press, 1981). Also see Gerald Horne, *Mau Mau in Harlem? The U.S. and the Liberation of Kenya* (New York: Palgrave Macmillan, 2009).

2. Eslanda Goode Robeson, testimony before the Executive Session of the Permanent Subcommittee on Investigations of the Committee on Government Operations of the U.S. Senate, 83rd Cong., 1st sess., *Congressional Record* 2 (1953): 1223.

3. Eslanda Robeson, "Mrs. Robeson Tells McCarthy about the 15th Amendment," *National Guardian*, July 20, 1953, 6.

4. "Mrs. Robeson Jars Joe McCarthy's 'All-White' Probe," *Daily Worker*, July 8, 1953, 1.

5. Eslanda Goode Robeson, testimony before the Executive Session of the Permanent Subcommittee on Investigations.

6. "Mrs. Robeson Jars Joe McCarthy's 'All-White' Probe," 1.

7. Prattis to Eslanda, Mar. 23, 1953, in "Correspondence," PERC.

8. Thelma Dale Perkins, "Untitled," in *Paul Robeson: The Great Forerunner*, by the editors of *Freedomways* (1965; New York: International Publishers, 1998).

9. Ibid., 306.

10. Eslanda Robeson, "Loyalty—Lost and Found," 1949, in "Writings of Eslanda Robeson," PERC.

11. Eslanda Robeson, "A Citizen's State of the Union," *Daily Worker*, Mar. 19, 1953.
12. Ibid.
13. Eslanda Robeson to James Hicks, Nov. 24, 1951, reel 1, PRC.
14. Paul Robeson Jr., *The Undiscovered Paul Robeson* (Hoboken, N.J.: Wiley, 2010).
15. Ben Davis to Essie Robeson; Apr. 27, 1943, Mar. 30, 1945, Nov. 5, 1947, and July 5, 1948, all in Correspondence files, PRAB.
16. Eslanda Robeson, "I Know a Communist," *Freedom* (Mar. 1952): 4.
17. Claudia Jones, *Ben Davis: Fighter for Freedom* (New York: National Committee to Defend Negro Leadership, 1954), 3.
18. Robeson, "I Know a Communist."
19. Jones, *Ben Davis*, 4.
20. Martin Duberman, *Paul Robeson: A Biography* (New York: Knopf, 1988), 294.
21. For a political biographical sketch of Ben Davis, see Gerald Horne, *Black Liberation/Red Scare: Ben Davis and the Communist Party* (Newark: University of Delaware Press, 1994).
22. Eslanda Robeson, "Negro Leadership," *Afro-American*, June 4, 1955.
23. "Thousands Greet Mrs. Eslande [*sic*] Robeson at American Committee for Protection of the Foreign Born (ACBFP) Picnic," press release, n.d., CBP.
24. Eslanda Robeson, essay defending Du Bois, 1951 (n.d.), PRC.
25. For more on the Trumbull Park housing struggle, which went on an entire year, see "Chicago Riot House on *CBS Sunday*," *New York Amsterdam News*, Apr. 24, 1954, 5; "CHA Hits City for Trouble at Trumbull Park," *Chicago Daily Tribune*, Apr. 27, 1954, 16; "Howard Denies Guilt in Trumbull Park Tilt," *Chicago Defender*, Apr. 24, 1954, 2; "Police Ring Project to Ban Racial Clash," *New York Times*, Aug. 12, 1953, 18; and "750 Cops Curb Mob in Chicago," *Pittsburgh Courier*, Aug. 22, 1953, 4. Also see Arnold Hirsch, "Massive Resistance in the Urban North: Trumbull Park, Chicago, 1953–1966," *Journal of American History* 82, no. 2 (Sept. 1995): 522–550.
26. Eslanda Goode Robeson, "Force and Violence in South Chicago: The Siege of Trumbull Park," Apr. 27, 1954, in "Writings," PERC.
27. Ibid.; also see Frank London Brown, *Trumbull Park* (1959; Boston: Northeastern University Press, 2005); and Sterling Stuckey, "Frank London Brown: A Remembrance," in *Black Voices: An Anthology of Afro-American Literature* (New York: New American Library, 1968), 669–676.
28. Robeson, "A Citizen's State of the Union."
29. Original copies of Essie's passports from the years 1940, 1946, 1950, and 1958 can be found in "Memorabilia," PERC. Records obtained April 10, 2012 from U.S. Department of State, Office of Legal Affairs indicate Essie did not have an active passport between 1950 and 1958.
30. The Chaplin quote is from "Border Concert," Jan. 1, 1954, Vancouver, B.C., box 33, folder 6, concert program, RBC.
31. Leonard Boudin to Eslanda Robeson, July 13, 1957; Boudin to Robeson, June 24, 27, 1958; Boudin to Robeson, July 3, 9, 10, 1958, in box 33, folders 4 and 5, RBC.
32. Eslanda Robeson, "Mother's Day," speech, May 11, 1952, PERC.
33. Susan Robeson, *The Whole World in His Hands: A Pictorial Biography of Paul Robeson* (Secaucus, N.J.: Citadel Press, 1981), 216–217.
34. Freda Diamond, "Corrections to Revised Galleys (Chapter 21, 1955–1956)," TAM 346, box 3, folder 2, ASP.

35. Paul Robeson Jr., *The Undiscovered Paul Robeson: Quest for Freedom, 1939–1976* (Hoboken, N.J.: Wiley, 2010), 441.

36. Eslanda Robeson to Cedric Belfrage and Peggy Middleton, 1957–1958, PRAB.

37. Duberman, *Paul Robeson*, 461 n.34, and 462 n.35.

38. Robeson to Belfrage and Middleton, 1957–1958.

39. Robeson Jr., *Undiscovered, 1939–1976*, 426.

40. Daisy Bates to Eslanda Robeson, Mar. 21, 1958, PERC.

41. David Levering Lewis, *W. E. B. Du Bois: The Fight for Equality and the American Century, 1919–1963* (New York: H. Holt, 2000), 558–559.

42. Duberman, *Paul Robeson*, 451 n.12.

43. "Mrs. Robeson Addresses Unionists" (no byline), *Evening News of the Trinidad Guardian*, April 29, 1959, 5; "Mrs. Robeson Lectures Tonight," *Evening News of the Trinidad Guardian* April 28, 1959, 7; Robert J. Alexander and Eldon M. Parker, *A History of Organized Labor in the English-Speaking West Indies*, by Robert J. Alexander, Eldon M. Parker (Westport, Conn.: Greenwood/Praeger, 2004), 282, 458.

44. Announcement of lecture by Eslanda Robeson on "The Negro in World Focus," and "Robeson to Address the Women's League of Peoples National Movement," both in *Trinidad-Evening* (newspaper), Apr. 24, 1958, 1–2; ad announcing that Essie would "speak to General Workers Trade members and National Union of Government employees at 68 Henry St.," *Trinidad-Evening*, Apr. 21, 1958, and Apr. 29, 1958.

45. John A. Lent, *Third World Mass Media and Their Search for Modernity: The Case of Commonwealth Caribbean, 1717–1976* (Lewisberg, Pa.: Bucknell University Press, 1977), 47, 49; also three photographs of Eslanda Robeson and T. A. Marryshow in Trinidad in 1958, PERC; and ibid., 39.

46. Edward L. Cox, "William Galwey Donovan and the Struggle for Political Change in Grenada, 1883–1920," *Small Axe* 11, no. 1 (Feb. 2007): 17–38; Jesse H. Proctor Jr., "The Development of the Idea of Federation of the British Caribbean Territories," *Revista de Historia de América* 39 (Jun. 1955): 61–105.

47. Paul Robeson, *Here I Stand*, 3rd ed. (1958; Boston: Beacon Press, 1988), 39, 68, 86.

48. Ibid., ix.

CHAPTER 13. A FAILING BODY AND A HOPEFUL HEART, 1958–1961

1. Shirley Graham Du Bois to Eslanda Robeson, Sept. 23, 2958, in "Correspondence," PERC.

2. Kwame Nkrumah to Eslanda Robeson, Aug. 10, 1960, in "Correspondence," PERC.

3. Jim Aronson to "Dear Paul and Marilyn and Paully [*sic*]," Dec. 16, 1965, in "Condolences," PERC.

4. Essie's appointments list (typed) in "Memorabilia," box 7, PERC.

5. Eslanda Robeson, Foreword to Claudia Jones, *Ben Davis: Fighter for Freedom* (New York: National Committee to Defend Negro Leadership, 1954), 3.

6. See Carol Boyce Davies, *Left of Karl Marx: The Political Life of Black Communist Claudia Jones* (Durham, N.C.: Duke University Press, 2007), 22, 95, 150, 275; and Eslanda Robeson to George Murphy, Oct. 23, 1959, and Feb. 6, 1962, in "Correspondence," PERC; *National Guardian*, July 21, 1958; and Claudia Jones, "The Robeson Legend," *West Indian Gazette* (June 1959).

7. Chatwood Hall, "Robeson Kin Is Back in Moscow after Three Years," *Chicago Defender*, Mar. 4, 1944. In his 1964 book *Black Man in Red Russia*, Homer Smith writes of his encounter with Frank Goode in January 1945. He describes Frank as "a great hulk of a man," someone referred to by his Russian circus promoters as the "Black Samson." By 1945, according to Smith, Frank had been let go by the circus and was nearly destitute. "It was a hungry, cold and depressed American Negro that I let into my apartment" on that day, Smith wrote. This was the last time that Smith saw Frank Goode, but later he heard rumors that Frank had re-established himself in Gorky and was living off of a state pension with supplements from Essie and Paul. See Homer Smith, *Black Man in Red Russia: A Memoir* (Chicago: Johnson Publishing Company, 1964), 196-199; Joy Carew, *Blacks, Reds and Russians: Sojourners in Search of the Soviet Promise* (New Brunswick, N.J.: Rutgers University Press, 2008), 200.

8. "Paul and Eslanda Robeson," *New World Review* 51, no. 3 (1983): 23; and Lily Golden, *My Long Journey* (1973; Chicago: Third World Press, 2002).

9. Essie's specific contributions are a bit unclear but several sources cite her as instrumental in the formation of the institute. Given her deep interest in Africa and her growing prominence as an expert writer and researcher on the politics and cultures of the continent, she is likely to have been as central in the discussions with Golden and Potekhin as Paul was. See George Skorov, "Ivan Potekhin: Man, Scientist and Friend of Africa," *Journal of Modern African Studies* 2, no. 3 (1964), which mentions that Essie and Paul were Potekhin's guests at the institute; and Marguerite Cartwright, "World Backdrop," *Pittsburgh Courier*, Feb. 14, 1959, A4, which reports that Eslanda and Potekhin were in Ghana together in 1958.

10. Esther Cooper Jackson, telephone interview with the author, Nov. 30, 2011.

11. Eslanda Robeson, *African Journey*, ed. Ivan Potekhin (Moscow: Foreign Literature Publishers, 1957). The book was translated into Russian by K. A. Chugunova.

12. Eslanda Robeson, "Learning How to Live Together," *Seamen's Journal* (Nov. 1960): supplement, 378-379, 383.

13. Eslanda Robeson, "Africa for the Africans," n.d., in "Writings of Eslanda Robeson," PERC. (There may be more than one essay by Essie with the same or similar title.)

14. Eslanda Robeson, "The Accra Conference," *New World Review* (Feb. 1959). This article was also reprinted posthumously in *Freedomways*, no. 4 (1966): 349.

15. Ahmed A. Rahman, *The Regime Change of Kwame Nkrumah: Epic Heroism in Africa and the Diaspora* (Basingstoke, Eng.: Palgrave Macmillan, 2007), 179.

16. Huuda Shaawari, *Harem Years: The Memoirs of an Egyptian Feminist (1879–1924)*, trans. Margot Badran (New York: Feminist Press at City University of New York, 1987). Note the various versions of the spelling of Nabarawi's name, including Naboury and Nabariwi. Saiza is sometimes Ceza.

17. Judy Mabro, *Veiled Half-Truths: Western Travellers' Perceptions of Middle Eastern Women* (London: B. Tauris, 1991); Margot Badran, *Feminists, Islam and Nation: Gender and the Making of Modern Egypt* (Princeton, N.J.: Princeton University Press, 1996); Margot Badran, "The Feminist Vision in the Writings of Three Turn-of-the-Century Egyptian Women," *British Journal of Middle East-*

ern Studies 15, no. 1 (1988); and Cynthia Nelson, *Doria Shafik, Egyptian Feminist: A World Apart* (Gainesville: University Press of Florida, 1996).

18. Notebook labeled "Africa 6/6/35" (erroneous date as archived; likely correct date is June 6, 1965), folder 445, PRAB.

19. Yevette Richards, *Maida Springer: Pan Africanist and International Labor Leader* (Pittsburgh: University of Pittsburgh Press, 2000), 182.

20. Robeson, "Africa for the Africans."

21. Robeson, "Accra Conference," 14.

22. Robeson, "Africa for the Africans."

23. Robeson, "Accra Conference," 13.

24. Ibid., 14.

25. Ibid.

26. Ibid. In this same article Essie also criticizes efforts by the thirty-person U.S. delegation to sow seeds of animus between President Kwame Nkrumah and Egyptian leader Gamal Abdul Nasser, a leader in the growing Non-Aligned Movement (which the United States opposed).

27. Eslanda Robeson, "African Leadership," *New World Review* (Mar. 1959): 24–25.

28. Eslanda Robeson to Freda Diamond, Dec. 12, 1958, PERC.

29. Eslanda Robeson, "A Call to the Negro People: Begging Should End Now Says Eslanda Robeson," *California Eagle*, Apr. 12, 1951 (microfilm), PRC.

30. Ibid.

31. Ibid.

32. Ibid.

33. Eslanda Robeson, letter to National Association of Colored Women (NACW), Oct. 3, 1954, Oakland, Calif., in "Correspondence," PERC.

34. Ibid., 5–7.

35. Eslanda Robeson, "Tribute to Jim Ford," eulogy, n.d. (1957), in "Writings," PERC.

36. Eslanda Robeson to George Murphy Jr., Oct. 14, 1956, GMP.

37. Eslanda Robeson to "Dear Bobby and Beautiful" (The Rockmores: Paul's lawyer-friend and his wife), Feb. 8, 1959, in "Correspondence," PERC. The letter indicated that as of Feb. 8, Essie had been in the hospital for five weeks.

38. Robeson to Marion Forsythe, in Duberman, *Paul Robeson*, 669 n.25; Robeson to Paul Jr. and Marilyn, Mar. 9, 1959, and Mar. 24, 1959, in "Correspondence," PERC; and ibid.

39. Eslanda Robeson to "Paul Jr. dear," Mar. 9, 1959, in "Correspondence," PERC. The long letter to Paul Jr. mentions that Paul is back in London and describes her treatments as well as her Women's Day meeting and speech.

40. Eslanda Robeson to "Hi There!!" (Marilyn Robeson), Jan. 31, 1959, courtesy of Paul Robeson Jr., copy in author's possession.

41. Robeson to Peggy Middleton, Mar. 20, 1959, folder 335, PRAB.

42. Robeson to Murphy, Dec. 2, 1959.

43. Robeson, *Undiscovered, 1939–1976*, 298.

44. Ibid., 300.

45. Robeson to Murphy, Dec. 2, 1959.

46. Eslanda Robeson to Claude Barnett, Dec. 2, 1959, from London, Connaught Square, box 294, folder 3, CBP.

47. Robeson to Murphy, Dec. 2, 1959.

48. "Mrs. Robeson Is Notable Too," *New Zealand Herald* (Auckland), Oct. 18, 1960; and "Mrs. Paul Robeson Is Anthropologist, Writer," *The Sun* (Melbourne), Nov. 16, 1960.

49. Union of Australian Women, "For the Rights of Women: Three Decades of Struggle, 1950–1980," Sydney, 1980, available online at www.reasoninrevolt.net .au/bib/PR0001505.htm (last accessed May 14, 2012), 1.

50. Ibid., 13.

51. "Women's Influence Needed in All Spheres," no byline, *Seamen's Journal* (Nov. 1960): supplement, 383, archived in folder 424, PRAB.

52. For a description of a challenge staff (or rakau/raki), see the online Maori dictionary at www.maoridictionary.co.nz (last accessed May 14, 2012), or Mervyn McLean, *Maori Music* (Auckland, N.Z.: Auckland University Press, 1996), 28–29.

53. Eslanda Robeson to George Murphy, Dec. 1, 1960, GMP.

54. Eslanda Robeson to Freda Diamond, Nov. 13, 1960, in "Correspondence," PERC.

55. Ibid.; Eslanda Robeson to Helen Rosen, cited in Duberman, *Paul Robeson*, 489, 739 n.61 (letter to Rosen in Duberman's possession).

56. Robeson Jr., *Undiscovered, 1939–1976*, 309–329. While the Robesons' Soviet ties were clearly a factor in the U.S. government's interest in them, more important were their popularity and influence among the masses of African Americans and within the Third World. Had that influence not been real, the couple's Soviet affiliations would have been less relevant. Moreover, both Essie and Paul continually made the point to Black audiences that their fate was linked to that of oppressed people, especially people in what was then called the Third World and is now called the Global South—a point that posed a threat to the ideological position that the CIA and State Department were promoting with great care and at great expense.

57. See Duberman, *Paul Robeson*, 498–499; and Paul Robeson Jr., "The Counterfeit Paul Robeson," unpublished version in author's possession, courtesy of Paul Robeson Jr., 24–25. Conclusions about Robeson's suicide attempt were based on interviews by Duberman and Paul Robeson Jr., as well as Paul Robeson Jr.'s eyewitness account when he visited his father some days after the hotel incident on Mar. 27, 1961.

58. Robeson Jr., "Counterfeit," 5, 22.

59. Ibid.

60. Eslanda Robeson to "Dear Paul Jr. and Marilyn," Hotel Moskva, Moscow, July 7, 1961, and July 14, 1961, in "Correspondence," PERC.

61. Bobby Rockmore to Essie, Oct. 5, 1961, in "Correspondence," PERC. For Essie's feeling about Bobby Rockmore, see Eslanda to "Mama Dear" (her mother), Jan. 20, 1935, in "Correspondence," PERC.

62. In addition to correspondence in the PERC, see letters between the two women archived in the Shirley Graham Du Bois Collection, Schlesinger Library, Harvard University.

63. Eslanda Robeson to Shirley Du Bois, Nov. 7, 1961, and Shirley Du Bois to Eslanda Robeson, Oct. 29, 1961, both in "Correspondence," PERC.

64. The Robesons were generous with their home. The young actors Ruby Dee and Ossie Davis were also invited to stay at the London flat when Paul and Essie were not there. See Ruby Dee and Ossie Davis, *With Ossie and Ruby: In This Life Together* (New York: William Morrow, 1998), 322.

65. Robeson Jr., *Undiscovered, 1939–1976*, n.p.

66. Essie to "Dear Friends," sent to George Murphy and others, Mar. 24, 1964, GMP.

67. Robeson to "Dear Bobby and Beautiful" (letter addressed to Paul's lawyer-friend and his wife), Oct. 29, 1961, in "Correspondence," PERC.

68. On Essie's relishing being in control, see Duberman, *Paul Robeson*, 504.

CHAPTER 14. ALWAYS THE FIGHTER:
A PEN AS HER WEAPON, 1961–1965

Epigraph. Eslanda Robeson, *African Journey* (New York: John Day, 1945), 152.

1. Eslanda Robeson, "Cuba Libre," *New World Review* (ca. May 1961), in "Writings of Eslanda Robeson," PERC.

2. Eslanda Robeson, "Island in Flames," unpublished, n.d., in "Writings," PERC. A typed, slightly different version of "Cuba Libre" is in box 294, folder 3, CBP.

3. The Associated Negro Press (ANP) series was a personal triumph for Essie because the ANP was a highly regarded news service that reached a wide audience through its many subscribing newspapers. When she first approached founder Claude Barnett in the 1940s about serving as a foreign correspondent, he rebuffed her. She gracefully persisted over the years, sending him clippings and pitching news stories. By the late 1950s, she had received ANP credentials.

4. In a 1950 article, just after her return from China, Essie criticized Jawaharlal Nehru for his alleged jailing of dissidents without trial. But over time she either privately reversed her view or reassessed her overall analysis of the situation in India. For early criticism, see Jimmy Hicks, "Mrs. Robeson Regrets Having Defended Nehru," *Afro-American*, n.d., PERC.

5. "So. African Woe Brings Clash in London at Rally," UPI, *Atlanta Daily World*, Mar. 23, 1961, 8; Eslanda Robeson to George Murphy, Feb. 25, 1961, GMP.

6. Robeson to Murphy, Feb. 25, 1961.

7. Marie-Noelle Little, ed., *The Poet and the Diplomat: The Correspondence of Dag Hammarskjöld and Alexis Leger* (Syracuse, N.Y.: Syracuse University Press, 2001), 136–138.

8. Eslanda Robeson, "Jomo Kenyatta," Jan. 22, 1961, in "Writings," PERC. The essay, which reads like an open letter, is typed but no publication details are listed.

9. London School of Economics class list, ca. 1932, courtesy of Holly Peters-Golden, copy in author's possession.

10. Robeson, "Jomo Kenyatta."

11. Jawaharlal Nehru to "Dear Essie," Aug. 5, 1955, in Eslanda Robeson Papers, box 17, "Writings," PERC.

12. Essie's informal "encyclopedia" from the 1960s is archived in PRAB.

13. Notebook labeled "Africa 6/6/35" (erroneous date as archived; likely correct date is June 6, 1965), folder 445, PRAB. All of the events described in Eslanda's "encyclopedia" notebook can be found in folder 445, PRAB.

14. Eslanda Robeson, "The New Negro Movement," *Sun-Reporter*, July 27, 1963, 16.

15. Eslanda Robeson to Helen Rosen, "The Report Continued" (daily journal-style letter that begins Oct. 1961, but stretches over several months), folder 338, 16–17, PRAB. Also, see Eslanda Robeson to Peggy Middleton, Nov. 3, 1961, folder 336, PRAB.

16. Eslanda Robeson to Shirley G. Du Bois, Berlin, Oct. 5, 1963 PRC.

17. Robeson, to "Robesons, Rosens and Rockmores," Nov. 12, 1962, 31, 32.

18. "Africa Women's Day" flyer with speech typed on it, in "Awards, Tributes, Memorabilia," box 2, folder "Programs," 1960–1961, PERC.

19. Robeson, to "Robesons, Rosens and Rockmores," Dec. 7, 1962, 42.

20. "Africa Women's Day" flyer.

21. Ibid.; photo with "Lumumba" sign, n.d., CJMC.

22. I. K. Chinebuah to Eslanda Robeson, folder 428, n.d., PRAB.

23. Donald S. Carlisle, "The Uzbek Power Elite: Politboro and Secretariat (1938–83)," *Central Asian Survey* 5, nos. 3–4 (1986): 91–132.

24. Essie Robeson to Mr. Mukhitdinov from her hospital at Barveekha (referencing a long conversation they had when he visited her), Apr. 28, 1960, folder 438, PRAB.

25. Frances W. Herring, *The World without the Bomb: Story of the Accra Assembly* (Berkeley, Calif.: Women's Strike for Peace, 1962), 1, 2, 11, 19 (Nkrumah quote).

26. Ruth Gage-Colby, cable to Eslanda Robeson, June 13, 1962, folder 428, PRAB; Eslanda Robeson to President Kwame Nkrumah, June 20, 1962, folder 441, PRAB. Gage-Colby's view of Jack may be hyperbolic and unfair. See Walter Francis White, *A Rising Wind* (Garden City, N.Y.: Doubleday Doran, 1945), 233.

27. Carlton Goodlett to Eslanda Robeson, Mar. 7, 1963, folder 427, PRAB. For background on jazz musicians visiting the Soviet Union and Khrushchev's responses in particular, see Penny Von Eschen, *Satchmo Blows Up the World: Jazz Ambassadors Play the Cold War* (Cambridge, Mass.: Harvard University Press, 2006), 100–109.

28. Essie Robeson to P. L. Prattis, Dec. 12, 1962, and May 30, 1964, in "Correspondence," PERC.

29. Jeffrey Herf, *Reactionary Modernism: Technology, Culture, and Politics in Weimar and the Third Reich* (Cambridge, Eng.: Cambridge University Press, 1984), 184. Hans Globke was a high-ranking civil servant in Nazi Germany who settled in West Germany after the war. After the construction of the Berlin Wall in 1961, the GDR (East Germany) engaged in some highly publicized trials in absentia of alleged Nazi sympathizers who were living in freedom on the other side of the wall. These high-profile trials were framed as indicators of the GDR's anti-fascist commitment and were designed to embarrass the West Germans in the eyes of the rest of the world. In July of 1963 Globke, called the "Eichmann of Bonn," was put on trial for nine days; Essie was one of the international witnesses who were invited to participate in the trial heard before the East German Supreme Court. See Jeffrey Herf, *Divided Memory: The Nazi Past in Two Germanys* (Cambridge, Mass.: Harvard University Press, 1997), 184; and Devin Owen Pendas, *The Frankfort Auschwitz Trial, 1963–1965: Genocide, His-*

tory and the Limits of the Law (Cambridge, Eng.: Cambridge University Press, 2005), 18. A July 3, 1963, photo and caption of Essie in the German Federal Archives documents her presence at the trial; see http://en.wikipedia.org/wiki/File:Bundesarchiv_Bild_183-B0708-0014-004,_Oberstes_Gericht,_Globke-Prozess,_Publikum.jpg (last accessed May 14, 2012).

30. "Eslanda Robeson in the German Democratic Republic," December 15, 1963, folder 384, PRAB; photo 1136 of Eslanda Robeson at Globke trial in 1963 (Berlin, 8. VII. 1963), PRAB; and Joanne Sayner, *Women without a Past? German Autobiographical Writings and Fascism* (Amsterdam: Rodopi Press, 2007), 210–211.

31. Eslanda Robeson diary, 1963, in "Writings," PERC.

32. O. Watson, "What Are Paul Robeson's Views on Russia Now?" *Daily Telegraph*, Sept. 25, 1963. Also see John Osman as the named reporter in Martin Duberman, *Paul Robeson: A Biography* (New York: Knopf, 1988), 516.

33. Eslanda Robeson, "Kidnapped?" in "Writings," PERC.

34. Eslanda Robeson, "Notes on Birthday Abroad GDR," in "Writings," PERC: also see Duberman, *Paul Robeson*, 518.

35. Eslanda Robeson, "Eslanda Robeson Visits East Germany," *New World* Review (Apr. 1964): 14 (reporting on the 1963 trip).

36. Eslanda Robeson, "Long Hot Summer," June 10, 1964, in "Writings," PERC.

37. "After 188 years . . . ," flyer for The Committee of Afro-Asian-Caribbean Organizations, July 9, 1964, PERC.

38. A photo in PRAB shows a sixty-something-year-old Essie in a hat speaking to a smiling Martin Luther King Jr., with an unidentified young man standing in the background; see Robeson to Helen Rosen "The Report Continued," 1961, folder 338, 16–17, PRAB.

39. Robeson, "Long Hot Summer," 3–5.

40. Eslanda Robeson, "The Funeral of Malcolm X," unpublished version, Mar. 2, 1965, PERC. In Robeson Jr., *Undiscovered, 1939–1976*, 633, Paul Jr. recalls an instance in which he was trying to arrange a meeting between Malcolm X and his father, and Essie objected strenuously. Paul dismissed her objections and agreed to the meeting, but Malcolm was killed before it could take place. There may be a number of explanations for Essie's objection, none of which necessarily have anything to do with politics. Perhaps most likely, Essie would have known that Malcolm was a target in 1965 and she was very protective of and concerned for Paul's safety in the wake of all he had endured. Indeed Malcolm X was assassinated a short distance from where Essie and Paul lived, less than a month after he had asked to meet with Paul. If Essie had fears about security, they were not unfounded.

41. Eslanda Robeson to George Murphy, Dec. 24, 1964, and George Murphy to Eslanda Robeson, Jan. 17, 1965 (about Hansberry), both in GMP.

42. "Eslanda Robeson Receives GDR Peace Medal," *New World Review* (Oct. 1963): 37.

43. "Remembrances of Eslanda," *Freedomways*, no. 4 (1966): 335 (comments by Victor Grossman).

44. Ibid.

45. Eslanda Robeson to George Murphy, Jan. 1, 1964, GMP.

46. Eslanda Robeson to Florence Luscomb, Oct. 27, 1965, Correspondence files, FLP.

47. "Remembrances of Eslanda," 329 (comments by Alice Childress).

48. Eslanda Robeson, letter to editors of the *Afro-American*, Nov. 23, 1956; Robeson to Murphy, Nov. 23, 1956, GMP.

49. Esther Cooper Jackson and Constance Pohl, *Freedomways Reader: Prophets of their Own Country* (New York: Basic Books, 2001), xxix, 149; Robin D. G. Kelley, *Monk: The Life and Times of an American Original* (New York: Simon and Schuster, 2009), 168; Philip S. Foner, *Freedomways' Salute to Paul Robeson*, box 10, folder 29, 44, Henry Foner Papers, The Tamiment Library and Robert F. Wagner Labor Archives, New York University; and Esther Cooper Jackson, telephone interview with the author, Nov. 30, 2011.

50. Robeson Jr., *Undiscovered, 1939–1976*, 607.

51. Robeson to Luscomb, Oct. 27, 1965. Also see Sharon Hartman Strom, *Political Woman: Florence Luscomb and the Legacy of Radical Reform* (Philadelphia: Temple University Press, 2001), 179, 210, 215.

52. Ruth Gage-Colby to John Henrik Clarke (associate editor of *Freedomways*), Aug. 24, 1966, Correspondence folder, 1959-1966, RGCP.

53. "A Great Lady Passes," *Sun Reporter*, Dec. 18, 1965, 10.

54. "Remembrances of Eslanda," 329, 331, 333, 338-339 (entries by multiple friends).

55. "Condolences" folder, PERC.

56. Vicky Garvin to Paul Robeson, Jan. 12, 1966; Langston Hughes to "the family," Dec. 15, 1965; Janet Jagan letter (no addressee), Dec. 14, 1965, all in "Condolences" folder, PERC.

57. Jessica Smith, "Eslanda Robeson, 1895-1965," *New World Review* (Jan. 1966): 8.

58. "Remembrances of Eslanda," 341-342 (comments by Ruth Gage-Colby).

EPILOGUE

1. Robin D. G. Kelley, *Race Rebels: Culture, Politics, and the Black Working Class* (New York: Free Press, 1996).

2. Vijay Prashad, *Darker Nations: A People's History of the Third World* (New York: New Press, 2008).

3. Martin Duberman, *Paul Robeson: A Biography* (New York: Knopf, 1988), 68, 70, 76.

BIBLIOGRAPHY OF SELECT
WRITINGS BY ESLANDA ROBESON

BOOKS

Paul Robeson, Negro. London: Gollancz, 1930.
African Journey. New York: John Day, 1945.
American Argument with Eslanda Goode Robeson. Pearl Buck, co-author. New York: John Day Company, 1949.

ARTICLES, ESSAYS, AND PARTS OF BOOKS

"Black Paris." *Challenge* (1936).
"About the Spanish Civil War." Unpublished. Circa 1937.
"Félix Éboué, First Negro Gov. General." Unpublished. 1940s.
"Southern Story." Unpublished. 1943.
"The Negro Problem: An Approach to the Problem of Race Relations." 1944. Thesis for Ph.D. degree, Hartford Seminary.
"A Negro Looks at Africa." *Asia and Americas* (Nov. 1944).
"Old Country for Thirteen Million." *Negro Digest* (Nov. 1944).
"Unofficial America Goes to the Conference," Unpublished. 1945.
"A Negro Looks at Africa." *This Month* (Mar. 1945).
"What Do the People of Africa Want?" *Council on African Affairs* (1945).
"Is Black a Handicap?" *Negro Digest* (Apr. 1945).
"Africa Tests World Drive to Win Permanent Peace." *San Francisco Daily World* (Aug. 15, 1945).
"Togoland Story." Unpublished. 1946–1957.
"Unrest in India: A Report from the Asian Women's Conference." *Far East Spotlight* 5, no. 12 (1950).
"World Woman Number One." *New World Review* 19, no. 5 (1951).
"The Cry for Freedom Rings through Africa." *New World Review* 20, no. 9 (1952).
"Is US-USSR Co-Existence Possible?" *New World Review* 20, no. 3 (1952): 14–15.
"Africa—No Longer the 'Dark Continent.'" *New World Review* (Aug. 1952): 3–6.
"Félix Éboué: The End of an Era." *New World Review* (Oct. 1952): 44–48.
"The Rising Tide." *New World Review* (Nov. 1952): 10.
"Which Way for Africa?" *New World Review* (Dec. 1952): 24–29.
"Unrest in Africa Due to Oppression." Unpublished. June 1953.
"Why I Am a Friend of the USSR." *New World Review* (Aug. 1953).
"A Lesson on Discrimination Is Drawn from a UN Incident." *New World Review* 22, no. 2 (1954).
"U.S. Smoke Screen at Caracas." *New World Review* 22, no. 4 (1954).
Foreword to Claudia Jones, *Ben Davis: Fighter For Freedom* (Brooklyn: National Committee to Defend Negro Leadership, Nov. 1954).

"Force and Violence in South Chicago: The Siege of Trumbull Park." Unpublished. Apr. 27, 1954.

"Loyalty, the Democratic Process, and Dr. Ralph J. Bunche." *National Guardian* (May 8, 1954).

"Ralph Bunche Cleared." *Afro-American* (June 1954).

"Ralph Bunche and the United Nations." *Freedom* (June 1954).

"140,000,000 Women Can't Be Wrong." *New World Review* 22, no. 6 (1954).

"Favorite and Step-Child in the United Nations." *New World Review* 22, no. 10 (1954).

"A Big Tree Has Fallen." *New World Review* 22, no. 12 (1954).

"Negro History Week." *New World Review* (Mar. 1955).

"Some Thoughts on Negro History Week." *New World Review* (Mar. 1955).

"The Ninth UN Session." *New World Review* (Apr. 1955).

"Asian Countries Conference." *New China News Agency*. Apr. 12, 1955.

"Trust in Trusteeship." *New World Review* (Apr. 1955).

"Powell at Bandung: The American Negro Abroad." *The Afro American*. May 25, 1955.

"How to Spot a You-Know-What." *Afro-American* (June 1955).

"Always to Resist, Always to Prevent!" *Jewish Life: A Progressive Monthly* 9, no. 8 (1955): 104.

"Negro leadership." (Editorial.) *Afro-American* (June 4, 1955).

"UN + Bandung = Peace." *New World Review* (June 1955).

"Before and After Bandung." *New World Review* (July 1955).

"Last Stand of Colonialism in the UN." *New World Review* (Oct. 1955).

"Nrinad Autherine Lucyove." *Malda Fronta* (July 19, 1956). Czech Republic.

"President Sukarno: Brother, Father, Son of the Indonesian People." *New World Review* (Aug. 1956).

"The New General Assembly." *American Journal of Law* 51, no. 4 (1957): 861.

"China and the U.N." *New World Review* (June 1957).

"Daniel Louis 'Satchmo' Armstrong." *International Life* (Oct. 1957).

"Ghana's Crusade." Unpublished. Oct. 1957.

"Nkrumah, Nasser Are Not Rivals." *Courier Magazine* (Apr. 18, 1959).

"The 21st Congress on Television." *New World Review* (Apr. 1959).

"Soviet Man in Space: No. 2." *New World Review* (Sep. 1961).

"Cuba Libre Island in Flames." *New World Review* (April 16–May [n.d.] 1961).

"Negro in American Life." *New Times: A Weekly Journal of World Affairs* (June 27, 1963).

"New Negro Movement." *The Sun-Reporter* (July 27, 1963).

"Determined to Be an American." *Journal of Negro History* 49, no. 1 (1964): 73.

"Long Hot Summer." Unpublished. June 10, 1964.

"Black Revolution and White Backlash." *West Indian Gazette* (Aug.–Sep. 1964).

"The Time Is Now." Unpublished. Nov. 28, 1964.

"Fresh Winds at the UN." *New Worker* (Dec. 20, 1964).

"The Funeral of Malcolm X." Unpublished. Mar. 2, 1965.

"Changes in Manuscript." Unpublished autobiographical sketch. N.d.

NOVELS AND PLAYS (UNPUBLISHED IN HER LIFETIME)

"Aunt Hagar's Children." Play. May 1, 1926.
"Black Progress," Play. Jan. 1931.
"Leave Them Alone." Script. 1930s.
"Uncle Tom's Cabin." Play. Mar. 4, 1932.
"Color." 1940.
"Congolaise." Film script. 1949.

INDEX

ER in the index stands for Eslanda Robeson. PR stands for Paul Robeson.

African National Congress (ANC),
107, 110, 151, 215
Africa: The Wonder and the Glory
(Graves), 309n86
Afrikaner National Party, 149–50. *See
also* Apartheid; South Africa
Afro-American newspaper, 5, 200, 206,
227–29, 272, 273
Alda, Frances, 57
Algeria, 209–10
All-African Peoples' Conference
(AAPC), 217, 242–46
All-African Women's Freedom Move-
ment (AAWFM), 263
All God's Chillun Got Wings, 39, 42,
44, 301n51
ALP (American Labor Party), 194,
197–98
Alpha Phi Alpha fraternity, 33
American Argument (Buck and
E. Robeson), 2, 65, 179–83, 203,
294n10
American Committee for Protection
of the Foreign Born, 229
American Communist Party. *See*
Communist Party USA
American Continental Congress for
Peace, 196
American Labor Party (ALP), 194,
197–98
Amitié Franco-Dahoméenne, 70
Amsterdam News, 5, 77, 95, 156, 175,
190, 198, 206, 326n20
ANC (African National Congress),
107, 110, 151, 215
Anderson, Carol, 7, 195
Anderson, Marian, 95
Angola, 150, 163, 260
ANP (Associated Negro Press), 5,
341n3
Anthropology, 2, 81, 87–91, 97, 152–56,
205, 259
Anti-colonialism. *See* Colonialism;
Council on African Affairs (CAA);
Decolonization
Anticommunism: accusations of com-
munist affiliations against Progres-

sive Party, 186, 187; of Buck, 181–82;
Cold War propaganda on generally, 124, 185, 186–87; and confiscation and later return of passports of
ER and PR, 5, 10, 217, 231–32, 234,
239, 241; and different responses to
red-baiting by those who were targeted, 224; and ER and PR targeted
as subversives, 5, 10, 176–77, 189–92,
195–96, 202–4, 223–38, 250, 253,
280, 330n48; ER's testimony before
McCarthy's Senate Investigating
Committee, 223–26, 228; and House
Un-American Activities Committee
(HUAC), 224, 226, 234, 273, 331n67;
internationalism of McCarthyism,
208; of McCarthy and his Senate
Investigating Committee, 5, 108,
207, 223–26; and NAACP, 235; and
Palmer Raids, 28; and Peekskill vio-
lent protest against PR, 195, 203;
and racism, 227, 228–29; of Yergan,
108, 135, 187–88. *See also* Cold War;
Communism
Anti-Semitism, 61, 62–63, 93, 207,
313n40. *See also* Holocaust
Apartheid, 111, 135, 149–50, 207, 215,
257–58. *See also* South Africa
Árbenz Guzmán, Jacobo, 208
Arbouin, Uvee Mdodana, 273
Armah, Kwesi, 263
Armitage, Teresa, 23
Arnold, Rev. Taschereau, 191
Arraleh, Mahmoud Abdi, 263
Ashcroft, Peggy, 65, 66, 82
Asia. *See* China; India
Asian Women's Federation, 197
Associated Negro Press (ANP), 5, 188,
206, 223, 251, 257–58, 341n3
Association des Femmes de l'Union
Française outre-mer et métropole,
170
Atlanta Daily World, 191
Atlantic Charter, 145
Augustin Guéry, Fortuna, 212
"Aunt Hagar's Children" (E. Robe-
son), 55, 56–57

Chibambo, Rose, 263

Chicago: housing desegregation in, 229-30, 245; schools in, 23, 298nn54-55; youth of ER in, 22-23

Chicago Defender, 24, 80, 95, 139, 190

Childress, Alice, 188, 206, 272, 334n34

China: Asian Women's Federation meeting in, 197; Buck in, 180; Chiang Kai Shek government in, 198, 200; civil war in, 199-200; compared with Deep South in U.S., 200-201; Shirley Du Bois in, 217; ER's lectures on, 201-4; ER's support for People's Republic of China (PRC), 208-9, 214; ER's trip to, 6, 197, 198-202; FBI monitoring of ER's trip to China, 198, 200; Mao Zedong in, 198-200; Nanking in, 199; *New World Review* on, 206; Peking in, 198; Shangai in, 198-99, 201; Soong Ching-ling in, 199; Tientsin in, 199; United Nations and People's Republic of China (PRC), 208-9; U.S. policy on People's Republic of China, 200, 201; women's rights in, 199, 201, 202, 203, 209, 248

Chinese Revolution and the Chinese Communist Party, The (Mao Zedong), 198

Chinn, May, 31, 46, 299n13

CIA, 208, 253, 258, 340n56

CIO (Congress of Industrial Organizations), 202

"Citizen's State of the Union, A" (E. Robeson), 227

City College of New York, 22, 23

Civil rights movement. *See* Black Freedom movement, U.S; King, Martin Luther, Jr.; NAACP

Cold War: anti-communist propaganda during, 124, 185, 186-87, 235; beginning of, 176; British intelligence agency during, 164-65, 250, 253; confiscation and later return of passports of ER and PR during, 5, 10, 217, 231-32, 234, 239, 241; and criticism of PR's political views, 189-92, 195-96, 235; different responses to red-baiting by those who were targeted during, 224; ER and PR targeted as subversives during, 5, 10, 176-77, 189-92, 195-96, 202-4, 223-38, 250, 253, 280, 330n48; and ER's testimony before McCarthy's Senate Investigating Committee, 223-26, 228; execution of Rosenbergs during, 223; and House Un-American Activities Committee (HUAC), 224, 226, 234, 273, 331n67; impact of, on Third World, 208, 222; and Korean War, 185, 186, 203, 232, 332n87; and McCarthy's Senate Investigating Committee, 223-26; and Peekskill violent protest against PR, 195, 203; and People's Republic of China (PRC), 198-200, 208-9; and Progressive Party, 185-86; Truman's policies on, 184; U.S. government surveillance of ER and PR during, 141, 145, 200, 207, 214, 250, 280, 298, 340n56; and World Congress of Partisans of Peace, 189-91. *See also* Soviet Union

Colonialism: accommodation as strategy of Africans regarding, 113-14; in Africa, 72, 100, 103, 113-15, 118-21, 161, 166, 175-76; and British Empire Exhibition (1924-1925), 50; compared with Hitler's occupation of Europe, 176; of England, 50, 113-14, 215, 257-58; films and movie script on, 97-98, 175-76; of France, 70, 161, 166, 209-11; Kojo's work for rights of Black colonial subjects, 70-71; and neo-colonialism, 246, 261, 265. *See also* Racism and discrimination; *and specific colonies*

"Color" (E. Robeson), 84-85

Color consciousness among blacks, 17-19, 83, 106

Columbia Presbyterian Hospital, New York City, 2, 34, 307n38

Columbia University, 94, 97, 118

Columbia University Law School, 29–30, 34, 38

Columbia University Teachers College, 3, 25, 28, 29–30, 294*n*6

Committee of African Organizations, 263–64

Committee of Afro-Asian-Caribbean Organizations, 270

Committee to Restore Paul Robeson's Passport, 231

Communism: accusations of communist affiliations against Progressive Party, 186, 187; appeal of, worldwide, 193; in China, 198–200; compared with socialism, 318*n*1, 321*n*49; and Council on African Affairs (CAA), 144, 145; in Cuba, 257; ER's refusal to answer questions about, before McCarthy's Senate Investigating Committee, 224–25, 228; ER's support for, 2, 4, 5, 132, 141, 181–82, 186–87, 193, 194, 214, 226, 280, 294*n*9, 318*n*1, 321*n*49; and *New World Review*, 5, 206; and Pan-Africanism, 193–94; PR's support for, 3–4, 132, 138, 141, 190–93, 227–28, 318*n*1; and Third World, 123, 145, 192, 193, 264–65; and Women's International Democratic Federation (WIDF) Conference, 331*n*67. *See also* Soviet Union; *and* Communist Party *headings*

Communist Party, British, 126

Communist Party, Chinese, 198–200

Communist Party in India, 244

Communist Party USA: and Black artists and intellectuals, 94; ER's refusal to answer questions about, before McCarthy's Senate Investigating Committee, 224–25; Ford's leadership of, 248; imprisonment of members of, 227; members and leaders of, 187, 188, 227–28, 274; newspaper of, 5; Patterson's leadership of, 57, 132, 133; PR's and ER's relationship with, 138, 191–93, 226,

227–28, 294*n*9. *See also* Communism

Congo: air travel to, 160; assassination of Lumumba in, 172, 258–59; Bakonjo-pygmy village of Ngite in, 117–18; Booth in, 149; Brazzaville in, 165, 167; British Intelligence surveillance of ER in, 164–65; and CIA, 258; colonialism in, 161; compared with Deep South in U.S., 163; conditions in, during ER's trip, 173–75; Congo River in, 2, 9, 165–66; d'Arboussier in, 167–68, 326*n*26, 326*n*32, 327*n*35, 327*n*37; diamond mines in, 166; Éboué in, 168–69, 171, 173–74, 327*nn*35–36; Elisabethville in, 171, 172–73; ER in, 4, 6, 9, 117–18, 151, 159–75, 256; funding for ER's travel in, 159–60, 171; Kasai in, 166; Leopoldville in, 160, 161–65, 170–71, 173; Lumumba in, 172, 242; migrant labor system in, 163, 164; missionary conference in, 170–71; prostitution in, 164; racism and discrimination in, 117, 163, 166, 229; resistance to colonialism in, 161; Scotti family as ER contacts in, 150; Toussaint in, 172–73; and travel to Chad, 173–74; and travel to Usumbura, 171–72; Tshombe in, 172; visa for travel in, 165; women in, 162, 164, 170; writing on, by ER, 256

"Congolaise," (E. Robeson), 175–76

Congress of American Women, 198

Congress of Industrial Organizations (CIO), 202

Conrad, Joseph, 161

Les Continents, 42, 71, 300*n*44

Cook, Corrine, 8

Cook, Marvel, 96

Cornell University, 143, 196

Costa Rica, 139–40

Council on African Affairs (CAA): communists and communist sympathizers in, 144, 145, 187–88; Du Bois as member of, 4–5, 144; on

Éboué, 168; and ER, 4–5, 75, 108, 134–35, 143–45, 148–52, 156, 159, 178, 184, 187–88, 323*n*35; and founding of International Committee on African Affairs (ICAA), 134–35, 144; political divisions within, 184, 187–88; and PR, 4–5, 134, 144, 156, 184, 188, 323*n*35; publications by, 148–49, 161, 323*n*35; and U.S. State Department, 144–45; women's involvement in, 144, 188, 201, 217; and Yergan, 4–5, 108, 134–35, 144, 184, 187–88, 323*n*35

Coward, Noel, 4, 67, 307*n*41

Crane, Mr., 79, 311*n*11

Crane, Mrs. Murray, 47

Crawford, Roberta Dodd, 307*n*50

Crisis magazine, 96

Cuba, 208, 214, 253, 257

Cullen, Countee, 4, 36

Czechoslovakia, 62, 197

Dahomey, 42, 70, 309*n*81

Daily Worker, 5, 132, 226–27

Daïnah la métisse, 72

d'Arboussier, Gabriel, 167–69, 190, 326*n*26, 326*n*32, 327*n*35, 327*n*37

Davenport, Millia, 299*n*7

Davis, Allison, 89–90

Davis, Ben, 187, 227–28

Davis, Ossie, 271, 273, 311*n*107, 341*n*64

Decolonization: in Africa, 2, 148–52, 183, 190, 214, 242, 242–46, 257–58, 259–61, 330*n*52; and African independence struggles of 1960s, 257–65; and Algeria, 209–10; and All Africa People's Conference, 217; d'Arboussier on, 190; ER on, 205, 206, 209–10; in Ghana, 217, 243, 244, 330*n*52; and radical Black internationalism, 194–95, 214, 216, 247–48; in South Africa, 257–58; and United Nations, 145–46, 148, 151, 152, 209–11. *See also* Africa; Council on African Affairs (CAA); Racial equality; *and specific countries*

Dee, Ruby, 271, 273, 311*n*107, 341*n*64

De Gaulle, Charles, 169

Delaney, Clarissa (Clare) Scott, 60, 144

Delaney, Hubert, 60, 144, 183

Delta Sigma Theta sorority, 25–26, 33, 60, 179, 183–84, 202

DeMille, Cecil B., 57

Depression. *See* Great Depression

De Prorok, Byron, 168–69

Desegregation. *See* Racial equality

Diamond, Freda, 142, 157, 173, 197, 233, 252, 306*n*27, 328*n*62

Diaspora. *See* African Diaspora

Dickerson, Earl, 270

Dillard University, 141

Discrimination. *See* Racism and discrimination

Divorce: ER on, 77, 310*nn*93–94; of Charlotte Haldane, 127; Haldane on, 127; PR's initiation of divorce proceedings, 65–69, 71–72, 74, 76–79; of Minnie Sumner, 127

Djilas, Milovan, 212

Dominican Republic, 208

Donaldson, J. S., 261

Donat, Richard, 98

Doolittle, Hilda (H.D.), 63–64, 306*n*23

Dorsey, Charlotte, 215

Douglass, Frederick, 17, 226

Douglass, Helen Pitts, 17

Dreiser, Theodore, 47

Duberman, Martin, 9, 79, 298*n*5, 299*n*15, 306*n*27, 307*n*38, 310*n*104, 328*n*62, 340*n*57

Du Bois, David, 217

Du Bois, Shirley Graham: and All-African Peoples' Conference (AAPC), 243, 244; and Council on African Affairs, 217; death of, 217; ER's friendship with, 216–17, 222; FBI surveillance of, 217; and *Freedom* newspaper, 215, 216, 217; Ghana citizenship for, 217, 239, 254, 334*n*38; marriage of, 217; and Sojourners for Truth and Justice, 188; at World Congress of Partisans of Peace, 190; writings by, 217

Houénou, (Prince) Kojo Touvalou, 4, 42, 44, 70–72, 74, 81, 99, 216, 307n50, 309n81

House Un-American Activities Committee (HUAC), 224, 226, 234, 273, 331n67

Howard family, 229–30

Howard University, 3, 19, 144, 184; Paul and Eslanda Robeson Collection (PERC) at, 8, 293

Howell, Catharine Romena, 15, 17

HUAC (House Un-American Activities Committee), 224, 226, 234, 273, 331n67

Hughes, Langston: and ER generally, 4; and ER's death, 276; and filming of *Black and White* in Russia, 92; in France, 73; and Harlem Renaissance, 27, 36, 73, 83; and Nehru, 90; and *New Challenge*, 308n65; on *Paul Robeson, Negro* by ER, 83

Humboldt University, 269–70

Humphrey, Hubert, 213

Hunter, Alberta, 95

Hunton, Alphaeus, 144, 188, 334n38

Hurston, Zora Neale, 4, 27, 36, 40, 90–91

"I Believe in Divorce" (E. Robeson), 77, 310n93

ICAA (International Committee on African Affairs), 134–35, 144

"If We Must Die" (McKay), 53

"I Know a Communist" (E. Robeson), 228

Imru, Hirtu, 244

Independent India, 86

India: Community Party in, 244; ER's interest in, 7, 75, 86, 109, 216, 268; and Gandhi, 85–86, 216, 220, 280; independence of, 258, 330n52; links between Black Americans' experience and, 86, 90; Menon from, 210–11, 240; Geeta Mukherjee from, 244, 245; Nan Pandit from, 148, 218–21; political prisoners in, 219, 220; students and intellectuals

from, in London, 88, 90; support for restoration of Robeson's passport in, 234–35; in United Nations, 210–11; women's rights in, 248; and Yergan, 108, 144. *See also* Nehru, Jawaharlal

Indonesia, 243, 248, 268

Ingram, Rosa Lee, 189, 203

Institute for African Studies, Soviet Academy of Sciences, 241–42

Integration. *See* Racial equality

Inter-American Conference, Tenth (Caracas, Venezuela), 207–8

International Committee on African Affairs (ICAA), 134–35, 144

Intersectionality, 189, 214, 278

Iran, 212

"Is Black a Handicap?" (E. Robeson), 121

Island in Flames, 257

Israel, 214

Italy, 101, 109, 169

Jack, Homer, 266, 342n26

Jackson, Ada, 197–200

Jackson, Esther Cooper, 123–24, 242, 273–74

Jackson, James, 274

Jackson, Yolande, 65–66, 68, 69, 71–72, 78–80, 82, 310n104

Jagan, Cheddi, 4, 215, 216, 221–22, 237–38

Jagan, Janet, 216, 221–22, 237, 238, 276

James, C. L. R., 87, 236

Jeffries, James, 297n43

Jericho, 124

Jews. *See* Anti-Semitism; Holocaust

John Day Company, 154

John Henry, 138

Johnson, Grace Nail, 68

Johnson, Jack, 297n43

Johnson, James Weldon, 27, 68

Johnson, Joe, 184

Johnson, Mordecai, 144

Johnson, Thomasina, 143

Jonah's Gourd Vine (Hurston), 91

Jones, Claudia, 187, 228, 240, 263

National Negro Congress, 108, 218
"Native," as derogatory term used by
  whites in Africa, 103
Nazism, 93–94, 125, 131, 207, 267–68,
  342n29
NCNW (National Council on Negro
  Women), 178
Neale, Gerry, 31
Negro Digest, 121
*Negro in the American Economic System,
  The* (Reid), 141
Negro Review, 40
Negro spirituals, 46, 47, 58
Negro World, 86
Nehru, Jawaharlal: and African in-
  dependence movement in 1960s,
  258, 259–60; archives of, 8; ER's
  relationship with, 4, 139, 216, 218,
  220–21, 259–60, 280, 335n50; and
  Langston Hughes, 90; imprison-
  ment of, 218, 219; in London, 4,
  90, 218; political career of, 148 218,
  219–20, 341n4; and restoration of
  Robeson's passport, 234–35; and
  Yergan, 108
Neo-colonialism, 246, 261, 265. *See
  also* Colonialism
New Africa, 144
New Challenge, 308n65
Newell, Jim, 74, 309n80
Newfoundland, 160
New Guinea, 88–89
New Masses, 231
"New Negro," 25, 27
New World Review, 5, 206–10, 234
New York City: black domestic
  workers in, 96; Chinese diplomatic
  community in, 200, 202; discrimi-
  nation in, during ER's childhood,
  14, 21–22; employment of ER as
  chemist in, 2, 34; ER's childhood
  in, 14, 20–22; Goode family home
  in, during ER's childhood, 22; Es-
  landa Goode's return to, from
  Chicago, 24–25; homes of ER and
  PR in, 5, 25–28, 30, 34–35, 137, 233,
  234, 239; Interracial Assembly in,

198; Liberty League in, 24, 25;
  low-income housing in, 215; protest
  against police brutality in, 22, 26,
  297n43; race riots in, 28, 297n43;
  return of ER to, after travels, 8,
  135, 137–38, 270–75; schools in, 22;
  South African activists' travel to,
  151; woman's suffrage movement in,
  25, 26. *See also* Harlem Renaissance
New York Herald Tribune, 83
New Zealand, 3, 251, 252
Nicaragua, 208
Nigeria, 87, 207, 243–44, 246
"Nigger": ER's use of, in her private
  diary, 304n44; "native" as deroga-
  tory term used by whites in Africa,
  103; racist use of term in workplace,
  39
Nigger Heaven (Van Vechten), 40,
  301n46
Njururi, Ngumbu, 261
Nkrumah, Kwame, 217, 239, 243, 245,
  258, 265–66, 334n38
Non-Aligned Movement, 339n26
North Korea. *See* Korean War
Northwestern University, 19
Ntumazah, Ndeh, 211
Nuclear disarmament, 261–62, 265–66
Nyabingi Movement, 114, 118
Nyabongo, Akiki, 112–13, 118, 316n55,
  317n63
Nyasaland, 242, 263

O'Dell, Jack, 273–74
"Old Man River," 61, 138
Olivier, Laurence, 250
O'Neill, Eugene, 4, 39, 49, 301n51
Orizu, Prince A. A. Nwafor, 156
Ornwu, 64
Orwell, George, 125
Othello, 62, 65, 138, 141–42, 156–57, 219,
  240, 249, 250
Othello Associates, 238
Oxford University, 112, 316n55

Padmore, George, 87
Palmer Raids, 28

dad, 236–38; in U.S. South, 141. *See also* England

Robeson, Eslanda Cardozo Goode, writings by: on Africa, 75, 107, 109, 115, 143, 148–49, 153–58, 175, 207, 312*n*19, 312*n*26, 323*n*35; *African Journey*, 109, 115, 143, 153–58, 160, 179, 224, 242, 312*n*19, 312*n*26; as allegedly "un-American," 224; *American Argument*, 2, 65, 179–83, 294*n*10; "Aunt Hagar's Children," 55, 56–57; bibliography of, 345–47; biographical sketches, 85–86; on Black Freedom movement in U.S., 270–71; "Black Paris," 69, 72; "Black Progress," 83; "A Call to the Negro People: Begging Should End Now," 247; "A Citizen's State of the Union," 227; "Color," 84–85; in diary, 36, 44, 47, 50, 54–56, 61, 62, 66, 68, 71, 74, 77, 79, 93, 103–5, 115, 127, 175, 256, 268, 269; for *Freedom* newspaper, 200–201, 206, 214–17, 271; as freelance journalist, 2, 5, 85–86, 97, 121, 205–13, 256–58, 341*n*3; general description of, 2, 9, 206, 256–57, 264; "I Believe in Divorce," 77, 310*n*93; "I Know a Communist," 228; "Is Black a Handicap?," 121; "Leave Them Alone," 84; "Loyalty–Lost and Found," 197; on marriage and divorce, 77–78, 182, 310*n*93–94, 310*n*100; movie script by, 175–76; for *New World Review*, 5, 206–10, 234; novels by, 55, 56–57, 83–85; *Paul Robeson, Negro*, 17–18, 81–83, 153, 154, 219, 295*n*12; plays, 55, 56–57, 76, 83–84; "Proud to Be a Negro," 318*n*89; *The Three Eslandas*, 67; typewriter for, 173; "Uncle Tom's Cabin," 83–84; as United Nations correspondent, 2, 5, 205–14, 220, 238, 256, 273, 276, 280; "What Do the People of Africa Want?," 148–49, 323*n*35; "What Is a Ghetto? Lessons from the Warsaw Ghetto Uprising for All People," 207; "Women in the United Nations," 211–12

Robeson, Marilyn Greenberg: children of, 250, 275; ER living with temporarily, 233; and ER's death, 275; and ER's health problems, 249, 272, 275; marriage of, 196–97, 203; and preservation of information on ER and PR, 8; and PR's depression, 254

Robeson, Paul: and abortions by ER, 31, 67, 299*n*13; acting career of, 35–39, 42–44, 46, 49–50, 52, 60–62, 79, 95, 138, 141–42, 156–57, 219, 240, 249, 250, 301*n*51, 303*n*27; African qualities and characteristics of, 76; archives of, 8, 293; in Australia and New Zealand, 251–52; awards and honors for, 157, 190, 273–74; biographers of, 8–9, 10, 217; birthday celebrations for, 234, 273–74; career of generally, 3–4, 5, 10; communism and Soviet Union supported by, 3–4, 6–7, 123–24, 132, 133, 138, 141, 181–82, 187, 190–93, 203, 227–28, 238, 318*n*1, 320–21*n*46; confiscation and later return of passport of, 5, 10, 231–32, 234, 239, 241; and Council on African Affairs (CAA), 4–5, 134, 144, 156, 188, 323*n*35; courtship of ER and, 28–31, 298*n*5, 299*n*15; criticisms of and protests against, for his political views, 189–92, 195–96, 235; defense of, regarding political attacks against, 191–92, 195–96, 231–32, 234, 268–69, 272, 279; and depression, 251, 252–55, 268, 269, 272, 274, 340*n*57; desire of, to return to U.S. permanently, 250; divorce proceedings initiated by, 65–69, 71–72, 74, 76–79; education of, 29–30, 34, 38; in England, 37–38, 49–50, 52, 60, 61, 79, 80, 87–92, 95, 126, 217–18, 239–40, 249–51, 253, 254–55, 339*n*39; ER as business manager, coach, and career strategest

Robeson, Paul (continued)
for, 4, 35–36, 38–39, 42–44, 47,
48, 55, 96–98, 279, 302*n*12; ER's
book on, 17–18, 81–83, 153, 154, 219,
295*n*12; and ER's death, 275; eulogy for Lorraine Hansberry by,
271; fame of, 112, 138–39, 323*n*35;
film career of, 42–43, 57, 63–64,
92, 94, 96, 97–98, 124–25, 134, 139,
259; finances of, 42, 47, 48, 49,
78–79, 96, 177, 231, 232–33, 310*n*101;
and *Freedom* newspaper, 206, 215,
217; Ghana citizenship declined
by, 239; health problems of, 10,
221, 249, 251, 252–55, 267, 268, 269,
270, 272, 274, 275; *Here I Stand*
by, 231, 238; homes of, in London,
61, 80, 87, 239; homes of, in New
York City, 5, 30, 34–35, 137, 233,
234, 239; investigation of, as communist supporter, 176–77, 330*n*48;
and Korean War, 203; as lawyer,
38–39; marital infidelities of, 6, 56,
64–66, 68, 69, 71–72, 78, 79, 80,
82, 98, 142, 157, 177, 233, 310*n*94,
310*n*104, 328*n*62; marriage of, 3,
5–6, 31–35, 43–44, 55–59, 79–80,
82, 139, 142, 156–58, 177–78, 228,
233, 250, 255, 279, 299*n*15, 301*n*52,
304*n*48; and marriage of Paul Jr.,
197; musical career of, 44, 46–49,
55–56, 58, 59, 62, 64, 96, 122, 138,
234, 239, 240, 242, 251; and Nehru,
221; as orator, 138; patrons of, 40;
Peekskill violent protest against,
195, 203; personality of, 5–6, 29,
30, 35, 64, 82; physical appearance
of, 29, 35, 76; political activism of,
126, 138, 176–77, 180, 189–90, 194–
95, 221, 238, 269, 272, 279; and Progressive Party, 184; in psychiatric
facility in London and electro-
shock treatments of, 254–55, 262,
267; racism and discrimination
against, 99–100; and radical Black
internationalism, 194–95; return
of, to U.S. in 1963, 270–75; sculpture of, 48; singing voice of, 29,
33, 46; son of, 6, 8, 59–62, 78, 80,
82, 99–100; in Soviet Union, 4, 6,
92–96, 122–24, 240–42, 249, 252–
54, 313*n*34; in Spain, 126–31; and
Spanish Civil War, 126–31; speech
by, at World Congress of Partisans of Peace in Paris, 189–92, 197;
suicide attempt by, 252–53, 340*n*57;
U.S. government surveillance of,
145, 250, 280, 340*n*56; vocal coach
for, 23. *See also* Africa; *and specific
plays and films*
Robeson, Paul, Jr.: on abortion by ER,
299*n*13, 307*n*38; African trip by,
during his childhood, 99, 100–121,
151; on African trip by ER, 314*n*;
in Air Force, 177; biography of PR
by, 8, 9; birth of, 59–60; childhood and youth of, 61, 62, 66, 68,
69, 74, 99–121, 124, 131, 133, 134, 135,
137, 305*n*15; children of, 250, 275;
education of, 99, 124, 142–43; in
England, 62, 74, 131, 133, 134, 135;
on ER's book *Paul Robeson, Negro*,
82; and ER's death, 275; and ER's
health problems, 249, 272, 275;
ER's relationship with, as adult,
233, 249–50, 255, 272; on Kazakov,
320*n*43, 321*n*46; and Kenyatta, 262;
on Malcolm X, 343*n*40; marriage
of, 196–97, 203; mental breakdown
of, 253; on Nehru, 335*n*50; and
Othello Associates, 238; and Pandit sisters, 219; personality of, 102;
and PR's depression and suicide
attempt, 253–55, 269, 274, 340*n*57;
and PR's desire to return permanently to U.S. from England, 250;
on PR's marital infidelities, 79,
306*n*27; PR's relationship with, 78,
79, 82; racism and discrimination
in childhood of, 99–100, 120–21,
135; return of, to New York City
in 1939, 135; in Soviet Union, 124,
133, 253; on Soviet Union's purges,
123, 133, 294*n*10, 321*n*46; typewriter

for, 173; during World War II in England, 134

Robeson, Susan, 250

Robinson, Jackie, 183

Robinson, Michael E., 332n87

Rockmore, Bess, 168

Rockmore, Clara, 160

Rockmore, Robert (Bobby or Bob), 157, 159, 173, 177, 254, 310n101

Rogers, J. A., 77

Romania, 198

Romilly, Rita, 47, 79

Roosevelt, Eleanor, 195

Roosevelt, Franklin D., 145, 149, 179, 184

Roseanne, 39

Rosenberg, Julius and Ethel, 223

Rossel, Agda, 211–12

Ruanda-Urundi, 171

Rumbough, Constance, 143

Russell, Gray, 162

Russia, 61, 62. *See also* Soviet Union

Rustin, Bayard, 54–55

Rutgers University, 29, 300n37

Rwanda, 171

St. John Irvine, Nell, 66–67

Salemme, Antonio, 48

Sanders of the River, 97–98, 259

Sands, Diana, 273

Savage, Augusta, 36

Schapera, Isaac, 104, 315n11

Schine, G. David, 224

Schmeling, Max, 104

Schomburg, Arturo, 53

Schomburg Center for Research in Black Culture, 8

Scotland, 64

Scott, Emmet, 60

Scott, Lavinia, 150

Scotti, Richard and Edith, 150

Seeger, Pete, 273

Segregation. *See* Apartheid; Racism and discrimination

Senegal, 103, 169

Senghor, Leopold, 73

Seton, Marie, 92, 93

Sexism. *See* Feminism

Sexuality: ER on, 65, 182; and prostitution, 164, 182

Sex workers. *See* Prostitution

Shaka Zulu, 75

Shakespeare, William, 62

Showboat, 60, 61, 79, 95, 96, 97, 218

Shuffle Along, 46

Shumlin, Herman, 154

Singh, Nikhil, 7

Sisulu, Walter, 107, 215

Slavery, 103

Smith, Beatrice Queen Victoria Louise Virginia (Bricktop), 73–74

Smith, Homer, 338n7

Smith, Lillian, 143

Smith Act (1940), 227

Smuts, Jan., 152

Socialism: appeal of, to worldwide, 193; compared with communism, 318n1, 321n49; of Hubert Harrison, 24–25; of McKay, 53

Society of African Culture, 264

Sojourners for Truth and Justice, 188–89, 217

Somali Student Association (London), 264

Somoza, Anastasio, 208

Soong Ching-ling, 199

South Africa: African National Congress (ANC) in, 107, 151, 215; Afrikaner National Party in, 149–50; All-African National Convention in Bloemfontein in, 111; and annexation of South West Africa, 151–52; apartheid in, 111, 135, 149–52, 207, 215, 257–58; Barnes in, 74–75; Basutoland in, 110; Bunch in, 155; Capetown in, 104–6; compared with Deep South in U.S., 106, 110, 151–52; employment of blacks in, 106–7; ER in, 3, 4, 9, 100, 102, 104–11, 314n65; ER's contacts in, 149–50; ER's political activism for, 151–52; independence for, 257–58; Johannesburg in, 110, 149, 150; Langa reserve in, 105–6; miners'

South Africa (continued)
strike in, 149, 151; mining in, 110–11, 121, 149, 151; mixed-race people in, 106; New Brighton reserve in, 108-9; Ntselamanzi reserve in, 109; Port Elizabeth in, 107-8; poverty in, 105, 108, 109, 110-11, 150; racism and discrimination in, 75, 105-11, 149-52, 237; resistance to racism in, 150, 188-89, 258; Sharpeville massacre in, 258; Sofiatown in, 110, 151; Treason Trials (1956) in, 107, 262; U.S. visit by activists from (1946), 151; visa for ER's trip to, 100–101; wedding celebration in, 109; women's activism in, 188-89, 215

South African Institute for Race Relations, 101

South Korea. *See* Korean War

Soviet Communism: A New Civilization? (Webb and Webb), 122-23

Soviet Union: Marian Anderson's concert in, 95; anti-racist and anti-colonial policies of, 122, 123, 138, 181, 187, 319*n*6; Black Americans in, 53, 85, 92, 94-95, 122, 241, 253; Buck's criticism of, 181-82; cold weather in, 95; and Cuba, 257; ER in, 4, 6, 92-96, 122-24, 131, 133, 197, 198, 217, 240-42, 249, 252-54, 264, 276, 313*n*34; ER's and PR's support of, 6-7, 123-24, 133, 138, 181-82, 187, 190-91, 194, 203, 214, 238, 320-21*n*46; ER's brothers in, 93, 94, 95-96, 123, 131, 133, 241, 305n15; ER's writings on, 294*n*10; films made in and film festival in, 92, 94, 95, 241; Emma Goldman in, 51, 52; Institute for African Studies in, 241-42; jazz performers in U.S. cultural exchange program with, 266-67; Khrushchev in, 241, 251, 264, 266-67, 321*n*46; Mukhitdinov in, 264-65; *New World Review* on, 206; Nan Pandit as ambassador to, 220; persecution and discrimination of Jews and ethnic minorities in, 313*n*40; PR in, 4, 6, 92-96, 122–24, 217, 240-42, 249, 252-54, 264; Progressive Party on dialogue with, 184; PR's concerts in, 122, 240; PR's interest in language and culture of, 122-23, 132; purges and persecutions in, under Stalin, 122, 123-24, 132-33, 181, 319*n*6, 320-21*n*46; schools in, 124; Stalin in, 7, 122, 181, 191, 294*n*10, 319*n*6, 320-21*n*46; theater in, 95; and Third World, 123, 145, 192, 193, 241-42, 264-65; Uzbekistan in, 241, 276; women in, 201; Women's International Democratic Federation (WIDF) Conference in, 197, 198; and World War II, 134; Yergan in, 108. *See also* Cold War; Russia

Spain: civil war in, 2, 125-31; ER and PR in, 126-31, 246, 320*n*26; Madrid during Spanish Civil War in, 128-31, 140; Republican Constitution (1931) of, 128; scenic beauty of, 127, 130-31; theatrical performances in, 129-30

Spanish Civil War, 2, 125-31, 140

Spirituals. *See* Negro spirituals

Springer, Maida, 178, 244

Stalin, Josef, 7, 122, 134, 181, 191, 294*n*10, 319*n*6, 320-21*n*46

State Department, U.S.: blacklisting of ER and PR by, 5, 340*n*56; and China, 200; and Council on African Affairs (CAA), 144-45; Division of African Affairs in, 144-45; and jazz performers in cultural exchange program with Soviet Union, 266-67; and Nehru's visit to U.S., 221; Supreme Court cases on revocation of passports by, 239

Stein, Gertrude, 50, 303*n*23

Stowe, Harriet Beecher, 83

Strange Fruit (Smith), 143

Straw, William St. John, 165-66

Student Nonviolent Coordinating Committee, 262

Sudan, 100, 120

Sumner, Minnie: clothing for ER made by, 41, 49; divorce of, 57, 95; and ER's health problems, 37; and ER's return home to New York City, 8, 137–38; as roommate of ER in Harlem, 28, 29, 30; and vacation with ER, 56

Sun-Reporter, 206, 261, 275

Sun Yat-sen, Madame, 199

Swaziland, ER in, 100, 104

Sweden, 211–12

Switzerland, 63, 66, 68

Taboo (later renamed *Voodoo*), 35–38, 39

Taiwan, 200, 208–9

Tchad. *See* Chad

Tendulkar, D. G., 90

Tenney, Jack, 176–77

Tenney Committee, California State Legislature, 176–77, 330n48

Terrell, Mary Church, 143, 144

Third World: and Black leadership in U.S., 195; ER and PR's influence with, 340n56; and ER as member of "world family," 7, 222, 278; ER's support for independence of, 183, 214; impact of Cold War on, 208, 222; internal struggles over politics and power in, 208; non-aligned nations of, 210; Prashad on Third World project, 278; solidarity among nations of, 220; and Soviet Union, 123, 145, 192, 193, 241–42, 264–65; and United Nations, 210. *See also* Africa; Colonialism; Decolonization; Latin America; *and specific countries*

Thomas, Nina, 140

Three Eslandas, The (E. Robeson), 67

Thunder, 222

Tilden-Hayes presidential compromise (1876), 16

Tobias, Channing, 144, 170–71

Toro, Kingdom of, 114–17, 121, 317n68

Toure, Sekou, 251

Toussaint, E., 172–73

Trilling, Lionel, 125

Trinidad, 236–38, 261

Trujillo, Rafael, 208

Truman, Harry, 177, 184, 185, 192

Trumbull Park (Brown), 230

Truth, Sojourner, 188

Tshombe, Moïse Kapenda, 172

Tubman, Harriet, 215

Tufts University, 148

Tuskegee Institute, 105, 118, 141

UAW (Union of Australian Women), 252

Uganda: Bahima people of, 148; British governor of, 118–20; as British protectorate, 113–15, 118–20; and Committee of African Organizations, 264; Entebbe in, 118–20; ER in, 4, 9, 100, 102, 112–20, 318n89; fieldwork by ER in, 115–17, 153; Kabarole village in, 114–17; Kampala in, 112, 118; mining in, 115; Nkole province in, 118; Nyabingi Movement in, 114; resistance to colonialism in, 113–14; scenic beauty of, 112, 114–15; Toro Kingdom of, 114–17, 121, 317n68

Ulric, Lenore, 54

"Uncle Tom's Cabin" (E. Robeson), 83–84

UNIA (United Negro Improvement Association), 71

Union of Australian Women (UAW), 252

United Nations: and Africa, 114, 145–46, 148, 151, 152; and Algeria, 209–10; and Black Freedom movement, 271; and Cameroon, 211; Commission on the Status of Women, 212; and Congo, 259; and decolonization, 145–46, 148, 151, 152, 209–11; ER as U.N. correspondent, 2, 5, 205–14, 220, 238, 256, 273, 276, 280; ER's interest in, 11, 146, 179, 272; founding convention of, 5, 145, 146–48, 179, 213, 280; friendships of ER with reporters and diplomats at, 213–14; and Guatemala, 208;

Women: at All-African Peoples' Conference (AAPC), 243–45; and All-African Women's Freedom Movement (AAWFM), 263; in China, 199, 201, 202, 203, 209; in Congo, 162, 164, 170; and Congress of American Women, 331n67; and Council on African Affairs (CAA), 144, 188, 201, 217; ER's criticism of American women, 147; ER's defense of, 147; *Freedom* contributors, 215; in Kenya, 262; in Nyabingi Movement, 114; and Progressive Party, 184–85, 274; and racial reforms, 143; role of, in Africa, 109, 113, 115–16, 149, 164, 170; roles for Black women actors, 124–25; and Sojourners for Truth and Justice, 188–89, 217; in South Africa, 188–89, 215; in Soviet Union, 201; in Toro Kingdom of Uganda, 115–16; and Union of Australian Women (UAW), 252; in United Nations, 146–48, 211–13; United Nations Commission on the Status of Women, 212. *See also* Feminism

"Women in the United Nations" (E. Robeson), 211–12

Women's International Democratic Federation (WIDF) Conference, 197, 198, 331n67

Women's International League for Peace and Freedom, 213

Women Strike for Peace, 213

Woolf, Leonard, 309n86, 311n1

Woolf, Virginia, 4, 309n86

World Congress of Partisans of Peace, 189–92, 197

World War I, 24–25, 27, 45, 53, 70, 145

World War II, 101, 133–34, 145, 169, 170, 241

"World without Bombs" assembly (1962), 265–66

Wright, Richard, 218

Xuma, Alfred Bitini, 8, 110, 151, 216, 324n49, 324n50

Yale University, 216

Yergan, Lena, (Max Yergan's second wife), 146

Yergan, Max: anticommunism of, during late 1940s and 1950s, 108, 135, 187–88; and Council on African Affairs (CAA), 4–5, 108, 144, 184, 187–88, 323n35; and ER in South Africa, 107–10; and International Committee on African Affairs (ICAA), 134–35; left-wing activism of, in 1930s, 108; Lena (second wife of), 146; and political divisions within Council on African Affairs (CAA), 108, 184, 187–88; travels to Indian and Soviet Union by, 108; and United Nations founding convention, 156

Yergan, Susie, 109

Yugoslavia, 211–12

Zanzibar, ER in, 100, 111, 264

Zetkin, Clara, 271

Zimbabwe, 149

Zohra, Princess Lalla Fatima, 263

Zola, Émile, 61

Printed in the USA
CPSIA information can be obtained
at www.ICGtesting.com
JSHW022342251223
54313JS00014B/63

9 781642 595826